Time Out

Brussels

www.timeout.com

TORONTO
PUBLIC
LIBRARY
Sale of this book
supports literacy programs

D1286555

Guides

Time Out Digital Ltd
4th Floor
125 Shaftesbury Avenue
London WC2H 8AD
United Kingdom
Tel: +44 (0)20 7813 3000
Fax: +44 (0)20 7813 6001
Email: guides@timeout.com
www.timeout.com

Published by Time Out Digital Ltd, a wholly owned subsidiary
of Time Out Group Ltd. Time Out and the Time Out logo are
trademarks of Time Out Group Ltd.

© Time Out Group Ltd 2015
Previous editions 1996, 1998, 2000, 2002, 2004, 2007, 2010.

10 9 8 7 6 5 4 3 2 1

This edition first published in Great Britain in 2015 by Ebury Publishing.
20 Vauxhall Bridge Road, London SW1V 2SA

Ebury Publishing is part of the Penguin Random House group of companies
whose addresses can be found at global.penguinrandomhouse.com

Distributed in the US and Latin America by Publishers Group West
(1-510-809-3700)

For further distribution details, see www.timeout.com.

ISBN: 978-1-84670-355-3

A CIP catalogue record for this book is available from the British Library.

Printed and bound in China by Leo Paper Products Ltd.

While every effort has been made by the author(s) and the publisher to
ensure that the information contained in this guide is accurate and up to
date as at the date of publication, they accept no responsibility or liability
in contract, tort, negligence, breach of statutory duty or otherwise for any
inconvenience, loss, damage, costs or expenses of any nature whatsoever
incurred or suffered by anyone as a result of any advice or information
contained in this guide (except to the extent that such liability may not be
excluded or limited as a matter of law). Before travelling, it is advisable
to check all information locally, including without limitation, information
on transport, accommodation, shopping and eating out. Anyone using
this guide is entirely responsible for their own health, well-being and
belongings and care should always be exercised while travelling.

All rights reserved. No part of this publication may be reproduced, stored in
a retrieval system, or transmitted in any form or by any means, electronic,
mechanical, photocopying, recording or otherwise, without prior permission
from the copyright owners.

Penguin Random House is committed to a sustainable future for our
business, our readers and our planet. This book is made from Forest
Stewardship Council® certified paper.

MIX
Paper from
responsible sources
FSC® C018179
www.fsc.org

Contents

43

118

128

158

Time Out Brussels

Editorial
Editor Peterjon Cresswell
Copy Editor Cath Phillips
Proofreader Jo Willacy

Editorial Director Sarah Guy
Group Finance Manager Margaret Wright

Design
Art Editor Christie Webster
Designer Kei Ishimaru
Group Commercial Senior Designer Jason Tansley

Picture Desk
Picture Editor Jael Marschner
Deputy Picture Editor Ben Rowe
Picture Researcher Lizzy Owen

Advertising
Managing Director St John Betteridge

Marketing
Senior Publishing Brand Manager Luthfa Begum
Head of Circulation Dan Collins

Production
Production Controller Katie Mulhern-Bhudia

Time Out Group
Founder Tony Elliott
Chief Executive Officer Tim Arthur
Managing Director Europe Noel Penzer
Publisher Alex Batho

Contributors
All content written by Peterjon Cresswell and Gary Hills, except Battle Stations (Derek Blyth), Getting Around, Resources A-Z and Further Reference (Lucy Mallows).

The Editor would like to thank Niki Daun (Ixelles & St-Gilles), Frédérique Honoré (Coudenberg Palace), Pierre Massart (Visit Brussels), Lynn Meyvaert (Ghent Tourism), Anita Rampall (Visit Flanders, London) and Vos Wietske (Ghent Tourism).

Maps JS Graphics Ltd (john@jsgraphics.co.uk)

Cover and pull-out map photography Richard Taylor/4Corners

Back Cover Photography Clockwise from top left: CRM/Shutterstock.com; Rostislav Glinsky/Shutterstock.com; Serge Anton; Fille Roelants Photography; Emi Cristea/Shutterstock.com

Photography Pages 5 (top), 118 Bart Van der Sanden; 5 (bottom left), 128, 129 Oliver Knight; 5 (bottom right), 13, 27 (top), 38, 68/69, 78, 79, 82, 84, 85, 86, 87, 94, 95, 96, 141, 152, 153, 157, 158, 159 Elio Germani; 7 eFesenko/Shutterstock.com; 11, 29, 88 josefkubes/Shutterstock.com; 14/15 (top), 260 Kiev.Victor/Shutterstock.com; 14/15 (bottom), 25, 132/133 pbombaert/Shutterstock.com; 15 Nathalie Du Four; 17 Patrick Despoix/Wikimedia Commons; 20/21 Ulrich Baumgarten/Getty Images; 22 Thierry Roge/AFP/Getty Images; 24, 44, 45 Joseph Jeanmart; 24/25 (top) johandehon; 24/25 (bottom) Blueclic.com/G.Miclotte; 26 (top) © www.atomium.be - SABAM 2009 - Frankinho; 27 (bottom), 63, 114/115, 150, 194, 233, 234 pavel dudek/Shutterstock.com; 28 (bottom), 62, 74, 180, 181 skyfish/Shutterstock.com; 30/31 © Avi&Gulli, Gaston Batistini, Labo River, Michel Block/Mathieu Paternoster; 32 F.Andrieu; 32/33 Eric Danhier; 33 Saskia Batugowski; 34, 35 CRM/Shutterstock.com; 36/37 (top) © Royal Museums of Fine Arts of Belgium; 42 Myrabella/Wikimedia Commons; 51 EmDee/Wikimedia Commons; 61 (top) Jérôme Lambot; 64 © éditions Jacques Brel; 68, 175 Michel wal/Wikimedia Commons; 75 Renata Sedmakova/Shutterstock.com ; 97 Alain Van Haecke; 98, 108, 116 Jonathan Perugia; 98/99 Fabio Mancino Photography; 102 Dieter Telemans; 103 Frédérique Honoré; 105 Tim Van de Velde; 107 Michael Paraskevas/Wikimedia Commons; 114, 119 © Xavier-Marquis; 120, 130 Karol Kozlowski/Shutterstock.com; 120/121 Anton Ivanov/Shutterstock.com; 132, 167 J.P.Remy; 135, 253 Ben2/Wikimedia Commons; 138 (top) Babelphoto; 138 (bottom) © Musée d'Ixelles, Belgium 2015; 144 Alexandre Van Battel; 149 (bottom) PHDPH.COM; 161 © www.atomium.be - SABAM 2009 - DJ Sharko; 162 Hudsonmanu/Wikimedia Commons; 166 ©KCAP; 168/169, 184, 185 Fille Roelants Photography; 172 ImageGlobe; 173 Stefan Dewickere; 177 (left) © Leen Lagrou; 178 © UGC De Brouckere; 179 October Films/Studio Canal+/Films du Fleuve/The Kobal Collection; 182/183 thedarlings@me.com; 187 Alexis Machet; 189 Badger Prod © Renaud Coppens; 195 Mikael Falke; 197 Erlikk/Wikimedia Commons; 202 Walencienne/Shutterstock.com; 203 Ad Meskens/Wikimedia Commons; 204 Torsade de Pointes/Wikimedia Commons; 208 mihaiulia/Shutterstock.com; 211 John Stapels; 212, 213 Yves Vermeulen; 217 Hit1912/Shutterstock.com; 222/223 Emily VDBroucke; 235 Pascale Cousaert ; 238/239 City of Brussels collection; 240 Marco Zanoli/Wikimedia Commons; 243 atelier Leyniers and Reydams/Wikimedia Commons; 244, 246, 248 (left) Wikimedia Commons; 248 (right) Musée de la ville de Bruxelles/Wikimedia Commons; 251 R. Sennecke/Paul Thompson/FPG/Getty Images; 256 Jean-Pol Grandmont/Wikimedia Commons; 258 (right) Jean-Alain/Wikimedia Commons; 262/263 Warburg/Wikimedia Commons; 264/265, 276 (right) Serge Anton; 266, 272 (left) Adrian Houston Limited; 270 (left), 271 Yoann Stoeckel; 275 Fabrice Rambert; 277 ABACApress/Didier Delmas; 278, 279 Sven Laurent; 290 Rostislav Glinsky/Shutterstock.com

The following images were supplied by the featured establishments: 36/37 (bottom), 38/39, 39, 49, 52, 54, 55, 56, 58, 61 (bottom), 66/67, 70, 71, 112, 123, 126, 131, 140, 142, 143, 145, 146, 149 (top), 160, 170, 174, 177 (right), 186, 192, 193, 196, 198, 215, 228, 229, 230, 261, 262, 267, 268, 269, 270 (right), 272 (right), 273, 276 (left)

© **Copyright Time Out Group Ltd**
All rights reserved

About the Guide

GETTING AROUND

Each sightseeing chapter contains a street map of the area marked with the locations of sights and museums (❶), restaurants and cafés (❶), pubs and bars (❶) and shops (❶). There are also street maps of Brussels at the back of the book, along with an overview map of the city. In addition, there is a detachable fold-out street map.

THE ESSENTIALS

For practical information, including visas, disabled access, emergency numbers, lost property and local transport, see the Essential Information section. It begins on page 264.

THE LISTINGS

Addresses, phone numbers, websites, transport information, hours and prices are all included in our listings, as are selected other facilities. All were checked and correct at press time. However, business owners can alter their arrangements at any time, and fluctuating economic conditions can cause prices to change rapidly. The very best venues in the city, the must-sees and must-dos in every category, have been marked with a red star (★). In the sightseeing chapters, we've also marked venues with free admission with a FREE symbol.

THE LANGUAGE

Although officially bilingual, Brussels is a largely French-speaking city (English is widely spoken too). For this reason, we have usually referred to Brussels' streets, buildings and so on by their French name. In town, street signs are given in both languages. French is also the language of Wallonia (the south), while Flemish, a dialect of Dutch, is the language of Flanders (the north). There, English is the first foreign language, with French frowned upon. You'll find a primer on page 290, along with some help with restaurants on page 291.

PHONE NUMBERS

The area code for Brussels is 02. You need to include this code even when calling from within the city. From outside Belgium, dial your country's international access code (00 from the UK, 011 from the US) or a plus symbol, followed by the Belgian country code (32), then 2 for Brussels (dropping the initial 0) and the number as listed in this guide. So, to reach the Brussels Info Point, dial + 32 2 563 63 99.

FEEDBACK

We welcome feedback on this guide, both on the venues we've included and on any other locations you'd like to see featured in future editions. Please email guides@timeout.com.

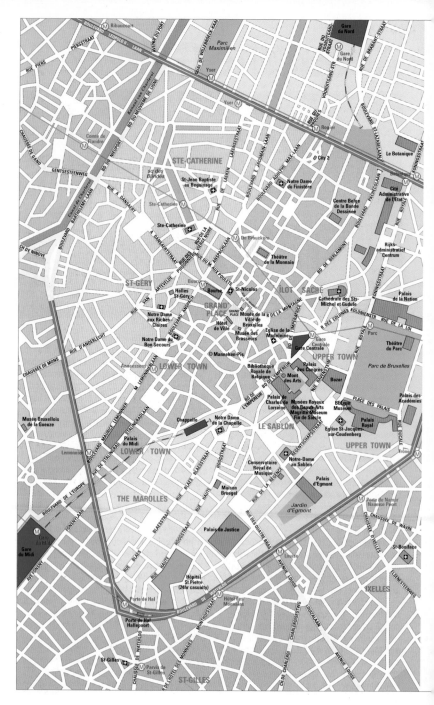

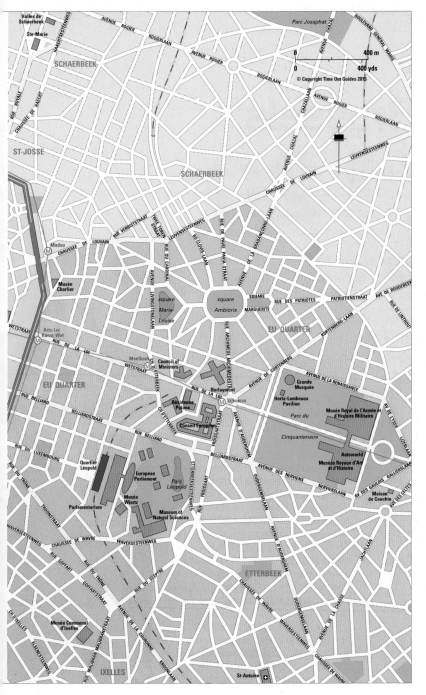

Brussels' Top 20

From cartoons to museums, we count down the city's highlights.

1 Grand'Place
(page 44)

This showpiece square has been the city's centrepiece since medieval times. Lined with attractive guildhouses, interspersed by the Hôtel de Ville and the Museum of the City of Brussels opposite, the Grand'Place owes its appearance to its renovation by mayor Charles Buls in the late 1800s. His revamp was faithful to the square's complete and sumptuous rebuilding by the guilds themselves immediately after the French bombardment 200 years before. The Grand'Place is busy at all times of the day, but changes character according to event. In December, it lights up for the Christmas market; in June and July, it becomes the backdrop for jousting and the pageantry of Ommegang.

2 Cartoon murals
(page 29)

The most colourful features around the city centre are the cartoon murals, more than 40 of them, that decorate previously blank, grey walls. The idea was formed in 1991 when it was decided that the centre needed a bright overhaul. Working in collaboration with the Belgian Comic Strip Centre, the city authorities commissioned the Art Mural association of local artists to create striking

②

representations of revered characters by Belgium's best comic-book artists. These include Hergé's Tintin on rue de l'Étuve, Astérix on rue de la Buanderie and Gaston Lagaffe on rue de l'Écuyer.

3 Éditions Jacques Brel
(page 64)

Belgium's most notable singer-songwriter, Jacques Brel, is still very much revered in Brussels. In 2011, his family decided on a new approach to the existing Brel foundation. Now, as well as filmed interviews with a dozen people who knew him, a wealth of archive material and film clips of Brel in Brussels, the Foundation offers an audio-guided walking tour of the places around the city centre that the Schaerbeek-born artist frequented or performed in.

4 Palais Coudenberg
(page 108)

Once Brussels had a royal palace as fine as anywhere in Europe. Established as a fort in 1047, it was turned into a residence in the early 1400s. Its Great Hall hosted the famous farewell speech by Charles V in 1555. By 1731, the palace was no more, destroyed almost beyond recognition by a terrible fire. It took decades for French architect Barnabé Guimard to rebuild the complex into the neoclassical huddle of buildings, streets and a park you see today. In recent years, the ruins of the original palace have been uncovered and put on display. Although by no means complete, it provides a memorable experience.

5 Galeries Royales St-Hubert
(page 52)

Still spectacular, still lined with lovely boutiques, the Galeries Royales were the first shopping arcade in continental Europe. Opened in 1847, they were commissioned by King Léopold I in 1836. The architect he hired, young Dutchman Jean-Pierre Cluysenaar, created a riot of glass and cast iron, stretching some 200 metres in length. Among the venerable outlets are the Cinéma Galeries, where in 1896 the Lumière brothers screened moving pictures for the first time outside Paris, and the Museum of Letters & Manuscripts, containing correspondence from Victor Hugo and sundry Surrealists.

6 Manneken-Pis
(page 55)

Bafflingly popular, the statuette of a boy with an infinite capacity to pee attracts wave after wave of curious onlookers

collection of musical instruments, including various types of saxophone dreamed up by its inventor Adolphe Sax before he hit upon something close to its final version. The museum hosts free concerts of all types, from school choirs to funk orchestras.

8 Place du Jeu de Balle
(page 96)

Deep in the heart of the Marolles – the city's working-class district between Sablon and Midi station – the main square of place du Jeu de Balle is the site of a daily flea market. Once occupied by a factory, this public space (created in the mid 19th century) became a popular place for a local version of the Spanish game *pelota* – hence the square's name. The flea market is at its best at weekends, when accordionists bash out a few tunes in the traditional bars alongside, and extra traders set up. More upscale vintage outlets and galleries have recently opened on the east side of the square.

9 Chocolate shops
(page 107)

The city's most elegant square, place du Grand Sablon, close to the royal quarter, provides a suitable showcase for Belgium's most prestigious chocolate manufacturers. Some, such as Wittamer and Godiva, have histories dating back around a century. Others, such as Pierre Marcolini and Planète Chocolat, are trying to take on these long-established dynasties by creating finer pralines or revealing the mysteries of manufacturing them by means of regular public workshops. And then there's the latest challenger – and he's not even Belgian: Patrick Roger, a veritable artist in chocolate, who made his name in Paris and has recently planted the *tricolore* on Sablon. Raising the bar with his Vanuatu-sourced chocolate truffles and exquisite ganaches, Roger has created a truly fabulous window display.

to this otherwise featureless corner, a short walk from the Grand'Place. In fact, you'll see him all round the Grand'Place, on T-shirts, magnets and postcards – the Manneken-Pis has become, somewhat embarrassingly, a symbol of the Belgian capital. Set behind railings, placed on a pedestal to give everyone a better look, the Manneken-Pis was created by Jérôme Duquesnoy in the 1600s and has been stolen and replaced several times since. The current version, from 1965, is dressed in various costumes according to events in the calendar. The costumes are displayed in the Museum of the City of Brussels on the Grand'Place.

7 Musée des Instruments de Musique
(page 106)

One of the most distinctive landmarks in Brussels, the Museum of Musical Instruments is set in the former Old England department store, designed in ornate fashion by Paul Saintenoy in 1899. Then, as now, the building features a rooftop café with a wonderful panorama of the city. The museum contains the world's largest

10 Musées-Royaux des Beaux-Arts
(page 106)

Some of the finest art of Belgium and the Low Countries, from the Old Masters of the 15th and 16th centuries to the modern day, is gathered under this one roof. Rembrandt, Rubens – including his *The Fall of Icarus* – and van der Weyden, they're all here. In a separate section are works from the 19th and 20th centuries. The Musée Magritte and the Fin-de-Siècle Museum can be found in the same complex.

11 Parlamentarium
(page 126)

Aware of the fact that the European Union remains a distant and unfathomable (and expensive) organisation for many member citizens, the powers that be opened this excellent visitors' centre in 2011. Free, accessible and informative, the three-floor Parlamentarium explains in an entertaining and visual way the history of its institutions and how they work. Highlights include 'United in Diversity', a vast floor map indicating places of particular interest around the 28-member states, and the 'Sky of Opinions' LED graphic of recent and varied surveys.

and Ixelles neighbourhoods – but the place is still a crowd-pleaser. The extravagant staircase is not to be missed, but even the details of the door handles and stained glass are worth noting.

13 Atomium
(page 165)

Another iconic symbol of the Belgian capital, the Atomium was created for the 1958 World's Fair. Reaching a height of just over 100 metres (330 feet), with a marvellous view from the upper of nine huge stainless-steel spheres, the Atomium towers above the nearby attractions of the Mini-Europe theme park and the national football stadium.

It's said that on a clear day you can see Antwerp's cathedral from the top. This is part of the permanent exhibition, which deals with the Atomium itself and its history – from André Waterkeyn's drawing board to a national treasure nearly 60 years on.

14 L'Archiduc
(page 75)

Brussels has many bars. Some are weird, some are traditional, some are tourist-friendly. L'Archiduc is, simply, unique. Firstly, in terms of pedigree: the former jazz club was once graced by Nat King Cole. Secondly, in terms of looks: the art deco interior makes you feel like you're on board a luxury ocean liner gliding across the Atlantic. Thirdly, in terms of location: right on ultra-fashionable rue Antoine Dansaert. And finally, in terms of sheer class: when Lady Gaga and Tony Bennett perform on the Grand'Place, there's only one place in town they'll enter arm-in-arm afterwards.

12 Musée Horta
(page 154)

Victor Horta was arguably the most influential figure in art nouveau at the end of the 19th century, creating works such as the Hôtel Tassel, the Hôtel van Eetvelde and the Maison Autrique. Built by and for Horta, the house and studio that make up the museum are actually not as ornate as his other creations around the St-Gilles

15 Restaurant Vincent
(page 53)

Just north of the Grand'Place, Îlot Sacré is a tangle of streets whose names echo their medieval origins. Rue des Bouchers is one such thoroughfare, heaving with a constant flow of tourists being ushered into garish restaurants locals would never dream of patronising. Not so, the Restaurant Vincent. Set off a little side street, newcomers here sometimes fail to see the entrance, which is, in fact, the kitchen. Be brave, walk past the chefs, and the maître d' will guide you into a beautifully tiled dining room dating from 1905, its piscine decorative theme a portent of the menu. The bounty of the North Sea will be served up by épauletted waiters more than happy to show off their flambé skills.

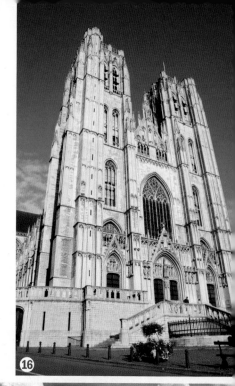

16 Cathédrale des Sts Michel et Gudule
(page 100)

Perched upon the 'Hill of Sorrows', Treurenberg, this magnificent cathedral bears the name of the twin patron saints of Brussels, male and female. This landmark gained its importance as an institution when Lambert II moved saintly relics here. Sts-Michel-et-Gudule has undergone several changes since, and suffered many sorrows, most notably the Gothic remake completed in 1499 and the destruction of its beautiful interior by French revolutionary soldiers in the 18th century. The church underwent major restoration in the 1990s, when remnants of the 11th-century Romanesque church were unearthed in the crypt.

17 Parc du Cinquantenaire
(page 127)

Created by Léopold II, who liked his imperial capital to be overblown and triumphant, the Parc du Cinquantenaire was laid out in celebration of the 50th anniversary of Belgium in 1880. Its main feature is the Arc de Triomphe, which features two grandiose colonnades

been transformed by a raft of new eateries and outlets, most with a terrace, giving a new dynamism and an alfresco Med vibe.

19 Hôtel de Ville (page 49)

Wherever you are in downtown Brussels, you can always find your way by using the signature tower of the Hôtel de Ville as your guiding post. Sadly, this was the tactic used by the French gunners when they laid waste to the Grand'Place and surrounding streets in 1695. Ironically, it was only the Hôtel de Ville that remained standing. Today, you can visit the Town Hall and its gilded official chambers, but not the tower. The 18th-century Council Chamber, all mirrors and tapestries, is the most noteworthy of these many rooms.

flanking either side. These contain three museums: the Musée Royal de l'Armée et d'Histoire Militaire, the Musée du Cinquantenaire, and Autoworld. Nearby stands the Horta-Lambeaux Pavilion, created by the art nouveau architect to show off the somewhat lewd relief of sculptor Jef Lambeaux, *Human Passions*. But Lambeaux wanted his work screened off from the public and the two artists argued – it was only in 2014 that this controversial landmark was renovated and opened to the public.

18 Place Ste-Catherine (page 82)

A short walk from the Grand'Place, place Ste-Catherine was once a working port, where goods were unloaded to be transported to the businesses of the city centre. This all stopped when the River Senne was covered over in the second half of the 19th century. The names of the surrounding streets hark back to their harbour heritage: quai aux Briques, quai au Bois à Brûler. For most of its modern life, Ste-Catherine was known for its rather smart fish restaurants – and little else. Of late, though, this rather staid image has

20 À La Mort Subite (page 54)

If there's anything that defines the fabulous pubs of Brussels, it is tradition. In place for generations, their interiors are lined with neon adverts for the finely brewed beers they serve, and they are staffed by waistcoated waiters of the old-school variety. Some of the brews have been concocted by Trappist monks, some are fruit-flavoured, some are improbably strong – hence the common fallacy that one such bar, À La Mort Subite, is named after some dark and devious ale guaranteed to cause 'Sudden Death'. In fact, this wonderful spot shares its name with a game of cards. But this doesn't stop it from being a mirrored gem of convivial ensozzlement, as Belgian as can be, giving visitors the impression that time has stood still. Maybe, though, that's just the beer.

Brussels Today

A city with politics at its heart.

TEXT: GARY HILLS

On a sunny Sunday in May 2014, Belgians went to place their votes in regional, federal and European elections. For Brussels – as a region in its own right, as the capital of Belgium and as the de facto capital of Europe – every electronic cross of this triple election impacted on its future. It's nothing new; the complexity of political life here is accepted and understood. And nothing could be as bad as the heady days of 2010-11, when Belgium took the world record for the time taken to form a coalition government, a full 541 days after the election.

This time round, it took only five months. The most successful party was the centre-right separatist New Flemish Alliance (N-VA), whose leader, Bart De Wever, sees Flemish independence as a slowly negotiated settlement (though this could be even slower than he expected). The King tasked De Wever to act as *informateur* to find agreement between parties to form a coalition. The job of prime minister eventually went to the leader of the liberal Reform Movement (MR) party, Charles Michel – at the tender age of 39, Belgium's youngest ever PM.

The election map shows Brussels Capital Region, sitting as it does in Flanders, surrounded by N-VA yellow – something that cuts the country in half horizontally. But zoom into the wannabe city-state and the palette is quite different. Here, it's cut in half again; the red of the Socialist Party (PS) to the north, the blue of the MR to the more affluent south – and both of them French-speaking. So, while N-VA won almost 32 per cent of the vote in the Flemish Parliament, it won only three of the 89 seats in Brussels. Overall, 72 seats were won by French-speaking parties and 17 by Flemish-speaking ones. Brussels, as ever, does its own thing.

It's no real surprise that the francophone parties did so well – Brussels is, after all, 85 per cent French-speaking. Nor is it a surprise that Brussels sits comfortably with centre-left politics, what with its multicultural mix, its liberal professions and its old-school, left-wing urbanites. On the street, nothing much changes. There are the usual grumbles about tax and bureaucracy, about the rising cost of living and about aircraft rising in the sky above the city (see p23 **Is it a Plane?**), along with a general anti-austerity sentiment. But most of these are federal issues and Brussels continues to concern itself with the cut of its own jib.

> '*The presence of the EU brings huge economic benefits and impact – without it, Brussels could well be just a middling European city.*'

EU RELATIONS

There's an old EU joke: 'How many people work in Brussels? About half of them.' This may tell you something about perceptions, but, joking aside, since Croatia joined the EU in 2013, there are more than 40,000 people employed by the European institutions in Brussels. That's without the attendant 10,000 lobbyists and one of the world's biggest press packs. All of these people need office space in an ever-expanding EU.

The European Quarter around Place Schuman is fast filling up. Some buildings are being refashioned; other, smaller ones are being demolished to make way for more space-efficient mega structures. Plans to develop a mini Manhattan along rue de la Loi have been simmering since 2009, when architect Christian de Portzamparc won the design tender. The plan involves doubling office space while keeping the scale human: mixed-use shops, homes, a school and even a tram running down the narrowed two-lane road.

Other options include developing EU outposts further out of the city centre to ease congestion. This has already happened to some extent in Beaulieu, south-east of the European Quarter, but Eurocrats and Brussels officials are now looking at Heysel, around the site of the Atomium, which is ripe for becoming an international hub.

Multicultural populations co-exist with few tensions in much of Brussels.

Previous suggestions to move the regular European Council summits to Laeken failed because it was felt that people needed to connect with the EU. Tell that to the local resident or worker who faces insurmountable security cordons and helicopter buzz every time national government ministers arrive for a conflab.

Despite best intentions and some serious investment in urban planning, there is still a disconnect between locals and the EU, who see the area as a city within a city, a white-collar ghetto for short-stay expats. On the other hand, the presence of the EU brings huge economic benefits and impact to the city – without it, Brussels could well be just a middling European city.

CHANGE AND CHALLENGE

To further complicate the political mix, Brussels is technically a region – Brussels Capital Region – rather than a city, and is made up of 19 devolved municipalities or communes. One of these communes,

Brussels (Ville de Bruxelles/Stad Brussel) is the main tourist and historic centre – the Town Hall on Grand'Place is for the commune, not the whole city region. Each commune has its own demographic and its own budget, with some facing more challenges than others.

It's often said that Brussels is harmonious, that there is an easy tolerance of different ethnicities and cultures. In general, this is true; places such as downtown Brussels, Etterbeek and St-Gilles have multicultural populations that co-exist with few tensions. The Matongé adds a splash of the Congo to an otherwise middle-class, upmarket Ixelles, while the posher European expats prefer to live in leafy Uccle.

Harmonious, yes, *laissez-faire*, yes, but there are parts where never the twain shall meet. Some of the poorer communes, such as Anderlecht and Molenbeek, are not so much no-go areas as sad relics of a more noble past. The big houses are chopped up into smaller apartments and bedsits, and there's a feeling that things are more fractured than

Soldier protecting prominent buildings following terror attacks.

cohesive. It also means some communities, particularly those from North African backgrounds, are living in segregated, close-knit communities where the much-lauded integration simply isn't happening. This is a major challenge for the city in the future.

Brussels is now looking at itself in a mirror to question its place in a changing world. It's estimated that between 300 to 400 Belgian Muslims have travelled to Syria to join Isis, with most coming from Brussels. For such a small country, this represents the highest per capita recruitment from western Europe. The issue was brought into focus by the Jewish Museum shootings in 2014, when four people were killed. Attacks like this are a rarity in Belgium, but the mood quickly changed, particularly among the Jewish population of the major cities.

The pace quickened with the 2015 police shoot-out in Verviers, when two suspected terrorists were killed. Since then, it's common to see armed soldiers out on the streets protecting government buildings, police stations, synagogues and Jewish schools. Like other western cities, the challenge now is to address root causes and look urgently at the disparity between the communes and at how the disaffected can feel part of the bigger Brussels success story.

CLEANING IT UP

As a region proud of its green credentials – around half of its total area is green space – Brussels is still blighted by pollution, mostly from road traffic. Despite attempts to get people to use public transport, and the creation of an impressive network of cycle lanes, there are still too many cars coming into the city, encouraged by free, ample parking.

To try to combat this, Brussels introduced a new mobility plan in summer 2015. At its heart are more pedestrianised zones, particularly around the Grand'Place, Sablon and rue Antoine-Dansaert areas. Traffic is being redirected around these zones to underground car parks, while street parking for local residents and deliveries only is being extended. Most importantly, the bicycle network is undergoing improvements too, with direct access to the city centre via a series of cycle-only lanes on main-road links and a more bike-friendly downtown area tied into the pedestrian zones. There's still resistance from the fervent motorist, but it helps to remember that Grand'Place was a car park until 1971. Even after that, you could still drive through it on your way to the supermarket.

Plus ça change – endearingly, though, Brussels will continue to do it at its own pace. They wouldn't want it any other way.

IS IT A PLANE?
New flight paths are creating controversy

Say the words 'Plan Wathelet' to any Brussels resident and they're likely to look skywards with a grimace. It's understandable. Since early 2014, there has been a huge surge in the number of flights taking off from Brussels National Airport then turning left over the city. The plan, which has redirected take-off routes away from the Flanders periphery and towards Brussels, is named after the man who implemented it: Melchior Wathelet, the then-minister for environment, energy and mobility.

This has, of course, impacted hugely on an urban area of over one million inhabitants – and, in particular, on those living under flight paths to the north-west and south-east of Brussels. These include the residential communes of Schaerbeek, Etterbeek and Auderghem. From living in peace and quiet with zero take-offs, these areas suddenly found themselves beneath an estimated 35,000 flights per year. The north-west canal route, taking in Molenbeek, Brussels City, St-Gilles and Uccle, among others, had always had moderate daytime take-offs, but the plan intensified this to include early-morning and night flights of heavier traffic, such as 747 cargo planes. All was not well down on the ground.

The trouble is, Wathelet hadn't gone through any public consultation or impact assessment. The public decided to fight back, and Pas Question (http://pasquestion.be) was born. Big yellow banners appeared on balconies and there was a festive demonstration where torches were lit along the sides of the canal to represent a runway at night. The usual political wrangling kicked off – federal government, Flemish government, Brussels Region and the communes all had their say. But nothing happened until Pas Question brought legal action in 2014 and a judge decided that the new routes were unlawful. He gave three months for a solution to be found, but there was another problem – the new coalition government had still not been formed.

Wathelet's party lost seats at the 2014 election and he was replaced as secretary of state by Jacqueline Galant. Despite a moratorium on the flight paths, Galant has won no admirers for her perceived dithering in trying to bring together complex negotiations. Observers say it could be at least 2016 before any decisions are made, let alone any permanent implementations.

In the meantime, when you see that ascending Airbus to Athens, remember it's not just loaded with passengers, it's loaded with a whole history of politics, in-fighting and popular protest.

Itineraries

*Plot your perfect trip
to the capital with our
step-by-step planner.*

10.30AM

9.30AM

Day 1

9.30AM What better way to start the day than with a stroll through the elegant **Galeries Royales St-Hubert** (p52). This glass-roofed shopping arcade was the first of its kind in continental Europe. Order a quick, affordable breakfast at **Mokafé** (p53), well known for its delicious waffles. It's then just a short walk to Europe's most picturesque square, the showpiece **Grand'Place** (p44). Lined with ornate guildhouses,

it's worth a circuit before heading over to the **Musée de la Ville de Bruxelles** (p50), which is housed in the former bakers' guild.

10.30AM Opposite the museum is the **Hôtel de Ville** (p49), its tower reaching up more than 100m (330ft) into the Brussels sky. You can't climb the tower, but you can admire the gilded chamber rooms and learn all about the history of the Grand'Place – the terrible bombardment of 1695, the rebuilding by

2PM

2PM

Clockwise from far left: **Manneken-Pis**; **Musée de la Ville de Bruxelles**; **Musées Royaux des Beaux-Arts**; **Bozar Brasserie**.

the guildhouses and renovation in the 1800s. There are guided tours in English. The next thing everyone wants to see is the **Manneken-Pis** (p55), the symbolic statuette of a peeing boy located on the corner of rue de l'Étuve and rue du Chêne (and invariably surrounded by tourists). On the way there, you'll pass **33 rue de l'Étuve**, home to a giant fresco of Belgium's most famous cartoon character, Tintin, with Snowy and Captain Haddock.

NOON A saunter up rue du Chêne and you're at the **Éditions Jacques Brel** (p64) on place de la Vieille Halle aux Blés. Revamped to provide a more complete picture of Belgium's most famous singer-songwriter, it now requires a commitment of 90 minutes – if you're pressed for time, maybe just pick up a CD or a copy of a classic concert poster instead.

2PM From there, it's a pleasant climb up the Mont des Arts to the cultural hub of the Upper Town, with panoramic views opening up as you ascend. Here, the **Musées Royaux des Beaux-Arts** (p106), the **Musée Magritte** (p106) and the **Musée des Instruments de Musique** (p106) should keep you occupied for the rest of the afternoon with Old Masters, Surrealist treats and crazy early versions of what would eventually become the saxophone. Eating may be a pressing necessity beforehand – for those happy to snack on the hoof, there'll be a *fritekot* (chip van) on any main square, dishing up the world's finest fries, served in a cone with mayonnaise. Alternatively, if you're after a sit-down treat, head for the **Bozar Brasserie** (p108). Run by TV chef David Martin, the Bozar serves a top-notch set lunch. Before ordering pudding, though, it's worth remembering that the Musée des Instruments de Musique has a pleasant rooftop café, perfect for late-afternoon post-culture coffee and cake.

7PM Once you're done around the Upper Town, walk up rue Royale to the métro station at Parc. From there, it's three stops and little more than five minutes to reach Ste-Catherine. Once a square of staid fish restaurants, the former port of **Ste-Catherine** (p81) is now awash with contemporary alfresco eateries, such as **Mer du Nord** (p87) and **Ellis Gourmet Burger** (p83).

8.30PM By now, the nearby bars of **St-Géry** (p70) and Ste-Catherine should be buzzing. Many line place St-Géry but are usually filled to the rafters with tourists. A real locals' haunt is **Au Daringman** (p85) on rue de Flandre. Later on, don't miss revered **L'Archiduc** (p75), a classy venue on rue Antoine Dansaert that stays open until silly o'clock.

Day 2

10AM Wherever you happen to be coming from, the métro station of Heysel is an easy trip on line 6. Towering overhead is the iconic **Atomium** (p165) – this crystal molecule of metal magnified 165 billion times was created for Expo 1958. As well as offering a wonderful view of the Belgian capital and its surroundings, the Atomium can also provide coffee and a panoramic mid-morning breakfast on level eight.

10AM

11AM Immediately beneath the Atomium are various family-friendly attractions, though this area will remain a construction site for much of 2016 and 2017 while the new national stadium is being built. Depending on the weather, it may be as well to head east for a wander around the nearby **Parc du Laeken** (p165). Though its major sights – the Royal Palace and the Royal Greenhouses – are closed or rarely open to the public, this English-style park contains curious landmarks such as the **Tour Japonaise** (p165) and **Pavillon Chinois** (p165) that testify to the folly of Léopold II. Back at Heysel métro, you can be whisked across town in no time on

11AM

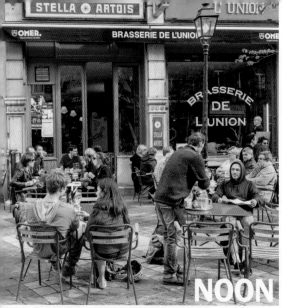

NOON

3.30PM

Clockwise from top left: **Atomium**; **Brasserie de l'Union**;
Parc du Cinquantenaire; **Tour Japonaise**.

spot of cheap lunch at one of
two recommendable spots
at its south-east and south-
west corners: **Brasserie de
l'Union** (p157) or **Brasserie
Verschueren** (p158).

2PM St-Gilles is best known
for its most famous son,
Victor Horta, and the art
nouveau houses he created
here and in neighbouring
Ixelles. Though by no means
his most ornate creation, the
one he built for himself is now
the **Musée Horta** (p154), no
more than a ten- to 15-minute
walk from the parvis. You're
now close to Ixelles, and the
upscale shopping of avenue
Louise. From nearby Trinité,
take tram 81 to Mérode,
which glides across avenue
Louise, past the pretty Ixelles
Ponds and the striking Flagey
radio building.

3.30PM Mérode is at the tip
of the **Parc du Cinquantenaire**
(p127). Its overblown features,
such as the Arc de Triomphe
and dramatic colonnades,
were created by Léopold II to
celebrate 50 years of Belgian
independence. Cut through
the park to soak up some
of the days-of-empire vibe.
At the other end of the park
is the Schuman roundabout,
and the towering institutions
of the **EU Quarter** (p122):
the Justus Lipsius Building,
Berlaymont and Résidence
Palace. If it's all a bit too
overwhelming, head down rue
Froissart to the attractive Parc
Léopold. This not only gives
you a sense of the tranquil
Quartier Léopold that stood
here before the EU came to
town, but also gives access
to **Parlamentarium** (p126), a
free and user-friendly visitors'
centre that explains the

line 6, which will take you
to Porte de Hal, one stop
beyond Gare du Midi.

NOON Once a medieval
gateway, now a neo-Gothic
museum piece, the **Porte
de Hal** (p154) stands on the
southern border of the Petit
Ring that encloses central
Brussels. After checking out
its modest historic exhibits

and the panoramic view from
its battlements, cross the
main road into chaussée
de Waterloo and walk for
a few minutes to the **parvis
de St-Gilles** (p154). This
pedestrianised main square,
with its busy market five days
a week, gives a real feel of
neighbourhood Brussels.
It also offers the chance to
have a well-earned drink and

7PM

6PM

Left: **Notre-Dame au Sablon**. Above: **Palais de Justice**.

Brederode – eerily described by Joseph Conrad in his *Heart of Darkness* – leads you to another showcase square, place du Grand Sablon. After a fortifying coffee in the **Café du Sablon** (p111) and a peep inside striking **Notre-Dame au Sablon** church (p109) – worth a look for its stunning stained-glass windows – enjoy a wander round Sablon's dainty chocolate shops and antiques stores as you slowly build up to dinner.

7PM If it's a nice evening, build up your appetite with a walk along rue Ernest Allard. At its south-western end is the vast **Palais de Justice** (p93), the largest building constructed in the 19th century. Adjoining place Poelaert provides great views across the city. Heading back to Sablon, you have a wide choice of restaurants for dinner: for somewhere lively

and Belgian, **Au Vieux Saint Martin** (p109) is a good choice. If it's full (they don't take reservations), then **Lola** (p110) is buzzy.

10PM For a nightcap, head down rue de Rollebeek, over boulevard de l'Empereur and down rue de l'Escalier. You're then close to rue du Chêne, where the **Poechenellekelder** (p58) is a typical pub with scores of classic Belgian beers. From there, if you're still full of beans, the nearby gay quarter of rue du Marché au Charbon is lined with late-night bars. Venues such as **Le Fontainas** (p58) and **Au Soleil** (p59) heave with a convivial gay/straight mix.

workings of the various parliamentary bodies in entertaining detail.

6PM From there, head to place du Luxembourg, then down rue du Luxembourg. Once you reach the Petit Ring, you're at the back of the Royal Palace. The rather creepy rue

Cartoon Capital

Belgium's cultural identity is forever linked to a young man with a blonde quiff and a white dog. The country is the spiritual home of the comic strip (*bande dessinée* or BD for short), and Tintin is its most easily identifiable cartoon icon. The cub reporter and his various friends and associates – his faithful fox terrier Snowy, gruff companion Captain Haddock – shift more postcards, T-shirts and books than anything else Belgian.

Born in 1907, Georges Rémi – or Hergé as he signed himself – is the father of what Belgians call the 'Ninth Art'. He transformed the genre, creating the clear graphic that would inspire the pop art of Warhol and Lichtenstein, and heading up a cottage industry that has now gone global. Publishing houses now churn out some 40 million comic albums a year, while tales of Tintin and other Belgian BD stars are animated for TV series or the big screen.

As well as being home to an excellent museum dedicated to the genre and no less than 40 BD stores, Brussels has also transformed several downtown façades with colourful murals of cartoon characters. These comprise the Comic Strip Walk, a tour of painted street corners. For a detailed outline of the six-kilometre route, follow the tour with a map from the tourist office (p289).

Walkers are welcomed at the corner of rue des Sables and boulevard Pachéco by a statue of Franquin's error-prone **Gaston Lagaffe**, before being pointed in the direction of the nearby **Centre Belge de la Bande Dessinée** (p63). This art nouveau former department store explores the history of cartoons across three floors of exhibits.

The route then runs past 116 rue de Laeken, and Willy Vandersteen's **Bob and Bobette** – Suske and Wiske, as they are known in their original Flemish, became the biggest post-war smash after Tintin. Next, the walk heads through the heavily muralled Ste-Catherine and St-Géry quarters, passing **Lucky Luke** at rue 't Kint/rue de la Buanderie, to myriad murals on and around lively rue du Marché au Charbon, including Frank Pé's **Broussaille**

at the top of the street. The trail winds through the Marolles (Hergé's wily **Quick and Flupke** at 191 rue Haute are suitably in character with the area) and down to Gare du Midi.

You're ushered on to the Eurostar by Philippe Geluck's **Le Chat** (87 boulevard du Midi) and, fittingly, the figures of **Tintin and Snowy** atop the Lombard Publications building (7 avenue Paul-Henri Spaak).

Diary

Your guide to what's happening when.

B russels is packed with special events and festivals throughout the year, though things really liven up in spring and summer, when the whole city seems to move outdoors. Locals love nothing better than a good street parade with the loudest possible music, from traditional bands to disco trucks – look out for Ommegang, Meyboom, Gay Pride and the biennial Zinneke parades. Arts, film and music events range from genteel family affairs to major festivals of recognised international standing. As winter descends and the nights draw in, the Christmas market is one of Europe's biggest, attracting crowds from across the Channel.

For more information on seasonal events and festivals around the city, see www.visitbrussels.be.

Foire du Midi. *See p33.*

Spring

Brussels International Festival of Fantastic Film
Palais des Beaux-Arts, Upper Town (02 201 17 13, www.bifff.net). **Date** Mar/Apr.
This two-week horror/sci-fi festival continues to pack in the gore-loving punters. There's the legendary Vampire's Ball too – entrance in costume only.

Klarafestival
Various venues (070 210 217 premium line, tickets 02 507 82 00, www.klarafestival.be). **Date** Mar.
This annual festival of international classical music is organised by Klara Radio. All the concerts are streamed live.

Brussels Pride
The Bourse & nearby streets, Grand'Place & Around (no phone, www.pride.be). **Date** May.
Pride happens during the first two weeks of May, culminating in the Parade on the second weekend. *See p183* **Be Proud of BePride.**

★ Kunstenfestivaldesarts
Various venues (information 02 219 07 07, tickets 070 222 199, www.kfda.be). **Date** May.
What makes this major three-week arts festival so different is that it appeals to all Belgians, refusing to identify solely with French or Flemish. It's on a par with the most important European festivals. Some 20 theatres and cultural centres are involved, hosting challenging, contemporary performing and visual arts.

Zinneke
Various venues (02 214 20 07, www.zinneke.org). **Date** May (next festival 2016).
The biennial Zinneke festival and street parade literally sets Brussels alight. Fire and noise, steam punk and wacky home-made carts bring a Burning Man vibe to the streets of the city.

FREE Jazz Marathon
Various venues in Brussels & nearby towns (02 456 04 86, www.brusselsjazzmarathon.be). **Date** May.
For three days, jazz-lovers can enjoy live music in bars, clubs and restaurants all over Brussels, including the Grand'Place and place Sainte-Catherine. It's a blast, with free concerts and free transport laid on to get you around the venues.

Brussels 20km
Race begins & ends in Parc du Cinquantenaire, EU Quarter (02 511 90 00, www.20kmdebruxelles.be). **Date** last Sun in May.
The race starts and finishes in the Parc du Cinquantenaire, passing through the Bois de la Cambre and avenue Louise along the way. Fewer than 5,000 runners started the inaugural event in 1980 – just under 40,000 set off in 2014, including 58 'VIPs' who had not missed a single event in 35 years.

Royal Greenhouses
Avenue du Parc Royale, Laeken (no phone,
www.monarchie.be). **Admission** €2.50;
free under-18s. **Date** Apr-May.
The magnificent Serres Royales, which were built
for Léopold II during the 1870s, are open to visitors
for a few weeks each year.

★ Concours Musical International Reine Elisabeth de Belgique
Bozar, 23 rue Ravenstein, Upper Town
(02 507 82 00, www.concours-reine-elisabeth.be).
Date May-mid June.
Regarded as one of the world's foremost music com-
petitions, the Concours was founded over 40 years
ago by Belgium's former Queen Elisabeth, a keen
violin player. Aimed at young professional musicians and singers, it has alternated between three
disciplines, but a new instrument – the cello – is
being introduced into the competition in 2017. Thus,
the new four-year cycle is: violin (2015), piano (2016),
cello (2017) and voice (2018).

Summer

Brussels Film Festival
Various venues (Flagey box office 02 641 10 20,
www.brff.be). **Date** early June.
This week-long festival, which is now mainly based
at Flagey, has European film at its heart.

Festival of Flanders
Various venues in Brussels & Flanders (tickets
070 77 00 00, www.festival.be). **Date** Mar-Oct.
One of the two major classical music festivals in
Belgium (the other is the Festival of Wallonia), the
Flanders version is, in fact, eight separate festivals,
with different themes being followed in Brussels and
the major Flemish cities.

Festival of Wallonia
Various venues in Brussels & Wallonia (081 73 37
81, www.festivaldewallonie.be). **Date** June-Oct.
Belgian and international orchestras perform in a
vast classical musical programme all across francophone Belgium, with major events taking place
in Brussels.

★ Ommegang
Grand'Place, Grand'Place & Around (070 660 601,
www.ommegang.be). **Tickets** Grand'Place €38-
€78. **Date** last Tue in June & 1st Thur in July.
This popular pageant is marked by a spectacular
procession of enthusiastic Belgians dressed as
nobles, guildsmen, jesters and peasants, marching
from the Sablon to the Grand'Place, some on horseback, others on foot, but all commemorating the
glorious entry into Brussels in 1549 of Charles V,
then new emperor of the Spanish Netherlands. The
event is held twice, to maximise viewing potential.

Brosella Folk & Jazz Festival
Théâtre de Verdure, Parc d'Osseghem, Laeken
(02 270 98 56, www.brosella.be/eng/brosella-folk-
jazz). **Tickets** €5 donation. **Date** July.
A weekend of music, played in the open-air amphi-
theatre in Osseghem Park, in the shadow of the
Atomium. It's popular with families, who take a picnic along for the Sunday afternoon.

Couleur Café
Tour & Taxis, 86 avenue du Port, Moleenbeek
(no phone, www.couleurcafe.be). **Tickets** 1-day
pass €39; 3-day pass €95. **Date** end June/early July.
Brussels' massive urban music festival, featuring
bands and food from around the world. Founded
in 1990, the event has come on in leaps and bounds
since moving from the Halles de Schaerbeek – the bill

Clockwise from left: **Ommegang;
Bruxelles les Bains; Brussels
Film Festival.**

for 2015 included Cypress Hill and Wu-Tang Clan.
And just so you get that true festival vibe, there's
even indoor camping.

FREE Bruxelles les Bains
*Quai des Péniches, Place Sainctelette, Molenbeek
(02 894 27 98, www.bruxelleslesbains.be).*
Admission free. **Open** 11am-10pm Tue-Thur,
Sun; 11am-11pm Fri, Sat. **Date** July-Aug.
Tonnes of sand are piled by the sides of the main
Brussels canal to create a city beach, full of games,
sports and cultural events. Sun permitting, natch.

Foire du Midi
*Boulevard du Midi, Marolles (no phone,
www.foiredumidi.be).* **Date** mid July-mid Aug.
The largest travelling funfair in Europe arrives and
sets up along a 1km stretch of the inner ring road
near the Gare du Midi. There's been a fair on this site
since the Middle Ages, but today's modern incarna-
tion bears no resemblance whatsoever to the spit-
roasted suckling pig event of yesteryear. *Photo p30.*

National Day
*Parc de Bruxelles, rue Royale & place des Palais,
Upper Town.* **Date** 21 July.
National Day (a public holiday) is taken seriously
in Belgium, and the festivities naturally focus on
Brussels. The royals are out in force and there's a
large military parade – with tanks, artillery, the lot.
Afterwards, the day settles down into more light-
hearted fairs, neighbourhood celebrations and fire-
works that last late into the night.

PUBLIC HOLIDAYS

New Year's Day
1 Jan

Easter Sunday
Varies each year

Easter Monday
Varies each year

Labour Day
1 May

Ascension Day
6th Thur after Easter

Whit Monday
7th Mon after Easter

Belgian National Day
21 July

Assumption
15 Aug

All Saints' Day
1 Nov

Armistice Day
11 Nov

Christmas Day
25 Dec

WINTER WONDERLAND

Sip mulled wine and skate beneath the stars.

Christmas in Brussels seems to get bigger every year. Since the decision was made in 2001 to move the **Marché de Noël** (see p35) out of the overcrowded Grand'Place, it has extended along the streets to Ste-Catherine, via the Opera House and the Bourse. The skating rink, previously on Ste-Catherine, moved in front of the Opera House in 2014.

Upwards of four million people tread the festive path during the five-week fair, passing 200-plus market stalls selling all manner of stuff, from garish candles to reindeer hats. Everything still starts on the Grand'Place, though, centrepieced by a vast tree transported from the Baltic slopes.

Traditionally, the last Friday in November is lighting-up time, a sparkling ceremony of song, dance and street performance, complemented by a parade of floats, vast prancing horses, parading drummers and amiable snowmen. The market proper begins at the back of the Bourse and follows a festively lit trail across boulevard Anspach and onward to Ste-Catherine. Each stall is a little wooden-roofed hut selling mainly arts and crafts or food and drink, all with a pan-European flavour, tying Brussels neatly in with the utopian single-market dream.

By the time you've reached Ste-Catherine and the quays beyond, you're at the heart of the festivities. The quaint chalets are punctuated every now and again by Heath Robinson-esque merry-go-rounds and the largest travelling Ferris wheel in Europe, which is adorned with 18,000 lights. It's here that the crowds gather and settle, at the beer tents, food stands and surrounding restaurants. The festive atmosphere is thick and warm, as are the plastic cups of mulled wine, helping to keep out the bitterly cold air.

FREE Royal Palace
Place des Palais, Upper Town (no phone, www.monarchie.be) **Admission** free. **Open** 10.30am-4.30pm Tue-Sun. **Date** late July-Sept.
A chance to nose around the Royal Palace for free, including the magnificent *Heaven of Delight* installation by Jan Fabre made from the wing cases of 1.6 million jewel scarab beetles.

FREE Meyboom
Rue des Sables & rue du Marais, Grand'Place & Around (no phone, www.meyboom.be). **Date** 9 Aug.
This ancient and unusual ceremony dates from 1308, when the first Planting of the Maytree took place. It's all to do with fighting off rebels from Louvain and the ensuing thanksgiving to the patron saint Laurent, whose symbol is the fabled tree. It's also an excuse to dress up, parade around the city with the tree, plant it before 5pm by the Centre Belge de la Bande Dessinée and then party into the night.

★ Tapis des Fleurs
Grand'Place, Grand'Place & Around (no phone, www.flowercarpet.be). **Date** mid Aug (next festival in 2016).
For three days every other year, the Grand'Place is the scene of a floral carpet (*tapis*) made up of a million cut begonia heads. For a superb aerial view, ascend the balcony of the Hôtel de Ville (€3).

Brussels Summer Festival
Various venues (tickets 070 660 601, www.bsf.be). **Date** Aug.
Organised by the city council, this is a ten-day festival of rock, pop and world music in venues throughout Brussels. There are two outdoor stages at Mont des Arts and Place de Palais, plus an indoor venue at La Madeleine.

Autumn

FREE Journées du Patrimoine
Across Brussels (no phone, www.journees dupatrimoinebruxelles.be). **Admission** free. **Date** 3rd weekend in Sept.
Brussels Heritage Days are a once-a-year chance to peek inside hundreds of historical buildings that are usually closed to the general public.

Brussels Marathon & Half Marathon
Starts at Parc du Cinquantenaire, EU Quarter (no phone, www.sport.be/brusselsmarathon). **Registration** €5-€85. **Date** early Oct.
The Brussels Marathon is known for its strenuous, hilly course and shouldn't be attempted by beginners. Places are limited to 2,000 runners. The gentler half-marathon is more popular and open to over-16s. There's also a five-kilometre mini-marathon and a one-kilometre run for kids.

Mini-Maxi Festival

Various venues (02 219 26 60, www.arsmusica.be/ mini-maxi). **Date** Nov (next festival in 2016).
This biennial festival of contemporary classical music, organised by the beloved Ars Musica, lasts a fortnight. The 2014 edition saw 60 concerts taking place in 15 venues across the city.

Brussels Independent Film Festival

Centre Culturel Jacques Franck, 94 chaussée de Waterloo, St-Gilles (02 649 33 40, www.fifi-bruxelles.be). **Date** early Nov.
Known as Le Fifi, this five-day festival began in 1974, when Super8 reigned supreme. Now incorporating a mix of media, its philosophy remains the same: to allow young directors to find a springboard for their work.

Winter

Ice skating

Place de la Monnaie, Grand'Place & Around (02 474 27 98, www.plaisirsdhiver.be). **Admission** €6; €4 reductions. **Open** noon-10pm Mon-Fri; 11am-10pm Sat, Sun. **Date** late Nov-early Jan.
See p34 **Winter Wonderland**.

Marché de Noël

Grand'Place to place Ste-Catherine, Lower Town (02 474 27 98, www.plaisirsdhiver.be). **Date** late Nov-early Jan.
Brussels takes its Christmas celebrations seriously, with five weeks of rejoicing that bring throngs of sightseers to the city. For more details, *see p34* **Winter Wonderland**.

IN THE KNOW THE DARK SIDE

Some regular events in Brussels only come into their own once the sun has dipped below the canals. The biggest of these is **Nuit Blanche** ('Sleepless Night'; www.nuitblanchebrussels.be), which takes place on the first Saturday in October. In 2014, more than 100,000 night owls turned out for this free urban arts festival around the city's squares, bars and arts venues.

In March, **Museum Night Fever** (www.museumnightfever.be) sees 23 museums stay open until 1am. It's not just a case of looking at exhibits – this wild night involves music, fashion, performance, bars and an after-party. The major museums are also open until 10pm every Thursday from October to December for **Nocturnes** (www.brusselsmuseumsnocturnes.be).

Finally, **Les Nuits Botanique** (www.botanique.be) fills the Serres Royales (old royal greenhouses) with indie, rock and electronic acts for three weeks in April and May. A friendly late vibe in the bars helps to make it a firm favourite.

New Year's Eve

Grand'Place, Grand'Place & Around. **Date** 31 Dec.
Crowds pour into the city centre. The heart of it all is Grand'Place, the Bourse and place de Brouckère, where fireworks are set off at midnight. Public transport is free from midnight to 5.30am (some central stations and stops are closed because of the crowds).

Ice skating, Place de la Monnaie.

Brussels' Best

There's something for everyone with our hand-picked highlights.

Musée Fin-de-Siècle.

Sightseeing

VIEWS

Atomium p165
Expo 1958 icon still a panoramic attraction.

Basilique du Sacré-Coeur p164
Way up in Koekelberg, get a bird's-eye view from under the dome.

Musée des Instruments de Musique p106
Brussels spread out before you from the rooftop café.

Palais de Justice p93
Dominating the downtown skyline, Joseph Poelaert's gargantuan creation overlooks the city.

Boat tours p283
See Brussels from a different angle on a canal or river cruise.

ART

Musées Royaux des Beaux-Arts p106
Old Masters and modern classics, all under one roof.

Musée Communal d'Ixelles p138
Home to Magritte, Delvaux and Spilliaert, in a comprehensive permanent collection.

Musée Magritte p106
Some 200 works by the master of Surrealism, inspired by everyday scenes of Brussels.

Musée Wiertz p123
Antoine's gruesome but striking oeuvre, ranged around his studio.

Musée Fin-de-Siècle p105
Recent arrival tells the story of Belgian art in the time of Khnopff, Meunier and Ensor.

Brussels Vintage Market. See p39.

Musée David et Alice van Buuren p148
Fabulous private collection – Bruegel, Van Gogh, Braque and more.

HISTORY
Musée de la Ville de Bruxelles p50
How the city came to be.
Musée Royal de l'Armée et d'Histoire Militaire p129
Battles, wars and campaigns.
Hôtel de Ville p49
Take a guided tour and discover the city's history.
BELvue Museum p104
The Belgian royals, from 1830 onwards.
Palais Coudenberg p108
How the other half lived – before 1731.

ONLY IN BRUSSELS
Centre Belge de la Bande Dessinée p63
Tintin, Lucky Luke, the Smurfs and others.
Belgian Chocolate Village p164
Just how do they make those scrumptious chocs?
Manneken-Pis p55
See what all the fuss is about.
Musée des Brasseurs Belges p50
Centuries of brewing tradition, depicted right on the main square.

CHILDREN
Musée des Enfants p172
Games, modelling, dressing up and tons of interactive fun.
Mini-Europe p170
Enjoy it while it lasts – a whole continent at your feet.
Planétarium p171
The cosmos and all its wonders presented in the space of 40 minutes.
Océade p170
Wet and wild – slides, chutes, pools and flumes.

Cartoon Walk p29
Cartoon capers on every street corner.

Eating & Drinking

BLOW-OUTS
Sea Grill p65
One of Belgium's finest seafood restaurants.
Bon-Bon p148
Michelin-starred brilliance in an out-of-town setting.
Comme chez Soi p57
Two Michelin stars and old-school service.

GLOBAL
Kamo p145
Award-winning Japanese newbie.
La Porte des Indes p145
Dishes from the royal court of Hyderabad and other maharajah faves.
Aux Mille et Une Nuits p157
The delights of Tunisia – tagines, couscous and chickpea soup.
Senza Nome p111
High-end Italian, providing imaginative if pricey fare in a prime spot on Sablon.
Toukoul p85
Authentic Ethiopian in Ste-Catherine – forget about knives and forks.
Thiên-Long p75
Steaming bowls of Vietnamese goodness.
Comocomo p74
Basque tapas in all forms and combinations.

LOCAL
Le Pré Salé p85
A white-tiled institution on rue de Flandre.
Aux Armes de Bruxelles p53
As authentic as it comes, with art deco to boot.

Crémerie de Linkebeek.

Musée Communal d'Ixelles. *See p36*.

Restaurant Vincent p53
Classic fish dishes and waiters in épaulettes.

La Roue d'Or p57
Time-honoured Belgian dishes as grandma would have made them.

Belga Queen p63
Not cheap but unquestionably Belgian, with seafood served by the platter-load.

Au Stekerlapatte p94
Tucked away in the Marolles, this is a locals' favourite for black pudding and grilled pig's trotters.

BARS

L'Archiduc p75
The Brussels bar for any occasion.

Au Daringman p85
Where the rue de Flandre set mingle amid wood panelling and old Stella ads.

Barbeton p75
Another classic spot created by bar guru Frédéric Nicolay, where trendy Volga beer is the drink *du choix*.

À la Mort Subite p54
Utterly classic Belgian bar near the Galeries St-Hubert.

Le Greenwich p76
Timeless hostelry where Magritte hustled pictures.

Ultime Atome p141
Beer, beer and more beer in a brassy brasserie.

Winery p146
Here's where to switch from grain to grape – and it's right on place Brugmann too.

Shopping

GIFTS & SOUVENIRS

Belgikie p141
One-off knick-knacks and off-beat accessories, with underscores of black, yellow and red.

Dandoy p51
Traditional Belgian ginger biscuits, speculoos and other comestible delights.

La Boutique Tintin p54
Postcards, figurines, soft toys and stationery – all featuring Belgium's most famous quiff.

Avec Plaizier p59
Original gifts, posters, postcards and calendars.

Wittamer p113
Belgium's most prestigious chocolate firm, with boxes wrapped in serious style.

BOOKS & MUSIC

Taschen p113
World-renowned art books, now with a store on Sablon.

Arlequin p59
Shelves and shelves of classic rock, punk and jazz – just two minutes from the Mannekin-Pis.

Fnac p66
The latest sounds of Belgium, France and Africa.

Sterling p67
Fiction, guides and albums at this independent outlet for English-language print.

FASHION

Stijl p80
First port of call for original Belgian design.

Martin Margiela p87
Blue-chip brand from the original Antwerp wave.

Isabelle Baines p142
Hand-finished jumpers, cardigans and sweaters.

Sandrina Fasoli p147
Refined womenswear, right on place Brugmann.

Wouters & Hendrix p147
Trendy jeweller from Antwerp's Royal Academy.

Carine Gilson p77
Sassy lingerie.

Christophe Coppens p77
Hats for every occasion. If it's good enough for Grace Jones…

Le Fabuleux Marcel de Bruxelles p77
Tank tops made fashionable by the tragic lover of Edith Piaf.

Winery.

Nightlife

CLUBS

Fuse p185
Still fizzing after all
these years.
Madame Moustache p185
The club of the moment
– hedonism in the heart
of Ste-Catherine.
Mirano Continental p186
Smarter than the average bar
set in a 1950s cinema.
Le You p186
Progressive house, breaks
and trance, with a decent
gay/straight mix.

MUSIC

Ancienne Belgique p187
A great live venue in the
heart of town with plenty
of pedigree.
Botanique p188
Sought-after sounds in a
former botanical garden.
Magasin 4 p188
Loud rock and indie in
an industrial setting.
Jazz Station p192
Affordable, atmospheric
and muso-friendly.

Hatshoe p78
Designer accessories from
Antwerp and elsewhere.

MARKETS

Place du Jeu de Balle p96
Eclectic junk spread out over
a neighbourhood square.
Châtelain Market p146
Popular purveyor of sought-
after produce.
**Brussels Vintage
Market** p70
Monthly bazaar of retro
togs, held in a historic
downtown market hall.
Midi Market p156
Sunday morning selection
of bright produce and
cheap gear, located by
the Eurostar terminal.

FOOD & DRINK

La Maison du Miel p60
Honey of every stripe
and every type.
Le Palais des Thés p60
More than 200 varieties
of tea from 30 countries,
with free tastings.
Crémerie de Linkebeek p77
The city's oldest cheese
shop, with rare examples
by small-batch domestic
producers.
Pierre Marcolini p113
Exquisite chocolates from
a master of the genre.
Beer Mania p141
Two decades of experience
in stocking, selling and
packaging beer – 400-plus
varieties on offer.

Performing Arts

VENUES

Théâtre de la Monnaie p194
Prestigious opera house
with a revolutionary past.
Bozar p194
Successfully rebranded
palace of the arts.
Flagey p194
Revived former home of the
National Radio Orchestra.
Les Brigittines p196
Imaginative multimedia space
and first-rate dance venue.
Beursschouwburg p197
Fifty years of innovative
performance.

Explore

Grand'Place & Around

Gazed over by the towering Hôtel de Ville, the Grand'Place is Brussels' showcase square. Lined on each side by fabulous guildhouses, each relating to a historic trade, the square owes its stunning appearance to its destruction – by the French forces of Louis XIV in 1695. What you see today stems from swift and lavish reconstruction by the guilds. Spreading out around the square is a tangle of historic streets, their width, shape and names echoing their medieval roots. This atmospheric hub is known as the Îlot Sacré. Its jewel is the gorgeous 19th-century shopping arcade of the Galeries St-Hubert. Further north stands the Théâtre de la Monnaie, the opera house with historic ties to Belgium's independence of 1830. South of the Grand'Place, a more vivid tableau is presented by niche boutiques, quirky bars and the gay quarter around rue du Marché au Charbon.

Musée de la Ville de Bruxelles.

Don't Miss

1 Grand'Place Brussels' showcase square (p44).

2 Musée de la Ville de Bruxelles The history of the city laid out in a former medieval courthouse (p50).

3 Hôtel de Ville Standing tall through invasions and bombardments (p49).

4 Galeries St-Hubert Europe's oldest shopping arcade (p52).

5 Centre Belge de la Bande Dessinée Tintin, Lucky Luke et al (p63).

EXPLORE

GRAND'PLACE

The **Grand'Place** is Brussels's most obvious and always outstanding set piece. It's hard to dispute former resident Victor Hugo's description as it being 'the most beautiful square in the world' – or UNESCO's designation of it as a World Heritage Site. The Place has always been a focus for the social and cultural life of the city, whether as a medieval market, a parade ground, a place of execution, a concert venue or, until the 1980s, a shortcut for traffic and a car park for coaches. Now a pedestrian zone, it changes colour and character according to the season: flower-strewn in summer, fairy-lit for Yule.

In its earliest days, it was a low-lying marsh. The main market originally ranged around the nearby early medieval Church of St Nicholas, by the banks of the Senne that used to run past here. Trade gradually extended to what was then a primitive thoroughfare. By the 12th century, when profits started rolling in from the lucrative textile trade, the 'Lower Market' was paved over, and the first permanent houses erected. The first guild on the block was the powerful drapers. Enclosed markets, proffering cloths, meat and bread, displayed the wares of the all-powerful Dukes of Brabant. Based at the imperial fiefdom of Leuven, the ruling dukes could easily assess and collect the taxes they were due from traders set up at individual outlets.

In turn, with Brussels and its focal market at a busy international trading crossroads, increased revenues allowed for the creation of a town hall in the early 1300s and, later, even a fountain to act as a centrepiece for the whole square. Fountains also flowed inside the Town Hall itself. Opposite, another powerful guild, the bakers, set up the Bread Hall (Broodhuys), which later became the law courts. In subsequent centuries, it housed the imprisoned Counts Egmont and Hoorn, among the leading nobles who had opposed the stern Catholic rule of Philip of Spain in the mid 1500s. The Grand'Place became the site of gruesome public torture and execution. One June day in 1568, the counts walked out on a scaffold built to lead from the law courts to the executioner's block, above the heads of anyone potentially able to rescue them. Their beheadings were only two of hundreds, perhaps thousands, in those few short brutal months. The Broodhuys, later known as the Maison du Peuple under the French, then

Grand'Place.

Neufville, aka the Duc de Villeroi, a dilettante soldier and poor military strategist, inexplicably ordered the senseless bombardment of Brussels by cannon and mortar. Using the tall tower of the Town Hall to guide them, his gunners achieved direct hits on every property on the Grand'Place – in fact, they laid waste to some 4,000 buildings in total. Ironically, the last edifice standing was, in fact, the Town Hall tower. Even today, it can be used as a beacon to direct you as you negotiate the confusing (and usually crowded) tangle of streets around the Grand'Place.

Under the command of the omnipotent mercantile guilds (*see p248* **The Gilded Guilds**), the square was rebuilt in less than five years, with fine bronze and gold detail. As each guild jostled for influence, it branded each house with individual markings and a name (although some pre-date the guilds). These wonderful houses suffered further damage in the string of uprisings, marches and ransackings in the immediate aftermath of the French Revolution of 1789. Almost worse, the Grand'Place was then left to neglect.

It was thanks to long-term, progressive city mayor Charles Buls that so much of historic Brussels was protected and immaculately restored, the Grand'Place included. In his near 20-year tenure at the end of the 1800s, he saw to it that all the gorgeous façades of the city's showpiece square appear as they do today. In his honour, the architects he commissioned collected money among themselves and created a monument to Buls at the L'Étoile house, no.8.

A century or more later, the fruits of their collective labour sparkle around the main square for all to see. The following are some of the most spectacular guildhouses worth investigating:

Nos.1-2, **Le Roi d'Espagne** ('The King of Spain'). This was also the bakers' guild and is now a near permanently busy pub. The bust on the front façade is the Roi d'Espagne in question, Charles II, the last Habsburg ruler of Spain, whose otherwise near disastrous reign ended with the Treaty of Karlowitz and the significant retreat of the Ottoman Empire. Turkish flags and prisoners in chains are depicted either side of the maligned monarch.

No.3, **La Brouette** ('The Wheelbarrow'). The tallow dealers' guild, merchants of oil and candles, whose patron St Gilles stands in statue form above the door.

No.4, **Le Sac** ('The Sack'). The joiners' and coopers' guild, with a carving of a man diving into a sack above the door, lending the house its name. In spring 2015, all buildings numbered 1-7 on the Grand'Place underwent restoration – the five above Le Sac were given completely new mouldings.

No.5, **La Louve** ('The She-Wolf'). The archers' guild, with a phoenix at the top to symbolise

the Maison du Roi, has been the home of the Musée de la Ville de Bruxelles since 1887.

It wasn't all blood and beheadings. Philip's predecessor, the popular, Dutch- and French-speaking Charles V who ruled over an empire that extended as far as distant Peru, oversaw the great Ommegang on the Grand'Place in 1549. Taking place shortly before his emotional handover of power at the Coudenberg Palace, this was a magnificent pageant set up for his Joyous Entry into Brussels, 30 years after he had become Holy Roman Emperor. Although other great pageants were staged later, most notably for Philip's daughter Isabella in 1615, when it came to reviving the concept in modern times, the model was the costumes and characters from 1549. Today, in late June and early July, a cavalcade of banner-bearing locals dressed as medieval nobles escort a present-day Charles V around the Grand'Place, accompanied by a parade of horses. Stilt-fighting and a jousting tournament also take place, and a grandstand is set up for paying customers. For details, s*ee p32* **Ommegang**.

The pageantry and the market trading ended on 13 August 1695. Commander of a 70,000-strong French force, Marshal Francois de

EXPLORE

EXPLORE

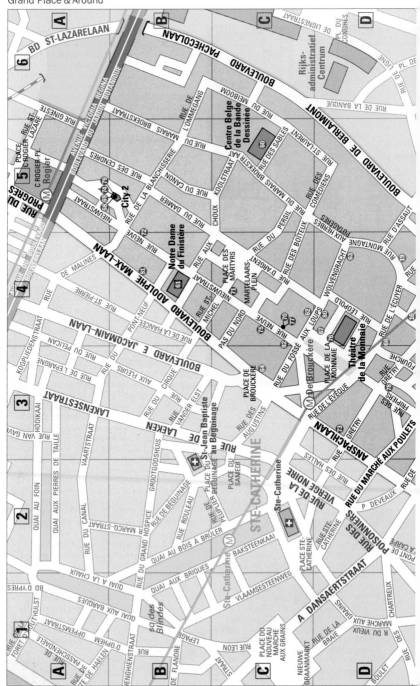

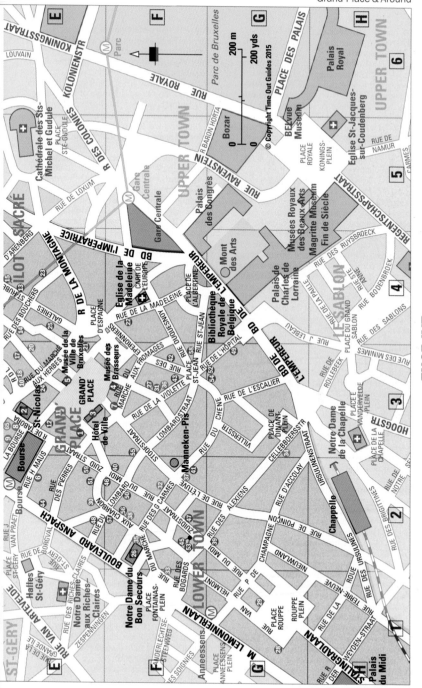

© Copyright Time Out Guides 2015

EXPLORE

the building's two burnings and rebuilds. The relief over the door relates to the legend of Romelus and Remus.

No.6, **Le Cornet** ('The Horn'). The boatmen's guild, with a façade designed to resemble the stern of a galleon. It also features another likeness of Charles II of Spain, the Habsburg monarch whose last years coincided with the rebuilding of the Grand'Place.

No.7, **Le Renard** ('The Fox'). The haberdashers' guild, with a female statue representing four of the world's continents. Created two centuries after the Age of Discovery, it signifies the far-flung destinations from which the finest materials have been brought to sell here in Brussels.

No.8, **L'Etoile** ('The Star'). This was knocked down in 1853 to accommodate the flow of tourist crowds – which says quite a lot about visitor numbers around the Grand'Place, even back then. Burgomaster Charles Buls was so incensed he had it rebuilt over an arcade. Today this serves as shelter to the much-caressed recumbent figure of Everard 't Serclaes, the guild leader who fought off a Flemish attack on Brussels in 1356. Soldiers from Gaasbeek wrested him from the property that once stood here and tore his tongue out, prompting locals to destroy Gaasbeek castle. Stroking the statue's worn limbs is supposedly meant to bring good luck.

No.9, **Le Cygne** ('The Swan'). This is the butchers' guild. Marx and Engels (who wrote the Communist Manifesto in Brussels) drank in a brasserie here, and the house witnessed the birth of the Belgian Workers' Party. Today, it's still a restaurant, La Maison du Cygne (www. greatmomentsinbrussels.be/fr/la-maison-du-cygne) and was renovated after a change of ownership in 2013.

No.10, **L'Arbre d'Or** ('The Golden Tree'). The brewers' guild and the only building still under guild ownership. Note the hop plant detail in the masonry. A tavern in the 1700s, today it houses the cellar **Musée des Brasseurs Belges**, with a permanent display of brewing techniques over the centuries. The statue outside is of Charles-Alexandre of Lorraine, the 18th-century benefactor to the brewers. *See p56* **Here for the Beer**.

Nos.24-25, **La Chaloupe d'Or** ('The Golden Galleon' – now a touristified restaurant of the same name, www.greatmomentsinbrussels. be/fr/la-chaloupe-dor); and **La Maison des Tailleurs** ('The House of Tailors'). The tailors' guild is topped by St Boniface, holding up a symbolic pair of scissors.

Nos.26-27, **Le Pigeon** ('The Pigeon'). This was home to the artists' guild. This was one of a handful of properties in Brussels that Victor Hugo stayed in during his Belgian exile in the early 1850s, commemorated with a plaque. His rooms above what was then a tobacconists

allowed Hugo a perfect view of the Town Hall opposite. He also stayed briefly at no.16.

Stretching across the east side of the Grand'Place, from rue de la Colline and rue des Chapeliers, is a terrace of six houses with a single façade, designed by Willem de Bruyn in 1698. The grouping is known as the **House of the Dukes of Brabant** because of their sculptures on the front. Restored at various stages in modern times, the building retains its gilded façade, though this striking ornamentation is its main purpose – except for, at one end, the Estaminet Kelderke (www.restaurant-estaminet-kelderke.be) tourist restaurant, newly converted boutique hotel **Le Quinze** (*see p270*) and, beneath them both, the Restaurant Kelderke.

Facing the **Hôtel de Ville** (Town Hall) is the Maison du Roi, which houses the **Musée de la Ville de Bruxelles**. As well as its permanent collection relating to the development of the city – including, on the first floor, the costume collection of the Manneken-Pis – the museum is presenting, for the foreseeable future, a series of exhibitions about Brussels and Belgium in World War I.

The bombardment that destroyed the Grand'Place in 1695 also flattened most of the buildings around it. These were also rebuilt, street by street, including the tower of the oldest surviving church in Brussels, **St Nicholas**. This was the original site of the market that gradually extended to what became the Grand'Place – St Nicholas is the patron saint of merchants. Today, it's slightly set back from the Roi d'Espagne on the corner of the main square, on rue au Beurre.

Diagonally opposite is the **Bourse**, the old stock exchange. This grand, neoclassical building boasts a decorative frieze by Carrier-Belleuse, with statues by Rodin adorning the top. It was built in the early 1870s, shortly after King Léopold II had ascended to the throne. Riches from the Congo, which was run as his own private fiefdom, allowed the notorious monarch to splurge on grandiose constructions around Belgium. It was here in the Bourse that the Welsh explorer Henry Morton Stanley, whom Léopold had commissioned to carve out and claim further African territory, gave a triumphant speech after the Emin Pasha Relief Expedition of the late 1880s. The price of rubber was about to go through the roof, and Stanley was greeted with rapturous applause – even though his mission had been chaotic and completely disastrous.

Stanley had also published a lucrative book detailing his travels. When stories of atrocities and disease came to light later from other sources, Stanley was posthumously discredited and the Congo passed from Léopold's hands to Belgium's. The explorer's daughter, Denzil, donated Stanley's archives to the Musée Royale de l'Afrique Centrale in Brussels, which is currently undergoing renovation.

Underneath the Bourse runs the pré-métro, the half-tram, half-underground network, instigated before a modern metro system was created in the late 1970s. Usefully, it runs below arterial boulevard Anspach to Gare du Midi and the Eurostar terminal. Unfortunately, it is notoriously rife with pickpockets.

Either side of the Bourse stand two venerable cafés: **Le Falstaff** and **Le Cirio**. The latter was created by and named after the king of the tinned tomato, Francesco Cirio, in 1886. Originally a *salon de dégustation* for the Italian's many products, it then became a café-brasserie but even today features posters displaying his wares.

Sights & Museums

Choco-Story

9-11 rue de la Tête d'Or (02 514 20 48, www. choco-story-brussels.be). Métro Gare Centrale or pré-métro Bourse. **Open** 10am-4.30pm Tue-Sun. Closed 2nd & 3rd wks Jan. **Admission** €6; €5 reductions; €3.50 6-12s; free under-6s. **No credit cards. Map** p47 E3 ❶
Renamed and refashioned in 2014, the former rather staid Museum of Cocoa & Chocolate is the fruit of a union between Peggy van Lierde, daughter of the museum's original founder, and the van Belle family, responsible for similar ventures in Bruges, Paris and elsewhere. The result is not only a history of this sweet treat – from its discovery by the Aztecs through its arrival in Europe and on to the development of the praline and other Belgian specialities

– but also includes demonstrations, tastings and workshops. Competition is fierce nowadays, with the main chocolate firms in town also providing workshops – not to mention the Belgian Chocolate Village in Koekelberg (*see p164*).
► *For advice on where to invest in the city's finest chocolate, see p107.*

FREE Église de St-Nicolas

1 rue au Beurre (02 513 80 22). Pré-métro Bourse. **Open** 10am-6pm Mon-Sat; 9.30am-6.30pm Sun. **Admission** free. **Map** p47 E3 ❷
Founded in the 12th century, this model of medieval sanctity still displays the curved shape that followed the old line of the River Senne, with tidy little houses (now shops) built into its walls. Over the centuries, the church became gloomy and stained but, of late, it has been lovingly and painstakingly renovated and now sits again in warm, honeyed splendour.

★ Hôtel de Ville

Grand'Place (02 279 43 76). Métro Gare Centrale or pré-métro Bourse. **Open** *Guided tours* (in English) 3pm Wed; 10am, 2pm Sun. **Admission** €5. **No credit cards. Map** p47 E3 ❸
Construction work on this superb edifice, adorned with elaborate sculptures, took no less than 50 years. The left wing (1406) was built by Jacob van Thienen; later, for balance, a right wing was introduced by an unknown architect. The old belfry was too small for the new structure, so Jan van Ruysbroeck added the splendid 113m (376ft) tower, an octagon sitting firmly on a square plinth. In 1455, a dramatic gilt

EXPLORE

Le Falstaff. See p50.

EXPLORE

IN THE KNOW TIPS & TIPPING

Brussels is not particularly cheap for eating out, nor do all its restaurants offer a set menu. The best bargains can be found at lunchtime (*midi*), when you can order the *plat du jour*, often with a free glass of wine or a coffee thrown in. Bills come with service included, so there is no obligation to tip. Most diners leave a little extra to round off the evening; in top-quality restaurants, a more generous contribution is expected.

For information on restaurants (and visitors' reviews), website www.resto.be is the most wide-reaching resource. The search engine works in French, Dutch and English, but is hyper-sensitive and not smart enough to find a restaurant if you misspell the name.

statue of St Michael slaying the dragon was erected at its pinnacle. The tower seems to unbalance the rest of the building and legend has it that, in despair, the architect climbed to the top of his masterpiece and threw himself from it. This is unlikely; the simple reason for the imbalance is that the left wing is smaller than the right in order to preserve the street pattern. Famously, the tower was used by French gunners during the terrible bombardment of 1695 – which is why it, mainly, survived.

You can't climb the tower, but the guided tour visits a series of elegant official rooms. The most flamboyant is the 18th-century Council Chamber, awash with gilt, tapestries, mirrors and ornate ceiling paintings. Brussels' only secular gothic building, the Town Hall remains in practical use as the seat of the Mayor of Brussels and is also the official marriage venue for Brussels commune residents.

Musée des Brasseurs Belges

10 Grand'Place (02 511 49 87, www.beer paradise.be). Métro Gare Centrale or pré-métro Bourse. **Open** *Apr-Nov* 10am-5pm daily. *Dec-Mar* 10am-5pm Mon-Fri; noon-5pm Sat, Sun. **Admission** €5. **No credit cards.** **Map** p47 F3 ❹
See p56 **Here for the Beer.**

Musée de la Ville de Bruxelles

Grand'Place (02 279 43 50, www.museedela villedebruxelles.be). Métro Gare Centrale or pré-métro Bourse. **Open** 10am-5pm Tue, Wed, Fri-Sun; 10am-8pm Thur. **Admission** €4; €2-€3 reductions; free under-6s; free 6-18s Sat, Sun. **No credit cards. Map** p47 E3 ❺
Constructed in the 13th century and thrice rebuilt, the Museum of the City of Brussels is known in Dutch as the Broodhuys ('Bread House') – a more accurate title since it was owned by the bakers' guild.

Shored up after 1695, it was left to crumble until Mayor Jules Anspach decided to rebuild it in fashionable neo-Gothic style in 1860. A museum since 1887, it now houses a somewhat dowdy collection of paintings, photographs, documents, tapestries and models that chronicle the history of Brussels. You'll find enlightening sections on the bombardment of 1695 and Léopold II's ambitious building programme, but the dizzying impression is one of constant invasion. The museum also contains the vast wardrobe of the Manneken-Pis (amounting to almost 800 costumes, of which around 200 are on permanent display), plus some impressive paintings, including Pieter Bruegel the Elder's *Wedding Procession*.

Restaurants

Le Falstaff

19-25 rue Henri Maus (02 511 87 89, www. lefalstaff.be). Pré-métro Bourse. **Open** 11am-2am daily. **Main courses** €12-€26.50. **Map** p47 E2 ❻ **Café**
An awning on one side of the Bourse barely prepares the first-time visitor for the eye candy of the art nouveau interior, which has been attracting diners and boozers for the better part of a century. The serviceable main dishes will never set your heart aflutter, but just being here is an experience. The extended opening hours are a major draw. *Photo p49.*

Hard Rock Café

12A Grand'Place (02 546 16 60, www.hard rock.com/cafes/brussels). Pré-métro Bourse. **Open** noon-11pm Mon-Thur, Sun; noon-midnight Fri, Sat. **Main courses** €14.50-€24.50. **Map** p47 F3 ❼ **Café**
See p140 **The Burgers of Brussels**.

Pubs & Bars

À la Bécasse

11 rue de Tabora (02 511 00 06, www.ala becasse.com). Pré-métro Bourse. **Open** 11am-midnight Mon-Thur, Sun; 11am-1am Fri, Sat. **Map** p47 E3 ❽
See p56 **Here for the Beer.**

Le Cirio

18-20 rue de la Bourse (02 512 13 95). Pré-métro Bourse. **Open** 10am-1am daily. **No credit cards.** **Map** p47 E3 ❾
Le Cirio is named after the Italian grocer, remembered on a million sauce cans, who shipped wagons of goodies over the Alps from Turin to his ornate delicatessen, set by the stock exchange. Both the Bourse and deli have since folded, but the decor remains – beautiful fittings and Vermouth promotions, cash registers and century-old gastronomy awards – along with the eternally popular *half-en-half* wine (half sparkling, half still, wholly Italian). Grandes dames and their lookalike poodles sip away

the afternoon, the former from a stemmed glass, the latter from a bowl of tap water. Pre-war toilets complete the experience. Le Cirio doesn't have a website but it is on Facebook.

À l'Imaige Nostre-Dame

3 impasse des Cadeaux, off 8 rue du Marché aux Herbes (02 219 42 49). Pré-métro Bourse. **Open** noon-midnight Mon-Thur, Sun; noon-1am Fri, Sat. **No credit cards. Map** p47 E3 ⑩
See p56 **Here for the Beer.**

Le Roi d'Espagne

1 Grand'Place (02 513 08 07, www.roidespagne. be). Pré-métro Bourse. **Open** 10am-1am daily. **Map** p47 E3 ⑪
The king of the guildhouses on the gilded square (it was the HQ of the bakers' guild), Le Roi is a classic spot in a prime location, taking full advantage of the tourist trade by filling its warren of dark rooms and corners with dangling marionettes, old prints and pigs' bladders. By all means pity the poor pigs, but also save some sympathy for the waiters in monk outfits, as they struggle to keep tabs on busy tables while tourists scrap it out for a seat with that view over the Grand'Place. Many a diplomatic incident has been caused grabbing one.
▶ *For a quick rundown of the guilds and their emblems, see p45.*

Shops & Services

★ Dandoy

31 rue au Beurre (02 540 27 02, www.biscuiterie dandoy.be). Pré-métro Bourse. **Open** 9am-7pm Mon-Sat; 10.30am-7pm Sun. **Map** p47 E3
⑫ **Food & drink**
The oldest and most renowned cookie shop in town sells the best melt-in-your-mouth *speculoos* (traditional Belgian ginger biscuits), *pains d'amande* (wafer-thin biscuits), *pain d'épices* and *pain à la grecque*. Altogether there are six Dandoy stores around Brussels and Waterloo – plus one in Tokyo. The branch at 14 rue Charles Buls south of the Grand'Place is also a tearoom. *Photos p52.*
Other locations throughout the city.

ILOT SACRÉ

Just north of the Grand'Place is the **Ilot Sacré** ('Holy Isle'), saved by locals and now one of the liveliest areas in the city centre. At the time of the World Expo of 1958, the city authorities were looking to redevelop the streets here to ease traffic flow. Shopkeepers in the neighbourhood were outraged and the plans were axed. After the Expo, the authorities decided to create seven protected 'isles' with stringent planning rules to protect their identity, and, in 1960, the Ilot Sacré was created.

Le Roi d'Espagne.

Dandoy. See p51.

It is an evocative medieval tangle of small streets, devoted almost entirely to restaurants, many of which entice tourists with stupendous displays of fresh fish and seafood reclining on mountains of ice. Rue des Bouchers is the main thoroughfare, with the street names around it appetisingly evoking the Middle Ages, with the likes of rue des Harengs ('Herring Lane') and rue du Marché aux Herbes ('Grassmarket'). Rue des Bouchers is today still full of original houses with stepped gables and wooden doors, mostly dating from the 17th century. At the end of the street, near no.58, a narrow passage leads to the **Résidence Centrale**, a modern development in a traditional style with a tranquil courtyard and an elegant bronze fountain. Not quite so elegant is **Jeanneke-Pis** (www.jeannekepisofficial. com), the female counterpart to the Manneken, installed in 1985 to raise money for charity, and still squatting in nearby impasse de la Fidélité.

Petite rue des Bouchers has more of the same brash restaurants, but it was here, at no.30, that La Rose Noire jazz club gave Jacques Brel his first success in 1953. The renowned **Théâtre du Toone**, a puppet theatre (see p199) and café, is in an alley off here in a building put up a year after the bombardment. Tradition dictates that performances take place in the authentic argot of Brussels, either Flemish or French – but the bar, signposted from the Grand'Place, is one of the most accessible and popular tourist destinations.

In contrast to the bustle of medieval markets evoked nearby, **Galeries St-Hubert** suggests the seeds of the modern mall. Europe's oldest glass arcade was designed by JP Cluysenaar and opened by Léopold I in 1847, at the time, as Karl Marx cynically observed, of a potato famine.

It still sparkles, equalling the glitter of the jewellery shops that it harbours. Set out in three sections (galeries de la Reine, du Roi and des Princes), it also houses keynote cultural venues such as the **Arenberg Galeries** (see p176), a fabulous independent arthouse cinema; the **Théâtre Royal des Galeries** (see p199), with a noted Magritte fresco on the ceiling, and the Théâtre du Vaudeville, which now boasts a fine pedigree as a restaurant and events venue. Restaurants such as **Ogenblik** and cafés such as **Mokafé** echo the splendour of their surroundings. In a more recent development, the **Hôtel des Galeries** (see p269) and its partner restaurant, **Comptoir des Galeries**, have brought contemporary lodging and dining to the age-old selection of outlets and boutiques.

Opposite the Comptoir des Galeries is one of the city's more obscure yet unique historic attractions: the **Museé des Lettres et Manuscrits de Bruxelles**, with the original writings of Churchill, Voltaire and Picasso. Leaving by the arcade's northern entrance, you come to one of the city's most venerable bars, **À La Mort Subite**.

EXPLORE

IN THE KNOW
THE MICHELIN MEN

In 2015, 127 Belgian restaurants were awarded Michelin stars, 18 of those being in Brussels. Impressive as this is, you don't need to fork out Michelin-rated money to eat well in this little country – or in Brussels, with its 2,000 or so restaurants. Most places have been around for years: if a new establishment arrives and doesn't come up to scratch, it soon closes. Brussels diners know what they like and are not prepared to compromise on their expectations.

By the arcade's southern entrance stands busy place d'Agora, an oasis of waiting taxi cabs with a small craft market on most days. The square is centrepieced by a statue of beloved city mayor Charles Buls, who did so much to revive the historic centre of the city, often in complete opposition to the wishes of the otherwise omnipotent 19th-century monarch, Léopold II. Buls is depicted relaxed and sitting down, his beloved dog pawing at his lap. It's marked on most maps as place d'Espagne, which is, strictly speaking, the desolate area behind, with the giant statue of Don Quixote looking over the old town.

Sights & Museums

Museé des Lettres et Manuscrits de Bruxelles

Galerie du Roi 1 (02 514 71 87, www.mlmb.be). Métro Gare Centrale. **Open** 10am-6pm Tue-Fri; 11am-6pm Sat, Sun. **Admission** €7; €5 reductions (€1 extra for a touchscreen guide). **Map** p47 E4 ⓭
This quirky but worthwhile attraction presents nothing less than the history of written communication. It was opened in 2011, inspired by a similar, longer-established institution in Paris. The shared collections run to some 140,000 artefacts, divided into the categories of science, art, music, literature and history. Relating to Brussels, you'll find the *chansons* of Jacques Brel and 3D drawings of Tintin by Hergé dating from the 1940s, while recent temporary exhibitions have focused on themes such as Victor Hugo, letters between the painters Magritte, Rops and Ensor, and rare documentation from the earliest days of Surrealism.

Restaurants

★ Aux Armes de Bruxelles

13 rue des Bouchers (02 511 55 98, www.arme brux.be). Métro/pré-métro De Brouckère. **Open** noon-10.45pm Mon-Fri; noon-11.15pm Sat; noon-10.30pm Sun. **Main courses** €19-€57. **Map** p47 E4 ⓮ Belgian

Sitting like a grounded galleon in the gaudy sea of fish restaurants near the Grand'Place, Aux Armes is a classically mullioned institution, beloved by business folk and middle-aged, middle-class Belgians since 1921. The art deco interior is as classy as the waiters, who slide around with the utmost professionalism, delivering plates of mussels, turbot and the occasional steak. It's seafood that the locals come for, including perfect *moules-frites* and creamy fish *waterzooi*. *Photos p54.*

Mokafé

9 galerie du Roi (02 511 78 70). Métro Gare Centrale. **Open** 7am-11.30pm Mon-Sat; 8am-11.30pm Sun. **Main courses** €8-€18. **Map** p47 E4 ⓯ Café
Located near the opera and opposite Brussels' best classical music shop, the Mokafé attracts a terrace full of arty types year round, protected from inclement weather by covered galleries. It's good for lunch, with reasonably priced Belgian café grub and pasta. On Sunday mornings, locals bring their newspapers and sit for hours with coffee and a croissant. Everyone pretends to be in their own little world, but just watch eyes dart and ears prick when a newcomer takes a table; knowing nods to regulars and faux lack of interest at strangers.

★ Ogenblik

1 galerie des Princes (02 511 61 51, www. ogenblik.be). Métro Gare Centrale. **Open** noon-2.30pm, 7pm-midnight Mon-Sat. **Main courses** €23-€35. **Map** p46 D4 ⓰ French
Set on the edge of the glamorous covered galleries, this place is a must for flash-the-cash professionals. The eclectic interior is sort of old-railway-station-meets-Conran, with a sprinkle of salt on the floor to give it that old soak feel. The menu is a polished affair: turbot, hare, and sweetbreads all make an appearance. Watch the prices, though, as the bill tends to mount up in an *ogenblik* (blink of an eye). Also be sure to look out for Madame, who takes the bookings and prepares the bills; she sits at an ancient shop till with a little wooden footstool, wearing dancing pumps, half-moon glasses and a mess-with-me-and-you're-dead look. Classic.

Restaurant Vincent

8-10 rue des Dominicains (02 511 26 07, www. restaurantvincent.com). Métro/pré-métro De Brouckère. **Open** noon-2.45pm, 6.30-11.30pm Mon-Sat; noon-3pm, 6.30-10.30pm Sun. **Main courses** €20-€35. **Map** p47 E3 ⓱ Fish & seafood
Up a little side street from the main glare of rue des Bouchers is the unassuming frontage of Vincent. Newcomers hesitate to enter because there seems to be only a kitchen entrance. Correct. Be brave, and walk past the steaming chefs, and the dry maître d' will meet you at the other side. Vincent's fame comes from its tiled dining room, with a 1905 mural depicting old-time fishing and wild seas. Some of the tables are shaped like fishing smacks, just in case

EXPLORE

you missed the theme. Ask for one when booking, or you could end up in the unexceptional dining room next door. This is one of those places where the final touches are rustled up at table by epauletted waiters.

Pubs & Bars

Délirium Café
4 impasse de la Fidélité Carmes (02 514 44 34, www.deliriumcafe.be). Pré-métro Bourse. **Open** 10am-4am Mon-Sat; 10am-2am Sun. **Map** p47 E3 ⑱ *See p56* **Here for the Beer**.

★ À la Mort Subite
7 rue des Montagnes aux Herbes Potagères (02 513 13 18, www.alamortsubite.com). Métro Gare Centrale. **Open** 11am-1am Mon-Sat; noon-midnight Sun. **Map** p46 D4 ⑲ *See p56* **Here for the Beer**.

Toone
21 petite rue des Bouchers (02 513 54 86, www.toone.be). Métro/pré-métro De Brouckère. **Open** noon-midnight Tue-Sun. **No credit cards. Map** p47 E3 ⑳
This might be a well-known spot on the tourist trail, but to call it a trap would be doing the Toone family a great injustice. Eight generations have worked the puppet theatre here, cynical in six tongues. This cosy, two-room, dark wood establishment is the old theatre bar, a familiar stop for many Brussophiles as it's quirky enough to show to first-time visitors (dangling marionettes and the like), quiet enough to enjoy in whispered intimacy, and not too quaint to put you off coming again. It's signposted by the Musée de la Ville de Bruxelles on the Grand'Place.

Shops & Services

La Boutique Tintin
13 rue de la Colline (02 514 51 52, www. tintinboutique.com). Métro Gare Centrale. **Open** 10am-6pm Mon-Sat; 11am-5pm Sun. **Map** p47 E3 ㉑ **Comics**

> **IN THE KNOW LIGHTING-UP TIME**
>
> Rules on smoking in bars are clear. Since 2011, when the ban was extended from establishments serving food to all places of public entertainment (including casinos), venues can set up a designated smoking room, provided it has suitable ventilation and does not take up more than a quarter of the overall area. Drinks can only be served in the non-smoking sections of the bar, though smokers can take their glasses with them.

If you're a Tintin fan, then it's going to be hard to walk into this shop and not leave without buying something, even though prices are high. The range includes clothes, stationery and soft toys, as well as the books themselves. If you're a serious collector, there are also some limited edition miniatures.

Corné Port-Royal
9 rue de la Madeleine (02 512 43 14, www. corneportroyal.be). Métro Gare Centrale. **Open** 10am-8pm daily. **Map** p47 F4 ㉒ **Food & drink**
A good-quality chocolatier (similar to Neuhaus and Godiva), with franchises around town. Look out for the rather theatrical store at 5 Galerie de la Reine. **Other locations** throughout the city.

Délices et Caprices
68 rue des Bouchers (02 512 14 51). Pré-métro Bourse. **Open** 2-8pm Mon, Thur-Sun. **Map** p47 E4 ㉓ **Food & drink** *See p56* **Here for the Beer**.

Grasshopper
39 rue du Marché aux Herbes (02 511 96 22, www.thegrasshoppertoys.be). Métro/pré-métro De Brouckère or métro Gare Centrale. **Open** 10am-7pm daily. **Map** p47 E3 ㉔ **Toys**
This fantastic toy store, with eye-catching window displays, begins with a ground floor of trinkets and classics (yoyos, kaleidoscopes), novelty lamps and lots more. Upstairs are puzzles, educational and craft-based games, and larger items.

Aux Armes de Bruxelles.
See p53.

Tropismes

11 galerie des Princes (02 512 88 52, www. tropismes.com). Métro/pré-métro De Brouckère or métro Gare Centrale. **Open** 11am-6.30pm Mon; 10am-6.30pm Tue-Thur; 10am-7.30pm Fri; 10.30am-7pm Sat; 1.30-6.30pm Sun. **Map** p47 E4 ㉕ **Books & music**

Occupying the premises of the legendary former jazz club Blue Note in the Galeries St-Hubert, Tropismes is the most convivial French-language bookstore in town. It has a separate entrance at no.4, specialising in comic and children's books.

SOUTH FROM THE GRAND'PLACE

The south side of the Grand'Place is quieter, but no less historic, its street names (Plattesteen, Cantersteen) reflecting the early medieval era when those rich enough could build houses from stone. Much was destroyed in the 1695 bombardment, of course, but the **Quartier St-Jacques**, as this neighbourhood is known, is characterised by idiosyncratic shops and odd vendors of strange plastic figurines.

Follow the crowds from the square, past the lace and tapestry shops into rue de l'Etuve, and you come across the **Manneken-Pis**, famous as a national symbol but eternally disappointing as a tourist spectacle. You wouldn't believe it when you see the crowds, though. Like the Mona Lisa, it's so much smaller than you expect, but the boy

is fortunately elevated on a Baroque pedestal to give him some grandeur. Around him are gated railings, only opened by the person whose sole job it is to dress him in his various costumes: Euro-jogger, Santa Claus, a condom on World AIDS Day and so on. A framed sign gives a calendar of upcoming costume days. The current statue was made in the 17th century by Jérôme Duquesnoy. Stolen by the British in 1745, then again by the French in 1777, it was smashed by a French ex-con in 1817, who was given life for doing so. Its origins are unknown, though it is naturally endowed with local myth as well as a never-ending pee.

A short walk east, up the hill and on the Vieille Halle aux Blés, is the **Édition Jacques Brel**, dedicated to the famed chanteur (*see p64* **Brel's Brussels**). A short walk west, rue du Marché au Charbon is the main gay quarter of town with a bar in almost every building. Perhaps the loveliest of the Lower Town's half-dozen churches also stands here: **Notre-Dame de Bon Secours**.

Further down, the Lower Town becomes more workaday towards the Gare du Midi, which used to stand on place Rouppe. It was here that Symbolist poet Paul Verlaine was arrested in 1873, his young lover Arthur Rimbaud having run to the police during an absinthe-fuelled farewell at the station. Verlaine had shot Rimbaud in the arm shortly before. Verlaine then spent two years in prison, mainly in Mons; Rimbaud caught

HERE FOR THE BEER

Discover the tradition and range of Belgium's famous brews.

EXPLORE

Belgians have a long and proud brewing tradition stretching back the best part of a millennium. And prominent too – just look at the magnificent Brewers' House right on the Grand'Place, home to the only functioning guild that remains of the numerous guildhouses that line the city's main square.

Founded in the 14th century, around the same time as the house itself was constructed in stone, the brewers' guild was rich enough to buy the building 200 years later. A century on, and 'the Golden Tree' and its neighbouring buildings were destroyed by the French bombardment of 1695. The still wealthy guild then hired renowned architect Guillaume De Bruyn to recreate it, adding flowery baroque touches. It was a tavern at some point afterwards, and the basement was converted into the **Musée des Brasseurs Belges** (see p50) in 1951.

Run by the brewers' confederation, who convene here annually, the museum provides the perfect introduction to the art of Belgian beer. An exhibition shows traditional brewing techniques with 18th-century equipment, alongside a contemporary section displaying the high-tech methods of today. A beer is offered at the end of your visit.

Belgium's beloved national treasure comes in some 600 varieties (1,000 if you count one-off specials) – unequalled for such a small country. These range from pump lagers to sublime, finely honed ales brewed by monks – even medieval recipes. As with fine wines, the brewing process can take years and there are strict controls governing how any company can describe its brew.

Only Achel, Chimay, Orval, Rochefort, Westmalle and Westvleteren carry the hexagonal Authentic Trappist Product logo, which means they have been brewed within the walls of a Trappist monastery. Aside from the dark, unclassifiable Orval, all are deep brown and creamy; for deep brown and creamy with a kick, select the *dubbel* or *trippel* versions, which deliver up to nine per cent ABV. The next ecclesiastical step down are the Abbey beers – never to be confused with the Trappists. These include Leffe and Grimbergen, frequently found on tap.

You can find an authentic range of beers in venues that are close to the Grand'Place but not obvious to the first-time visitor. Hidden between a tacky souvenir shop and the Naracamicie shirt emporium, at no.8 rue des Marché aux Herbes, an alley is signposted 'impasse des Cadeaux'. Within, a graffitied sign reading **À l'Imaige Nostre-Dame** (see p51) leads to a 130-year-old rustic tavern straight out of a Flemish painting. This is the place to try Kwak, the amber ale from the Bosteels Brewery in the East Flanders forest of Buggenhout. As at all other bars in Brussels, it's served in its own special glass – a vessel that resembles something from a science lab.

Another age-old tavern, **À la Bécasse** (see p50) is where a young Jacques Brel held his stag night in 1950. No doubt then, as today, aproned waiters poured local, naturally fermented, draught lambic beer from a traditional jug. Sour in taste, lambics are produced in the Cantillon Brewery near Brussels' Gare du Midi, along with the rarer and younger faro, and spontaneously fermented gueuze.

Only a select few bars in Brussels sell lambic, this champagne of Belgian beers – another is the legendary **À la Mort Subite** (see p54), named after a card game and a variety of fruit beer whose hangovers can easily assume the mantle of sudden death. Earning such post-booze pain is a pleasure in this narrow, wood-and-mirror haven by the northern entrance of the Galeries St-Hubert.

For sheer selection, head for the **Delirium Café** (see p54), another alleyway find. It's named after the powerful pale ale brew, Délirium Tremens, from the Huyghe Brewery in East Flanders. The pink elephant tells you all you need to know. But don't think you're hallucinating when you see the menu of 2,000 Belgian and global beers. Do keep an eye on the alcohol strengths unless you want to become a victim of the tricky pachyderm.

Finally, to buy for home consumption, at the far end of rue des Bouchers, **Délices et Caprices** (see p54) is run by a Swiss beer expert, Pierre Zuber. In addition to ale, you can buy beer glasses and other paraphernalia, and tastings are held on site.

his train and quickly wrote what would prove to be his solitary but hugely influential published work, 'Une Saison en Enfer'.

Sights & Museums

FREE Église Notre-Dame de Bon Secours

89 rue du Marché au Charbon (02 514 31 13, www.goedebijstand.be). Pré-métro Anneessens. **Open** 9am-5.30pm daily. *Services* 11am Sun. **Admission** free. **Map** p47 F2 ⓯

Built in the late 1600s, this Baroque masterpiece, designed as a collaboration between Jan Cortvrindt and Willem de Bruyn, remains a superb example of Flemish Renaissance style.

Restaurants

Cécila

16 rue des Chapeliers (02 503 44 74, www. restaurantcecila.com). Métro/pré-métro Bourse. **Open** noon-2pm, 7-10pm Tue-Fri; 7-10pm Sat. **Set menu** lunch €49-€59, dinner €59-€89. **Map** p47 F3 ⓱ **French**

Mélanie Englebin has worked with Brussels Sea Grill chef Yves Mattagne and at Joel Robuchon in London. She's now landed firmly back in town with a fresh and modern restaurant just off the Grand'Place. The restaurant is named after her mother but that's where the apron strings end – the sea-inspired tasting menus are exquisitely presented with fine attention to detail. Sous-vide turbot, cream of urchin, sea cucumber and tiny vegetables give you an idea of what's in store. No wonder restaurant guide *Gault et Millau* named it as the find of 2014.

Comme chez Soi

23 place Rouppe (02 512 29 21, www.comme chezsoi.be). Pré-métro Anneessens. **Open** 7-9pm Tue, Wed; noon-1.30pm, 7-9pm Thur-Sat. **Main courses** €49-€173. **Map** p47 G1 ⓲ **French**

Lionel Rigolet heads up this Michelin two-star food mecca. Immaculate dishes are served in a mannered art nouveau dining room: typical offerings might include sole with a mousseline of riesling and shrimps, or fillet of Aubrac beef with black truffles. Old habits die hard, though: after a beautifully sculpted course arrives at your table, waiters return with an unassuming bowl of second helpings, proving that artistically small portions are never enough in Belgium.

Houtsiplou

9 place Rouppe (02 511 386, www.caat.be/ houtsiplou). Pré-métro Anneessens. **Open** noon-2pm, 6-10.30pm Mon-Fri; noon-3pm, 6-10.30pm Sat, Sun. **Main courses** €14-€16. **Map** p47 G1 ⓴ **Café**

See p140 **The Burgers of Brussels.**

IN THE KNOW TGI FRIDAY

In Brussels, the late-opening shopping evening of the week is Friday, not Thursday. Typically, a major shop – or, indeed, shopping mall – will stay open for an extra half an hour on a Friday. On the other hand, few major shops open on a Sunday; it's generally restricted to independent boutiques in tourist-friendly neighbourhoods.

Plattesteen

41 rue du Marché au Charbon (02 512 82 03). Pré-métro Bourse. **Open** 11am-midnight daily. **Main courses** €12-€25. **Map** p47 E2 ⓵ **Café**

This multifunctional bar-café acts as both a neighbourhood bar and an inexpensive restaurant. It's something of a melting pot, joining shopping Brussels to gay Brussels and the rue du Marché au Charbon, so the clientele might include ladies with poodles, ladies with men and men with men. As a result, it makes for a great meeting place – especially in summer, when you can sit on the terrace and watch the world cruise by arm-in-arm. It's a true Brussels contradiction, with homely and unexceptional decor slap in the middle of the new trendsville.

La Roue d'Or

26 rue des Chapeliers (02 514 25 54, www2. resto.be/rouedor). Pré-métro Bourse. **Open** noon-midnight daily. **Main courses** €18-€27. **Map** p47 F3 ⓵ **Belgian**

The Golden Wheel takes its name from the gold motif at the heart of a stained-glass window above the open kitchen. Through the window you can watch the team of chefs toiling away at what can be described as grandma's cooking. The fine spread of time-honoured Belgian classics includes mussels, oysters, lamb's tongue, pig's trotter, brawn, rabbit and slabs of beef; not surprisingly, vegetarians will feel rather left out. While the ingredients are no-nonsense, presentation and flavours are impeccable; it remains a favourite with locals, who adore the wholesomeness of the place. To help you know what you're letting yourself in for, the menu is also offered in startling pidgin English.

Pubs & Bars

Le Cercle des Voyageurs

18 rue des Grandes Carmes (02 514 39 49, www.lecerdedesvoyageurs.com). Pré-métro Bourse. **Open** 11am-midnight daily. **Map** p47 F2 ⓵

As the name suggests, the Cercle des Voyageurs is a place for travellers to meet. So as well as drinking in a laid-back, colonial-inspired setting in a grand old Brussels house, there are lots of events and talks about all aspects of travel. Check the website for upcoming turns. It's perfect for those on the road

EXPLORE

Le Fleur en Papier Doré.

As the haunt of the surrealists, this quirky venue would make a mint from the tourist trail were it not stuck on an obscure, steep, grey street whose only function is to connect the Lower and Upper Towns. It's not that La Fleur is far from the action: it's just that it's the wrong side of a pleasant stroll. It attracts the more unusual tourist, happy to gawp at the doodles and sketches and stagger around in Magritte's wonky footsteps. A modest but artistically active bunch of regulars alleviate their solitude.

★ Le Fontainas
91 rue du Marché au Charbon (02 503 31 12). Pré-métro Anneessens or Bourse. **Open** 10am-1am Mon-Thur; 10am-2am Fri; 11am-2am Sat; 11am-1am Sun. **No credit cards. Map** p47 F2 ⑤

Possibly – no, probably – the best bar on Brussels' best stretch for bar crawling, the Fontainas is wonderfully understated. Set opposite the equally enjoyable Au Soleil, it is full of lovely little retro touches – old beaded curtains, Formica chairs with chrome legs, vintage advertising – that would do justice to a 1950s milk bar. Yet the place is as determinedly 21st century as the gay/straight mixed clientele: reliably excellent sounds from fiery resident DJs; strong cocktails; rare Orval and Maredsous brews. Throw in a few terrace tables when the sun's out and you have somewhere that's head and shoulders above anything going on in St-Géry. Search for Le Fontainas on Facebook.

Goupil le Fol
22 rue de la Violette (02 511 13 96). Métro Gare Centrale. **Open** 7.30pm-5am daily. **No credit cards. Map** p47 F3 ⑥

Goupil – the stocky, grey-haired gent handing out sweets by the front door at the end of the night – can't fail to cash in. He has his staff urge questionable house fruit wines upon many a tourist, while only providing standard Jupiler (at €3.80 a glass!) by means of any beer alternative. So, what is there to recommend? Well, Goupil is a kooky labyrinthine junk-shop of a bar, where all trace of time can be lost thanks to a jukebox of 3,000 choice slices of French pop. It's eccentric, velvety and nostalgic; check the beads and commie kitsch. On the right night – in a group, or better still, à deux – it can be fun. Pricey but fun.

★ Poechenellekelder
5 rue du Chêne (02 511 92 62, www. poechenellekelder.be). Métro Gare Centrale or pré-métro Anneessens. **Open** 11am-1am Tue-Sun. **Map** p47 F2 ⑦

In any other European city, the nearest bar to the main tourist sight would be a hideous, overpriced tourist trap. Not so Michel de Triest's convivial Poechenellekelder near the Mannekin-Pis. Round the corner and up the slight incline of rue du Chêne – and up its own flight of steps once you enter – this *estaminet* specialises in lesser-found Belgian beers.

wanting some inside information – speak to the regulars or consult books and periodicals in the library. There are even dance classes in salsa and flamenco.

★ Chez Moeder Lambic Fontainas
8 place Fontainas (02 503 60 68, www.moederlambic. com). Pré-métro Anneessens. **Open** 11am-1am Mon-Thur, Sun; 11am-2am Fri, Sat. **Map** p47 F2 ⑥

The thoroughly modern daughter of the older St-Gilles Moeder Lambic (*see p158*) makes a splendid addition to the city's bar scene. This bright young thing sits in an old townhouse on the unglamorous place Fontainas, right at the end of the Marché au Charbon crawl, providing an ideal punctuation mark to a long evening of drinking. Its 40 lesser-known draught Belgian beers make this a place of real discovery, along with a menu more befitting a wine bar. The crowd ranges from nouveau goth to clipped professional, all there for a glass or two of something rather special.

La Fleur en Papier Doré
55 rue des Alexiens (02 511 16 59, www.lafleur enpapierdore.be). Pré-métro Anneessens. **Open** 11am-midnight Tue-Sat; 11am-7pm Sat, Sun. **No credit cards. Map** p47 G3 ⑥

Bottles of Forestinne Ambrosia, Noir de Dottignes and Zinnerbir cost just over the €3 mark, and there are well over 50 other varieties to choose from. Faro Lindemans and St Feuillien Blonde are included in the draught options. Plates of dried sausage, young gouda cheese and salami may accompany.

Au Soleil
86 rue du Marché au Charbon (02 513 34 30). Pré-métro Anneessens or Bourse. **Open** 10am-1am daily. **No credit cards. Map** p47 F2 ❸
Set in an extravagant old tailor's premises, Au Soleil is filled with a constant buzz from early on – so much so that passing by without popping in can be difficult. Everyone seems to be talking on top of one another, when they're not looking impossibly interesting amid the din. It's all a pose, of course, but it's quite fun for all that, and it lures punters to tumble down Charbon like lemmings. The somewhat stern interior features plenty of marble and weighty metal, backdropped by picture windows.

Shops & Services

Ali Photo Video
150 rue du Midi (02 512 34 55). Pré-métro Anneessens. **Open** 9am-6pm Mon-Fri; 10am-6pm Sat. **Map** p47 G2 ❸ **Cameras**
Ali Photo Video sells new still and video cameras of all makes, as well as buying, selling and exchanging second-hand ones. Staff develop photos, slides and black-and-whites.

Arcane
54 rue du Midi (02 511 91 42, www.arcane bijouterie.com). Pré-métro Bourse. **Open** 11am-6.30pm Mon-Sat. **Map** p47 F2 ❹ **Accessories**
Arcane trades in affordable jewellery in all shapes and sizes, some incorporating leather, satin ribbons and beads. Many pieces are made from silver; some are classic, simple designs, while others come from India, Mexico, Thailand and Israel.

Arlequin
7 rue du Chêne (02 514 54 28, www.arlequin.net). Métro Gare Centrale or pré-métro Anneessens. **Open** 11am-7pm Mon-Sat; 2-7pm Sun. **Map** p47 F2 ❹ **Books & music**

IN THE KNOW ANNUAL SALES

Strict rules govern when shops in Brussels may hold a sale. The two times of the year are *soldes d'été* (summer sales), 1-31 July, and *soldes d'hiver* (winter sales), 3-31 January. Apart from those specified slots, and certainly in the two weeks running up to them, outlets may not offer their goods at visibly discounted prices.

Not ten paces from the Manneken-Pis, Arlequin has all kinds of second-hand music, but focuses on rock, punk, import and jazz; its sister store specialises in soul, funk, jazz, rap, reggae, classic and world music. Quality is high and staff are friendly. Both branches open on Sundays – the one in St-Gilles has more choice of hip hop, funk and reggae.
Other location 90 rue d'Andenne, St-Gilles (02 512 15 86).

★ Avec Plaizier
50 rue des Eperonniers (02 513 99 29, www. avecplaizier.be). Métro Gare Centrale. **Open** *Jan-Nov* 11am-6pm Mon-Sat. *Dec* 11am-6pm daily. **Map** p47 F3 ❹ **Gifts & souvenirs**
Most people come here for the excellent postcards, generally original and artistic, but there's also a well-chosen selection of books, posters and diaries. Opened by the Plaizier family in 1977, it also specialises in photos of Brussels from the 1940s and '50s – look out for the annual retro calendar. In the run-up to Christmas, the shop is open daily.

Azzato
42 rue de la Violette (02 512 37 52, www.azzato.eu). Métro Gare Centrale. **Open** 9.30am-6pm Mon-Sat. **Map** p47 F3 ❹ **Musical instruments**
In business since 1919, Azzato specialises in stringed instruments of all kinds, and also has two workshops for essential repairs.

Brüsel
100 boulevard Anspach (02 511 08 09, www.brusel.com). Pré-métro Bourse. **Open** 10.30am-6.30pm Mon-Sat; noon-6.30pm Sun. **Map** p47 E2 ❹ **Comics**
One of the best comic shops in Brussels, with a huge choice of national favourites, as well as the most popular European and US comic strips in English, French and Dutch. The shop also stocks accompanying plastic and resin miniatures, posters and lithographs.
Other location 29 place Flagey (02 649 02 11).

Connections
119-121 rue du Midi (02 550 01 30, www. connections.be). Pré-métro Bourse. **Open** 9.30am-6.30pm Mon, Tue, Thur, Fri; 10.30am-6.30pm Wed; 10am-5pm Sat. **Map** p47 F2 ❹ **Travel services**
Flights, tours, last-minute bookings and sundry travel deals, all arranged in person just a few steps from the Grand'Place.

★ Conni Kaminski
102 rue du Marché au Charbon (02 502 51 55, www.connikaminski.com). Pré-métro Anneessens. **Open** 11.30am-6.30pm Tue-Sat. **Map** p47 F2 ❹ **Fashion**
This is the flagship of the German-born designer of chic, seasonal womenswear in fine materials – there

EXPLORE

IN THE KNOW A RING TO IT

Central Brussels is enclosed within the Petite Ceinture or Pentagone, the five-sided ring road that follows the city walls, built after the Flemish invasion of 1356 and modernised 200 years later. The medieval defensive system featured seven main gates, correlating to the ones created as part of the first city walls in the early 1200s. Gradually, these walls and towers were destroyed and, from the early 19th century, boulevards laid out to replace them. Porte de Hal remains in place, however, having been transformed into a romanticised neo-Gothic tower later in the 1800s. Some eight kilometres (five miles) long in total, these boulevards were modernised after World War II. Tunnels were created to follow part of the ring road, then métro lines. Today, this main, heart-shaped boundary is called Ring 20, as opposed to Outer Ring 0 that serves the city's agglomeration.

are now some two dozen outlets across Belgium and Switzerland. Conni works with asymmetrical shapes that seem to drape effortlessly on the body.

Le Dépôt
108 rue du Midi (02 513 04 84, www.depotbd. com). Pré-métro Anneessens. **Open** 10am-6.30pm Mon-Sat. **Map** p47 F2 ⑰ **Comics**
This store buys and sells all types of new and old comic strips, as well as figurines, cards, posters, limited-edition lithographs and DVDs.

Dyers
4 rue des Teinturiers (02 840 84 45, www. facebook.com/dyersbrussels). Pré-métro Bourse. **Open** 11am-7pm Mon-Sat. **Map** p47 E2 ⑱ **Fashion**
This recently opened streetwear shop sells fashionable sneakers, sweaters and wristwatches for men and women, in a chic, minimalist space where quarterly changing original artworks are also displayed.

De Geest
41 rue de l'Hôpital (02 512 59 78, www. degeestteinturerie.be). Métro Gare Centrale. **Open** 8am-7pm Mon-Fri; 9am-6pm Sat. **Map** p47 G3 ⑲ **Laundry services**
Spilled some wine? Dropped the jam? In business since 1846, De Geest will launder virtually anything, including leather and suede items and upholstery.

Gillis
17 rue du Lombard (02 512 09 26, www.gillis modistes.be). Pré-métro Bourse. **Open** 10am-6pm Mon-Sat. **Map** p47 F2 ⑳ **Accessories**

Gillis is something of a Brussels institution, dating from 1910 and also known for supplying theatrical costumes. There's a small range of ready-made hats, mostly for women, with a few men's hats available in winter. However, the real speciality is made-to-measure hats, which are created on the premises using more than 300 wooden blocks.

Hill's Music
37-39 rue du Marché au Charbon (02 512 77 71, www.hillsmusic.be). Pré-métro Bourse. **Open** 9.30am-12.30pm, 1.30-5.30pm Tue-Sat. **Map** p47 E2 ㉑ **Musical instruments**
Hill's Music specialises in quality acoustic string instruments, from guitars to harps.

★ Johnny Velvet
1 rue de l'Hôpital (02 513 23 12). Métro Gare Centrale. **Open** 11am-7pm Mon-Sat; 2-7pm Sun. **Map** p47 G3 ㉒ **Fashion**
'Where the street meets the chic' is the motto of this boutique for urban gear, trainers, tops, watches and so on. Woollen jackets and leather boots are sold too, mostly for men. The shop is on Facebook.

La Maison du Miel
121 rue du Midi (02 512 32 50, www.lamaison dumiel.be). Pré-métro Anneessens. **Open** 9.30am-6pm Mon-Sat. **Map** p47 F2 ㉓ **Food & drink**
Make a beeline for this shop, which was founded in 1887 and sells all things honey-themed, scented and flavoured, from edible goodies to toiletries.

Le Palais des Thés
45 place de la Vieille Halle aux Blés (02 502 45 59, www.palaisdesthes.com). Métro Gare Centrale. **Open** 11am-6.30pm daily. **Map** p47 G3 ㉔ **Food & drink**
A stylish shop, with around 250 varieties of tea from 30 countries, including Georgia and Turkey. Free tastings are offered, while gift ideas include beautiful teapots and scented teas.
Other location 25 chaussée de Charleroi, St-Gilles (02 537 89 07).

Planète Chocolat
24 rue du Lombard (02 511 07 55, www. planetechocolat.be). Pré-métro Bourse. **Open** 10.30am-6.30pm Mon-Sat; 11am-6.30pm Sun. **Map** p47 F3 ㉕ **Food & drink**
As well as being a chocolate shop and a tea house, Planète Chocolat offers (bookable) group demonstrations of chocolate-making. The chocolate itself is among the funkiest in town: chocolate lips and bouquets of chocolate 'flowers' are specialities.

Privejoke
76-78 rue du Marché aux Charbon (02 502 63 67, www.privejoke.com). Pré-métro Bourse. **Open** 11am-7pm Mon-Sat; 2-7pm Sun. **Map** p47 F2 ㉖ **Fashion**

TRUCKING ON

Meals on wheels, Brussels-style.

Brussels has recently joined the motorised street-food club, in a way that has energised locals looking for something new and oh-so-cool. The city has always had food on wheels, but in a camping-trailer kind of way where a booth is unhitched and left permanently to dole out chips or waffles. As an example, check out Chez Jef & Fils opposite the Bourse, where Jef has seemingly been stewing whelks for most of his life.

But change is in the air. In 2014, Brussels Ville unveiled its food truck trail (a first in Europe, according to the city authorities). It comes with strict criteria, the most important being that food should be high quality and always cooked to order – and vendors must not be in direct competition with fixed restaurants. The city has licensed 25 trucks, which can visit 13 locations in rotation, all chosen for their potential trade, such as tourists and office workers. Vendors include Keep on Toasting (www.keepon toasting.be), which deals in toasties and was one of Brussels' first street-food stars; and Urban Cook (www.urbancook.be), which celebrates the gourmet burger (*see also p140* **The Burgers of Brussels**).

The trail doesn't yet have a dedicated website, but search for 'food truck trail' on www.brussels.be and you'll find a link to the trucks with individual web addresses, as well as a list of locations. The trucksters

are social-media savvy too; many post their GPS location daily on Facebook.

Also in 2014, the city held the first **Brussels Food Truck Festival** (www.brusselsfoodtruck festival.be), along the boulevards between the Grand'Place and Mont des Arts. Around 80 street-food vendors fed upwards of 80,000 people over three days in May. Billed as the biggest event of its kind in Europe, it's intended to be an annual event. There's even a Belgian Food Truck Association (www.belgianfoodtruckassociation.org) to represent and offer training to mobile chefs. It looks like street food is here to stay.

EXPLORE

Privejoke, another of Brussels' original streetwear boutiques, is a funky choice. At least, it is if you make your way to the back of the shop, where the men's clothes are to be found in a dark room. The women's section at the front, dotted with chandeliers, is far more bright and girlie. Brands stocked include Kangol, Pringle, Seven Jeans and Puma.

Ramon & Valy
19 rue des Teinturiers (02 511 05 10). Pré-métro Bourse. **Open** 11am-7pm Mon-Sat. **Map** p47 F2 ⑤ Fashion & accessories
An elegant corner shop that stocks only the best vintage clothes from French designers such as Yves Saint Laurent, Dior, Givenchy and Christian Lacroix, as well as Italian labels such as Gucci and Roberto Cavalli. Vintage shoes and accessories are aimed at women, but there are also a few offerings for men and children. There's no website, but the store is on Facebook.

Ride All Day
39 rue St-Jean (02 512 89 22, www.rideallday.be). Métro Gare Centrale. **Open** noon-6pm/6.30pm Tue-Sat. **No credit cards. Map** p47 F3 ⑤ Sports
Ride All Day sells boards, shoes and clothing to the skate rats who congregate around the skating hotspot of the neighbouring Mont des Arts. The staff,

die-hard skaters, are happy to provide tips. The shop opens on Mondays in the school holidays.

Utopia
39 rue du Midi (02 514 08 26, www.utopiacomics. be). Pré-métro Bourse. **Open** 10am-6pm Mon-Fri; 10am-7pm Sat. **Map** p47 E2 ⑤ **Comics**
Utopia specialises in American comic strips, plus TV and film merchandise, with a good collection of Batman and Simpsons gear.

NORTH FROM THE GRAND'PLACE

Much of the historical heart of Brussels was tragically lost when the River Senne was covered over and straight avenues and formal squares were constructed between the Gares du Nord and Midi. Distinguished architectural ensembles included place De Brouckère, whose grandeur – and fountain – gave way to build the métro station. Although home to the classy **Hotel Métropole** (*see p267*) and its lovely café, these days it is merely a traffic intersection, dominated by the awful Centre Monnaie shopping mall. It overshadows the neoclassical opera house **Théâtre de la Monnaie** (*see p194*), built here in 1819. As well as being historically significant (in 1830 it staged the opera that led to the uprising

Notre-Dame du Finistère.

for Belgian independence), the venue is worth visiting for its ornate interior. The square was also the site of the mint, hence its name. After nearly 500 years here, the mint moved out to St-Gilles in 1890.

Arrowing north from the plaza in front of the theatre is gaudy rue Neuve. It could be any high street in any town, a crowded, pedestrianised stretch of brand names culminating in the ugly shopping centre **City 2**. It's hard to believe that this was the site of the Duchess of Richmond's famous musical ball on the eve of the Battle of Waterloo – although the airy **Notre-Dame du Finistère** does provide some architectural relief. Nearby is the place des Martyrs, home to a large monument to the 445 revolutionaries who gave their lives for Belgium in 1830. It was a cobbled ruin until the Flemish authorities took the initiative to restore some buildings as government offices. Their French counterpart then responded in turn by renovating another part of the square. It is lined with fine neoclassical buildings, including the impressive **Théâtre des Martyrs** (*see p198*).

Around the corner is one of Brussels' most popular museums, the **Centre Belge de la Bande Dessinée**. Located in a beautifully restored Victor Horta department store (whose ground-floor café can be visited free of charge),

it features a Tintin section, as well as displays on lesser-known Belgian comic characters – many of whom feature on a comic-strip walk of the city (*see p28*).

Running parallel to rue Neuve is the grand boulevard Adolphe Max, with some stunning buildings if you look up beyond the ground-level shops. Max was the heroic mayor of Brussels who refused to cooperate with his German overlords after the invasion of 1914 – and was locked up for his troubles until escaping in 1918. The boulevard rises steeply to meet the Rogier Tower skyscraper, office blocks and business hotels of wind-blown place Rogier, recreated when the Gare du Nord was moved slightly further north to link with the rail axis with Gare du Midi (*see p277* **First Class**). Before World War II, place Rogier was a pleasant, open square and tram terminus, lined with pretty terrace cafés.

The ring road that divides today's place Rogier from the city centre spread out below forms the northern edge of the Petite Ceinture, the pentagonal ring that contains the historic centre of the Belgian capital (*see p60* **In the Know**).

Sights & Museums

★ Centre Belge de la Bande Dessinée

20 rue des Sables (02 219 19 80, www.comics center.net). Métro/pré-métro De Brouckère or Rogier. **Open** 10am-6pm daily. **Admission** €10; €6.50 12-25s; free under-12s. **Map** p46 C5 ⑩

Set on three floors of a beautiful Horta-designed department store, the Comic Strip Museum greets you with a statue of Tintin, Snowy and the iconic red and white rocket they took to the moon. The Tintin collection (revamped for the 75th anniversary celebrations in 2004) is the highlight of the exhibition, which covers the history of comics and cartoons from Winsor McCay's early Gertie the Dinosaur (1914) to the heroes of today. Cartoon artists from around the world are featured in themed temporary exhibitions on the third floor.

FREE Notre-Dame du Finistère

76 rue Neuve (02 217 52 52). Métro/pré-métro De Brouckère or Rogier. **Open** 1-6pm Mon-Fri. **Admission** free. **Map** p46 B4 ⑪

Largely built in the early 18th century on the site of a 15th-century chapel, the church features a Baroque interior most notable for its almost stupendously over-the-top pulpit. Its location on the shopping drag of rue Neuve, directly opposite the Galeria Inno department store, lends it a somewhat incongruous air when the sales are on.

Restaurants

Belga Queen

32 rue du Fossé aux Loups (02 217 21 87, www.belgaqueen.be). Métro/pré-métro

EXPLORE

BREL'S BRUSSELS

Follow in the footsteps of Belgium's finest singer-songwriter.

EXPLORE

For a man who's not been with us since 1978, Brussels-born singer-songwriter Jacques Brel still feels very much alive. Created by his widow, Miche, and their family in 2011, the **Éditions Jacques Brel** (11 place de la Vieille Halle aux Blés, 02 511 10 20, www.jacques brel.be) aims to make best use of the archives he left behind. It creates a new approach to Brel's legacy, a walk-through tour of his life and relationship to Brussels and Belgium, featuring interviews with 16 people who knew him best and clips from some three dozen places in the city.

For those who remember the foundation that operated in this same building, this is a far more structured attraction than the previous drop-in-and-dip-in exhibition. On the downside, the new walk-through audio-guide demands 90 minutes of your time and maximum concentration, plus an annoying voiceover translation for non-French speakers. Although the foundation offers an extremely detailed database of the 750-plus books and publications focusing on Brel, plus more than 100 concert posters including many originals, it no longer screens on video-loop the concert he gave at the famous Olympia in Paris, a near cathartic experience.

On the plus side, the new attraction gives a much more rounded picture of 'Jef', one of the finest *chansonniers* of the post-war era. In addition, the foundation provides a tour through Brussels, with audio-guide, for a combined price of €13 and a further two

hours and 40 minutes. For Brel lovers, of course, this is all manna from heaven.

Alternatively, you could create your own tour. Many of the venues Brel played and the places he frequented still exist today – such as the **Ancienne Belgique** concert hall (*see p187*), **La Taverne du Passage** (30 Galerie de la Reine) where he liked to take his post-show meals, and the **À la Bécasse** tavern (*see p50*) where he drank on his last night as a bachelor in 1950. You could also make a pilgrimage to Schaerbeek, where Brel spent part of his childhood and set up home once he gained success in the early 1960s. A plaque at 138 avenue du Diamant marks where he was born in 1929; the house he purchased later, at 31 boulevard Général Wahis, is a grander affair.

Equally, grey Anderlecht, where the young Brel moved after his father got a job at a cardboard factory, has a modest selection of sights promoted by the local tourist office (www.anderlecht.be). You'll find a métro station named after Brel and, on a wall at square Henri Rey, the words from his song 'Madeleine', which was partly inspired by the no.33 tram that used to run through here.

Finally, in leafy Uccle (where Brel bought an apartment near Bois de la Cambre for his wife and three daughters), there's the pleasant Parc Jacques Brel near Uccle Stalle station – though it's perhaps not as pleasant as the singer's last resting place, near that of artist Paul Gauguin in Hiva Oa, Atouna, in the Marquesas Islands in the south Pacific.

De Brouckère. **Open** noon-2.30pm, 7pm-midnight Mon-Fri; 7pm-midnight Sat. Set menu €35-€52. **Map** p46 C4 ㉒ **Belgian**

Everything about this glitzy place is unashamedly Belgian. The design, the menu, the produce; even the wine is sourced from Belgian producers abroad. The restaurant sits in a vast bank building with original pillars and a massive stained-glass skylight, giving it a lofty, spacious air. Yet once you're seated at your table, it can feel surprisingly intimate (though couples alone are rare – this seems to be a place to go with a crowd). The BQ is renowned for its oyster bar, where heaving seafood platters are composed. Other dishes are inventive and thoroughly modern; the famous farm bird, Coucou de Malines, is sat on gingerbread with a hot pear sauce, though more traditional methods, such as braising in beer, are also used. The unisex toilet doors are transparent and it's up to you to work them out – don't expect us to give the game away.

Sea Grill

Radisson SAS Royal, 47 rue du Fossé aux Loups (02 227 91 25, www.seagrill.be). Métro/ pré-métro De Brouckère. **Open** noon-2pm, 7-10pm Mon-Fri. **Main courses** €50-€80. **Map** p46 D4 ㉓ **Fish & seafood**

The Sea Grill – which is regarded by many Belgians as the country's top seafood restaurant – is buried inside the five-star Radisson SAS Royal Hotel, so while the entrance may appear rather corporate, the interior is seriously luxe. Chef Yves Mattagne seems to win every award going for his masterful pairing of traditional French techniques with modern international touches. Red mullet with truffle risotto, and roast tuna with sautéed goose liver are among the specialities. Be aware, however, that a starter here could set you back more than an entire meal elsewhere in town.

Pubs & Bars

Café Métropole

31 place de Brouckère (02 217 23 00, www. metropolehotel.com). Métro/pré-métro De Brouckère. **Open** 9am-1am Mon-Fri; 11am-1am Sat, Sun. **Map** p46 C3 ㉔

For a little fin-de-siècle finesse, pop into the café of the grand Hotel Métropole. This place is of a different age: over-burdened chandeliers, mirrored walls, ornate ironwork and a hush that hasn't changed for a century. A pillar of guests' autographs features Emerson Fittipaldi and Vera Lynn; Sarah Bernhardt also stayed here, and is reincarnated in the ladies with elaborate hairdos who sit on the terrace in sunglasses and fur coats all year round. Aperitifs dominate the drinks menu, along with champagnes offered by the bottle, half-bottle and quarter-bottle, delivered with aplomb by bow-tied waiters. Alongside, the evening-only Bar 31 piano bar appeals to the pre-theatre crowd. *Photos p66.*

Celtica

55 rue Marché aux Poulets (02 513 33 08, www.celticpubs.com/celtica). Métro/pré-métro De Brouckère or pré-métro Bourse. **Open** 1pm-5am Mon, Tue, Sun; 1pm-7am Wed, Thur; 1pm-8am Fri, Sat. **Map** p47 E3 ㉕

Just look at those opening hours – when you're in for a sesh at the Celtica, you're in for the long haul. True, weekends are chivvied along with a disco upstairs, but downstairs can be just as wild. Set on the edge of the Ilot Sacré, the Celtica proves that you don't have to serve overpriced beer and dumb down to expat accountants to be a real pub on continental Europe. Football is shown on high-definition TV screens.

Churchill's

20 rue de l'Écuyer (02 514 27 10, www.churchills.be). Métro/pré-métro De Brouckère. **Open** 11am-last guest Mon-Sat; noon-last guest Sun. **Map** p46 D4 ㉖

Under English management, Churchill's is one of the better places in town to watch the match. It has plenty of space, for a start, with rows of tables ranged around pictures of the Small Faces and the Kinks – Winston might even get a look-in here and there. Beer-wise, there's Bishop's Finger, Adnam's and Newcastle Brown, and happy hours are basically all day Monday to Friday – up to 7pm.

▶ *A similar pub-like space in which to watch TV sport is down adjoining, narrow rue de la Fourche – although Six Nations (48-50 rue Grétry, 02 203 07 33, www.sixnations.be) veers more to the oval-ball game.*

La Lunette

3 place de la Monnaie (02 218 03 78). Métro/ pré-métro De Brouckère. **Open** 9am-1am Mon-Thur; 9am-2am Fri, Sat; 10am-1am Sun. **No credit cards. Map** p46 D4 ㉗

This has become a bit of an institution, partly because of its location near the commercial zone and partly because of its beer list, with eight on-tap varieties. Measures come in a standard glass or a *lunette*, which is like a magnum champagne glass. That's a polite way of putting it; a *lunette* is a bucket. The sleek two-floor interior of curved green banquettes would be much admired elsewhere; in Brussels, it's par for the course. The clientele includes shoppers, drifters and folk waiting for a film to start.

Shops & Services

City 2

123 Rue Neuve (02 211 40 60, www.city2.be). Métro/pré-métro Rogier. **Open** 10am-7pm Mon-Thur, Sat; 10am-7.30pm Fri. **Map** p46 B5 ㉘ **Mall**

There's something very 1980s about the city's main shopping centre, set on the main pedestrianised commercial thoroughfare of rue Neuve. Belgium's largest urban mall, with four storeys and 100-plus outlets, still feels parochial, provincial and unwittingly retro. The prime attraction here is the Fnac

EXPLORE

shop for DVDs, computers and film equipment. Of the other major emporia, there's the Inno department store, a Carrefour supermarket and a Mothercare – but fashion-wise, the selection is pretty naff.

Fnac

City 2, 123 rue Neuve (02 275 11 11, www.fr. fnac.be). Métro/pré-métro Rogier. **Open** 10am-7pm Mon-Thur, Sat; 10am-8pm Fri. **Map** p46 B5 ⑳ **Books & music**
Head to the top of the City 2 shopping centre to find this ever-dependable mammoth store. The book stock is excellent in all disciplines and languages (the French section is particularly strong), and prices aren't bad. There are also CDs, DVDs, computer games and assorted audio-visual and computer equipment. By the door is a ticket office for concerts.

Hema

13 rue Neuve (02 227 52 10, www.hema.be). Métro/pré-métro De Brouckère. **Open** 9am-6.30pm Mon-Wed; 9am-7pm Thur-Sat. **Map** p46 C4 ⑰ **General store**
Hema is like a Flemish Woolworths. Its two floors are filled with basics – candles, underwear, kitchenware and other random goods – of varying quality but at ludicrously cheap prices. Have a good rummage around and you may just leave triumphant.
Other locations throughout the city.

Ici Paris XL

37 rue Neuve (02 219 22 07, www.iciparisxl.be). Métro/pré-métro De Brouckère. **Open** 9.30am-6.30pm Mon-Sat. **Map** p46 C4 ⑰ **Health & beauty**

Founded in Belgium in the late 1970s, this is the largest chain of perfumeries in the country. Each shop is stylish, while the range of luxury fragrances in most branches includes all the top brands.
Other locations throughout the city.

Inno

123 rue Neuve (02 211 21 11, www.inno.be). Métro/pré-métro Rogier. **Open** 9.30am-7pm Mon-Thur, Sat; 9.30am-8pm Fri. **Map** p46 B5 ⑫ **Department store**
Inno is Brussels' main department store. Established in 1897, it has 15 shops in Belgium. This is the largest, with five floors featuring all the usual departments: menswear, womenswear, childrenswear, shoes, home furnishings and so on. The handbag, jewellery and lingerie departments are notably good.
Other locations throughout the city.

Maisons du Monde

Anspach Shopping Centre, boulevard Anspach & rue Grétry (02 217 66 41, www.maisonsdumonde. com). Métro/pré-métro De Brouckère. **Open** 10am-7pm Mon-Thur, Sat; 10am-7.30pm Fri. **Map** p46 D3 ⑬ **Homewares**
This homewares chain sells cushions, glassware, beds, cupboards and chairs with an Indian influence. The sections are organised by colour.

Media Markt

City 2, 123 rue Neuve (02 227 15 70, www. mediamarkt.be). Métro/pré-métro Rogier. **Open** 10am-7pm Mon-Thur, Sat; 10am-8pm Fri. **Map** p46 B5 ⑭ **Computers & electronics**

Café Métropole. *See p65.*

This giant German electronics emporium has taken over the top floor of the Inno department store. Great prices in a superstore environment.
Other locations throughout the city.

Pearle

22 rue Neuve (02 223 05 40, www.pearle.be). Métro/pré-métro De Brouckère. **Open** 9.30am-6.30pm Mon-Sat. **Map** p46 C4 ⑦ **Health & beauty**
Pearle is one of Belgium's main optician chains, offering walk-in eye tests and a wide range of glasses and sunglasses. Prescriptions take around five days to process.
Other locations throughout the city.

Planet Parfum

Centre Monnaie, 18 place de la Monnaie (02 218 48 58, www.planetparfum.be). Métro/pré-métro De Brouckère. **Open** 9.30am-6.30pm Mon-Sat. **Map** p46 D4 ⑦ **Health & beauty**
Ubiquitous fragrance store selling a wide selection of perfumes and some cosmetics.
Other locations throughout the city.

Primark

13-15 rue Neuve (no phone, www.primark.com). Métro/pré-métro De Brouckère. **Open** 9.30am-7pm Mon-Thur, Sat; 9.30am-8pm Fri. **Map** p46 C4 ⑦ **Fashion & accessories**
Yes, Brussels has a Primark. Not only that, but 2,000 shoppers queued like it was Oxford Street on Boxing Day when it opened in December 2014. Pandemonium was how TV news described it. If anything sums up the state of the retail industry on rue Neuve...

Sacha Shoe Design

27-31 rue des Fripiers (02 218 79 65, www.sacha.be). Métro/pré-métro De Brouckère. **Open** 10am-7pm Mon-Wed, Fri, Sat; 10am-8pm Thur. **Map** p46 D3 ⑦ **Accessories**
This funky, Dutch-owned shoe emporium sells everything from eccentric clubbing heels and boots to conventional office shoes for men and women. All the latest trends and top brands are covered, including Le Coq Sportif, Converse, Diesel and Dr Martens.
Other locations City 2, 123 rue Neuve, Grand'Place & Around (02 218 12 67); 66 chaussée d'Ixelles, Ixelles (02 511 58 36).

Sports Direct

City 2, 123 rue Neuve (02 217 88 15, www.sportsdirect.com). Métro/pré-métro Rogier. **Open** 10am-7pm Mon-Thur, Sat; 10am-7pm Fri. **Map** p46 B5 ⑦ **Sports**
A massive depot of reduced-price sportswear and equipment including cycle, gym and hiking gear from this UK chain.
Other locations 63 chaussée d'Ixelles, Ixelles (02 511 5022); 112 rue de Birmingham, Anderlecht (02 305 18 00).

★ Sterling

23 rue du Fossé aux Loups (02 223 62 23, www.sterlingbooks.be). Métro/pré-métro De Brouckère. **Open** 10am-6pm Mon-Sat. **Map** p46 D4 ⑧ **Books & music**
This popular and friendly English-language bookshop moved to a new location just across the road from the old one. It has an excellent range of contemporary fiction, children's books, classic fiction and non-fiction. There's also a comprehensive section of books on Brussels.

Waterstones

71-75 boulevard Adolphe Max (02 219 27 08, www.waterstones.com). Métro/pré-métro Rogier. **Open** 9am-7pm Mon-Sat; 10.30am-6pm Sun. **Map** p46 B4 ⑧ **Books & music**
The local Waterstones has a good collection of English-language reading material (books, magazines and newspapers) on its two floors. Prices are on the steep side, though.

Women'Secret

2 rue Neuve (02 217 10 28, www.womensecret.com). Métro/pré-métro De Brouckère. **Open** 10am-6.30pm Mon-Sat. **Map** p46 C4 ⑧ **Fashion**
This successful Spanish chain stocks an excellent selection of fun and reasonably priced lingerie, nightwear, beachwear, maternity wear and comfortable clothes for anyone looking to lounge in style around the home.
Other locations 1349 Chaussée de Waterloo, Uccle (02 374 63 35); Woluwe Shopping Center, 70 boulevard de la Woluwé, Woluwé-Saint-Lambert (02 772 20 02).

EXPLORE

St-Géry & Ste-Catherine

Fish restaurants, hip bars and fashion boutiques are the typical features of St-Géry and adjoining Ste-Catherine, two small, self-contained quarters across boulevard Anspach from the Bourse. Both neighbourhoods have undergone major renovation, turning once-shabby districts into likeable but more commercial versions of their former selves. As opposed to the area around the Grand'Place, where little changes, these twin hubs of the Lower Town are as dynamic as any in Brussels, particularly the former port of Ste-Catherine. Instead of reliable but staid fish restaurants, there's now a mishmash of new eateries, most of them best enjoyed alfresco. As for St-Géry, site of the city's beginnings at the start of the last millennium, this is where bar entrepreneur Frédéric Nicolay started his empire of fashionable drinkeries that take Belgian history and iconography as their theme.

L'Archiduc.

Don't Miss

1 Rue Antoine Dansaert Street of chic (p70).

2 Halles St-Géry Former market hall, now one large drinking hub (p70).

3 L'Archiduc Where Tony Bennett and Lady Gaga clink glasses (p75).

4 Place Sainte-Catherine Alfresco eateries line this ex-fish market (p82).

5 Église de St-Jean-Baptiste au Béguinage Flemish Baroque at its best (p83).

ST-GÉRY

St-Géry is centred on the square of the same name, itself centred on a covered market hall converted in modern times to house a large bar and exhibition space. The grand **Halles St-Géry** were opened in 1881, soon after the River Senne was covered and boulevards constructed in its place. Place St-Géry was, in fact, the Île St-Géry, the original historic island heart of Brussels. A church was built here to honour Saint Géry, the Bishop of Cambrai of the late sixth and early seventh centuries, who had previously opened his own chapel on this same site. Though no remains of it were ever found, the chapel is thought to have contained the body of Sainte Gudule, before it was transferred to the cathedral that partly bears her name.

The fortifications built around the island by Charles, Duke of Lower Lorraine, in 979, have given the city authorities as much excuse as any to nominate the year of their construction as the notional foundation of Brussels. The streets immediately encircling this enclave – Borgwal ('Fortress Wall'), rue de la Grande Île – hark back to these little-recorded times. For most of the following centuries, the surrounding Senne was clean enough to provide ample fish, and therefore a market, for the islanders.

This gradually changed as dyes from the nearby tanneries leaked into the waters. The industrial revolution did the rest. After 1789, the invading French demolished the medieval church and built a fountain in its place, soon surrounded by market stalls. This became the self-standing Halles St-Géry, now a bar hub both inside and out. St-Géry was originally revived by entertainment mogul Frédéric Nicolay, who set up a string of fashionable cafés and spread word of a cool scene. On summer nights, the busy terraces of bars, such as **Mappa Mundo** and **Zebra**, create a Mediterranean atmosphere around the square. More recently, the Halles are the setting for the **Brussels Vintage Market** (*see below* **In the Know**) on the first Sunday of the month.

This former desolate inner-city quarter, which is literally a stone's throw from the Bourse, was ripe for modernisation. It wasn't so long ago that **rue Antoine Dansaert** was just another scruffy Brussels thoroughfare, a quick route out of the centre towards the ring road. You may still get much the same impression as you dodge the hefty traffic, but look more carefully at its constituent parts and you begin to realise that this is a street with attitude. Simply put, Dansaert is a Flemish heartland of fashion, style and culture, spawning myriad little hotspots in and around its main artery.

Regeneration started in 1984, with the opening of a small fashion shop, selling designs that had never been seen before. **Stijl**, the brainchild of Sonia Noël, championed the work of young graduates from the fashion wing of the Antwerp Art Academy: the Antwerp Six. Brussels-based designers also found a home on Antoine Dansaert. **Annemie Verbeke**'s sober silhouettes belie an enfant terrible of fashion who likes to push limits in line and form. Other highlights include

IN THE KNOW VINTAGE FAIR

Vintage clothing stores have always been popular in Brussels, so when Charlotte Brabant and Gordon Laloux conceived of a regular vintage fair, they knew they were on to a winner. Set in the grand old Halles St-Géry, the **Brussels Vintage Market** (0473 74 10 19, www. brusselsvintagemarket.be) is held on the first Sunday of the month. The ground floor is packed with rails of men's and women's clothes, bags, sunglasses and vinyl. Bunting is strung up to give a fête feel, a vibe emphasised by the tea and homemade cake stands. A DJ spins records from another era and the place packs out. The first-floor gallery has more vintage wares, plus modern crafts and jewellery made by young designers who can't afford shop costs. Outside and under the glass canopies, there are more vendors, including someone who specialises in old radios and another in nylon '70s Adidas tracksuits.

Kat en Muis, a wacky clothes shop for children with floral wellies and funky knits. There are art-deco accessories at **Les Précieuses**, run by architect and fashion designer Pili Collado; designer eyewear at **Hoet**; exotic footwear at **Hatshoe**; and fine hats at **Christophe Coppens**. As if to offer some kind of global seal of approval, **Marc Jacobs** also set up on Antoine Dansaert in 2012. All this contemporary fashion is offset by fabulous **L'Archiduc**, the stylish jazz bar of Nat King Cole vintage, which reopened in the mid 1980s to resemble something akin to the ballroom of a grand ocean liner. Bands at the Ancienne Belgique across boulevard Anspach tend to finish the night here. After performing songs on the Grand'Place to promote their new album in Europe, Lady Gaga waltzed in here arm in arm with Tony Bennett in 2014. No other venue in Brussels would have been suitable.

The Flemish revitalisation of the area has also been driven by the innovative **Beursschouwburg** theatre (*see p197*), which celebrated its 50th anniversary in 2015 under the banner of being 'unpredictable and unpronounceable since 1965'.

Running at an angle from fashionable rue Antoine Dansaert, quainter, quieter **rue des Chartreux** stands strong against corporate or chain store development. It's never been a main thoroughfare because it leads to the place du Jardin aux Fleurs, part of a residential area. This creates a village effect and a sense of community among both residents and retailers. This is a street of shopping baskets, bicycles and dogs on leads, although the dawning of the new millennium didn't pass it by completely. Of constant interest to tourists is the life-size statue of a peeing dog that appeared as part of the City of Culture shenanigans in 2000. He stands in mid-spray on the corner with rue du Vieux Marché aux Grains.

An independent spirit reigns supreme in the neighbourhood. Near the dog, at no.27, is another half-cocked sight: a 1960s mannequin standing skew-whiff outside **Gabriele**'s impossibly packed vintage clothes shop. Sticking with the clothes theme, Chartreux has some slick little boutiques – don't be afraid to venture inside. **AM Sweet** is a real treat, full of old-fashioned charm. This is the village tearoom, where you can get a pot of leaf tea and a delicious slice of own-made cake. It also sells goodies by hot Brussels chocolatier Laurent Gerbaud. At no.66, **Den Teepot** (02 511 94 02) also serves tea and cake, but of the organic variety. In its grocery you can find a vast selection of eco-friendly goods, from kitchen roll to fresh veg. Add in concept lifestyle boutique **Hunting & Collecting**, funky homewares shop **Toit**, a couple of watchmakers and clock repairers, and you have one of the most offbeat streets in town. Oh, and there's timeless bar **Le Greenwich**, an institution where Surrealists (including Magritte) hustled pictures and played chess.

Even previously unsung **rue Léon Lepage** is muscling in on this mini-scene, taking advantage of its location as the connection between the main twin streets of chic, rue Antoine Dansaert in St-Géry and rue de Flandre in Ste-Catherine.

Brussels Vintage Market.

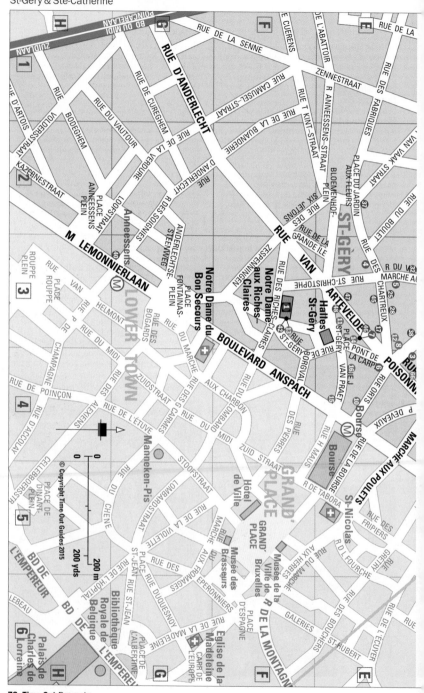

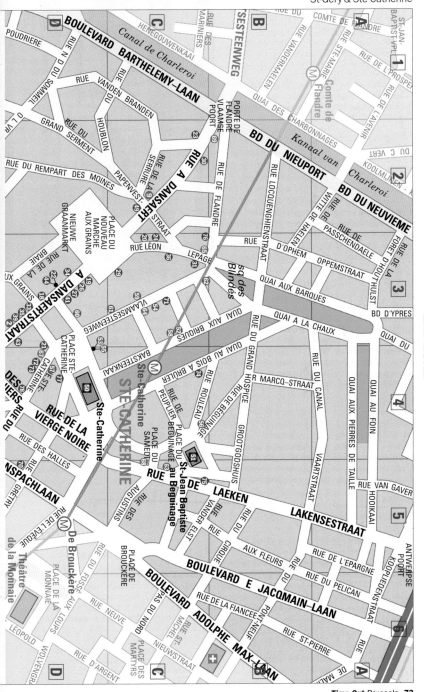

Describing itself as the 'missing link', an association of Lepage shop-owners has been set up, with its own Facebook page (www.facebook.com/leonlepagebrussels) promoting joint events and shopping vouchers.

The whole scene, within a walking radius of ten minutes, has led to an influx of young professionals, and made St-Géry popular with the gay community.

Sights & Museums

Eglise de Notre-Dame aux Riches Claires
23 rue des Riches Claires (02 511 09 37). Pré-métro Bourse. **Open** 8.30am-5pm daily. *Services* 10am, 11.30am (Spanish) Sun. **Map** p72 F3 **①**
This charming asymmetrical structure, which was built in 1665, is probably the work of Luc Fayd'herbe, a pupil of Rubens.

Restaurants

★ Bonsoir Clara
22-26 rue Antoine Dansaert (02 502 09 90, www.bonsoirclara.com). Pré-métro Bourse. **Open** noon-2.30pm, 7-11.30pm Mon-Thur; noon-2.30pm, 7pm-midnight Fri; 7pm-midnight Sat; 7-11.30pm Sun. **Main courses** €14-€27. **Set menu** €25-€50. **Map** p73 D3 **②**
Modern European
Bonsoir Clara is the restaurant that started it all off for rue Antoine Dansaert, a beacon of trend in an area that was just waiting to happen. It still pulls in the crowds with its understated sophistication and brilliantly eclectic food. The menu borrows from around the world, incorporating Asian spices, Italian delicacies and Californian reductions. Sweet and sour peking veal rib in Trappiste beer, or tuna tartare with pine nuts and wasabi mayo give some idea of what to expect. The look is clean and streamlined, with white tablecloths and white lilies, while a vast panel of back-lit coloured glass adds flair.

Comocomo
19 rue Antoine Dansaert (02 503 03 30, www.comocomo.com). Pré-metro Bourse. **Open** 6.30-10.30pm Mon, Tue; noon-2pm, 6.30-10.30pm Wed-Sun. **Dishes** €9.50-€22.50. **Map** p72 E4 **③** Tapas
Set amid designer shops and other chic eateries, Comocomo has proved a roaring success. It owes its popularity to both the food and the concept: it's a Basque *pintxo* (tapas) bar, with a sushi-style conveyor belt. Clean and modern, with splashes of coloured light, the interior feels inviting and up-to-the-minute. The *pintxos* wend their way around the snaking belt on colour-coded plates, depending on theme: purple for pork, blue for fish, green for veggie and so on. Try fried quails' legs, boar, octopus or black olives and mushrooms.

Divino
56 rue des Chartreux (02 503 39 09, www.divinoresto.be). Pré-métro Bourse. **Open** noon-2.30pm, 6.30-11pm Tue-Thur; noon-2.30pm, 6.30-11.30pm Fri; 6.30-11.30pm Sat; 6.30-10.30pm Sun. **Main courses** €10-€16. **Map** p72 E3 **④** Italian
The influence of the St-Géry area is spreading slowly along this charismatic street of idiosyncratic shops and eateries. Divino is a splash of inspiration in a row of old houses still waiting to find an identity. The buzzy dining space is retro-minimalist in style. Food includes carpaccio of beef, gigantic pizzas with a vast array of toppings, and pasta dishes that make liberal use of seafood and fresh vegetables. A lovely brick-walled terrace means the front of the restaurant is usually empty in summer, but don't think for a moment that it's fallen out of favour. Booking is advised.

Les Filles – Plaisirs Culinaires
46 rue du Vieux Marché aux Grains (02 534 04 83, www.lesfillesplaisirsculinaires.be). Pré-metro Bourse. **Open** noon-2pm, 6-9pm Mon-Fri; 10am-4pm, 6-9pm Sat, Sun. **Set menu** €16 lunch; €18 weekend brunch; €25 dinner. **Map** p72 E3 **⑤** Modern European
There's not much to see from the outside, just a blackboard and some window signage. Everything that goes on at Les Filles happens beyond the double carriage doors of this imposing grey-stone townhouse. And there's a lot that does go on. This isn't just an informal restaurant, it's a whole concept dedicated to the joy of food that includes cookery classes and a high-end grocery shop (open 10am-4pm daily). Les Filles prefer to call the restaurant a guesthouse. You can chat about the daily organic menus, help

EXPLORE

Eglise de Notre-Dame aux Riches Claires.

yourself to bread, to the fridge, serve yourself from the stove and sit with like minds at communal tables. A simple but celebratory experience.

Hotel Orts Café

38-40 rue Auguste Orts (02 517 07 00, www.hotelorts.com). Pré-métro Bourse. **Open** 9am-10.30pm daily. **Main courses** €10-€20. **Map** p72 E4 ❻ **Café**

Once upon a time, a tired and moody café called the White Horse sat on this busy corner. After it closed, the building slowly deteriorated. Then renovation work began, a three-star hotel opened upstairs and locals were thrilled to discover that an original belle époque canopy had been lurking under the plywood. Tourists and locals use Orts for different purposes throughout the day – breakfast, lunch, evening drinks or a good late-night booze-up on Guinness or the excellent collection of Belgian brews. The heated terrace is open year-round, despite the traffic.

Thiên-Long

12 rue van Artevelde (02 511 34 80). Pré-metro Bourse. **Open** noon-2.30pm, 6-10.30pm Mon, Tue, Thur-Sun. **Main courses** €9.50-€16. **No credit cards. Map** p72 E3 ❼ **Vietnamese**

First impressions of this Vietnamese restaurant are of a wooden-tabled caff incongruously set in a jungle of kitsch artefacts from the Far East, including the obligatory fluoro waterfall and red-tasselled lanterns. Despite the outlandish decor, this place is too self-effacing for its own good. It calls itself a snack-resto, but it's so much more than that. Steaming bowls of hot chilli soup, lacquered duck, and beef with bamboo and crunchy stir-fried vegetables appear on one of the longest menus this side

of Hanoi. The food is sublime, the portions are huge and they're concocted by one of the smallest chefs you've ever seen.

Pubs & Bars

★ L'Archiduc

6 rue Antoine Dansaert (02 512 06 52, www. archiduc.be). Pré-métro Bourse. **Open** 4pm-5am daily. **Map** p72 E3 ❽

The duke of all dives, the baron of all bars, the art deco L'Archiduc was reopened by Jean-Louis and Nathalie Hernant in 1985 in time to be part of the cultural wave that swept down rue Antoine Dansaert and washed over the rest of Brussels. Its predecessor dated from 1937 and boasted an impeccable jazz pedigree. Charlie Parker played here, as did Nat King Cole. Class will out, and L'Archiduc proved the perfect vehicle for fashionistas and their chic cohorts, with its curvaceous, two-floor interior resembling an ocean-liner's ballroom drifting across the Atlantic. By day, it's the ideal spot to sip a cocktail and reflect on your afternoon's shopping.

▶ *L'Archiduc also appeals to the demi-monde and those who prefer to do their drinking well past midnight – see p191.*

Barbeton

114 rue Antoine Dansaert (02 513 83 63, www. barbeton.be). Métro Ste-Catherine. **Open** 8am-2am Mon-Wed; 8am-4am Thur-Sat; 9am-midnight Sun. **No credit cards. Map** p73 C2 ❾

Halfway down Antoine Dansaert between the Bourse hub and the canal, Barbeton is one of a new generation of bars that has left St-Géry to the tourists and appeals to a more local crowd. Early evening

EXPLORE

IN THE KNOW
SETTING THE SENNE

Brussels is a rare European capital without a river. Originally, though, it had a waterway, the Senne, which meandered around what is today's city centre. In fact, the churches of St-Géry and St Nicholas were built around it. As the Senne became more and more polluted from industrial waste, and the Canal de Willebroeck and Charleroi served the city's cargo boats, the Senne was seen as sullied and superfluous. The terrible cholera of 1866 sealed its fate. Mayor Jules Anspach had the Senne covered over and boulevards created above. The main boulevard took his name after Anspach died, relatively young, in 1879. A fountain, first erected at De Brouckère and later moved to Ste-Catherine, bears a plaque listing his achievements.

is as good a time as any to visit, when the terrace fills and €5 cocktails set everyone up for another night's bar crawl around the Antoine Dansaert/rue de Flandre beat. Occupying the entire ground floor of a single building at a busy downtown junction, Barbeton also attracts much passing trade – trendy Volga beer also helps.

Le Coq

14 rue Auguste Orts (02 514 24 14). Pré-métro Bourse. **Open** 10am-late daily. **No credit cards.** **Map** p72 E4 ⑩

It's hard to know why some unassuming, plain-looking bars make a mark on the Brussels scene. You could walk past Le Coq without giving it a moment's thought, its wood-panelled walls and flat lighting resembling any bar in any town. But there's magic inside, from the indifferent professionalism of the older-generation staff (who close up when the last customer has left) to the eclectic mix of daytime boozers and night owls, all there for an unpretentious drink and deep philosophical banter.

Gecko

16 place St-Géry (02 502 29 99, www.gecko cocktailbar.be). Pré-métro Bourse. **Open** 9am-2am Mon-Thur; 10am-3am Fri, Sat; 11am-midnight Sun. **No credit cards. Map** p72 E3 ⑪

Formerly an in-the-know splinter of St-Gery, narrow of interior and thin in customers, Gecko is now a full-blown bar attracting an across-the-board clientele with cut-price lunches, zingy cocktails and – after a welcome expansion – cosy alcoves and casual furnishings. Come in and pull up a wooden folding chair or commandeer one of the dinky cushions. It's characterful and jazzy on certain nights; check the website for the latest line-up.

★ Le Greenwich

7 rue des Chartreux (02 540 88 78, www.greenwich-cafe.be). Pré-métro Bourse. **Open** noon-midnight daily. **No credit cards. Map** p72 E3 ⑫

The Greenwich is one of Brussels' institutions, a traditional 'brown' bar whose older patrons spend entire lifetimes over its chessboards. Grab a chair, a beer, a board and a Tupperware box of chess pieces and become part of the furniture. Or order up a drink, open up a book and observe. It's got history too: Magritte hustled pictures and Bobby Fischer hustled chess here. Of late, realising that the consumption of a single drink per evening per customer may not balance the books, the Greenwich has gone big on food, offering *moules-frites* lunchtime deals and hulking great steaks.

Java Bar

22 rue de la Grand Île (02 512 37 16). Pré-métro Bourse. **Open** 5.30pm-4am Mon-Thur, Sun; 5.30pm-5am Fri, Sat. **No credit cards. Map** p72 F3 ⑬

An imposingly cool bar composing the bow of St-Géry as it meets rue de la Grande Île, Java makes the best of its corner plot. The interior is dominated by a heavy circular bar counter, foot-railed by Gaudi-esque twisted metal and offset by half a tree and half a globe. Early-evening specials complement Bel Pils and Steendonk beers on draught, all served with the same smile that welcomed you in. Cocktails are available too.

Mappa Mundo

2-6 rue du Pont de la Carpe (02 514 35 55, www.mappamundo.com). Pré-métro Bourse. **Open** noon-1.30am Mon-Wed, Sun; noon-2.30am Thur; noon-3.30am Fri, Sat. **Map** p72 E3 ⑭

A mainstay of the St-Géry scene, Mappa Mundo feels as big as the world, a huge pub with a huge marble bar counter and an equally huge terrace. Somehow it fills, the terrace at least, almost every night, with tourists sipping Guinness, picking at plates of tapas and watching the crowds walk by, many looking for a free table on warm summer evenings. Occasional live music – jazz, latin – also brings in the punters.

▶ *For a similar funky feel, with live ska and African sounds, nearby Zebra (35 place St-Géry, 02 503 41 12, www.facebook.com/thezebrabar) is in the same family.*

O'Reilly's

1 place de la Bourse (02 552 04 80, www.oreillys. com/brussels.html). Pré-métro Bourse. **Open** 11am-2am Mon-Thur, Sun; 11am-4am Fri, Sat. **Map** p72 E4 ⑮

It's not to everyone's taste in a city where the quirky and the individual take pride of place, but there's no denying O'Reilly's part in the grand scheme of serious drinking and partying. For a start, it occupies the most in-your-face site in the Lower Town, immediately opposite the Bourse and at the entry to the St-Géry bar zone. Its bright green exterior is hard to miss, with customers spilling out on to the terrace and prime-seating mini balcony. It is from here that the stags, hens and footie fans shout their allegiance to the bewildered crowd below. There's a mix of Belgian and Irish draughts, along with sustaining Irish breakfasts from 11am.

Le Roi des Belges
35 rue Jules van Praet (02 513 51 16, www.facebook.com/leroidesbelges). Pré-métro Bourse. **Open** 9am-1am Mon-Thur, Sun; 9am-3am Fri, Sat. **Map** p72 E4 ⓰
One of the first venues from bar entrepreneur Frédéric Nicolay to set up and get St-Géry in motion, the King of the Belgians also set the tone for many of his other establishments. Here, the Belgian theme touches on Expo 58, with a kitschy representation of the Atomium on the bar counter, offset by sundry cycling iconography. It's a breakfast-to-past-bedtime operation, with DJ sets at weekends and a decent selection of cocktails to complement the standard beer range.

Shops & Services

AM Sweet
4 rue des Chartreux (02 513 51 31). Pré-métro Bourse. **Open** 9am-6.30pm Tue-Sat. **No credit cards. Map** p72 E3 ⓱ **Food & drink**
This lovely old-fashioned teahouse and shop sells biscuits, chocolate by Laurent Gerbaud, cakes, sweets, teas and coffees, some of which are made in-house. The foodstuffs range from traditional recipes (such as *pain d'épices*) to the latest innovative concoctions, such as French crystallised flowers, made from real rose, lavender, violet and mint leaves.

★ Annemie Verbeke
64 rue Antoine Dansaert (02 511 21 71, www.annemieverbeke.be). Pré-métro Bourse. **Open** 11am-6pm Mon, Wed-Sat. **Map** p73 D3 ⓲ **Fashion**
Fashionistas flock to Annemie Verbeke's shop, in a beautiful old building, for her classic clothes. The exquisite knitwear is simple, but often features subtle detailing around the sleeves and neckline.

Carine Gilson
87 rue Antoine Dansaert (02 289 51 47, www.carinegilson.com). Métro Ste-Catherine or pré-métro Bourse. **Open** 10am-6.30pm Tue-Sat. **Map** p73 D3 ⓳ **Accessories**
Carine Gilson's unique, sensual lingerie is laid out in art deco surroundings. Her collections are shown around the world, such as her Alba show in Dubai in summer 2015.

★ Christophe Coppens
2 rue Léon Lepage (02 512 77 97, www.christophecoppens.com). Métro Ste-Catherine. **Open** 11am-6pm Tue-Sat. **Map** p73 C3 ⓴ **Accessories**

Flemish designer Christophe Coppens creates amazing hats (mainly for women) using all kinds of materials and ranging in price from around €150 to seriously pricey. This is, after all, an artist who has created headwear for the likes of Grace Jones, Rihanna and the Scissor Sisters.

★ Crémerie de Linkebeek
4 rue du Vieux Marché aux Grains (02 512 35 10). Pré-métro Bourse. **Open** 9am-3pm Mon; 9am-6pm Tue-Sat. **No credit cards. Map** p73 D3 ㉑ **Food & drink**
The oldest cheese shop in Brussels, founded in 1902 by a family from the outlying village of Linkebeek. The sawdust on the floor, the white tiles: all looks similar to how it would have done during the reign of Léopold II – except that current owners Laurence Duhot and Jordan Greenwood have filled the display trays and shelves with 100-plus cheeses from mainly small producers in Belgium, France and the Netherlands. The pair traverse the Benelux for the best cheese – soft and creamy, hard and piquant – they can find. Milk from Lier is also sold in glass bottles, alongside cold meat, eggs, biscuits, wine and a signature cheesecake created to a secret recipe. *Photos p78.*

Essentiel Antwerp
76 rue Antoine Dansaert (02 290 01 38, www.essentiel-antwerp.com). Métro Ste-Catherine or pré-métro Bourse. **Open** 10.30am-6.30pm Mon-Fri; 10.30am-7pm Sat. **Map** p73 D3 ㉒ **Fashion**
The husband-and-wife team of Esfan Eghtessadi and Inge Onsea created this successful concept in 1999, gradually moving from T-shirt collections to jackets, dresses and knitwear, and branching out from their original Antwerp base to spread across Belgium. Still producing colourful, affordable, ready-to-wear fashion, the duo have since gained a foothold in Paris and are looking to establish EA as a key Belgian brand further afield.
Other location 66 avenue Louise, Ixelles (02 513 18 91).

La Fabrika
182 rue Antoine Dansaert (02 502 33 25, www.lafabrika.be). Métro Ste-Catherine. **Open** 11am-6pm Mon-Sat. **Map** p73 C2 ㉓ **Homewares**
Set at the canal end of Antoine Dansaert since 2010, this two-floor store has plenty of room to show off sought-after brands of contemporary furniture such as Ercol, Another Country and SCP. More often than not, La Fabrika has nationwide exclusivity on the latest sleek designs from Scandinavia, the States and the UK. An interior architect is on hand to advise and provide after-sales service.

Le Fabuleux Marcel de Bruxelles
10 rue Léon Lepage (02 201 03 61, www.fabuleuxmarcel.com). Métro Ste-Catherine. **Open** 11am-6.30pm Mon-Sat. **Map** p73 C3 ㉔ **Fashion**

Named after the tank top made famous by French boxer Marcel Cerdan, the famous tragic lover of Edith Piaf, Marcel creates casual tops for fashion-conscious men and women.

★ Gabriele Vintage

27 rue des Chartreux (02 512 67 43). Pré-métro Bourse. **Open** 1-7pm Mon, Tue; 11am-7pm Wed, Fri, Sat; 11am-8pm Thur. **Map** p72 E3 ㉕ **Fashion**
Owner Gabriele Wolf started collecting period hats when she worked in the theatre. She also sells elegant evening dresses, coats and shoes, all dating from the 1920s onwards.

Hatshoe

89 rue Antoine Dansaert (02 512 41 52, www. hatshoe.be). Métro Ste-Catherine or pré-métro Bourse. **Open** 12.30-6.30pm Mon; 10.30am-2pm, 2.30-6.30pm Tue-Sat. **Map** p73 D3 ㉖ **Accessories**
Designer footwear for men and women by Patrick Cox, Costume National and Belgian designers Dries van Noten and Veronique Branquinho. Hats and scarves are by Cécile Bertrand.

Hoet

97 rue Antoine Dansaert (02 511 04 47, www. optiekhoet-brussel.be). Métro Ste-Catherine or pré-métro Bourse. **Open** 10.30am-6.30pm Tue-Sun. **Map** p73 D3 ㉗ **Accessories**
The former Théo, purveyor of trendy specs and sunglasses with distinctive, brightly coloured, thick frames, has moved to bigger premises along the same fashionable street and changed its name – but has stayed in the same family, as it has done for six generations. Hoet still displays the Théo collection as well as custom-made glasses created from titanium by a 3D printer.

Hunting & Collecting

17 rue des Chartreux (02 512 74 77, www.hunting andcollecting.com). Pré-métro Bourse. **Open** 2-6pm Mon; noon-8pm Tue-Sat. **Map** p72 E3 ㉘ **Fashion**
'Where No Store Has Gone Before' they proudly boast and, sure enough, this experimental space is first of all a blank canvas for regularly changing menswear (Patrik Ervell, Kenzo, Christophe Lemaire) and womenswear (Jacquemus, Christian Wijnants, Cédric Charlier). Art and fashion happenings are frequently programmed.

★ Icon

5 place du Vieux Marché aux Grains (02 502 71 51, www.icon-shop.be). Métro Ste-Catherine. **Open** 10.30am-6.30pm Mon-Sat. **Map** p73 C3 ㉙ **Fashion**
Michèle Bogaert's trendy multi-brand store, set in an 18th-century townhouse, stocks seasonal womenswear by the likes of Each X Other, Marc Philippe Coudeyre and Marjorie Vermeulen. Crop tops, jeans, skirts and sweaters, accessories too.

Joya Brussels

175 rue Antoine Dansaert (02 203 18 14, www. joyabrussels.net). Métro Ste-Catherine. **Open** 11am-6.30pm Tue-Sat. **Map** p73 C2 ㉚ **Accessories**

Established in 2011, Joya Brussels provides an outlet for some of the city's most radical designers of rings, bracelets and necklaces. If you like your jewellery out-there and contemporary, this is the place to come.

Just In Case

63 rue Léon Lepage (02 511 50 01, www.justin case.be). Métro Ste-Catherine. **Open** 11am-7pm Tue-Sat. **Map** p73 C3 **㉛ Fashion**

Vicky Vinck and Katrien Strijbol established their label in their native Antwerp – this is their Brussels flagship. There's a distinctive romantic streak in their womenswear – you only need look at their recent collections, 'Are You The One I've Been Waiting For', 'Take This Longing' and 'Baby Won't You Please Come Home'.

Kat en Muis

35-37 rue du Vieux Marché aux Grains (02 514 32 34). Pré-métro Bourse. **Open** 10.30am-6.30pm Mon-Sat. **Map** p72 E3 **㉜ Children**

Recently moved from nearby Antoine Dansaert, this is the children's version of the cutting-edge fashion store Stijl. Expect designer clothes for the little ones at high prices.

Kure

48 rue Antoine Dansaert (02 265 12 17, www.kure-eshop.com). Pré-métro Bourse. **Open** 10.30am-7pm Mon-Sat. **Map** p73 D3 **㉝ Fashion**

This luxury multibrand store of 200 desirable sq m right on Antoine Dansaert, specialises in 'premium attainable' womenswear – meaning tops, bottoms and shoes by the likes of Raiine, Anine Bing and Chiara Ferragni.

Marc by Marc Jacobs BXL

90 rue Antoine Dansaert (02 511 05 82, www. marcjacobs.com). Métro Ste-Catherine or pré-métro Bourse. **Open** 11am-7pm Mon-Fri; 10.30am-7pm Sat; noon-6pm Sun. **Map** p73 D3 **㉞ Fashion & accessories**

With more than 200 stores worldwide, it was inevitable that New York's prince of fashion would set up in Brussels – and indicative that he chose Antoine Dansaert to do so. Men's, women's and children's ready-to-wear gear, shoes, bags and accessories are stocked over two floors.

Marianne Timperman

50 rue Antoine Dansaert (02 675 53 82, www.mariannetimperman.be). Pré-métro Bourse. **Open** 10.30am-6.30pm Mon-Sat. **Map** p73 D3 **㉟ Accessories**

Marianne Timperman makes the majority of the jewellery on display herself, but there are a few pieces by Italian designer Tiziana Redavid. Marianne's speciality is silver; some items are oxidised so that they appear black, while others are made from granulated silver, resulting in a bobbly effect. She also incorporates semi-precious stones and pearls, and sells gold work too. Prices are reasonable.

EXPLORE

Crémerie de Linkebeek. *See p77.*

NN70

47 rue Léon Lepage (02 502 24 08, www.facebook.com/nn70conceptstore). Métro Ste-Catherine. **Open** 11am-6.30pm Wed, Thur; 11am-8pm Fri, Sat. **Map** p73 C3 ⬤ **Concept store**

Beautician, stylist, art gallery, fashion boutique with a barista corner – Sylvie Kettel's NN70 covers all contemporary bases and also stages sundry art and fashion happenings.

Own Shop

5 place du Jardin aux Fleurs (02 217 95 71). Pré-métro Bourse. **Open** 10.30am-6.30pm Mon-Sat. **Map** p72 E2 ⬤ **Fashion**

From, literally, their own shop selling their own brand of men's and women's clothing, Thierry Rondenet and Hervé Yvrenogeau branched out to stock the likes of Atelier 11, Acne and Comme des Garçons, amid a multi-mirrored interior.

Le Pain Quotidien

16A rue Antoine Dansaert (02 502 23 61, www.lepainquotidien.be). Pré-métro Bourse. **Open** 7.30am-7pm Mon-Sat; 7.30am-6pm Sun. **Map** p72 E3 ⬤ **Food & drink**

This successful chain of café-bakeries has branches around the world. This flagship Brussels branch is the most centrally located, though the one on avenue Louise is a favourite for its conservatory. Shoppers can pick up a loaf or croissant, or delicacies such as raspberry clafoutis, tarte au citron and the legendary chocolate bombe cake. Enjoy brunch in a warm, rustic setting of shared tables.

Other locations throughout the city.

Passa Porta

46 rue Antoine Dansaert (02 502 94 60, www.passaporta.be). Pré-métro Bourse. **Open** 11am-7pm Mon-Sat; noon-6pm Sun. **Map** p73 D3 ⬤ **Books & music**

Referring to itself as 'an international house of literature', wonderful multi-language bookstore Passa Porta ('your passport to contemporary world literature') collaborates with important cultural institutions across the city to stage readings and sundry literary encounters. It also organises a biennial international literary festival – most recently in March 2015.

Pêle-Mêle

55 boulevard Maurice Lemonnier (02 548 78 00, www.pele-mele.be). Pré-métro Anneessens. **Open** 10am-6.30pm Mon-Sat. **No credit cards.** **Map** p72 G3 ⬤ **Books & music**

Pêle-Mêle is stuffed with books, comics, magazines, CDs, records, videos, DVDs and computer games, which it buys and sells. There is a decent English section too. Patient delving usually proves rewarding and prices are more than fair.

Other location 566 chaussée de Waterloo, Ixelles (02 888 95 44).

Les Précieuses

83 rue Antoine Dansaert (02 503 28 98). *Pré-métro Bourse.* **Open** 11am-6.30pm Mon-Sat. **Map** p73 D3 ⬤ **Accessories**

Pili Collado (Belgian of Portuguese descent) designs beautiful jewellery, using velvet ribbons, fine strands and polished, chunky, semi-precious stones and pearls. She also sells Jamin Puech's sequinned and embroidered bags, and flamenco-inspired shawls, Diptyque candles and perfume, and scarves and tops by Japanese label Antipast. Check for Les Précieuses on Facebook.

Other location 20 place Brugmann, Ixelles (no phone).

Ramona

21 rue de la Grande Île (0478 68 65 25). *Pré-métro Bourse.* **Open** noon-6pm Tue-Sat. **Map** p72 F3 ⬤ **Fashion**

Enter this boudoir and you're likely to find Chilean designer Ramona Hernández Collao lying on a chaise longue, knitting her latest creation. She will turn her hand to any kind of clothing, including jumpers, trousers, coats, dresses and tops. Each piece is unique, being a different colour, texture and design. There's a Facebook page.

Rue Blanche

39-41 rue Antoine Dansaert (02 512 03 14). *Pré-métro Bourse.* **Open** 11am-6.30pm Mon-Sat. **Map** p73 D3 ⬤ **Fashion**

Two Belgian designers, Marie Chantal Regout and Patrick van Heurck, launched Rue Blanche (also on Facebook) in 1987, with seven different styles of cotton knitted jersey. From such lowly beginnings their business has gone from strength to strength to include more than 100 timeless items in gorgeous fabrics, as well as beautiful evening bags, scarves and shoes. Household items, such as candles, vases and glossy books, complete the stock and ensure beautiful surroundings.

★ Stijl

74 rue Antoine Dansaert (02 512 03 13, www.stijl.be). Pré-métro Bourse. **Open** 10.30am-6.30pm Mon-Sat. **Map** p73 D3 ⬤ **Fashion**

The stark interior of Stijl contains some of the most cutting-edge design that Belgium has to offer – at a price. Owner Sonia Noël has a knack for spotting home-grown talent, having signed up first-time collections from Ann Demeulemeester, Dries van Noten and Martin Margiela, as well as Olivier Theyskens and Xavier Delcour.

Other location 6 place du Nouveau Marché aux Grains, St-Géry (02 513 42 50).

Toit

46 rue des Chartreux (02 503 33 38, www.facebook.com/toit.chartreux46). Pré-métro Bourse. **Open** 11am-7pm Wed-Sat. **Map** p72 E3 ⬤ **Homewares**

EXPLORE

This bright boutique sells glass, vases, framed pictures, CDs and bags. It also has a natty line in tinned and bottled food – squid in its own ink, for example.

Valérie Berckmans

8 rue Van Artevelde (02 502 94 00, www. valerieberckmans.be). Pré-métro Bourse. **Open** 11am-6.30pm Tue-Sat. **Map** p72 E3 ⓮ **Fashion**
Tops, skirts and shoes in muted colours for the contemporary woman, created by this Belgian designer and on display in her atelier-boutique.

Velodroom

41B rue Van Artevelde (02 513 81 99, www. velodroom.net). Pré-métro Bourse. **Open** 9am-1pm, 2-6pm Tue-Fri; 11am-1pm, 2-5pm Sat. **Map** p72 E3 ⓱ **Sports**
Velodroom is run by a non-profit organisation that promotes cycling in Brussels as an environmentally friendly alternative to driving in the city. It also does bike repairs.

★ Het Witte Gras

7 rue Plétinckx (02 502 05 29, www.facebook. com/hetwittegras.be). Pré-métro Bourse. **Open** 9am-6pm Mon, Tue, Thur, Sat; 9am-7pm Fri. **Map** p72 E3 ⓲ **Florist**
Houseplants and flowers spill on to the pavement from this pretty corner shop. Inside you'll find an abundance of attractive vases and pots, plus plenty of expert advice.

Y-dress?

102 rue Antoine Dansaert (0496 45 38 57, www.ydress.com). Métro Ste-Catherine. **Open** noon-7pm Tue-Sat. **Map** p73 C2 ⓳ **Fashion**
Aleksandra Paszkowska describes her creations as a 'new way of dressing', a multiple-choice concept of easily matching cheerful colours, off-the-peg and ready to roll. You'll find tops and dresses for about-town wear, for girls who cycle and mums to be, plus signature reversible coats and jackets.
Other location 8 rue des Renards, Marolles (no phone).

STE-CATHERINE

Similar to adjoining St-Géry, Ste-Catherine, set around the quays of an old harbour that once served a thriving traffic of fishing boats, became solid land with the filling in of the Senne in 1870. Nevertheless, it still feels like a port. The street names tell of its past – quai au Bois à Brûler ('Firewood Quay'), quai aux Briques ('Bricks Quay') – when cargo vessels would dock here to unload goods close to the town centre.

Fountains, including one to the mayor behind the Senne project, Jules Anspach, and paved walkways now cover what locals (but not maps) refer to as the Marché aux Poissons, the Fish Market, either side of the métro stop. But, just

IN THE KNOW
PINBALL WIZARDS

Belgium is maligned for many things – lack of identity is one. Yet so many things are quintessentially Belgian. Walk into any local bar and you'll find one such example, exotic, colourful and mysterious. Pinball. Belgian pinball. The same flashing lights, the same glass-topped machine, the same shiny steel balls catapulted with satisfying dexterity. But this isn't pinball, it's bingo. Belgian bingo. Balls don't whizz between flippers, but float capriciously into any of 25 holes, rows of numbers that represent byzantine combinations of potential winnings by line or pattern. The rest of the world might prefer to cross off numbers on a card and await the fateful patter of the caller – not here. This is planet Belgium – quirky, confusing and simply unique.

as its riverside legacy exists in name only, so too the once-thriving fish market. Significantly, in recent years, stalls have set up here on Wednesday mornings, selling organic produce (salamis, poultry and the like). In similar vein, where there were only long-established fish restaurants, characteristically lit with vast red neon lobsters, so Ste-Catherine is now home to all manner of new, independent eateries, most with a terrace, giving a real open-air feel to the area. Most prominent are the **Mer du Nord**, where shoppers and snackers fill a busy corner with chatter over herring and mussels, and **Charli**, an artisanal bakery and pâtisserie with a popular sit-down section – *see p82* **Moving On Up**.

Still dominating proceedings, of course, is the **church** that gave Ste-Catherine its name, built around the time the Senne was covered over; its predecssor, dating from the Middle Ages, was as insalubrious as the waters that surrounded it. Only its Italianate belfry survives. In December, Ste-Catherine's forms the backdrop for the Christmas market that extends here from the Grand'Place – although the open-air skating rink has moved and is now in front of the Opera House. Behind the church is the Tour Noire ('Black Tower'), a rare remaining remnant of the second city wall, rescued from demolition by Mayor Charles Buls in the late 19th century.

Place Ste-Catherine, beside the church, has been completely rebuilt: it's lost some of its old character, but no one bemoans that it is no longer a car park. Still very much in place is the church of **St-Jean-Baptiste au Béguinage**, once the centre of the city's largest *béguinage*, a charitable community for single women that was founded in the 13th century.

EXPLORE

EXPLORE

MOVING ON UP

Sassy Ste-Catherine sizzles with new venues.

There's something about downtown Brussels that keeps it in a kind of time warp. Maybe it's the Grand'Place effect or an if-it-ain't-broke attitude. There's something reassuring about being in a city centre where locals still live, where their favourite bars, restaurants and shops stay put and everyone knows how things should be.

The flipside is that regeneration can be limited, that there's no room for the new or adventurous. Ste-Catherine is a case in point. It's always been a traditional, fairly middle-class *quartier* resting on its fish restaurant laurels, with trendy rue Antoine Dansaert attracting only the fashionistas that can afford it. In recent times, though, a younger professional class has moved in, populating the eating and drinking terraces around place Ste-Catherine and rue de Flandre. In turn, this has fast become a destination in its own right.

Rue Sainte-Catherine, the street that links the area to the Bourse, has always had its share of indie shops and quirky buildings, but they were becoming rundown. A terrace of Dutch-gabled 17th-century houses had lain in ruins for years, but suddenly it seems as if money is being injected into the street and handsome renovations have been completed.

At the bottom of one such house is the new **Jack O'Shea Chophouse** (*see p84*), brainchild of the Irishman who took over the old Ghysel butcher at no.24 and filled the windows with Aberdeen Angus steaks and ibérico pork. The butchery theme continues with the restaurant, its big window doubling

up as the cold store, so you can gawp at haunches of dry-aged beef. Inside, a flaming charcoal grill cooks everything to perfection. Along the road is **Charli** (*see p87*), an artisanal bakery. People cross town to pick up its crusty loaves, sublime tarts and delicious pastries; there's also a tearoom at weekends.

On the other side of the square, rue de Flandre has been going through a quiet regeneration of its own. Once a street of tired shops, now it's home to stylish wine merchants, cooks, books and bicycles. Informal eating is becoming the norm. Try **Chicago Eet Café** (*see p83*), an ex-industrial space lightened by a glass roof and serving cakes, pastries and hot plates, from eggs on toast to pasta and burgers. On the other side of the street, **John & Rose Art Café** (*see p84*) is a daytime bar, café and exhibition space with rotating art shows each month. Have lunch here (tapenades, soups, salads, posh sandwiches on organic bread) and you'll have touched the nerve of what Flandre is all about.

Back at place Ste-Catherine, it's all about the outdoors. Restaurant terraces line one side of the square, but it's **Mer du Nord** (*see p87; pictured*) that punters flock to, come rain or shine. They stand and eat at high tables or huddle under the huge awning to tuck into plates of mussels, squid, herring – whatever's in season. Or there's **Jean's** (known to locals as Jeannot), an oyster stall that's there almost every day of the year. To add colour, in summer a red cocktail van turns up and you can pick up a mojito for €5 – *¡salud!*

Ste-Catherine has also benefited from the knock-on effect of St-Géry's modernisation. Everyday Belgian bars, cafés and shops are now interspersed with temples to minimalist chic. A classic example is **De Markten** on rue Vieux Marché aux Grains, an old refurbished building with a café on the ground floor and a popular Flemish arts centre behind. In summer, the square out front packs with drinkers and diners and live sound stages. Turn in to rue de Flandre and you're presented with a vivid image of how Ste-Catherine used to look – traditional restaurants, old-fashioned shops selling caged birds, a launderette – and how it is developing now, with establishments such as **John & Rose Art Café** and the **Chicago Eet Café** leading the way.

Further down rue de Flandre, west of central Ste-Catherine, on the edge of the Lower Town, more bars and clubs in the Nicolay Group – **Walvis**, **Au Laboureur** – have breathed new life into this long-forgotten stretch. On balmy evenings, where rue de Flandre and Antoine Dansaert meet, just before the canal, these one-time bleak streets now have a more downtown feel. Newer venues such as **Bravo** (*see p191*) have brought in more crowds.

Beyond, the Canal de Charleroi, a narrow stretch of water separating the city centre from the grey stretches of west Brussels, is all that remains of the Senne. But even the canal is coming back to life. In 2014, **Canal 05** (www.canal05.com) art gallery opened on the quayside, with regular workshops and debates alongside exhibitions. Every second September, a five-day multimedia arts event, **Festival Kanal** (www.festivalkanal. be), brings installations to both embankments. Further north, a waterbus service has been reintroduced to put the canal to regular use.

Sights & Museums

Église de Ste-Catherine
50 place Ste-Catherine (0497 99 53 02 mobile, www.eglisesaintecatherine.be). Métro Ste-Catherine. **Open** 9am-8pm Mon-Sat; 9.30am-7pm Sun. *Services* 6pm Mon; 12.15pm, 6pm Tue-Fri; 12.15pm Sat; 10.30am Sun. **Map** p73 D4 ⑩
Designed in neo-Gothic style by Joseph Poelaert, of Palais de Justice fame, Ste-Catherine almost became the stock exchange before opening as a church in 1867. It stands on the site of an earlier chapel sullied by the polluted waters of the Senne that once ran beside it. One treasure is a 15th-century statue of a Black Madonna, supposedly rescued from the river after being thrown in by angry Protestants.

Église de St-Jean-Baptiste au Béguinage
Place du Béguinage (02 217 87 42). Métro Ste-Catherine. **Open** 10am-5pm Tue-Sun. *Services* 5pm Sat; 10am, 8pm Sun. **Map** p73 C4 ⑪

One of the best examples of Flemish Baroque architecture in the city, this large church, attributed to Luc Fayd'herbe, has a fluid, honey-coloured façade. Its light-filled interior houses a beautiful pulpit and 17th-century paintings by Theodoor van Loon.

Restaurants

Bij den Boer
60 quai aux Briques (02 512 61 22, www.bijden boer.com). Métro Ste-Catherine. **Open** noon-2.30pm, 6-10.30pm Mon-Sat. **Main courses** €18-€27. **Set menu** €29.50. **Map** p73 C3 ㉒
Belgian/Fish & seafood
The Farmer's can seem a little intimidating from the outside as it's always packed with local customers – you get the feeling you're gatecrashing a private do. The decor is unremarkable, but made up for by the noisy, chattering atmosphere. The restaurant is famous for its mussels and bouillabaisse, and prices are good for the area – especially if you opt for the four-course set menu. Service is infuriatingly slow, though. Staff are friendly enough, and dash around at quite a rate, but never, it seems, towards your table. Persevere, though, and you will leave feeling mightily satisfied.

La Brasserie du Jaloa
5-7 place Ste-Catherine (02 512 18 31, www. brasseriejaloa.com). Métro Ste-Catherine. **Open** 11.45am-2.15pm, 6-10pm Mon-Thur; 11.45am-2.15pm, 6-10.45pm Fri; 11.45am-10.45pm Sat; 11.45am-10pm Sun. **Main courses** €18-€26. **Map** p73 D4 ㉝ Belgian/ Fish & seafood
Jaloa is a restaurant of three parts. First, there's the *écailler* of seafood at the front; sit on a stool and look over Ste-Catherine with a plate of oysters and a glass of something cold. Then there's the 1980s-style interior, all smoked glass and pastels with a strange mini-mezzanine overlooking the bar. Finally comes the courtyard, one of the biggest outside dining areas in town. Brick-walled and with huge awnings in case of rain, it's a perfect spot to attack the well-executed fish, seafood and meaty brasserie-style dishes. The only downside? The decision to cover the original flagstones with fake turf, which gives a sense that you're eating on a decommissioned five-a-side pitch. That apart, it's a reliable choice.

★ Chicago Eet Café
45 rue de Flandre (02 502 18 41, www.caat.be/ chicago). Métro Ste-Catherine. **Open** 9am-5pm daily. **Main courses** €10-€14.50. **Map** p73 C3 ㉞ Café
See p82 **Moving On Up**.

Ellis Gourmet Burger
4 place Ste-Catherine (02 514 23 14, www.ellisgourmetburger.com). Métro Ste-Catherine. **Open** 11.30am-11pm Mon-Thur,

EXPLORE

Sun; 11.30am-midnight Fri, Sat. **Main courses** €8.50-€16. **Map** p73 D4 ❺❺ **Burgers** *See p140* **The Burgers of Brussels**.

La Guinguette en Ville

9 place du Béguinage (02 229 02 22, www. facebook.com/laguinguetteenville). Métro Ste-Catherine. **Open** 6-10.30pm Mon, Sat; noon-3pm, 7-10.30pm Tue-Fri. **Map** p73 C4 ❺❻ **Belgian/French**

With its little pavement terrace looking directly on to the church of St-Jean du Béguinage, this relative newcomer has an envious location. It also has an envious reputation as a bistro to be reckoned with. The small green-tiled dining room with its metal lamps, banquettes and café tables has a casually flung-together look, though it's obvious that everything about the place is considered – especially the food. Classic seasonal dishes involve slow-cooked meats, super-fresh fish (try the swordfish ceviche) and vegetarian dishes such as wild mushroom risotto with verjus. Brussels is gushing about it and Michelin has already given it a *petit* nod, so don't expect to get in without a reservation.

★ Jack O'Shea Chophouse

32 rue Sainte-Catherine (02 503 36 31, www. jackoshea.com). Métro Ste-Catherine. **Open** noon-2.30pm, 7-10.30pm Mon, Thur-Sat; 11.30am-4pm Sun. **Main courses** €14-€85. **Map** p73 D4 ❺❼ **Steakhouse** *See p82* **Moving On Up**.

Jacques

44 quai aux Briques (02 513 27 62, www. restaurantjacques.be). Métro Ste-Catherine. **Open** noon-2pm, 6.30-10pm Mon-Sat. **Main courses** €25.50-€46.50. **Map** p73 C3 ❺❽ **Fish & seafood**

A favourite with locals, Jacques oozes traditional Belgian charm, especially in summer when the huge windows are open and the restaurant meets the street. An old-fashioned, wood-panelled interior, tiled floors and globe lamps give the place its atmosphere, although the back room is lacklustre and merely acts as a sounding board for the kitchen. Service is efficient but abrupt. Jacques is famous for its sublimely light and buttery turbot with sauce mousseline, though it's a costly choice.

John & Rose Art Café

80-84 rue de Flandre (02 318 15 38, www.john androse.be). Métro Ste-Catherine. **Open** 11am-4pm Mon-Fri; 11am-6pm Sat, Sun. **Main courses** €3.50-€9.50. **No credit cards. Map** p73 C3 ❺❾ **Café** *See p82* **Moving On Up**.

De Markten

5 rue du Vieux Marché aux Grains (02 512 91 85, www.demarkten.be). Métro Ste-Catherine. **Open** 8.30am-midnight Mon-Sat; 10am-6pm Sun. **Main courses** €7-€12. **No credit cards. Map** p73 D3 ❻⓪ **Café**

Before you enter this ground-floor café, take a step back and admire the magnificent building. The café is part of a cultural centre and, as such, attracts

young arty types from the Flemish school of thought. Inside, the style is postmodernist industrial chic. OK – it looks like a school canteen, but minimalism is just what these folk want. A terrace, filled with deckchairs in summer, looks on to the square.

Le Pré Salé

20 rue de Flandre (02 513 65 45). Métro Ste-Catherine. **Open** noon-2.30pm, 6.30-10.30pm Wed-Sun. **Main courses** €14-€24.50. **Map** p73 C3 ⑤ **Belgian**

What an institution this is. A white-tiled dining room leads to an open kitchen at the back, where you can see Madame slaving away with her little helpers, cooking everything to order. When she's done, she comes out for a drink and a chat with friends. Friday night is cabaret night, a decades-old tradition with Bruxellois jokes, bawdy humour and a bit of a knees-up; it's so popular, you'll need to book at least three weeks in advance. Food comprises hefty meat and fish dishes, with excellent cod, salmon and mussels and a huge beef rib for two people. There's absolutely no subtlety at the Pré Salé – it's all bright lights, big noise and vast plates of food, which is why we love it.

Selecto

95 rue de Flandre (02 511 40 95, www.leselecto. com). Métro Ste-Catherine. **Open** 7-10.30pm Tue-Thur; noon-2pm, 7-11pm Fri, Sat. **Set menu** lunch €14-€18, dinner €34-€40. **Map** p73 C3 ⑥ **Modern European**

Selecto refers to the fact that this is essentially a pick 'n' mix restaurant, where you create your own fixed-price menu from permanent dishes and daily specials chalked on the blackboard. As ever, more expensive ingredients such as foie and fillet will have a supplement, but it's all down to personal choice. It's certainly hit the mark with a buzzy, professional crowd packed in under the astonishing sea of 1960s ceiling lights. It's easy, it's a good brasserie and it gets you to the heart of happening rue de Flandre.

Toukoul

34 rue de Laeken & 1 rue du Marronier (02 223 73 77, www.toukoul.be). Métro Ste-Catherine. **Open** noon-2.30pm, 6.30-10.30pm Tue-Thur; noon-2.30pm, 6.30-11pm Fri; noon-3.30pm, 6.30-11pm Sat; noon-3.30pm, 6.30-10.30pm Sun. **Main courses** €16-€21. **Map** p73 C5 ⑤ **Ethiopian**

We don't know if the pun is intentional, but Toukoul really is. The sprawling space stretches between two streets and has a clever post-industrial tribal feel, where metal harmoniously meets wood and leather. The food is resolutely Ethiopian and designed for sharing. Veg, meat and fish are served on large rounds of *injera*, a spongy, pancake-like 'bread' (made from the tef grain), which acts as both plate and an eating implement when torn and rolled. Toukoul is more than a restaurant, though. It's also a cultural space with live world music acts (9-11pm Thur-Sat) and a bar where you can drink Ethiopian beer or try tej, the national drink of yeast wine with honey and water. See? Too cool.

Pubs & Bars

★ Au Daringman

37 rue de Flandre (02 512 43 23). Métro Ste-Catherine. **Open** noon-2am Tue-Sat; noon-8pm Sun. **No credit cards. Map** p73 C3 ⑥

Also known as Chez Haesendonck or Chez Martine, this entertainingly retro 'brown' bar is hidden between the fashion quarter and the canal. It attracts an enjoyably varied clientele, with theatregoing older couples squeezing in with folk of a younger, more boho bent. Surrounding them, jumble-sale shots of Elvis, Ella and others contrast with the wood panelling and an iconic Stella sign from the 1950s. It's bookended by a modest bar counter and regularly topped up with flyers and listings leaflets covering every art form, over- and underground.

★ Au Laboureur

108 rue de Flandre (02 512 13 82). Métro Ste-Catherine. **Open** 8.30am-10pm Mon-Thur, Sun; 8.30am-midnight Fri, Sat. **No credit cards. Map** p73 C3 ⑥

Once upon a time, in that seedy area of falling-down hotels in the estuary of bleak streets leading to Midi station, there was a museum-piece of a bar called 'Le Laboureur'. Railway workers and unpretentious older drinkers would nurse a beer over the course of

Jack O'Shea Chophouse.

EXPLORE

an afternoon. A decade or so ago, it served its last Stella. Now, either by deference or coincidence, an authentically retro bar of similar character has opened at the canal end of hip rue de Flandre, peanut dispenser, Belgian pinball machine and all. Old men play cards on baize tables and regulars shoot the breeze in a large wooden interior complemented by a sun-catching terrace.

Kafka

21 rue des Poissonniers (02 513 66 31, www. cafekafkabrussels.com). Pré-métro Bourse. **Open** 11am-2am Mon-Fri; 1pm-2am Sat, Sun. **Map** p72 E4 ⑥⑥

If it's late and you're lashing back the vodkas, chances are you're in the Kafka. Not that you'll remember the next day, but this place boasts a heady array of vodkas, genevers and other assorted white spirits, plus all the usual beers to chase the chasers down with. Images of the eponymous Czech writer set a somewhat incongruous tone in downtown Brussels, but the Kafka isn't so literary-minded that it can't pull down a big screen on football nights.

Monk

42 rue Sainte-Catherine (02 511 75 11, www. monk.be). Métro Ste-Catherine. **Open** 11am-1am Mon-Thur; 11am-3am Fri, Sat; 1pm-1am Sun. **No credit cards. Map** p73 D4 ⑥⑦

Occupying a 17th-century gabled house close to the main square, Monk is set apart by its big picture window and contemporary logo. The interior consists of a long, dark-wood bar, softly lit by railway carriage wall lights above a row of mirrored panels. Jazz sounds go with the territory – that's Monk as in Thelonious Monk, just so you know.

La Tentation

28 rue de Laeken (02 223 22 75, www.centrogalego. be/la-tentation). Métro Ste-Catherine or métro/ pré-métro De Brouckère. **Open** 9am-4am Mon-Fri; 5pm-4am Sat, Sun. **Map** p73 C5 ⑥⑧

Oozing urban chic, this converted drapery warehouse has huge windows, brick walls and effective low lighting. Staff are relaxed and friendly, and the vibe is stylish and civilised, making it a good spot to start the evening or head to for a quiet drink. It's run by Brussels' Galician community, hence the menu (Spanish liqueurs, tapas, cheese and cold meats) and the odd flamenco night.

Walvis

209 rue Antoine Dansaert (02 219 95 32). Métro Ste-Catherine. **Open** 11am-2am Mon-Thur; Sun; 11am-4am Fri, Sat. **No credit cards. Map** p73 B2 ⑥⑨

Down at the dark, canal end of Antoine Dansaert, the Whale is beached between kebab joints and shabby phone centres – but this bar is no small fry. It's another venture from the Nicolay team, responsible for revamping St-Géry at the more fashionable end of the same street. This venue has more gaudy retro touches than most of the others in the empire. Traffic-light red is the *couleur du choix* in an otherwise bare interior, offset by a quite bizarre ceiling. You'll find Tsing-Tao beer among the usual Belgian

Charli.

least a dozen in variety, according to season. Truffles are also seasonally available, plus oils, preserves and other own-grown produce.

★ Charli
34 rue Sainte-Catherine (02 513 63 32, www. charliboulangerie.com). Métro Ste-Catherine. **Open** 7.30am-7pm Mon-Sat; 8am-1.30pm Sun. **Map** p73 D4 ⓻ **Food & drink**
See p82 **Moving On Up**.

Färm Sainte Catherine
43 quai au bois à Brûler (02 218 24 81, www. farmstore.be). Métro Ste-Catherine. **Open** 9am-8pm Mon-Sat. **Map** p73 C4 ⓻ **Food & drink**
This is the large flagship supermarket of a local collective that produces organic meat, cheese, fruit and vegetables. There's also body-care and house-cleaning products, a kids' corner and fairtrade coffee.
Other location 176 rue de Linthout, Etterbeek (02 735 26 35).

Fash'n'Flash
60 rue de Laeken (0495 23 96 78, www.fashnflash. com). Métro Ste-Catherine. **Open** noon-7pm Tue-Sat. **Map** p73 C5 ⓻ **Concept store**
After years in the image business, Vincent Laurent set up this space for young designers to display their clothes and accessories. Shoppers can have their photos taken by a professional while debating whether to buy or fly – the results can be shared and debated on social media.

★ Martin Margiela
114 rue de Flandre (02 223 75 20, www.martin margiela.com). Métro Ste-Catherine. **Open** 11am-7pm Mon-Sat. **Map** p73 C3 ⓻ **Fashion**
Keep an eye on the street numbers, as Margiela's store, like his men's and women's clothes and accessories, is unlabelled. The Paris-based Flemish designer opened this shop (the first branch in Europe) in 2002. It's run by Sonia Noël, owner of the Stijl designer emporium (*see p80*) and renowned fashion connoisseur.

★ La Mer du Nord
45 rue Sainte-Catherine (02 513 11 92, www. vishandelnoordzee.be). Métro Ste-Catherine. **Open** *Fishmonger & delicatessen* 8am-6pm Tue-Fri; 8am-5pm Sat. *Food counter* 11am-6pm Tue-Sat; 11am-8pm Sun. **Map** p73 D4 ⓻ **Food & drink**
See p82 **Moving On Up**.

Super Dragon Toys
6 rue Sainte-Catherine (02 511 56 25, www. superdragontoys.com). Métro Ste-Catherine or pré-métro Bourse. **Open** 10am-6pm Mon-Thur; 10am-6.30pm Fri, Sat. **Map** p73 D4 ⓻ **Comics**
Everything a manga fan could possibly want or need, from DVDs to figurines, video games and music. A huge range of manga comics is available in French, English and Flemish.

faves, a modest snack menu, and an up-for-it clientele. Occasional jazz and regular DJs on Saturday nights bring in crowds from across Brussels.

Shops & Services

L'Ame des Rues
49 boulevard Anspach (02 217 59 47). Métro/ pré-métro De Brouckère. **Open** noon-6pm Mon-Sat. **Map** p73 D5 ⓻ **Books & music**
A real mecca for film buffs, packed as it is with film stills, posters and postcards, plus television- and film-related books and memorabilia.

★ Bel'Arte
53 rue de Flandre (0492 76 22 74 or 0497 86 61 83 mobile, www.bel-arte.be). Métro Ste-Catherine. **Open** 11am-7pm Mon-Sat. **Map** p73 C3 ⓻ **Concept store**
Original arts and crafts might be a simplified description of what's on offer here – 'cultural gifts store' is one preferred term by the Belgian creatives who opened it. With wacky one-offs to brighten up your interiors, jewellery, textiles, photographs and ceramics, Bel'Arte covers many bases, invariably in a colourful and entertaining fashion.

Champigros
36 rue Sainte-Catherine (02 511 74 98, www. champigros.com). Métro Ste-Catherine. **Open** 8am-6pm Tue-Sat. **Map** p73 D4 ⓻ **Food & drink**
In the Schoorman family since 1950, Champigros purveys all kinds of fresh mushrooms, usually at

EXPLORE

The Marolles

The Marolles is the traditional working-class district of Brussels, where weavers, dyers and labourers rubbed along together. These days, it's all too rapidly gentrifying – but, for the moment at least, you don't need to look too far to find a tatty but durable resistance to the urban expansion and standardisation of the 19th and 20th centuries. Much of what you might be looking for will be hidden under centuries of myth and misfortune. So much else has disappeared, either gone the way of the 3,000 properties razed to make way for the gargantuan Palais de Justice in the 1860s and '70s, or gone the way of the houses destroyed in order to create the Nord-Midi rail link in the early 1950s – or simply gone the way of various slum clearances. Yet tourists still flock here, to the bustling main square, place du Jeu de Balle, and its daily flea market, to the off-beat boutiques and, somewhat trepidatiously, to the authentic local bars whose interiors resemble scenes painted by Bruegel himself.

EXPLORE

Place du Jeu de Balle.

Don't Miss

1 Place du Jeu de Balle
Focal flea-market square, gradually gentrifying (p96).

2 Palais de Justice Take a look inside this vast courthouse (p93).

3 Pinpon Contemporary Belgian cuisine in a former fire station (p94).

4 Notre-Dame de la Chapelle Here (maybe) lies Bruegel the Elder (p93).

5 La Brocante Keeping it real: accordion players, rare beers and more (p95).

Public lift between Upper Town and the Marolles.

Though some historians point to credible Spanish roots, the name 'Marolles' derives from an order of nuns, the Mariam Colentes (Latin for 'devotees of Mary'), who lived in a convent on the corner of rue Montserrat and rue des Prêtres. In terms of a physical presence, the only reminder of them today is a statue of the Virgin in rue Prévoyance. The area stretches haphazardly from the slopes of Joseph Poelaert's imposing Palais de Justice down to the Gare du Midi. To the east it runs up against adjoining Sablon: up the hill and suitably upmarket. A public lift links the Upper and Lower Towns; around its base the once noticeably grimy Marolles is very slowly changing character as more antiques shops open.

Before the Soeurs Maricolles nuns arrived in the late 1600s, this area between Sablon and St-Gilles had no official title – but its down-at-heel characteristics changed little before, between or after Bruegel's and Poelaert's times. Set outside the city walls, the Marolles housed lowly workers from across Wallonia from the Middle Ages onwards. Rough, affordable and prone to the spread of diseases such as the Black Plague and leprosy, the Marolles developed its own two-fingered stance to authority. Generations of immigrants – Spaniards, Polish Jews, Turks, Italians, Moroccans – drifted in and settled here, influencing everyday life and speech. A few deep-rooted locals still speak odd words of Marollien, a fantastically rude dialect distinct from the indigenous patter of Brussels.

It was no coincidence that Léopold I, the first (German) king of independent Belgium, sited his vast **Palais de Justice** here. Sat atop Galgenberg (Gallows Hill), where generations of local criminals had met a grim fate, the Palace of Justice was to impose authority should the arsy Marolles ever get uppity. Léopold's favourite architect, Poelaert, was appointed, but just as the Brussels-born graduate of the Académie Royale des Beaux-Arts installed himself on-site – billetted on rue des Minimes, a shady thoroughfare of paupers and prostitutes – the king died in Laeken. Poelaert saw the first stone of Léopold's palace laid the following year, 1866. By the time the last brick was put in place in 1883, he was long dead, mad and soon to be completely discredited. In between, 3,000 houses had been razed, and many of their residents forcibly relocated to the suburbs.

Quite incredibly, the Palais de Justice is the largest building constructed in the 19th century. Anywhere. It dwarfs St Peter's in Rome. For all this forced sacrifice and endeavour, as a piece of work, it embraces no particular style. When trying to define it, experts reach for terms such as 'Assyrian-Babylonian' – but they may be doing both Assyrians and Babylonians a complete injustice.

Poor Poelaert. First, having to accommodate the bidding of Léopold I, then follow the grandiose caprices of his successor, Léopold II, the 'Builder King', the maligned architect is not honoured with a plaque. Rue des Minimes just survived another urban cull of the Marolles,

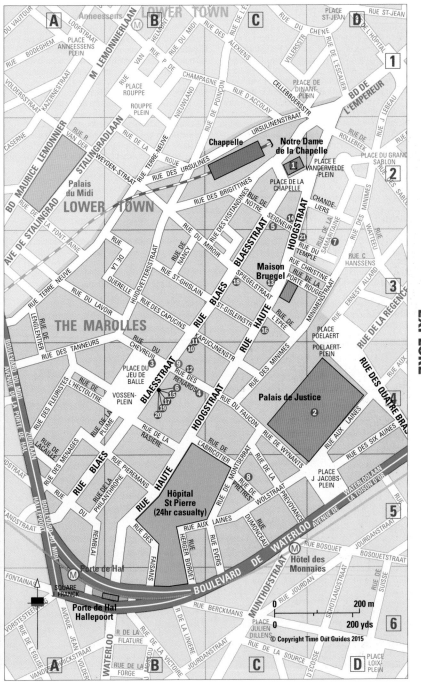

EXPLORE

to make way for the Nord-Midi rail link in the early 1950s. Instead, Poelaert's memory is kept by the epithet of *skieven architek* that Marolliens bestowed upon him – 'wonky architect', a play on words that questions his credibility to lead such a project. It also provided the name for a quirky local bar-brasserie that, sadly, folded in 2013.

Ironically, in recent years, the Palais de Justice is most visible when there's a demonstration on its steps; there were even riots in 2006 after the death in custody of a young Moroccan. The building itself is so long in the tooth that it always seems to need renovating and is invariably festooned with scaffolding.

The palace presides over an incongruous mix of shabby shops, boutiques purveying restored antiques, and dingy bars. Nouveau-riche interlopers are now interspersed with the locals. At night, legions of trendy drinkers congregate in the Sablon before making their way down the hill to eat, or move on to Brussels' top techno spot **Fuse** (*see p185*). As they tip out at daybreak, and the flea market on place du Jeu de Balle sets up, so the cyclical life of the Marolles starts all over again.

The two parallel main streets, rues Haute and Blaes, which cut through the heart of the Marolles, have completely different histories. **Rue Haute** existed in some form or other back in Roman times; rue Blaes is named after the local official who created it in the 1850s. Here, the Marolles has as its apex **Notre-Dame de la Chapelle** church, the only historic attraction in the neighbourhood, with parts dating as far back as the 13th century. It contains a memorial plaque to Pieter Bruegel the Elder, mounted by his son, Jan. The house where Bruegel and his family lived, the 16th-century **Maison de Bruegel**, is nearby at 132 rue Haute. Although it doesn't contain any of the artist's works or artefacts, it's open to groups by written request. Otherwise, rue Haute is more or less dedicated to interior design shops: kitchens, bathrooms, sofas and an impressive selection of colonial stores selling teak furniture or bits and bobs from India. Look out for art deco gems too.

Left and right, up and down the hill, narrow little streets give the best idea of how the Marolles must once have looked, with its diminutive dwellings and unsanitary conditions. Names echo historic roots: rue des Orfèvres ('Goldsmiths' Lane'); rue des Tonneliers ('Barrelmakers' Lane') and rue des Ramoneurs ('Chimneysweeps' Lane').

If you continue along the whole length of rue Haute, past the free public lift that whisks you up to the Palais de Justice, you'll come to the busy ring road and see the imposing old city gate, Porte de Hal. Alternatively, you can take a right-hand turn into any of the hilly streets leading

Palais de Justice.

down to the other thoroughfare, **rue Blaes**.
This is a little more higgledy-piggledy than its
haughtier cousin Haute. The shops here are full
of random jumble and ethnic curiosities, as well
as reclaimed antiques and second-hand clothing.
All the shops are independent, and browsing is
expected. Feel free to pop in and out and have a
nose. Zigzagging away from the main street will
give you another taste of the area and show that
there is still life in the old streets. The best
examples are provided by radical culture space
Recyclart (*see p188*) under Chapelle station
and, alongside, the extraordinary multimedia
space of **Les Brigittines** (www.brigitinnes.be).

Midway along rue Blaes is **place du Jeu de
Balle**, epicentre of the Marolles, where a daily
flea market is surrounded by earthy bars and
cafés. Although you'll still see a few locals jigging
to the accordionist on a Sunday, nowadays
tipplers are more likely to be shoppers back
from a browse in the local bric-à-brac shops –
see p96 **A Different Ball Game**.

Sights & Museums

FREE Notre-Dame de la Chapelle
*Place de la Chapelle (02 512 07 37). Pré-métro
Anneessens, or bus 27, 48.* **Open** 9.30am-4.30pm
Mon-Fri; 12.30-5pm Sat; 8am-7pm Sun. *Services*

4pm Sat; 8am, 10.30am, 4.30pm, 6.30pm Sun.
Admission free. **Map** p91 C2 ❶
Just as it straddles Romanesque and Gothic styles, so
the parish church of the Marolles spanned several
centuries in its construction. Part of the chapel dates
from the 13th century, while the nave is 15th-century
Gothic. The belfry was replaced soon after the French
bombardment of 1695, and most of the paintings
within date from the 19th century. Pieter Bruegel the
Elder is said to have married his much-younger bride
here, and then, just a few years later, been buried here.
However, little evidence remains of either event.

FREE Palais de Justice
*Place Poelaert (02 508 65 78). Métro Louise, or
tram 92, 93.* **Open** 8.30am-12.30pm, 1.30-4pm
Mon-Fri. **Admission** free. **Map** p91 D4 ❷
Providing there's no trial on, you're free to wander
into the main hall of this vast building and see what
45 million Belgian francs would have bought you in
the 1870s. Best accessed by the automated public
lift with a café at its foot, the Palace of Justice took
nearly two decades to build, costing architect Joseph
Poelaert his sanity and thousands of local residents
their homes. Its exterior is permanently clad in scaffolding – and permanently filthy. Pity the staff who
have to keep its 1,500-plus windows clean… Urban
myth has it that this was Adolf Hitler's favourite
building – although his soldiers tried to burn it down
on the eve of the Liberation of Brussels in 1944.

Restaurants

À La Clef d'Or
*1 place du Jeu de Balle (02 511 97 62). Métro/
pré-métro Porte de Hal, or bus 27, 48.* **Open**
5am-5pm Tue-Sun. Main courses €6.50-€11.
No credit cards. Map p91 B4 ❸ **Café**
This large, loud caff is a favourite with locals, so
it can be a bit of a squeeze for the casual visitor.
Sunday mornings are the best and busiest, thanks
to the earnest accordionist and party atmosphere.
Unintentionally retro, the interior sports vinyl chairs
and pink neon advertising signs. The food is of the
croque monsieur and fried egg variety. Madame
skates around in her mules and black leggings, while
monsieur stands at the coffee machine, barking
orders to the overworked staff; he's also in charge of
the *soupe du jour* pot.

L'Eau Chaude/Het Warm Water
*25 rue des Renards (02 513 91 59, www.
hetwarmwater.be). Métro/pré-métro Porte de
Hal, or bus 27, 48.* **Open** 10am-6pm Thur-Sun.
Main courses €3.50-€12. **No credit cards.**
Map p91 B4 ❹ **Vegetarian**
Warm Water is so rock 'n' Marolles, it hurts. Looking
over its shoulder at the neighbourhood's socialist
past, its collective heart is a canteen rather than a restaurant, providing freshly cooked vegetarian food
sourced as locally as possible and sold at democratic

EXPLORE

EXPLORE

prices. On Thursdays and Fridays, drop in for breakfast or a plat du jour; on Sundays, there's a selection of savoury and sweet small plates. Small-brewery artisanal beers offer a kick. Add to this a programme of political cabaret, concerts and *chanson* – and you may well get a feel for those glorious, edgy Marollien days of yore.

★ L'Idiot du Village
19 rue Notre-Seigneur (02 502 55 82, www. lidiotduvillage.be). Bus 27, 48, 95. **Open** noon-2pm, 7-10.30pm Mon-Fri. **Main courses** €19-€32. **Map** p91 C2 ❺ French
This small bistro, beloved by celebs, is hidden away in a side street off the antiques hub of rue Blaes. The chairs and tables are of the type you'd hope to find in the nearby flea market, the walls midnight blue and deep carmine, the flowers dried, the chandeliers camp. It sounds clichéd but works perfectly, as does the eclectic food, which is down to earth but well executed. Rabbit in tamarind, duck with rhubarb, you get the picture. Although it can be expensive for what it is, there's something theatrical about the place that makes it all worthwhile.

Pinpon
62 place du Jeu de Balle (02 540 89 99, www. facebook.com/apero.pinpon). Métro/pré-métro Porte de Hal, or bus 27, 48. **Open** 8am-11.30pm daily. **Main courses** €6-€18. **Map** p91 B4 ❻ Belgian
See p96 **A Different Ball Game**.

Soul
20 rue de la Samaritaine (02 513 52 13, www. soulresto.com). Bus 48, 95. **Open** noon-2.30pm, 7-10pm Wed-Fri; 7-10pm Sat, Sun. **Main courses** €8-€14. **Map** p91 D3 ❼ Organic
The warren of tiny streets between rue Haute and the Palais de Justice gives a sense of the old character of the Marolles. Soul, hidden away down a narrow lane, has built its reputation on healthy eating, so expect plenty of vegetarian dishes. The likes of duck breast and fish are also on the menu, but *sans* cream or butter. Produce is traceable, wines are organic and Soul can accommodate diners with allergies such as gluten intolerance.

★ Au Stekerlapatte
4 rue des Prêtres (02 512 86 81, www. austekerlapatte.be). Métro Louise or Hôtel des Monnaies. **Open** noon-2.30pm, 7-11pm Tue, Wed; noon-2.30pm, 7pm-midnight Thur-Sat; noon-3pm, 7-11pm Sun. **Main courses** €15-€29. **Map** p91 C5 ❽ Belgian
Back in business after a three-year renovation, this is a place for traditional food at decent prices. At first glance, you may think it full and turn to leave, but there's a warren of rooms and corridors: you're bound to find a table somewhere in the maze. It's a friendly place, despite a slightly offbeat location behind the Palais de Justice. Prepared in the time-honoured way are steaks with big fat fries, grilled pig's trotter, spare ribs and black pudding (vegetarians, beware).

Pinpon.

EXPLORE

Pubs & Bars

★ La Brocante
170 rue Blaes (02 512 13 43). Métro/pré-métro Porte de Hal, or bus 27, 48. **Open** 6am-6pm Mon, Sat; 6am-7pm Tue-Fri, Sun. **No credit cards.** **Map** p91 B4 ❾
See p96 **A Different Ball Game.**

Shops & Services

Bali-Africa
154-156 rue Blaes (02 514 47 92, www.bali africa.com). Métro/pré-métro Porte de Hal, or bus 27, 48. **Open** 10am-5pm Tue-Sun. **Map** p91 B4 ❿ **Gifts & souvenirs**
It's easy to get lost in this giant maze of a shop, though, luckily, the owners have signposted the rooms and provided a painted yellow line on the floor and stairs to help you find your way around. Wares include statuettes, masks, bongos and furniture from across the globe.

Bernard Gavilan
146 rue Blaes (02 502 01 28, www.bernardgavilan. be). Métro/pré-métro Porte de Hal, or bus 27, 48. **Open** 2-7pm Mon; noon-7pm Tue-Sat. **No credit cards.** **Map** p91 B4 ⓫ **Fashion & accessories**
Local gay celebrity Bernard runs this stylish shop, selling classy second-hand and customised vintage clothes, including trainers, sports bags and a huge selection of accessories.

Books & Plus Gallerie
14 rue des Renards (0471 204 265, www.facebook. com/booksenplusgallerie). Métro/pré-métro Porte de Hal, or bus 27, 48. **Open** 10am-6pm Tue-Sun. **No credit cards.** **Map** p91 B4 ⓬ **Gifts & souvenirs**
An eclectic range of pieces from Africa – musical instruments, jewellery, masks, paintings – fill the interior of this attractive little store, tucked between a row of eateries just off place du Jeu de Balle.

Cap Orient
123 & 133 rue Haute (no.123: 02 513 13 02, no.133: 02 513 13 05). Métro/pré-métro Porte de Hal, or bus 27, 48. **Open** noon-6.30pm Mon-Thur; 10am-6.30pm Fri-Sun. **Map** p91 C3 ⓭ **Antiques**
The shop at no.123 specialises in Chinese antiques and reproduction furniture, while the sister shop at no.133 focuses on Indian antiques, antique-style furniture and artefacts.

★ Cartoonist
11 rue Haute (02 511 21 33, www.thecartoonist.be). Bus 27, 48. **Open** 11am-5pm Thur, Sat; 1.30-7.30pm Fri; 11am-3pm Sun. **Map** p91 C2 ⓮ **Comics**
Marec, himself a cartoonist, and his daughter Marloes, opened this gallery/shop in 2014. Its goal is to provide a showcase for Marec's colleagues, such as Kamagurka, Kroll and Cécile Bertrand, who work in today's Belgian press. The Cartoonist is also attempting to bridge the Franco-Flemish divide – general themes of political polarisation and social alienation are dealt with by both sides. Signed original works

A DIFFERENT BALL GAME

The two sides of place du Jeu de Balle.

EXPLORE

To visit place du Jeu de Balle – as so many tourists do for its daily flea market, an easy jaunt from Midi station – tells you much about the Marolles. It's not just the junk on display, particularly random and near worthless during the week. It's not just the vendors, most of them Moroccan, a demographic also reflected in the patronage of the many bars lining this focal square. It's the name itself.

Where place du Jeu de Balle now spreads, a factory once stood. When it was knocked down in the mid 1800s, councillor Blaes (of rue Blaes fame) decided that a public space would be beneficial to locals who lived hugger-mugger in grimy surroundings. A popular game that these folk played was a bastardised version of *pelota*, more than likely brought over by the significant Spanish population who had settled in the Marolles. This is the ball game that gives the square its name: place du Jeu de Balle. The market arrived here from place Anneessens in 1873.

Where once may have been credenzas and coal scuttles, there is now… junk. At weekends especially, when more traders turn out, some of this junk – paintings, ornaments, vinyl LPs, carpets – is worth raking over. Whatever you do find, make sure you bargain

over it, having already ensured you're carrying euros in small denominations. If there's any ongoing gentrification of the Marolles, you wouldn't notice it amid the chipped dinner plates and worn-out shoes laid out for all to see and the sky to rain on. Nor in the down-at-heel bars on three sides of the square, where traders gather for glasses of tea.

Where things really are changing is on the eastern flank of place du Jeu de Balle, formed by a continuation of rue Blaes. This little hub, incorporating a small courtyard set back from the action, contrasts with the rest of the square – and the rest of the Marolles. It contains the old fire station built by Joseph Poelaert, a decade or more before he started work on the fateful Palais de Justice. Recently converted, the building and its forecourt provide spaces for boutiques and galleries.

Appealing to the tourists and out-of-towners who fill the square at weekends, some shops here don't even bother to operate during the week. **Jeu de Bulles** (*see p97*), for example, which specialises in sought-after old comic books and figurines of cartoon characters, opens its doors on a Friday and is done by Sunday afternoon. In similar vein, **Passé Passion** (*see p97*), a trove of tastefully

Jeu de Bulles.

Macadam Gallery.

and high-quality prints are on offer, and there's a regular schedule of personal appearances. Many works are also in postcard form – perhaps a better option to send home than an image of a urinating urchin.

House of Wonders
76 place du Jeu de Balle (0497 670 037, www.facebook.com/houseofwondersbelgium). Métro/prémétro Porte de Hal, or bus 27, 48. **Open** 11am-6pm Sat, Sun. **Map** p91 B4 ⑮ **Gifts & souvenirs**
See p96 **A Different Ball Game.**

Idiz Bogam
180 rue Haute (02 512 10 22). Bus 27, 48. **Open** 10am-6pm Tue-Sun. **Map** p91 C3 ⑯ **Fashion & accessories**
This quirky little shop sells second-hand and vintage clothing, for both men and women, from London, New York and Paris, much of it customised with sequins, ruffs and so on. There are also some wacky wedding dresses, as well as a fairly decent array of old and new shoes, hats and retro furniture.

Jeu de Bulles
79 place du Jeu de Balle (0475 697 538, www.jeudebulles.be). Métro/pré-métro Porte de Hal, or bus 27, 48. **Open** 10.30am-2pm Fri-Sun or by appointment. **Map** p91 B4 ⑰ **Comics**
See p96 **A Different Ball Game.**

Les Mémoires de Jacqmotte
92 rue Blaes (02 502 50 83, www.lesmemoires dejacqmotte.com). Bus 27, 48. **Open** 10am-6pm Mon, Tue, Thur-Sat; 10am-4pm Sun. **Map** p91 C3 ⑱ **Antiques**
The warehouse of the Jacqmotte coffee emporium has been converted into this space, where dealers can rent a pitch and display their goods. Expect to find art deco antiques, including furniture, porcelain and jewellery, plus earlier pieces.

Modes
70 place du Jeu de Balle (02 512 49 07, www.modes-antique-textiles.com). Métro/pré-métro Porte de Hal, or bus 27, 48. **Open** 10am-3pm Tue-Sun. **Map** p91 B4 ⑲ **Fashion & accessories**
See p96 **A Different Ball Game.**

Passé-Passion
53 place du Jeu de Balle (0475 939 184, www.passe-passion.com). Métro/pré-métro Porte de Hal, or bus 27, 48. **Open** 10am-3pm Tue, Thur; 10am-4pm Sat, Sun (or by appt). **Map** p91 B4 ⑳ **Gifts & souvenirs**
See p96 **A Different Ball Game.**

Technoland
22-24 rue Haute (02 511 51 04, www.technoland. be). Bus 27, 48. **Open** 11am-7pm Tue-Sat. **Map** p91 C3 ㉑ **Computers & electronics**
Come here for second-hand high-end audio-visual equipment and computers, usually at fair prices.

presented toys, ornaments and curiosities spanning the length of the 20th century, complements its busiest weekend trading days with a by-appointment-only service.

Alongside, Steve Angri's **House of Wonders** (*see right*), aka Fossilmar, also deals in antiquities – fossils, to be precise, for use as conversation pieces and as more unusual items of interior design. Nearby **Modes** (*see right*) specialises in vintage clothing made prior to 1950. Most pieces are for women, including furs, coats, dresses, shirts, skirts and hats, plus glasses, gloves, hatpins, purses and boas. There's also a limited range of linens, laces, ribbon and fabric.

Another new arrival is the **Macadam Gallery** (www.macadamgallery.com), set up in a former photographer's workshop, which showcases pieces by contemporary Belgian and international artists. Recently featured have been Call Me Frank, Obetre, FSTN and the photographer himself, Damien Gard.

Sharing the same courtyard, the **Pinpon** restaurant (*see p94*) is the creation of Charli (of Charli bakery fame; *see p87*) and Philippe Emmanuelli (of the once-lauded Café des Spores in St-Gilles). Light, seasonal Belgian cuisine is on offer, using scallops, boletus mushrooms, grey shrimps and the like.

If you'd rather save discerning dining for Sablon and what you're after is authentic, in-yer-face Marolles, then Sunday morning at age-old bar **La Brocante** (*see p95*) is ideal. Keeping marketplace hours (you can sink beers from 6am onwards), the bar – whose name, suitably enough, means 'junk' – brings out the squeezebox, and delighted tourists tuck into cold meats and hearty omelettes between the odd twirl around the tables. This is still a corner of place du Jeu de Balle that is forever Belgium.

EXPLORE

Upper Town

Just as central Brussels comprises Lower and Upper Towns, separated by a charmless main road, so the Upper Town itself is easily divided into the Royal Quarter and Sablon. Characterised by palaces and parks, and museums and institutions of national importance, the former has had regal connections ever since Lambert II sited his fortress here in the mid 11th century. Coudenberg ('Cold Hill') provided the ruling classes with a lofty (and defensible) vantage point. When the sumptuous palace here burned down in 1731, the large area it occupied was completely revamped by French architect Barnabé Guimard, who created a series of neoclassical buildings and streets in between. Ever since, the royals have preferred the leafier climes of Laeken. Parts of the old palace now house the Musées Royaux des Beaux-Arts, itself a multi-floored mansion containing centuries of Belgian art. Sablon, meanwhile, which was once a sandy-floored horse market, is today given over to exclusivity: fancy restaurants, antiques shops and luxury chocolatiers.

EXPLORE

Musées Royaux des Beaux-Arts.

Don't Miss

1 Musées Royaux des Beaux-Arts Old Masters to modernists (p106).

2 Cathédrale des Sts Michel et Gudule Landmark cathedral, with stunning glass (p100).

3 BELvue Museum Discover how Belgium became Belgium (p104).

4 Musée Magritte Man with bowler (p106).

5 Place du Grand Sablon Showcase square, antiques aplenty (p109).

GARE CENTRALE & CATHEDRAL

Central Brussels wasn't created as two separate entities – there was simply a Royal Quarter and a rest of town. A half-baked attempt by King Léopold II at the end of the 19th century to create a cultural area on the slope between them – the Mont des Arts – simply allowed for streets of old buildings to be demolished and an urban wilderness left in their place. With them went what was left of a Jewish Quarter in Brussels.

Eventually, a public park was created here and, with its pretty cascades and rock gardens, very popular it was too. But then, after World War II, came a number of random projects – the Nord-Midi rail link, Expo 58, the return of the concept of a Mont des Arts – and so concrete came to the rescue. The capricious laying down of main roads and throwing up of buildings in the Belgian capital was so infamous it was even honoured with its own globally recognised term in the field of modern architecture: Bruxellisation.

The end result was a plug-ugly arterial road between Notre-Dame de la Chapelle church (*see p93*) at the apex of the Marolles, and the Gare Centrale. It then has the good grace to snake around the Cathédrale des Sts Michel et Gudule before rising up to reach the Botanical Gardens. Given a different name for each section (boulevard de l'Empereur, de Berlaimont and Pachéco) the road – built above the rail line that sliced up the city in order to provide an easy cross-town connection between the three main stations – runs pretty much parallel to the traditional royal route that links the Palace Quarter with Laeken.

Gare Centrale is an excellent introduction to the no-man's land between the city centre and the regal sights of the Upper Town. Designed by guiding architect Victor Horta himself, on the eve of World War I, the central station project was shelved during the conflict and its aftermath. It was eventually revived as part of the Nord-Midi rail link in the early 1950s, and built partly according to Horta's design four decades before – note the fabulous sweeping front entrance. Unfortunately, the urban façades around it scream 'concrete jungle', and the first-time arrivee is happy to get out as quickly as possible. Fortunately, a new crop of stylish hotels has opened nearby to serve rail travellers – *see p277* **First Class**.

If you use the other main exit to the Gare Centrale, it takes you away from the Carrefour de l'Europe and within 100 metres of a historic building no-one dared to tear down: the **Cathédrale des Sts Michel et Gudule**.

Although it is isolated from the city by a crowd of modern buildings, it's easy to imagine the Cathédrale dominating the medieval skyline, a constant reminder of the power of the Church. Like Coudenberg ('Cold Hill') behind, where

IN THE KNOW BRUXELLISATION

Many look back on Brussels Expo 58, the first major World's Fair after 1945, with its Atomium and scale model of Sputnik, as a golden era. But the price for having millions come to admire this brave new mini-world was the City tearing up townhouses to create rapid transport links, with little overall plan. So extreme was the case in the Belgian capital that it made its way into textbooks relating to urban architecture: Bruxellisation. Brussels was held up to the world as a living example of how not to lay out a city in the post-war era. The low point came in 1965, when Victor Horta's Maison du Peuple was knocked down – and a bland skyscraper thrown up in its place. It wasn't until the early 1990s that laws were passed to prevent the demolition of historic buildings.

Lambert II sited his fortress, so Treurenberg ('Hill of Sorrows') was the perfect location for him to transfer the remains of Sainte Gudule from the former church at St-Géry and thus grant the one that stood here special status. He even founded his own chapter here. The building, over the course of 300 years, would become the city's cathedral. To the left and rear is rue du Bois Sauvage where, between nos.14 and 15, stands a solitary scrap of the old city wall.

Sights & Museums

FREE Cathédrale des Sts Michel et Gudule

Place Ste-Gudule (02 217 83 45, www.cathedral isbruxellensis.be). Métro Gare Centrale or Parc, or tram 92, 93. **Open** *Cathedral* 7.30am-6pm Mon-Fri; 7.30am-3.30pm Sat; 2-6pm Sun. *Archaeological site* 8am-6pm daily. *Treasury* 10am-12.30pm, 2-5pm Mon-Fri; 10am-3pm Sat; 2-5pm Sun. *Crypt* by appointment. **Admission** *Cathedral* free. *Archaeological site* €1. *Treasury* €1. *Crypt* €3. **No credit cards. Map** p101 C2 ❶

This wonderful cathedral is dedicated to the male and female patron saints of Brussels – and while St Michel is the better known, Ste Gudule is by far the more popular of the two in local lore. Her symbol is a lamp, blown out by the devil but miraculously relit when she prayed. The cathedral stands on the site of a Carolingian-era chapel on Treurenberg, which gained importance when Lambert II decided to move the saint's relics there from St-Géry in the 11th century. The current Gothic building (replacing a second church that had been built in 1072) was begun in 1226 and completed in 1499, with later chapel additions in the 16th and 17th centuries. The cathedral's

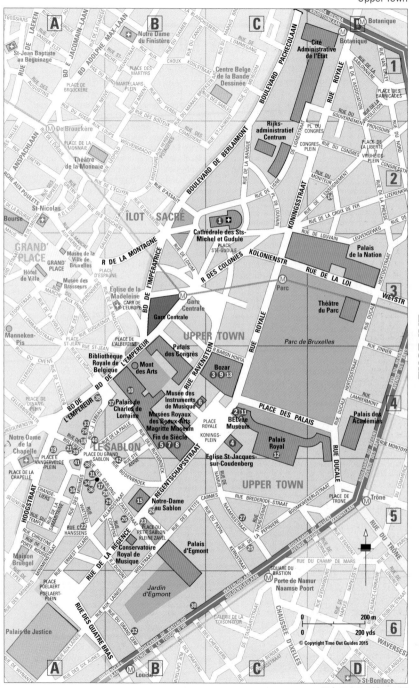

MEET THE ROYALS

From 2016, the Palais Coudenberg ruins and newly revamped
BELvue Museum will encompass 1,000 years of history.

On National Day, 21 July 2016, the **BELvue Museum** (*see p104*) reopens after an eight-month revamp. In March 2015, the museum threw open its doors after hours to allow the public to meet the people behind the overhaul: a 20-strong team of youngsters under the age of 25, who are laying out the permanent exhibition according to how they would most like to experience it.

This democratic approach is laudably bold, considering that the BELvue and the adjoining underground relics of the **Palais Coudenberg** (*see p108*) are the most accessible way for anyone, Belgians especially, to appreciate the royal history beneath their feet. In the decade from the BELvue's opening to its temporary closure, the public have flocked here in great numbers, keen to see how former rulers ruled.

After this sumptuous, mainly medieval complex was irretrievably scarred by fire in 1731, the decision was made decades later to raze it and start again. Today's Royal Quarter, all fenced-off parks and neat, neoclassical buildings, is the work of French architect Barnabé Guimard in the late 1700s. Another decision, by the Fondation Baudouin, to make a more all-embracing museum out of the former Musée de la Dynastie and have it connect to the Coudenberg excavation site,

created two compelling visitor attractions and brought a millennium of history full circle.

Since 1047, when Lambert II first built a fort on Coudenberg, heads of state were able to escape the murk of the marshes below and to defend their seat of power both psychologically and physically. In the Middle Ages, Brussels had to defend itself aggressively against powerful Leuven as the seat of power of the Dukedom of Brabant. Philip the Good (1396-1467) decided that the fort on the hill should become his main residence, and it was during this period that the palace helped Brussels firmly on the path to diplomatic ascendancy. Philip had a great hall built – the Magna Aula – with an open-beam, unsupported roof and wooden ceiling. This was a magnificent setting for receptions, assemblies and celebrations. Jousting was just part of the merriment. On a different note, there wasn't a dry eye in the house when popular Charles V gave his abdication speech in the great hall in 1555.

It was Charles V who had commissioned the massive chapel, renowned throughout Europe for its Gothic splendour. In fact, the palace at Coudenberg was regarded as one of Europe's greatest royal residences. Hunting grounds stretched beyond it. Imagine, then, the horror, when, during the night of 3 February 1731, a large vat of boiling sugar overheated and set fire to the palace kitchen. Attempts to put it out failed and the building was engulfed in flames. Everything apart from a portion of the library and a few works of art was destroyed, and the palace remained in ruins until 1774.

To accommodate Guimard's plans, parts of the old palace were blown up or simply built over. The ruins remained under place Royale for centuries and were largely forgotten until the 1990s, when they were finally excavated and underwent extensive archaeological research before being fully restored and opened to the public.

It's now possible to recreate the footsteps of the illustrious residents and visitors of the past and visit the palace in its underground setting, just beneath street level. Walking around this ancient site is evocative and eerie. You find yourself in a hugely atmospheric pink-brick space, gently lit and strangely silent.

One thing you'll notice is the contour of the hill and how the construct of this vast palace was cleverly designed to follow the steep drop

EXPLORE

while keeping everything on the level. Don't expect anything overly grand or spectacular; these are ruins at their most basic and you'll need to visualise the structures above their base levels. But you'll also see the footprint of the Magna Aula, remains of the chapel, parts of kitchens, store cupboards and courtyards. Piecing it all together with the help of the excellent free guide brochure (and the film) is a fascinating exercise in and of itself, as is trying to place your bearings in relation to the modern world still rolling on above you.

Of special note are the crumbling remains of rue Isabelle. Guimard had the street vaulted over for use as cellars, so you need to use your imagination to visualise it as an exterior street running along the natural contours of the Coudenberg. It had existed since the Middle Ages, but the Archduchess Isabelle wanted it widened and lengthened so she could slip out of the palace and make her way down the hill to the cathedral without fuss. It was here that Charlotte Brontë lived at no.32 – the site of that house is now under the entrance hall of the Palais des Beaux-Arts in rue Ravenstein.

It's an enchanting experience; apart from patches of the old city walls and the remaining gates, the palace ruins are the best of what is left of medieval Brussels. The rest of the city's story is taken up by the BELvue, and its remit to cover Belgium from 1830 to today, taking in independence, war, modernisation and the role of the royals. How the new, young design team chooses to represent these further layers of history should prove just as fascinating.

darkest moments came with the mass defacement in 1579, perpetrated by Protestant iconoclasts, and in the late 18th century, when French revolutionary armies largely destroyed the inside, along with priceless works of art. The renewed interior is splendidly proportioned and, happily, retains a host of its original treasures. Most impressive are Bernard van Orley's stunning 16th-century pictorial stained-glass windows in the transepts, and the 13th-century choir. Both the interior and exterior were heavily renovated during the 1990s, when remnants of the 11th-century Romanesque church were unearthed in the crypt.

ROYAL QUARTER

Lambert II's fortification on Coudenberg, gradually transformed from stronghold to palace, gave subsequent royals a psychological advantage over their subjects as they looked loftily down on them from on high. There were practical reasons too – it provided a defence against enemies, and was a good distance from the infested River Senne on the marshland below.

The ever-expanding Coudenberg Palace occupied a vast territory, large enough to accommodate rolling hunting grounds behind it. Even today there remains an air of superiority, reflected in the neoclassical architecture that replaced the palace in the late 1700s. Here are the seats of royalty and government, the stately squares and public spaces, as well as the city's most illustrious museums, all linked by the grand, stern rue Royale. From the Lower Town, it's a right royal climb, though the ascent is gentler if you start from the classy Sablon.

From the Cathédrale, walk up the steep hill and you come to the determinedly straight **rue Royale**, the main artery of the Upper Town, punctuated at one end by the Palais de Justice (*see p93*) and at the other by the Church of Ste-Marie (*see p119*). This is the 'Royal Route', linking the Royal Palace in Laeken (*see p165*), home to the royal family, with the Royal Palace off place Royale, used for state ceremonies. The king is driven along it most days. Tourists can jump on the 92 or 94 tram and let it take them along the road with as many stop-offs as they like for the hour validity of a standard STIB transport ticket.

Running alongside rue Royale is 18th-century **Parc de Bruxelles**. First laid out in classic French style, the design of its avenues is largely based on a masonic pair of dividers. It's dotted with strange classical statues – armless, but with toes peeking out at the bottom. You'll notice that some also have their noses missing. Lord Byron was believed responsible for this vandalism, but eventually the Austrian Count Metternich owned up to the not-so-statesman-like behaviour. The park was once a chic strolling ground, although in the revolution of 1830 its avenues ran with blood.

EXPLORE

These days, it's packed full of joggers and office workers on their lunch breaks. It also makes the perfect setting for the chocolate-box **Théâtre Royal du Parc** (*see p199*).

At the park's northern end stands the Belgian parliament building, the **Palais de la Nation**, graced by a lovely 18th-century façade by Barnabé Guimard, the architect responsible for the homogeneous nature of the area. At the southern end is the king's starkly imposing official residence, the **Palais Royal**. It has never been much in favour with the royals, who prefer the airiness of Laeken, and the flag only flies on the rare occasions when the monarch is home and on official duties. It's open to the public in summer.

At the western end of the palace is the Hôtel Belle Vue, built as a swanky hotel in 1777. It was Wellington's headquarters at the time of Waterloo, but now houses the **Musée BELvue**, where memorabilia, documents and photographs chronicle the short history of the Belgian monarchy since 1831 (*see p102* **Meet the Royals**). Directly behind the palace is the narrow rue Brederode, where Joseph Conrad first visited the Congo Trading Company in 1889; it's as creepy today as when it was first described in his novel *Heart of Darkness*.

West of the Palais Royal stands place Royale, built on the site of the 15th-century Coudenberg Palace, a name remembered in the **Église St-Jacques-sur-Coudenberg** at the top of the same square. The statue here is of Godefroid de Bouillon, who led the successful first Crusade in the 11th century; he remains blissfully unaware of the trams that now circle beneath him. From here, you get one of the best views in Brussels, looking directly down to the Grand'Place.

Underneath these streets are the remains of the original Palais Coudenberg, which burned down in 1731 when a fire started in the kitchens. When the square was rebuilt under the orders of Empress Maria Theresa, the ruins were buried for cost reasons and then forgotten about until the 1930s. They were re-exposed in 2000 during major renovations and – in typical Brussels style – were subsequently earmarked as the site for an underground car park. Now mercifully intact, they are open to the public (*see p102* **Meet the Royals**).

At the western corner of place Royale are two major art galleries, the Musée d'Art Ancien and the Musée d'Art Moderne. Linked by an underground passage, they make up the **Musées Royaux des Beaux-Arts**. Attached and alongside the galleries is the splendid **Musée Magritte**, which opened in 2009. Below ground, unveiled in late 2013, the equally excellent **Musée Fin-de-Siècle** presents a multi-faceted Brussels at the cultural crossroads of the late 1800s and early 1900s. At nos.2-4 is the main Brussels Info Point (BIP) centre (*see p289*).

Downhill from place Royale on rue Montagne de la Cour are two architectural landmarks. The first is one of the great triumphs of art nouveau in the city: the spiky Old England department store, long ago shuttered up but reopened in 2000 as the **Musée des Instruments de Musique**. It's one of the most distinctive and best-known buildings in Brussels. Just as a century ago, you'll find a panoramic roof terrace where you can dine and drink with a whole cityscape in view.

Further down the street, as it sweeps right into rue Ravenstein, is the red-brick, gabled Hôtel Ravenstein. This 15th-century building is the only significant survivor from the original Coudenberg quarter. Descending rue Ravenstein, to the left is the classic shopping arcade Galerie Ravenstein, now sadly faded and echoingly empty. To the right is the main entrance to the city's rebranded and revived cultural centre, the **Palais des Beaux-Arts**, aka 'Bozar' (*see p195* **Bozar for All**), and, alongside on rue Baron Horta, the **Cinematek**, both a film museum and working picture house.

From here, you can climb the steps back up to rue Royale, or take the steep descent down Ravenstein to the **Mont des Arts**. Here, you can see the solution town planners eventually came up with to link the Upper and Lower Towns. Where there was once a pretty park is now a staircased piazza, created in the 1950s – before the invention of the skateboard. Patrolled by teenagers throwing shapes, the Mont des Arts is flanked on one side by the **Palais du Congrès** and on the other by the **Bibliothèque Royale de Belgique**, irredeemably plain in appearance and opened more than a decade later.

By contrast, alongside stands the **Palais de Charles de Lorraine**, built in the mid 1700s. This particular Charles of Lorraine was Charles Alexander, Governor-General of the Austrian Netherlands until his death in 1780. Today, his palace houses a modest museum dedicated to the period in which he lived. It was in the court records of Charles of Lorraine that historians found the first mention of Barnabé Guimard in connection with Brussels – it was during this time that the Amboise-born architect transformed the Palace Quarter into the carefully planned complex of stately buildings and green spaces we see now.

Sights & Museums

BELvue Museum

7 place des Palais (02 500 45 54, www.belvue.be). *Métro Trône, or tram 92, 93.* **Open** *Jan-June, Sept-Dec* 9.30am-5pm Tue-Fri; 10am-6pm Sat, Sun. *July, Aug* 10am-6pm Tue-Sun. **Admission** €6; €4-€5 reductions; free under-18s. Free 1st Sun of mth. *Combined ticket with Palais Coudenberg* €10; €7-€8 reductions. **Map** p101 C4 ❷
See p102 **Meet the Royals**.

Cinematek.

Cinematek

Palais des Beaux-Arts, 9 rue Baron Horta (02 551 19 00, www.cinematek.be). Métro Gare Centrale or Parc, or tram 92, 93. **Open** *Library* Jan-July, Sept-Dec 9.30am-5pm Mon & Wed; 9.30am-1pm Fri. **Admission** €4; €2 under-12s. **Map** p101 C4 ❸

This modest but fascinating little museum was rebranded from the Musée du Cinéma to the Cinematek after an overhaul in 2009. It traces the early days of cinema and the inventions that led to the development of cinematography by the Lumière brothers. Even the museum itself has its own history. Originally a pre-war cinema club set up by a pioneering distributor of Soviet films, including *Battleship Potëmkin*, it became a cinema and museum in 1962.
▶ *This place is still used as a working cinema, with piano accompaniment to silent films in the two projection rooms; see also p177.*

FREE Église St-Jacques-sur-Coudenberg

1 impasse de Borgendael, place Royale (02 502 18 25, www.paroisse-militaire-saint-jacques-sur-coudenberg.be). Métro Trône, or tram 92, 93, 94. **Open** 1-6pm Tue-Sat; 8.45am-5pm Sun. *Services* 12.30pm Mon, Fri; 12.30pm, 5.15pm Tue-Thur; 9am, 11am, 6pm Sun. *Tour* (French) 4pm 1st Thur of mth. **Admission** free. **Map** p101 C4 ❹

This church was built by Barnabé Guimard, of Royal Quarter fame, in 1775. Much as the surrounding buildings he created after the Coudenberg Palace fire are neoclassical in style, so St-Jacques resembles a Roman temple. An incongruous bell tower was added in the 19th century, giving the church a strange Pilgrim Fathers-New England sort of look. The interior is as peculiarly imposing as the exterior, and you can imagine that it served perfectly as a temple of reason and then as a temple of law when Brussels was under the sway of revolutionary France – before being returned to Catholicism in 1802. Léopold I, the first king of Belgium, took his oath on these steps in 1831, a scene depicted in a painting by Edouard De Biéfve at the nearby Palais Royal.

★ Musée Fin-de-Siècle

3 rue de la Régence (02 508 32 11, www.fin-de-siede-museum.be). Métro Gare Centrale, or tram 92, 93. **Open** 10am-5pm Tue-Fri; 11am-6pm Sat, Sun. **Admission** €8; €6 reductions; €2 under-25s; free under-6s. *Combined ticket with Beaux-Arts & Musée Magritte* €13; €9 reductions; €3 under-25s. **Map** p101 B4 ❺

Opened in December 2013 and put together at a cost of nearly €9 million, the Fin-de-Siècle Museum has a lot to live up to – the last newbie unveiled at the illustrious Musées Royaux des Beaux-Arts was the smash-hit Musée Magritte. Occupying the lower four floors, the Fin-de-Siècle takes as its starting point 1868, and the formation of the Société Libre des Beaux-Arts, and runs up to 1914. Covering, therefore, half a century rather than the decade or so either side of the 1899-1900 divide, it has bitten off quite a big chunk of cultural history. This includes the development of film, cinema and opera, not to mention Realism, Symbolism, Impressionism and art nouveau. Hand-in-hand is the depiction of Brussels as an imperial capital, the covering of the River Senne, the Palais de Justice and the opening of the Gare du Midi.

English documentation guides you around the open-plan, well-signposted space, and many works previously exhibited in the main Museum of Fine Arts are now given context: Constantin Meunier's dour scenes of coal mining, for good example. Pieces by James Ensor and Fernand Khnopff, founding members of the influential XX ('Les Vingt') Group, are shown as pointers towards later movements such as Expressionism and Surrealism. Do leave time to admire the art nouveau furniture by, among

EXPLORE

others, Horta, part of the wonderful Gillion-Crowet collection garnered from the 1960s onwards and donated here. The Fin-de-Siècle is the second of three planned specialised sections at the Musées Royaux – a Museum of Modernism is slated for 2017.

★ Musée des Instruments de Musique

2 rue Montagne de la Cour (02 545 01 30, www. mim.be). Métro Gare Centrale, or tram 92, 93. **Open** 9.30am-5pm Tue-Fri; 10am-5pm Sat, Sun. **Admission** €8; €2-€6 reductions. Free from 1pm 1st Wed of mth. **No credit cards. Map** p101 B4 ❻ Designed by Paul Saintenoy in 1899, with curving black wrought ironwork framing large windows, the former Old England department store emerged a century later – and after a decade of restoration – as a museum housing a 6,000-strong collection of instruments (the world's largest), of which 1,500 are on display at any one time. Look out for the bizarre saxophones dreamed up by the instrument's inventor Adolphe Sax. The top-floor restaurant offers panoramic views of the city.
▶ *Free music events take place regularly, from funk orchestras to school choirs.*

★ Musée Magritte

1 place Royale (02 508 32 11, www.musee-magritte-museum.be). Métro Gare Centrale, or tram 92, 93. **Open** 10am-5pm Tue-Sun. **Admission** €8; €2-€6 reductions; free under-6s. Free from 1pm 1st Wed of mth. *Combined ticket with Beaux-Arts and Fin-de-Siècle museums* €13; €9 reductions; €3 under-25s. **Map** p101 B4 ❼
Until 2009, the only place of homage to René Magritte was the museum in his little house. That all changed when the Musées Royaux des Beaux-Arts opened this museum in a stunning building on place Royale. The collection is ordered chronologically. On entering, you ascend to the third floor, then work your way back down, with each floor representing a period in the artist's life. It's all very theatrical, and of course you get to see some of Magritte's most famous works. The museum has been an astounding success. Book online to avoid the queues. *Photo p108.*
▶ *For a more intimate look at Magritte, visit his modest former home in Anderlecht where he lived and painted for 24 years (see p164).*

★ Musées Royaux des Beaux-Arts

3 rue de la Régence (02 508 32 09, www.fine-arts-museum.be). Métro Gare Centrale, or tram 92, 93. **Open** 10am-5pm Tue-Fri; 11am-6pm Sat, Sun. **Admission** *Old Masters* €8; €6 reductions; €2 under-25s; free under-6s. *Modern* €8; €6 reductions; €2 under-25s; free under-6s. Free from 1pm 1st Wed of mth. *Combined ticket with Fin-de-Siècle & Musée Magritte* €13; €9 reductions; €3 under-25s. **Map** p101 B4 ❽
The collection at the Fine Arts Museum covers the art of the Low Countries from 15th-century Gothic to 20th-century Surrealism, in two museums, Modern,

and one now described as Old Masters. It's almost too much to take in in one go, so pick up a map at the information desk and head straight across the grand main hall and up the stairs to the blue section (rooms 10-45), featuring 15th- and 16th-century art and pieces by Roger van der Weyden and Hieronymus Bosch. Up a grey marble staircase is the vast 17th- and 18th-century section, home to works by Rubens, Rembrandt and masters from the Low Countries. Rubens' *The Fall of Icarus* (room 51) is the key work there. An escalator links to the Musée d'Art Moderne, through the red section, with its temporary exhibitions, to the green area (19th and 20th centuries). Four spacious floors hold a huge collection spanning a range of styles and movements, including Jacques-Louis David's groundbreaking masterpiece *The Death of Marat*. Several works by Belgians James Ensor and Fernand Khnopff have been moved to the new Fin-de-Siècle Museum below ground, but there's enough here to satisfy most tastes. Finish your grand tour with a peep at Georges Seurat's *La Seine de la Grande Jatte* – a sun-lit, soothing expanse of blue.

A wing carved out of two landmark buildings (one art nouveau, the other neoclassical), adjacent to the museum, contains a bookstore, a sleek café and an upscale restaurant, all accessible from the street. This expansion has made more room for the museum's marvellous collection of 17th- and 18th-century Flemish paintings, now cleaned, restored, and exhibited in superior numbers. A colossal gallery, the Patio, has been created for the display of a rare suite of eight vast Renaissance tapestries made in Brussels, and the museum is now finally looking like the world-class repository of art that it always promised to be.

Palais des Beaux-Arts (Bozar)

23 rue Ravenstein (02 507 82 00, www.bozar.be). Métro Gare Centrale or Parc, or tram 92, 93. **Open** *Exhibitions* 10am-6pm Tue, Wed, Fri-Sun; 10am-9pm Thur. *Box office* In person 11am-7pm Tue-Sat. By phone 11am-7pm Tue-Fri; 1-7pm Sat, Sun. **Admission** varies. **Map** p101 C4 ❾
The Bozar is the most dynamic element in the cluster of cultural attractions around the Mont des Arts. Once a moribund site of disparate arts disciplines, the Beaux-Arts has been transformed by director Paul Dujardin into a modern, multi-purpose cultural institute not unlike the Barbican in London. Designed by Victor Horta in 1928, the fabulous art deco building has also been revamped, with its false ceilings ripped out and original features restored. Exhibitions, classical concerts, films, plays and family-friendly events, mainly on Sundays, comprise its colourful agenda.

Palais de Charles de Lorraine – Musée du XVIIIème Siècle

1 place du Musée (02 519 53 03, www.kbr.be). Métro Gare Centrale, or tram 92, 93. **Open**

EXPLORE

LET THEM EAT CHOCOLATE

There's a French rival to Belgium's top choc shops.

The age-old dynasties of Belgium's world-renowned chocolate industry have lined Sablon for decades. Belgian chocolatiers base their luxury creations on three concepts: freshness, generosity and heritage. So it's almost impossible to go wrong in Brussels when choosing chocolate, except around the Grand'Place where the more obvious tourist-trap emporia can sometimes offer boxes of disappointment.

Here in Sablon, each boutique also contains its own history. **Wittamer** (*see p113*), easily spotted with its lurid pink canopies, was founded by Henri Wittamer in 1910 and is still a family-run business. Today, descendents oversee three operations: grandchildren run the chocolate shop at no.6 and pâtisserie at no.12; next door, the upmarket tearoom at no.13 is run by great-granddaughter Leslie. Chocolates are still made at the back of the store, which features eye-catching window displays that change every three months.

Known for its inventive pralines, **Godiva** (*see p113*) dates from 1926, when the Draps family set up their chocolate and sweet-making workshop. It was Joseph, having joined the firm at 14, who then took it to the next level, creating a prestige range that has defined the brand ever since. Today, a trio of 'chef chocolatiers', headed by Thierry Murret, devise new tastes and flavours. A current trend is to match specific chocolate types to fine wine.

Such innovation comes at a price. But even at the cheaper end, century-old **Leonidas** (*see p113*) is a brand with its own myth. In 1913, a young Greek chocolatier, Leonidas Kestekides, fell in love with a local girl and settled here, opening a series of tearooms. These evolved into city-wide outlets for his value-for-money pralines, adorned with a profile of the eponymous king of Sparta, sold through the famous 'guillotine windows' straight to the streets.

Across Sablon's grand square stands **Pierre Marcolini** (*see p113*), pretender to the Wittamer crown. Brussels-born with Italian lineage, Marcolini stole much dynastic thunder with his award-winning cocoa creations: a ganache with earl grey tea, a Brittany caramel with salted butter and four spices. Pedestrians soon made a point of stopping by to gawp at his elegant window displays and gaze at the edible works of art. Marcolini has branches in London, New York, Tokyo and Paris, and even the Belgian PM took a box of his chocs to Washington to sweeten the most pressing of deals.

With competition fierce, firms began to explore other avenues to garner trade, offering workshops so that the public could learn how to prepare their own pralines. Ahead of the pack is artisanal **Planète Chocolat** (*see p60*), with demonstrations every weekend afternoon and regular ateliers. Some of Sablon's bigger names have also followed suit.

Industry locals, justifiably proud of their heritage – which is outlined in **Belgian Chocolate Village** (*see p164*), a new, family-friendly attraction in Koekelberg – were shocked to find a new kid on the block: **Patrick Roger** (*see p113*). Not only foreign but French, Paris-based Roger is not just a chocolatier – he's an artist. An apprentice to a pâtissier at 15, working under a renowned chocolatier at 18, Roger was making waves with his elaborate chocolate sculptures at the same time as he was opening his first store in the French capital. Now with six boutiques in Paris and his mantelpiece lined with Lauréats and Grand Prix, Roger recently set up in Sablon, firmly planting his French *tricolore* among the black, yellow and reds. Worse, this interloper's got talent.

Walk into his boutique opposite Wittamer and you're surrounded by fine-lined recreations, masterpieces in chocolate, centrepieced by Roger's sculpture du jour, tens of kilos' worth of it. His pralines and ganaches aren't slapped together in the back room – the cocoa beans from which he composes his chocolate truffles are sourced in Ecuador and Vanuatu. Almost worse, he's modest, happy to introduce what's on offer if he happens to be in his Brussels outpost, keen to make his staff as informatively welcoming. It seems the Marcolinis and Wittamers of this world have to up their game.

EXPLORE

Musée Magritte. *See p106.*

1-5pm Wed, Sat. **Admission** €3; €2 reductions; under-13s free. **Map** p101 B4 ⑩

This *palais* was the residence of Charles of Lorraine, governor-general during the mid to late 1700s and brother-in-law twice over to Habsburg Empress Maria Theresa. It's now home to a five-room museum dedicated to the 18th century. For the nominal admission fee, it's probably worth a look to see how the other half lived 250 years ago. Along with furnishings and ornaments – a sedan chair, porcelain, a table laid for dinner – there are a couple of musical scientific instruments.

Palais Coudenberg

Entrance through BELvue Museum, 7 place des Palais (02 500 45 54, www.coudenberg.com). Métro Trône, or tram 92, 93. Open Sept-Dec 9.30am-5pm Tue-Fri; 10am-6pm Sat, Sun. July, Aug 10am-6pm Tue-Sun. **Admission** €6; €4-€5 reductions; free under-18s. Free 1st Sun of mth. *Combined ticket with BELvue Museum* €10; €7-€8 reductions. **Map** p101 C4 ⑪ *See p102* **Meet the Royals**.

FREE Palais Royal

Place des Palais (02 551 20 20, www.monarchie.be). Métro Trône, or tram 92, 93. Open 22 July-1st Sun Sept 10.30am-4.30pm Tue-Sun. **Admission** free. **Map** p101 C4 ⑫

Immediately after National Day, 21 July, the royals throw open their doors and let the public in for free. What you'll see is a series of rooms mainly created originally by Dutch king William I, remodelled in 1825 and again in 1904. Highlights include a series of tapestries of Goya scenes created in Madrid, Brussels-born Edouard De Bièfve's painting of

Léopold I taking his oath as Belgium's first king in 1831, and contemporary works by Marthe Wéry, Jan Fabre and Dirk Braeckman.

Restaurants

★ Bozar Brasserie

Palais des Beaux-Arts, 3 rue Baron Horta (02 503 00 00, www.bozarbrasserie.be). Métro Gare Centrale or Parc, or tram 92, 93. Open noon-11pm Tue-Sat. Main courses €24-€42. Map p101 C4 ⑱ French

Walk in through the main Bozar entrance, look to the left and there's the brasserie, a long retro-look room with deco lamps and marble tables. Created by famed television chef David Martin, the restaurant aims to present classic brasserie food with the best produce and authentic techniques. So a steak comes from Bavarian Simmental beef, aged in the cellars of La Paix 1892 (Martin's Michelin-starred restaurant across town, *see p162*), cooked in a Josper oven using charcoal from Argentina. It may be air-mile hefty but the end result is astonishing. This is top cooking in one of the city's most important artistic hubs.

Pubs & Bars

Le Bier Circus

57 rue de l'Enseignement (02 218 00 34, www.bier-circus.be). Tram 92, 93. Open 11.30am-2.30pm, 6pm-midnight Tue-Fri; 6pm-midnight Sat. Map p101 D2 ⑭

Near the Royal Circus, hence the name, this brick-lined bar offers a quite astonishing range of beers. There are around 200 to choose from, filling 17 pages of a menu that's handed to you by a well-informed barman. Vintage beers – Oude Kriek 35% at €25 a bottle, Gueuze aged in Cognac barrels at €20 – warrant four pages. It's then that you notice the mounted beer mats and a blackboard of seasonal beers breaking the monotony of brick. Delve a little deeper and you'll find an intimate side room, and a back room decked out in cartoon characters.

SABLON

Stroll on south past the Musées Royaux des Beaux-Arts on rue de la Régence and you come to upmarket and sophisticated Sablon. The local landmark is **Notre-Dame au Sablon**, most likely the loveliest Gothic church in Brussels. Across busy rue de la Régence from the church is **place du Petit Sablon**. In its centre is a small park, whose railings, by art nouveau architect Paul Hankar, are carefully divided by 48 columns, each with a statuette representing one of the ancient guilds of Brussels. Its chief dedicatees are the 16th-century counts Egmont and Hoorn, both of them executed on the Grand'Place in 1568.

It was when the Egmonts and other noble families set up here that Sablon gained the prestigious cachet it still has today. At the top end of the square stands the **Palais d'Egmont** itself. Begun in the 16th century, it was enlarged in the 18th century and had to be rebuilt at the start of the 20th after a fire. It is now used for receptions by the Ministry for Foreign Affairs; it was here that Britain, Ireland and Denmark signed their entry to the then EEC in 1972. The rooms are superb, but only the gardens are open to the public. Look for the statue of Peter Pan, a copy of the one in London's Kensington Gardens.

Another noble resident was Thomas Bruce, 2nd Earl of Elgin, an associate of England's Charles II, who was forced to flee Britain after being locked up in the Tower of London. Happily resident in Brussels for many years thereafter, he bequeathed the city the Fountain of Minerva that was erected in 1751. It stands behind Notre-Dame on the **place du Grand Sablon**, a major square lined with glitzy restaurants and high-price antiques shops. Small independent art galleries and some of Brussels' finest chocolate shops (*see p107* **Let Them Eat Chocolate**) complete the picture. At weekends, an antiques market adds colour to the foot of the church. Grand Sablon is full of life and verve, with white lights at Christmas and numerous festivals.

The frivolity was shattered in May 2014 when a lone attacker, armed with a handgun and a Kalashnikov, opened fire and killed four people at the **Musée Juif de Belgique** (Jewish Museum) on rue des Minimes. A few paces away, unwitting Sablon was still trading in antiques and fine chocolate. Within minutes, the attacker had fled, police cars were screeching and the world's press had descended. The drama continued as

a manhunt ensued. With a legal process ongoing, Sablon has now returned to its antiques and chocolates, though the terrible memory remains. Armed guards, meanwhile, keep close watch outside the museum.

Rue des Minimes, which has been a thoroughfare since medieval times, leads from Sablon to the gargantuan **Palais de Justice** (*see p93*). The Palais' architect, Joseph Poelaert, lived along the street as he drove himself mad with creating the world's largest building. It forms the border between classy Sablon, the Upper Town, and impoverished Marolles, the Lower Town.

Sights & Museums

FREE Église Notre-Dame au Sablon

38 rue de la Régence (02 213 00 65, www.catho-bruxelles.be). Métro Porte de Namur, or tram 92, 93. **Open** 9am-6.30pm Mon-Fri; 9am-7pm Sat, Sun. *Services* 6pm Mon-Sat; noon, 6pm Sun. **Admission** free. **Map** p101 B5 ⑮

Built during the 15th and 16th centuries, Notre-Dame au Sablon was once home to a statue of Mary shipped in from Antwerp on account of its reputed healing powers. A carving of the boat can be seen in the nave, but the statue was demolished by Protestants during the Iconoclastic Riots. The current impressive structure boasts some stunning 14m (46ft) high stained-glass windows. *Photo p110.*
▶ *The statue's arrival is still celebrated in July, with the Ommegang parade; see p32.*

Musée Juif de Belgique

21 rue des Minimes (02 512 19 63, www.new. mjb-jmb.org). Tram 92, 93, or bus 27, 48. **Open** 10am-5pm Tue-Sun. **Admission** €5; €3 reductions; free under-12s. Free 1st Sun of mth. **Map** p101 A5 ⑯

Forever desecrated by the awful events of May 2014, when a gunman burst in and killed four people, including a museum employee, this now heavily guarded institution carries on with its mission to tell the history of the Jews in Belgium. Part of the permanent collection comes from the Beth Israel School that operated in Molenbeek from 1946 to 2004, showing the rituals of family and communal life from the cradle to the grave. In all there are 750 artefacts and more than 1,000 works of art, including pieces by Chagall and El Lissitsky. A substantial archive comprises 20,000 photographs and literally millions of documents.

Restaurants

★ Au Vieux Saint Martin

38 place du Grand Sablon (02 512 64 76, www.auvieuxsaintmartin.be). Tram 92, 93, or bus 27, 95. **Open** 10am-midnight Mon-Sat; 10am-11pm Sun. **Main courses** €17-€32. **Map** p101 A5 ⑰ Belgian

Bang in the middle of Sablon, the popular Saint Martin is usually humming and frequently stretched to find a table for everyone. It doesn't take reservations – that's not a London-like trend, it never has done. That means you have to pick your moment or risk waiting. Once in, the food is resolutely Belgian, with steaks, *stoemp* and *waterzooi* in generous portions. The decor is more contemporary; clean white walls with statement modern art. This is a great choice – if you can get in.

Le Cap Sablon

75 rue Lebeau (02 512 01 70, http://sites.resto. com/capsablon). Métro Gare Centrale, or bus 95. **Open** noon-midnight daily. **Main courses** €9-€17. **Map** p101 A4 ⑱ **Modern European**

Among all the upmarket glitz of the Sablon, this understated little brasserie continues to shine, year after year. Its simple, understated art deco interior gives a homely, comforting feel, which is reflected in the menu. Basic but succulent roasts and grills, fish livened up by oriental spices, and wicked desserts – all make for a satisfying, reasonably priced meal. The chattering Sablon set knows all about this place, but the Cap has thus far resisted any social pressure to trendify. If you want to dine on the small terrace, specify when booking.

Jef

20 rue Haute (02 437 35 73, www.jefresto.be). Bus 27, 48, 95. **Open** noon-2.30pm, 7-10pm Tue-Fri; 7-10pm Sat; noon-2.30pm Sun. **Set menu** lunch €19, dinner €33. **Map** p101 A4 ⑲ **Belgian/French**

This small, Scandi-look restaurant has simple tables lined up like a school exam room. The fabulous original tiled floor gives colour and texture, as does the wall made entirely of corks. The menu is short, which makes sense considering the size of the place, and decided by what's available at market; all ingredients are organic and traceable. Dishes are deceptively simple but cooked decisively: roasted monkfish with chicory and lemon cream, pigs' cheeks slow-cooked, and a tarte tatin to die for are examples of Jef's contemporary Belgo-French kitchen.

Lola

33 place du Grand Sablon (02 514 24 60, www. restolola.be). Tram 92, 93, or bus 27, 95. **Open** noon-2.30pm, 7-11pm Mon-Fri; noon-11pm Sat, Sun. **Main courses** €16-€34. **Map** p101 B5 ⑳ **Modern European**

Lola is one of those institutions loved by urban professionals and consistently recommended in guidebooks. It has the name, it has the location, it has the right clientele. The food is absolutely fine, in a modern brasserie way: duck, steaks, cod en croûte and pastas. This is not a place to whisper sweet nothings – it's loud and gregarious and has everything the young set needs. Go for the buzz but, as with so many places of this genre, you may leave wondering if anyone noticed you were there.

Église Notre-Dame au Sablon. See p109.

★ Peï & Meï

15 rue de Rollenbeek (02 880 53 39, www.peietmei. be). Bus 27, 48, 95. **Open** noon-2pm, 7.30-10pm Tue-Sat. **Set menu** €39-€55. **Map** p101 A4 ㉑ **French**

The name is Brussels dialect for boy and girl, though there's nothing childish about the latest gastrobistro (from chef Gauthier De Baere and sommelier Melissa Triantopoulos) to hit the smart Sablon. Set in an old house, the walls are original raw brick or startlingly white, leading the eye through to the open kitchen. It's all about clean lines and clean plates; warm feta with truffle honey, pig's trotter croquettes, sweetbreads in champagne sauce. Be sure to book: P&M's reputation means it's always a full house.

Le Perroquet

31 rue Watteau (no phone). Tram 92, 93, or bus 27, 95. **Open** noon-1am daily. **Main courses** €7-€12. **Map** p101 A5 ㉒ **Café**

An authentic art-nouveau café, Le Perroquet features mirrors aplenty, plus stained glass, a striking black and white tiled floor and a summer terrace. A popular haunt of well-to-do young things in summer, before it's reclaimed by the autumnal flock of EU *stagiaires* (trainees), it's a stylish complement to the bland upmarket terrace bars of place du Grand

Sablon, which is a two-minute walk away. It's quite dinky inside, so expect a scramble for a table after office hours on a Friday. Plentiful salads and imaginative stuffed pittas form the core of the menu.

Senza Nome

1 place du Petit Sablon (02 223 16 17, www. senzanome.be). Tram 92, 93, or bus 27, 95. **Open** noon-2pm, 7-9.30pm Mon-Fri; 7-9.30pm Sat. **Set menu** €90-€115. **Map** p101 B5 ㉒ Italian

The Michelin-starred Senza Nome steers clear of predictable Italian fare with a short, seasonal menu, offering the likes of white truffle with cuttlefish ink or confit of veal shank with its marrow in a saffron purée. Nadia and Giovanni Bruno opened the place in 1997 and since then it has won international acclaim. From its original home in Schaerbeek, it now occupies a prime position overlooking the Sablon, giving it an even more upmarket vibe.

Pubs & Bars

★ Café du Sablon

26 rue de la Régence (02 503 39 99, www. facebook.com/lecafedusablon). Tram 92, 93. **Open** 7.30am-8pm daily. **Map** p101 B5 ㉓

This café fills a handy gap in the local market and offers fine views of Notre-Dame church opposite. Sablon, though glitzy, lacks contemporary urbanity but this namesake café has it in spades. 'We Brew Here' says the sign and, sure enough, beans of (mainly) Central American provenance help create a distinct aroma. Young professionals perch on low-backed chairs for eager pow-wows about potentially game-changing start-ups. Customers can create their own hot drinks, but it's far quicker to allow the smiling staff to barista for you. Enticing cookies and superior sandwiches are also served.

Flat

12 rue de la Reinette (02 502 74 34, www.theflat. be). Métro Porte de Namur, or bus 34, 54, 71. **Open** 6pm-2am Tue-Sat. **Map** p101 C5 ㉕

This unusual bar may seem a bit theme park-ish at first glance, but it works well as a sophisticated place to drink with friends and colleagues after work. The rooms are laid out as if part of someone's home, so you can quaff a beer in the lounge, the dining room, the candlelit bedroom or even the bathroom. Screens flash a stock market-type pricing index for drinks, which change according to how they're selling; get stuck into the margaritas, say, and the price comes down.

Shops & Services

Baobab Collection

15 rue des Sablons (02 513 80 64, www.baobab collection.com). Tram 92, 93, or bus 27, 95.
Open noon-6.30pm Tue-Fri; 10am-6.30pm Sat, Sun. **Map** p101 B5 **㉖ Gifts & souvenirs**
This domestic brand of fragrant candles owes its scents and colours to Tanzania, where the waxes originated. Throw in elegant Belgian craftsmanship and glasswork, wicks of fine Egyptian cotton and luxurious presentation boxes, and you have a gift of exquisite taste and originality.

Bensimon

70 rue de Namur (02 503 55 92, www.bensimon. com). Métro Porte de Namur. **Open** 10am-6.30pm Mon-Sat. **Map** p101 C5 **㉗ Concept store**
This is the Brussels branch of a perennially popular Parisian lifestyle boutique, which sells a nicely coordinated mix of clothes, bags, toiletries, home furnishings, stationery and accessories in various colours and prints, teamed with classic designs. Highlights include leather jackets and coats, simple tops and jumpers.

★ Christa Reniers

61 rue Lebeau (02 514 91 54, www.christareniers. com). Bus 27, 95. **Open** 12.30-6.30pm Tue-Sat; 1-5pm Sun. **Map** p101 A4 **㉘ Accessories**

Since she sold her first piece of jewellery in the early 1990s, Christa Reniers has become Belgium's most famous jewellery designer. Self-taught, she creates several new designs each season, adding to the already exquisite collection. Each piece is hand-cast and finished in her workshop, for display in this shop, now her only outlet in town.

Claire Fontaine

3 rue Ernest Allard (02 512 24 10). Tram 92, 93. **Open** 10am-6.30pm Tue-Sat. **Map** p101 B5 **㉙ Food & drink**
It's pretty well impossible to walk past Claire Fontaine, located just off the Sablon. As well as sandwiches, quiches, soups and pastries to take away, there's a host of international gastronomic delights such as foie gras, lobster soup, olives, dry goods, teas and tisanes, absinthe and Belgian fruit wines.

★ Delvaux

27 boulevard de Waterloo (02 513 05 02, www. delvaux.com). Métro Porte de Namur. **Open** 10am-6.30pm Mon-Sat. **Map** p101 B6 **㉚ Accessories**
Delvaux is a Belgian institution, creating top-quality leather products since 1829. You'll find handbags, wallets, belts, a small range of hand luggage, silk scarves and ties, and desk accessories, all at suitably luxury prices.
Other location 31 galerie de la Reine, Grand'Place & Around (02 512 71 98).

Godiva.

EXPLORE

Godiva

47-48 place du Grand Sablon (02 502 99 06, www.godivachocolates.eu). Tram 92, 93, or bus 27, 95. **Open** 10am-7pm Mon-Fri, Sun; 10am-8pm Sat. **Map** p101 A5 ⓷❶ **Food & drink**
See p107 **Let Them Eat Chocolate.**

Greta Marta

18 rue du Grand Cerf (02 514 50 01, www. gretamarta.be). Métro Louise. **Open** 10am-6.30pm Mon-Sat. **Map** p101 B6 ⓷❷ **Fashion**
The shop may bear the owner's name, but 80% of the stock carries the label of Diane von Furstenberg, the Belgian designer who made her name in the 1970s with her classic wrap dress and is now experiencing a renaissance. The boutique aims to sell unique pieces within Belgium; naturally, such exclusivity comes at a price.

Knott Shop

57 rue Lebeau (02 511 66 56, www.jean paulknott.com). Bus 27, 95. **Open** 11am-6.30pm Tue-Sun. **Map** p101 A4 ⓷❸ **Fashion & accessories**
Former costume designer for the Béjart Ballet and creative director for Cerruti, Jean-Paul Knott opened this store in 2009. Striking, elaborate, original contemporary wear for men and women, touching on haute couture, is on display, with some items designed by Knott's collaborator Greg Van Rijk. Knott's equally classy jewellery is also available.

Leonidas

41 place du Grand Sablon (02 513 14 66, www.leonidas.com). Tram 92, 93, or bus 27, 95. **Open** 10am-7pm Tue-Sat; 10am-6pm Sun. **Map** p101 A5 ⓷❹ **Food & drink**
See p107 **Let Them Eat Chocolate.**

Ma Maison de Papier

6 galerie de la rue de Ruysbroeck (02 512 22 49, www.mamaisondepapier.be). Métro Gare Centrale, or bus 27, 48, 95. **Open** 1-7pm Wed-Fri; 3-7pm Sat and by appointment. **No credit cards.** **Map** p101 A4 ⓷❺ **Gifts & souvenirs**
A store of treasures, with drawers of prints, plaques and posters of art exhibits and adverts from the late 1800s to the present.

Patrick Roger

43 place du Grand Sablon (02 514 70 46, www. patrickroger.com). Tram 92, 93, or bus 27, 95. **Open** 10.30am-7pm Tue-Fri, Sun; 10.30am-7.30pm Sat. **Map** p101 A5 ⓷❻ **Food & drink**
See p107 **Let Them Eat Chocolate.**

Philippe Lange

2A place de la Justice (02 503 46 18, www. philippelange.be). Métro Gare Centrale, or bus 27, 48, 95. **Open** 11am-1pm, 2-6pm Tue-Sat. **Map** p101 B4 ⓷❼ **Antiques**

Art deco, art nouveau, 20th-century antiques and new design are the specialities here, plus Panton chairs and Knoll furniture from the 1950s and '60s.

★ Pierre Marcolini

1 rue des Minimes (02 514 12 06, www.marcolini. be). Bus 95, 96. **Open** 10am-7pm Mon-Thur, Sun; 10am-8pm Fri, Sat. **Map** p101 A5 ⓷❽ **Food & drink**
See p107 **Let Them Eat Chocolate.**
Other locations throughout the city.

Pistolet Original

24-26 rue Joseph Stevens (02 880 80 98, www. pistolet-original.be). Tram 92, 93, or bus 27, 95. **Open** 9am-4pm Mon-Fri; 9am-6pm Sat, Sun. **Map** p101 A4 ⓷❾ **Food & drink**
A *pistolet* is a soft-centred, crunchy-crusted bread roll. At this popular, newly opened delicatessen, artisanal baker Yves Guns delivers two loads a day, so that award-winning chefs Pierre Wynants and Freddy Vandecasserie can add their own-made steak tartare, salt-pork hash or Zeebrugge grey shrimp. These satisfying superior snacks can be devoured *sur place* or as you wander around the Sablon.

Taschen

16-18 rue Lebeau (02 513 80 23, www.taschen. com). Bus 27, 95. **Open** 11am-7pm Mon-Sat; noon-6pm Sun. **Map** p101 A4 ❹⓪ **Books & music**
Hollywood, Beverly Hills and New York… now Brussels has its own temple to Taschen, Cologne-based producer of the finest (and dearest) art books in the world today. Photography, fashion, design, architecture and film, Taschen presents a cornucopia of global culture in its own innovative fashion. This store, designed by Philippe Starck, more than does justice to the subject matter, and was the setting for the visit of renowned pop photographer Gered Mankowitz for the launch of his 500-page tome *The Rolling Stones* (priced at €4,000) in December 2014.

★ Toni & Guy

31 rue Joseph Stevens (02 880 66 99, www.toni andguy.be). Tram 92, 93 or bus 27, 95. **Open** 10am-7pm Mon-Wed; 10am-8pm Thur, Fri; 9am-6pm Sat. **Map** p101 A5 ❹❶ **Health & beauty**
Prices at Toni & Guy depend on who cuts your hair – ranging upwards from a lowly stylist to the dizzy heights of the creative director. This new, intimate outlet at the lower end of Sablon comes with multilingual staff and discounts for students from certain international schools.
Other locations 184 rue Stévin, EU Quarter (02 737 52 80); 1489 chaussée de Waterloo, Uccle (02 374 29 40).

★ Wittamer

12 place du Grand Sablon (02 546 11 14, www. wittamer.com). Tram 92, 93, or bus 27, 95. **Open** 9am-6pm Mon; 7am-7pm Tue-Sat; 7am-6.30pm Sun. **Map** p101 B5 ❹❷ **Food & drink**
See p107 **Let Them Eat Chocolate.**

EXPLORE

St-Josse & Schaerbeek

Hugging the north-east corner of the inner ring road, St-Josse-ten-Noode is both the smallest and most densely populated of the city's 19 municipal districts. Referred to as St-Josse, it's predominantly North African and Turkish in character. Set close to the stately heights of the Royal Quarter, and home of the original Botanical Gardens, St-Josse was one of the first districts to urbanise. Once the Gardens were moved out of town, the area was left to neglect. Adjoining Schaerbeek was once a hunting ground, famed for its cherry orchards. Before the construction of the Gare du Nord in 1841, it was a mellow backwater of family-run bakeries and breweries. Urbanisation also brought the Halles de Schaerbeek, a large covered market, in 1865. Abandoned decades later, the Halles were converted in modern times to become a cultural venue of international renown.

Botanique.

Don't Miss

1 **Train World** New Schaerbeek railway heritage attraction (p119).

2 **Maison Autrique** Must-visit early Horta creation (p119).

3 **Le Botanique** Old botanical gardens, now a major music venue (p116).

4 **Halles de Schaerbeek** Capital culture (p118).

5 **138 avenue du Diamant** Birthplace of Belgium's greatest singer-songwriter, Jacques Brel (p118).

EXPLORE

Halles de Schaerbeek. *See p118.*

ST-JOSSE

Vibrant St-Josse is full of busy fruit shops and intimate little ethnic eateries, reflecting its mainly Moroccan and Turkish make-up. Shaped in a right-angle around the Petit Ring, its eastern fringes bumping up against the fancier streets of the Quartier Léopold and the EU Quarter, the district exudes faded grandeur. After all, St-Josse once contained the Botanical Gardens, laid out in 1829 – and, alongside the gardens, six years later, the first public train service on continental Europe set off to Mechelen. The station, Allée-Verte, was then replaced by the **Gare du Nord**, and the gardens were moved out of the city.

While the grounds and grand buildings of the former gardens were left derelict, something of a red-light district grew up around the Gare du Nord. The station building itself was moved back, into adjoining Schaerbeek, with the creation of the North-South rail link in the 1950s. In 1978, the Ministry of the French Community acquired the former gardens, with the intention of establishing a cultural centre. In 1984, the Rotonde and the Orangerie, relics of a botanical past, were transformed into **Le Botanique** (*see p188*), a venue for concerts, film festivals, theatre and literary evenings. The stage and seating in the Rotonde maintains its circular aspect, making it one of the city's most unusual and vibrant

performance spaces. 'Le Bota' also stages arguably the most important music festivals in Brussels: **Les Nuits Botanique** (*see p35*).

SCHAERBEEK

Schaerbeek stretches over great swathes of north-east Brussels, from the borders of St-Josse almost to the city limits. On its furthest north-western flank, only rows and rows of railway lines and the canal separate Schaerbeek from verdant, palatial Laeken – but the contrast could not be greater. Without its own métro station, Schaerbeek is a visibly poor neighbourhood – poor street lighting, erratic refuse collection and no glamorous shops – but don't let that deter you from a visit.

Once an international hub, the grandiose but neglected Schaerbeek train station up in this north-western corner is soon to house **Train World**, a museum dedicated to the history of Belgian rail. It's scheduled to open in late 2015.

As a commune, Schaerbeek expanded during the latter part of the 19th century and developed with the new Belgian state. At independence in 1830, there were 1,600 people living here; by 1900, there were 65,000, travelling to work in trams rattling down busy boulevards and past grand houses – many built in art nouveau style for and by the country's new bourgeoisie.

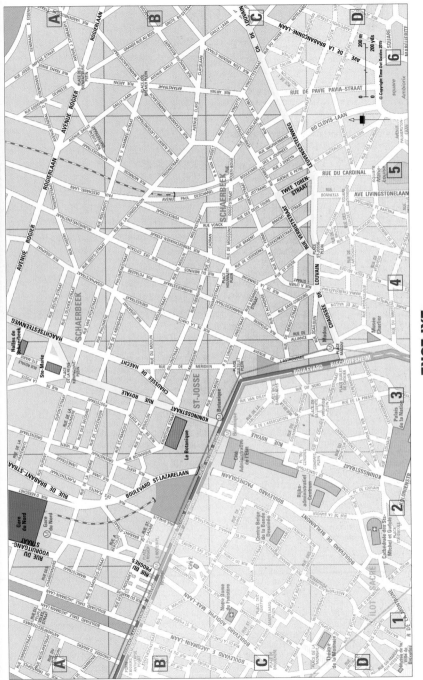

EXPLORE

Such grandeur had faded by the time the prodigal son of Schaerbeek, *chanteur* Jacques Brel, grew up here. A plaque at **138 avenue du Diamant** marks the house where he was born. Schaerbeek shaped his eye for everyday detail in his songwriting, and when Brel found fame and fortune, he bought a house not in Ixelles or St-Gilles but back in Schaerbeek. Although it has no plaque or memorial outside, **31 boulevard Général Wahis** is a much grander affair than Brel's modest childhood homes in Schaerbeek and Anderlecht. *See p64* **Brel's Brussels**.

Similar stately properties at this other, eastern end of Schaerbeek, nearest the Quarter Léopold and the EU Quarter, are now sought after – but in general, modern times have left Schaerbeek behind. In the area to the west of rue Royale, around the Gare du Nord, drab sex shops have been replaced by Moroccan stores selling halal meat, miniature indoor waterfalls and suitcases. Chaussée de Haecht is the place to find Turkish bakeries, Muslim butchers and cafés filled with Turkish football flags.

Renowned cartoonist François Schuiten, who has lived in Schaerbeek all his life and used its peeling grandeur as inspiration for epic urban comic tales (such as his seminal *Brüsel*), has also renovated and converted the commune's most treasured art nouveau legacy, the **Maison Autrique**. Persuading the local authorities to buy this 1893 gem, and collaborating with his co-author Benoît Peeters, Schuiten has transformed it into an imaginative exploration of the city's past. Another art nouveau landmark, restaurant **De Ultieme Hallucinatie** (316 rue Royale, 02 217 06 14), reopened in 2014, but is probably best visited for a drink and a gawp at its gorgeous interior.

Branching off from (and parallel to) rue Royale, the royal route leading past the palaces of the Upper Town down to the jaws of the Palais de Justice, **chaussée de Haecht** is the spine of Schaerbeek. Built on a rather grandiose scale with long avenues sweeping down to monumental buildings overlooking the city, it links the local landmarks of the churches of Ste-Marie and St-Servais, the Halles de Schaerbeek and the **Hôtel Communal** on place Colignon. The Hôtel itself was inaugurated in 1887 by Léopold II. Damaged by fire soon afterwards, the Flemish Renaissance-style building is made from red brick, with numerous towers and windows. Place Colignon was constructed around the Hôtel, and its houses are equally grand with their gables, turrets and flagpoles.

South down rue Royale Ste-Marie from the square is the large, beautiful and dilapidated church of **St-Servais**. It holds services in Spanish and Italian, and has a commanding view over avenue Louis Bertrand. This formerly grand boulevard leads east to pretty **Parc Josaphat**.

Here you'll find ponds, an animal reserve, a sculpture museum, sporting facilities and free concerts on summer Sundays.

Not far from St-Servais stand the **Halles de Schaerbeek** (*see p196*). A rare example of 19th-century industrial architecture, the Halles are another example of a Brussels renovation success story. The Halles were a product of the industrial age, a market hall of glass and riveted iron. After a fire in 1898, World War I and changes in shopping habits, the building stood empty by the 1920s. The Halles were used as a warehouse, workshops and even a car park until they were finally sold to a development agency that planned to convert them into housing. A group of influential locals petitioned for the building to be spared and reconfigured as a cultural centre for the commune and city. It was saved when the Ministry of the French Community took it on and raised the money to start renovations, completed in 1997.

Now the Grande Halle can seat 2,000 people, while the Petite Halle – once the fish market – presents smaller concerts and theatre. The original cellars accommodate the bar and small performance spaces. The Halles are big enough to hold major rock concerts and touring operas, but not to the detriment of its use as a place for kids, circus workshops, local Arabic-speaking groups or the international dance and theatre companies who represent the commune's neighbourhoods. Beside the Halles, and dominating the northern

EXPLORE

Le Botanique. *See p116.*

end of rue Royale, the church of **Ste-Marie** is a neo-Byzantine mosque-like building, arched and curvaceous, with an octagonal dome. It marks the border with the commune of St-Josse, as does the Gare du Nord.

Sights & Museums

★ Maison Autrique
266 chaussée de Haecht (02 215 66 00, www. autrique.be). Tram 92, 93. **Open** noon-6pm Wed-Sun. **Admission** €7; €3-€5 reductions.
The first design commission for the city's most renowned architect, Victor Horta, the Maison Autrique is a must-visit for anyone interested in art nouveau and its era. This typical three-storey Brussels townhouse is known here as an *enfilade*: tall, narrow and four rooms deep. Behind a white stone façade, a sober domesticity is enlivened by characteristic details such as the carved wooden staircase and the swirling mosaics on the ground floor. Revamped by François Schuiten and Benoît Peeters, illustrators who use surrounding Schaerbeek for inspiration for their strip-cartoon books, the Maison Autrique is half-museum and half-theatrical mise-en-scène; visitors can walk through the rooms, from the laundry to the attic, experiencing local life the way it was lived a century ago. Currently undergoing renovation, it is due to reopen in December 2015.
▶ *For more on art nouveau and its special place in Brussels, see pp256-260.*

★ Train World
Place Princesse Elisabeth (www.trainworld.be). Schaerbeek rail, or tram 92.
Due to open in September 2015, this €20.5 million project funded by the national train company celebrates the pioneering heritage of Belgian rail. Originally scheduled for 2013, a century after the unveiling of Schaerbeek's own impressive station alongside, Train World has been partly designed by renowned local illustrator François Schuiten. The collection starts with Belgium's oldest locomotive, and is housed in two adjoining historic buildings on the otherwise unused station concourse. Models, audio-visual displays and artists' impressions feature throughout, with a special section on mail trains and a vintage poster collection to die for.

Shops & Services

Smets
650-652 chaussée de Louvain (02 325 12 30, www.smets.lu). Tram 7, 25. **Open** 11am-7pm Mon-Sat. **Concept store**
Family-run Smets brings together design, art and fashion under one roof. A cornucopia of contemporary goodies is ranged around a cool space of bare brick, including furniture and furnishings by Moooi, Carl Hansen and Opinion Ciatti, shoes by Aquazzura, Christian Louboutin and Lolo, T-shirts by Stella McCartney and sneakers by Valentino Garavani. You'll have to pass a prosaic landscape of car showrooms and arterial traffic to get here, though.

EU Quarter & the East

EXPLORE

It may be years before the scars of EU expansion have healed. While the needs of locals are set against those of the Eurocrats, east Brussels remains a mix. This is the city at its most fractured. In the 1960s, an attractive 19th-century quarter around the Schuman roundabout was torn down to make room for the growing European institutions. In the 1980s, the Quartier Léopold suffered a similar fate when the European Parliament complex was built. Most Bruxellois are appalled at the damage that has been done to the fragile urban fabric of their city, with soaring glass and steel office blocks nudging out lovely townhouses, and local communities gone forever. Now, there are moves to make the EU Quarter more appealing to workers and residents alike. Meanwhile, sweeping below the Eurozone are the quiet streets of Etterbeek, and the triumphalist Parc du Cinquantenaire.

Parlamentarium.

Don't Miss

1 Parlamentarium Major new presentation of the EU's workings (p126).

2 Museum of Natural Sciences Find out how early Man survived (p126).

3 Maison de Cauchie Klimt-influenced art nouveau (p129).

4 Parc du Cinquantenaire Triumphal arch and stately museums (p127).

5 Square Marie-Louise Pond life, waterfowl and echoes of WH Auden (p123).

EU QUARTER

The EU Quarter is a series of office and policy-makers' buildings linked by streets that echo an older Brussels. The area has long been the focus of attention of urban heritage action groups, who refer nostalgically to pre-EU days when it was the lively Quartier Léopold with its characteristic local bars and beautiful houses. Patches of these still exist, but, as the heritage activists lament, the heart has been torn out. Recent times have at least seen a more decisive architectural style, and many of the heavy grey office blocks are being replaced by more daring sculptured buildings that may one day be seen as standard bearers of their time.

When the most recent EU member, Croatia, joined in 2013, more than 40,000 people were employed by the various European institutions in this compact area, along with 10,000 lobbyists and the press. With space now a pressing concern, plans to develop a more streamlined zone have come into focus, particularly with architect Christian de Portzamparc being given the green light to relandscape rue de la Loi. His blueprint calls for a doubling of office space while also bringing a more human element to the everyday infrastructure. When all this will happen is still unclear. For the time being, the EU Quarter remains in its own bubble, disconnected from the rest of Brussels while providing it with huge economic benefits.

To find out why such radical and costly solutions are needed, hop on the métro to Schuman. Exiting on the Schuman roundabout, your attention is snagged by the (in)famous **Berlaymont building**, a star-shaped symbol not just of the EU, but of the bureaucratic

nightmares associated with it. This was the original home for the European Commission until 1991, when it was deemed too dangerous because of its asbestos content. It would have been cheaper to pull it down, but local disquiet – yes, the locals learned to love it – and its tricky foundations meant renovation was the only option. It reopened in 2004, late and millions over budget, and now houses the whole Commission and 3,000 officials.

Opposite is the **Justus Lipsius building**, first opened in 1995 for the Council of Ministers. Its frontage of pink granite and fluttering flags will be familiar as the backdrop to countless newscasts. Away to the south, shining like a crystal palace in the far distance, is the **European Parliament**. It is known locally as the Caprice des Dieux ('Folly of the Gods'), the name of an identically shaped supermarket cheese. Aware of its negative image Europe-wide, in 2011 the EU opened an excellent (and free) visitors' centre, the **Parlamentarium**, in which the history and day-by-day activity of administering Europe is entertainingly outlined – *see p130* **Euro Vision**.

Nearby, across rue Wiertz and offering the best view of the EU's nerve centre, lies the attractive but unexceptional **Parc Léopold**. One of the world's first science parks in the late 19th century, it remains dotted with impressive research institutes. One of the public attractions is the **Museum of Natural Sciences**, famous for its dinosaur skeletons, a hit with kids. On the other side of the same street is the **Musée Wiertz Museum**, home and studio of the oddball 19th-century artist, Antoine Wiertz, and now a showcase for his works.

Turn left out of the park and you'll see the back of the **Résidence Palace**, a superb honey-brick art deco block built in the 1920s as an apartment complex, complete with a swimming pool, theatre and roof garden. It was later the Nazi administrative headquarters. It now houses the International Press Centre.

Following the train tracks brings you back to place du Luxembourg and the original **Luxembourg station building**. This became another chapter in the saga of resistance to development when squatters moved in to protest against its demolition. To no avail: bulldozers wiped away the waiting room, and with it a cherished piece of urban history. The remaining booking hall looks like an afterthought to appease the critics, a strange, lonely piece of old Brussels.

North of place du Luxembourg run two major roads, rue Belliard and rue de la Loi, parallel to rue du Marteau, a charming street full of eclectic architectural styles. This pleasant, residential no-man's land, neither the EU zone nor the grimy heart of adjoining St-Josse and Schaerbeek, is where you'll find the **Musée Charlier**,

---

IN THE KNOW POETIC TIMES

In 1938, poet WH Auden lived in Brussels for six months. He stayed at two addresses in what is now the EU Quarter: 83 rue des Confédérés and 70 square Marie-Louise. He wrote a raft of poems during his stay, including 'Brussels in Winter' and 'Gare du Midi'. One of his most famous works, 'Musée des Beaux-Arts', was inspired by a visit there to admire Bruegel's *Landscape with the Fall of Icarus*. Apart from an unfortunate disease picked up from a local boyfriend he referred to as 'Petit Jacques', his stay was uneventful until fellow writer Christopher Isherwood turned up. After several adventures together, and with war looming, the two decided to leave Europe. On 18 January 1939, Auden and Isherwood left Brussels, returned to England and boarded a boat bound for New York.

Musée Wiertz.

an art-filled, Horta-designed house where the fin-de-siècle portrait painter and sculptor Guillaume Charlier lived. Follow rue du Marteau to the end, and you arrive at **square Marie-Louise**. This bucolic park-cum-lake, barely five minutes' walk from the Berlaymont building, was designed and developed by Gédéon Bordian, who took advantage of its hilly relief to create a cascade of gardens with water features running over the rocks. These also provide shelter (and a shower) for the wildfowl that make the pond home. Dotted among them are sculptures by Constantin Meunier and Victor Rousseau. In the middle of the pond, a powerful fountain adds grace and spectacle.

Surrounding the square is an eclectic assortment of houses, mid 20th-century purpose-built blocks with neat gardens to the north and west, stately terraces of 19th-century townhouses opposite. In 1938, the poet WH Auden lived at no.70, composing the poem 'Brussels in Winter' ('Ridges of rich apartments loom tonight, where isolated windows glow like farms'). At ground (and water) level, sandy footpaths allow breathing space for both city dwellers and EU functionaries. Toddlers waddle with the ducks, old men sit and stare, young lovers canoodle and business deals are done down the phone. This is green urban living at its most attractive and individual.

East again, along avenue Palmerston (named after the British prime minister, a staunch supporter of Belgian independence, who lived at no.26), is square Ambiorix, its grassy expanse surrounded by lovely art nouveau houses.

Sights & Museums

Musée Charlier

16 avenue des Arts (02 220 26 91, www. charliermuseum.be). Métro Arts-Loi or Madou. **Open** noon-5pm Mon-Thur; 10am-1pm Fri. **Admission** €5; €4 reductions. **No credit cards. Map** p124 A1 ❶
Guillaume Charlier was an active figure in Brussels in the early 1900s, when he was taken under the wing of Henri van Cutsem, a patron of the arts. Charlier moved into van Cutsem's house, the site of the museum, where he hosted concerts and salon discussions. The house, whose interior was redesigned by Horta, is filled with tapestries, furniture and works by Ensor, Meunier and Charlier himself.

FREE Musée Wiertz

62 rue Vautier (02 648 17 18, www.fine-arts-museum.be). Métro Trône. **Open** 10am-5pm Tue-Fri. **Admission** free. **No credit cards. Map** p124 C5 ❷
Antoine Wiertz (1806-65) painted vast canvases of the most gruesome subjects: biblical and mythical scenes with gratuitous violence thrown in. Well regarded in his time (not least by himself – he put his own work on a par with that of Michelangelo and Rubens), Wiertz persuaded the state to buy him this house and studio in return for inheriting his works when he died. The museum contains 160 pieces and

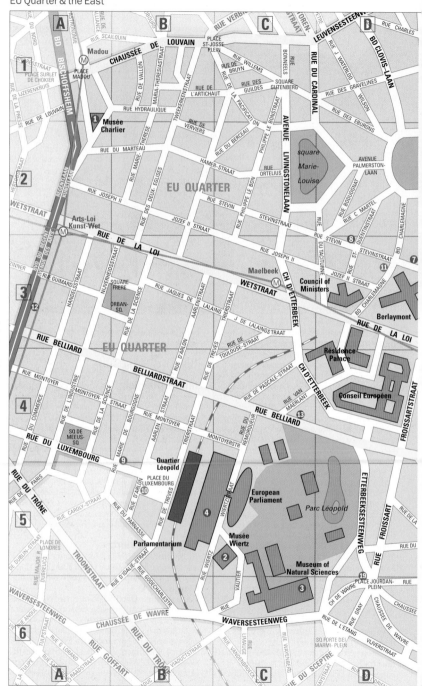

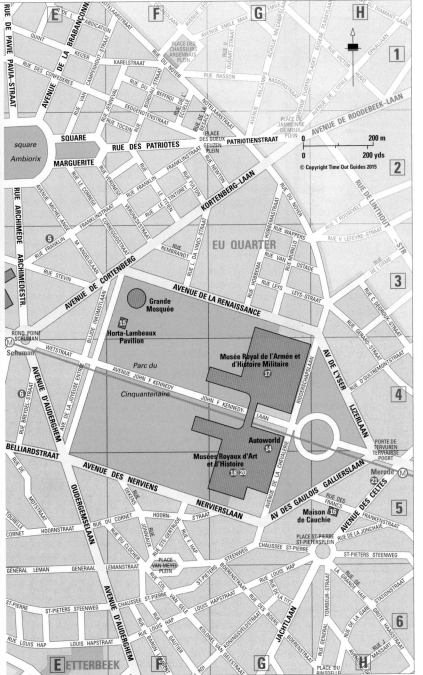

EXPLORE

Maison du Luxembourg.

makes for an unusual, if slightly bizarre, diversion. It forms part of the six-strong Musées Royaux des Beaux-Arts, whose big hitters of Old Masters and Magritte are nearby in the Upper Town.

★ Museum of Natural Sciences

29 rue Vautier (02 627 42 11, www.natural sciences.be). Bus 34, 38, 80, 95. **Open** 9.30am-5pm Tue-Fri; 10am-6pm Sat, Sun, school hols. **Admission** €7; €6 reductions; €4.50 6-17s; free under-6s. Free 1st Wed of mth after 1pm. **Map** p124 C6 ❸

The museum of the Royal Belgian Institute of Natural Sciences contains one of the world's finest collections of iguanodons, as well as a new Gallery of Humankind that reveals how we and our bodies developed. Its opening coincides with the long-term closure for redevelopment of the halls dedicated to whales and mammals and the Polar rooms. In 2017, a new gallery will open, dedicated to biodiversity and ecology on Earth. Even when it's fully operational, the museum can only exhibit a fraction of its 37 million specimens, the most important collection in the field of natural history in Europe after Paris and London.

★ FREE Parlamentarium

60 rue Wiertz (02 283 22 22, http://europarl. europa.eu/parlamentarium). Bus 21, 34, 64, 80, 95. **Open** 1-6pm Mon; 9am-6pm Tue-Fri; 10am-6pm Sat, Sun. **Admission** free. **Map** p124 B5 ❹

See p130 **Euro Vision**.

Restaurants

★ L'Atelier Européen

28 rue Franklin (02 734 91 40, www.atelier-euro.be). Métro Schuman. **Open** noon-2.30pm, 7-10.30pm Mon-Fri. **Main courses** €14-€28. **Map** p125 E3 ❺ Belgian/French

A former wine warehouse, with a leafy courtyard out front, was converted into a studio and then a restaurant, though the studio feel remains – it's light and airy, with a beamed roof and whitewashed brick walls. The food is a mix of Belgian and French, and prices are reasonable for the area, which makes the place lively – especially in summer.

Au Bain Marie

46 rue Breydel (02 280 48 88). Métro Schuman. **Open** noon-2pm Mon-Fri. **Main courses** €10-€15. **No credit cards. Map** p125 E4 ❻ Mediterranean

A favourite of EU types, the little Bain Marie is always crowded and always worth booking ahead. Organic quiches, tarts, salads and a crisp *pissala-dière* (caramelised onion and olives from Nice) are the order of the day here. The small garden is lovely in summer and adds to the lunchtime-only, weekday-only buzz.

Cool Bun

168 rue Stevin (02 230 52 11, www.cool-bun.be). Métro Schuman. **Open** noon-3pm, 6-10pm

Mon-Fri; 6-10pm Sat. **Main courses** €14-€28.
Map p124 D3 **❼ Burgers**
See p140 **The Burgers of Brussels**.

Kafenio

134 rue Stevin (02 231 55 55, www.kafenio.be).
Métro Schuman. **Open** 11am-11pm Mon-Fri;
6-11pm Sat. **Main courses** €7-€14. **Map**
p124 D3 **❽ Greek**
It's at lunchtimes that this Greek-inspired restaurant
and bar really swings into action, with every table
taken and a queue forming at the door. The reason
is the buffet meze bar, where – accompanied by a
waiter – you make your selection from 50 hot and
cold dishes, sit down with a drink and await delivery.

Maison du Luxembourg

37 rue du Luxembourg (02 511 99 95, www.
maisonduluxembourg.be). Métro Trône. **Open**
noon-2.30pm, 7-10pm Mon-Thur; noon-2.30pm
Fri. **Set menu** €32. **Map** p124 B4 **❾ French**
Occupying a prominent corner position in the heart
of the EU Quarter, the Maison is a stylish restaurant
on two floors, offering a classic take on Belgian-
French cuisine. Because of its location, it's lunchtime
that takes the busy hit with Eurocrats and their pals
discussing the latest directive or budget deficit. It
also explains why it doesn't open at weekends, as the
majority of its clientele disappears to the suburbs.
The menu is excellent value, with a choice of six
plates for each course.

Pubs & Bars

★ Fat Boy's

5 place du Luxembourg (02 511 32 66, www.
fatboys-be.com). Métro Trône. **Open** 11am-
late daily. **Map** p124 B5 **❿**
Fat Boy's is the city's main expat sports bar, conveniently set in the considerable shadow of the
European Parliament. Although it's American in
style, its scarves and shirts, donated by customers,
reflect Europe's rich tapestry: Brittany, Macedonia
and Tyrol. Brits flock here in droves to spend beery
Sunday afternoons gawping at any of several
screens showing Premiership action and scoffing
their way through the meaty menu of ribs and burgers. The place improves when the after-work crowd
descends to fill its long interior, spilling on to the terrace on summer evenings.
▶ *The more pub-like Fat Boy's 2 has opened close*
to Schuman métro at 36 avenue de Cortenbergh
(02 280 65 21; open from 11am daily).

Kitty O'Shea's

42 boulevard Charlemagne (02 588 42 35,
www.kittyosheas.eu). Métro Schuman. **Open**
noon-1am daily. **Map** p124 D3 **⓫**
Of the several expat-friendly pubs that are located
within a short stagger of each other around the
EU Quarter, Kitty O'Shea's provides the best

experience across the board. Hearty pub grub, serious TV sports and a decent range of draught brews
– Guinness, Boddingtons, Murphy's and Kilkenny –
are a given. What's extra are the themed nights, the
odd set by a Ukrainian singer-songwriter and a real
international atmosphere.

Shops & Services

Filigranes

39-42 avenue des Arts (02 511 90 15, www.
filigranes.be). Métro Arts-Loi. **Open** 8am-8pm
Mon-Fri; 10am-7.30pm Sat; 10am-7pm Sun.
Map p124 A3 **⓬ Books & music**
This labyrinthine bookstore has a decent English
books section, as well as international magazines
and newspapers. The art department is outstanding,
and the kids will love the children's area. You can
also enjoy a drink in the central café, surrounded by
books and browsers. Filigranes is totally un-Belgian
in that it's open 365 days a year.

Pauz

166 rue Belliard (02 230 07 80, www.pauz.be).
Métro Schuman. **Open** 10am-6pm Mon-Fri.
Map p124 C4 **⓭ Health & beauty**
Right in the heart of the EU Quarter, this is a bar with
a difference. It's a nap bar with a row of neat, spacious cubicles in a relaxation zone, with various levels of aids to rest – massage chairs, a shiatsu bed and
a hydro-massaging corner are all provided. Sessions
are broken up into 15-minute periods, the full package being a 45-minute zonk-out on three different
types. There's no booking, just walk in when you're
feeling bushed and recharge.

ETTERBEEK & PARC DU CINQUANTENAIRE

Etterbeek stretches across a large area of east
Brussels, between the EU Quarter and Ixelles.
When Georges Rémi was born here in 1907,
in rue Philippe Baucq, Etterbeek had not long
been transformed by Léopold II from a quiet
residential zone to an expanse of triumphant
boulevards, monuments and parks. Whether it
inspired the later Hergé (the reversed initials of
'RG') when he came to produce his Tintin cartoon
strips is not known.

If it's overblown and neoclassical in Brussels,
it's probably the work of Léopold II. The king had
300 labourers working day and night to complete
the massive **Arc de Triomphe** that stands at
the centre of **Parc du Cinquantenaire**, the
single largest, most impressive and best-known
Brussels park. The overdrive was an attempt to
meet the deadline of Belgium's 50th anniversary,
celebrated in 1880. In the event, construction
was not completed in time and the Arc had to be
substituted with a wooden stand-in for official
ceremonies. It wasn't completed until 1910, a year

EXPLORE

EXPLORE

after Léopold's death. Hugely impressive in scale, it is a monument that singularly fails to stir the emotions – a reflection perhaps of Léopold's own failed ambitions of glory.

On either side of the Arc, colonnades stand in front of wings that house three museums. The northern wing is the site of the **Musée Royal de l'Armée et d'Histoire Militaire**, which provides an enjoyably retro journey for military buffs of all ages; the southern wing is shared by motor vehicle museum **Autoworld** and the **Musée du Cinquantenaire**.

Over in the north-west corner of the park, the rather unexpectedly neoclassical and austere **Horta-Lambeaux Pavilion** is an early piece (1889) by the architect who was later to become synonymous with art nouveau in Brussels (*see pp256-260*). The real interest, however, is inside with Jef Lambeaux's luxuriant reliefs *Les Passions Humaines*. After years of being locked away – they were considered too lewd – the pavilion was renovated in 2013-14 and is open to the public on specific afternoons during European Summer Time. Ironically, this controversial landmark stands within the grounds of the city's largest mosque. On the south side of the park, on rue des Francs, is the **Maison de Cauchie**, home of painter Paul Cauchie.

From the east side of the park, the equally processional avenue de Tervuren was built by Léopold II to link it with his **Musée Royal de l'Afrique Centrale** (www.africamuseum.be) in the well-to-do Flemish community of Tervuren. Closed in 2013, this vast, echoing, controversial institution is due to reopen in 2017, following a major rehaul. What will be interesting is how it deals with Belgium's sordid colonial past – the museum holds the archives of Welsh explorer Henry Morton Stanley (of 'Dr Livingstone, I presume' fame). During the four-year hiatus, various pop-up exhibitions have been promised in Tervuren and Brussels.

The museum used to provide a somewhat bizarre bookend to the most convivial tram journey in Brussels: the no.44, from Montgomery, and the statue of the World War II hero the square is named after, to Tervuren and the assorted artefacts of Stanley and Livingstone. It's still a lovely ride, through the leafy fringes of the Forêt de Soignes.

Sights & Museums

Autoworld

11 parc du Cinquantenaire (02 736 41 65, www. autoworld.be). Métro Merode. **Open** *Apr-Sept* 10am-6pm daily. *Oct-Mar* 10am-5pm Mon-Fri; 10am-6pm Sat, Sun. **Admission** €9; €7 reductions; €5 6-12s; free under-6s. **Map** p125 G4 ⓮

The venue for Belgium's motor show since 1902 and one of the biggest automobile museums in Europe.

All in all, some 250 vehicles are gathered in this huge hall, built at the same time as the surrounding Parc du Cinquantenaire. A section on sport and competition is the most recent development.

Horta-Lambeaux Pavilion

11 parc du Cinquantenaire (02 741 72 11, www. kmkg-mrah.be/horta-lambeaux-pavilion). Métro Merode. **Open** *Late Mar-late Oct* 2-4pm Wed; 2-4.45pm Sat, Sun. **Admission** €7; €3-€6.50 reductions. **No credit cards. Map** p125 F3 ⓯

Now called, somewhat diplomatically, the Horta-Lambeaux Pavilion, the former Temple of Human Passions is at least open to the public these days – for a couple of hours on three days a week, in the summer months between the clocks changing. So what is so radical about this much-maligned work of art? The relief within, created by Jef Lambeaux, is a tangle of naked, writhing bodies. When a young Victor Horta was commissioned to design a neoclassical pavilion to house it, for the Brussels International Expo of 1897, he envisioned Lambeaux's relief to be on permanent view. The sculptor was horrified, as were the art critics of the day. *Les Passions Humaines* was heavily criticised for its lewd, derivative nature. Horta and Lambeaux fell out, but the master of art nouveau kept to the sculptor's wishes after the latter's death in 1908 – Horta built a front wall in 1909. In 1967, King Baudouin I offered the pavilion to the

ruler of Saudi Arabia, visiting the nearby Great Mosque. Decades later, the Saudis returned it to the Belgian State, and the pavilion was renovated in 2013-14. After more than a century, it's on public display once more. Visits are limited to one hour: you shouldn't need more than 15 minutes to look over the 17 blocks of Carrara marble, depicting extremes of pleasure, and wonder what all the fuss was about.

★ Maison de Cauchie

5 rue des Francs (02 733 86 84, www.cauchie.be). Métro Merode. **Open** 10am-1pm, 2-5.30pm 1st wknd of mth & by appt. **Admission** €5; free under-12s. **No credit cards. Map** p125 H5 ⓰

The former home of painter and architect Paul Cauchie was built in 1905 in the twilight of Brussels' art nouveau period. It shows the influence of the Vienna Secession with its geometric shapes – the gilded mural of the lovely maidens in long gowns is slightly reminiscent of Gustav Klimt and was actually designed to be an advertisement of Cauchie's art. *See also pp256-260* **Art Nouveau**.

FREE Musée Royal de l'Armée et d'Histoire Militaire

3 parc du Cinquantenaire (02 737 78 33, www. klm-mra.be). Métro Merode. **Open** 9am-5pm Tue-Fri; 10am-6pm Sat, Sun. **Admission** free. **Map** p125 G4 ⓱

Napoleon, the uprising of 1830, two world wars – all major areas of Belgian history are covered in this somewhat old-school museum. A revamp added a section covering international conflict from 1918 to the present day: the European Forum on Contemporary Conflicts. The display dealing with 1830 and the hangar filled with wartime aircraft are the highlights.

★ Musées Royaux d'Art et d'Histoire

10 parc du Cinquantenaire (02 741 72 11, www. kmkg-mrah.be/cinquantenaire-museum). Métro Merode. **Open** 9.30am-5pm Tue-Fri; 10am-5pm Sat, Sun. **Admission** €5; €1.50-€4 reductions. Free 1st Wed of mth after 1pm. **Map** p125 G5 ⓲

Also referred to as the Musée Cinquantenaire, this expansive and somewhat unwieldy attraction is divided into four sections. The antiquity department contains artefacts from the ancient worlds of Egypt, Greece, the Near and Far East, and pre-Columbian America. Other collections include European art from the Middle Ages, art deco glass and metalwork, lace and 18th-century carriages.

Restaurants

★ L'Esprit de Sel Brasserie

52-54 place Jourdan (02 230 60 40, www.esprit desel.be). Métro Schuman. **Open** noon-2.45pm,

Maison de Cauchie.

EXPLORE

EXPLORE

EURO VISION

The free-entry Parlamentarium gives the EU a human face.

One of the criticisms often levelled at the EU is that there is a disconnect between the European institutions and citizens, with few people really understanding how the whole shebang works. The EU has been fully aware of this, particularly in recent years as anti-European rhetoric has grown across its member states. Enter the idea of a parliamentary visitors' centre that could help put that to rights, a centre that would naturally be at home in Brussels, but more than that – be part of the Parliament complex itself.

Thus in 2011, **Parlamentarium** (*see p126*) opened after six years in the thinking and making. It cost €21 million, but there's plenty of bang for your buck. Entrance is free (a wise democratic move) and once inside you can easily spend a couple of hours learning about the European project from its inception and how the institutions operate. And, it turns out, this is one of the most entertaining educational spaces in Europe.

It's the use of technology that does it. Upon entry, you're given a small personal media guide, set to the language of your choice (of the 24 official EU ones). This device allows you to navigate the three-floor exhibition and activate the electronic displays. A powerful 360° surround-screen takes you to the heart of the parliament, where, via touchscreens, you can see debates, vote and meet any of the 751 MEPs (each has recorded a video). The most stunning room is United in Diversity, containing a huge floor map dotted with places of particular EU interest. Roll a mobile display over it and more information is revealed. Look up and the Sky of Opinions reflects the map in LED form, flashing up graphic information such as details of recent Europe-wide surveys.

In early 2015, Parlamentarium welcomed its millionth visitor, quite impressive for a politically themed venue. Careful thought has gone into making it work for everyone: there's a special one-hour tour for eight- to 14-year-olds; the media guides have audio files for the visually impaired and sign-language videos for visitors with hearing difficulties; there are Braille maps and the whole place is induction-looped. This is the EU at its best – democratic, inclusive and reaching out to all its citizens equally. It's a truly amazing space. Who knew European politics could be so engaging?

6.30-11.30pm daily. **Main courses** €14-€27.
Map p124 D5 ⑲ **Brasserie**
What used to be two restaurants have now become one. The menu is the same, but the looks are different: one section is slightly more traditional, with an amazing Murano glass chandelier, while the other is all wood, marble and copper. But it matters not a jot when you get round to tucking into the best of Belgian cuisine, from simple roast chicken and chips to rabbit in sour beer or beef tournedos with port. It's a popular spot with artistes, free thinkers and the odd celebrity.

▶ *Place Jourdan also contains another Belgian culinary destination. The most famous friterie in town, the Maison Antoine (no.1, 02 230 54 56, www.maisonantoine.be; open 11.30am-1am Mon-Thur, Sun; 11.30am-3am Fri, Sat) has been here since 1948.*

Midi 50

Musées Royaux d'Art et d'Histoire, 10 parc du Cinquantenaire (02 735 87 54, www.restauration-nouvelle.be). Métro Merode. **Open** 9.30am-4.30pm Tue-Sun. **Main courses** €12-€20. **Map** p125 G5 ⑳ **Modern European**
This classy, distinctive restaurant attracts not just visitors to the museum, but the movers and shakers of the EU Quarter too. Renowned for its pasta dishes, Le Midi is all about generous portions, perfectly prepared and cleanly presented. Also on offer are innovative soups and lighter dishes, as well as Moroccan tagines and oriental-inspired salads.

As befits so grand a building, the dining room is elegant; the lovely terrace overlooking the park is packed solid in summer.

La Terrasse

1 avenue des Celtes (02 732 28 51, www.brasserielaterrasse.be). Métro Merode. **Open** 8am-midnight Mon-Wed; 8am-1am Thur, Fri; 10am-1am Sat; 10am-midnight Sun. **Main courses** €16-€25. **Map** p125 H5 ㉑ **Belgian**
Set on the other side of the Parc du Cinquantenaire from the EU institutions, this eaterie makes an ideal meeting spot thanks to its proximity to Merode métro and a sun-dappled terrace. Set far enough back from the traffic of avenue de Tervueren to give the illusion of rustic dining, La Terrasse is more than just a summer retreat; in autumn, while the kitchen is cooking mussels in eight varieties, the respectable clientele moves inside to the convivial, old-style brasserie.

Shops & Services

Oliviers & Co

242 rue Linthout (02 734 96 00, www.oliviers-co.com/en). Métro Merode. **Open** 10.30am-6.30pm Mon-Sat. **Food & drink**
This atmospheric boutique specialises in olive oils from around the world. You can buy in bottles or old-fashioned tins, and pick up the paraphernalia to go with it – pourers, jugs and table sets. Exotic ranges include truffle oils and pastas, bags of chillies and olive oil-based skin products.

La Terrasse.

Ixelles & the South

Ixelles covers south-east Brussels, right down to the woods surrounding the city's southern fringe. In fact, the Bois de la Cambre, once part of the greater Forêt de Soignes, was the reason for the urbanisation of this once bucolic and independent district. In 1859, construction began on a great boulevard to give easy access from the city centre to the wide, open green spaces where the wife of Léopold II, Marie-Henriette, liked to ride her horses. When Ixelles citizens protested, Léopold simply annexed the avenue, ran a horse-drawn tram down it and renamed it after his eldest daughter, Louise. Ixelles gradually developed either side. Today, avenue Louise is an exclusive address for high-end stores and luxury hotels. By contrast, the streets to the east of the avenue are more workaday, particularly the parallel chaussées d'Ixelles and de Wavre.

EXPLORE

Châtelain Market.

Don't Miss

1 Musée Communal d'Ixelles Magritte, Delvaux and attractive temporary shows (p138).

2 Bois de la Cambre Bucolic park with an island restaurant (p147).

3 Maison Particulière Contemporary gallery in an old townhouse (p144).

4 Châtelain Market Foodie delight (p146).

5 Place Brugmann Happening boutique and wine bar hub (p147).

Abbaye de la Cambre.

EAST OF AVENUE LOUISE

Avenue Louise begins at the square and métro station of the same name, at the south-east corner of the Petit Ring. Backdropped by the vast Palais de Justice, this top end of the imperial avenue has human proportions. Sophisticated stores line each side – perhaps it is no coincidence that the avenue was named after an inveterate shopaholic who blew several fortunes on the French Riviera before declaring bankruptcy and spending six years in an asylum. Princess Louise would barely recognise her boulevard today, though she would surely approve of its luxury outlets.

One tramstop along, you reach place Stéphanie, named after the younger and equally unhappy sister of Louise. Here the reality of the avenue hits home: double-lane highways on each side of a central tree-lined reservation lined with tram tracks. Scale and traffic render pedestrians insignificant – don't even think about trying to cross the road. From a pretty boulevard lined with Léopold II's favourite chestnut trees, avenue Louise was transformed into a busy arterial road in preparation for the Expo of 1958.

By the early 1960s, shopping arcades opened along several streets east of the boulevard, providing convenience but helping to further homogenise this once regal thoroughfare. The portentously named **Galeries de la Toison d'Or** ('Golden Fleece Galleries') is a typical mixed bag, with everyday shops nestling in among the jewellery and fake furs. Two small pedestrianised streets, rue Jordan and rue Jean Stas, are full of small restaurants, and in summer the terrace tables are packed with chattering shoppers.

For a different take on Ixelles, keep heading east from avenue Louise to Porte de Namur (one stop on the métro), where the twin chaussées of Wavre and Ixelles fan out. Between the two is the **Matongé** area, taking its name from an area of

Kinshasa in the Congo. After independence from Belgium in 1960, Congolese students came to Brussels, gathering in clubs and bars around Porte de Namur métro. At the heart of the area is the **Galerie d'Ixelles**, the post-Expo arcade that links chaussées de Wavre and d'Ixelles. Its two sides take their names from Kinshasa's two main streets of Inzia and Kanda-Kanda. Hairdressers double up as social centres, where customers debate local goings-on.

Chaussée de Wavre is lined with grocery stores, their fronts piled high with imported plantains, manioc leaves, yams, sugar cane and guava; inside, the shelves are stacked with giant sacks of rice, huge drums of palm oil and heaps of fragrant dried fish. Traders thrust forward cheap shoes 'direct from Abidjan', cotton *kangas* (shawls) and colourful *bazin* (wraps). By night, pedestrianised rue Longue Vie comes to life, packed with upbeat bars and restaurants, all blazing forth the sounds of Salif Keita and Manu Dibango. Most open late and offer spicy stews, fiery chicken piri-piri, *foufou* and *chikwangue*, a starchy cassava root mash, washed down with Congolese Tembo beer or palm wine. Around the corner on rue Francart, they serve grilled gazelle or *n'dole*, a powerful meat and dried fish stew.

In the immediate vicinity are smaller hubs with more familiar names, smells and sounds. Just north of chaussée de Wavre, rue de Dublin, with the **London Calling** bar on the corner, leads to place de Londres, a tranquil square with a growing bar scene, including the **Golden Stones** sports pub. Just south of chaussée de Wavre, place St-Boniface, overlooked by the sinister, turreted church of the same name, shiny brasseries such as **Ultime Atome** attract a professional, beer-savvy crowd.

Further south, down chaussée d'Ixelles, the uneven square of place Fernand Cocq is an attractive evening option. In summer, when customers sip their drinks alfresco, the square mutates into a Mediterranean terrace, overlooked by the Riviera-styled **Maison Communale** at the far end. Surrounded by gardens, this large, pleasant residence belonged to the violinist Bériot and his Spanish wife, the famous singer La Malibrán, who bought the house as a monument to their newly wed love.

As it slowly meanders southwards, chaussée d'Ixelles becomes both sparser and significantly darker, dotted with little more than the occasional low-range retail name. There's one notable bright spot, just off the chaussée up steep rue Van Volsem: the **Musée Communal d'Ixelles** is an art museum housed in a former abattoir that's renowned for the quality of its exhibitions.

The chaussée ends at place Flagey and the Etangs d'Ixelles (Ixelles Ponds), popular with ducks and fishermen. It's not the tranquil locale that it once was, though, thanks to the rebirth of **Flagey**. When it was completed in 1938, this corner building with the ocean-liner profile was the world's most advanced communications centre. Its moment passed, however, and the place fell into disrepair. It was quite literally left to rot throughout most of the 1990s. A later revival as a studio, concert venue (*see p194*) and cinema (*see p177*), with a stylish bar, **Café Belga,** has

brought thousands down to this once-forgotten corner of Ixelles. Finally, after many years of major roadworks and deep digging, the whole square has become sparkling and sophisticated.

The two lakes that form the **Ixelles Ponds** sit north to south. The eastern side of the ponds is flanked by upmarket *maisons de maître*: swanky townhouses built for families at the turn of the 19th century. Many have fabulous art nouveau façades, often designed by Ernest Blérot (1870-1957), a lesser-known architect who created homes for those who couldn't afford a Horta pad. One façade worth noting stands at 29 avenue des Klauwaerts – a hulking behemoth of a building, whose aesthetic lies somewhere between a stone tomb and a Wurlitzer organ. The western side of the ponds contains a rag-bag mix of 1930s art deco apartment blocks and some tasteful art nouveau terraced houses. At the northernmost tip of the top lake, the Saturday market's stalls sell giant vats of fresh olives, Italian deli produce, home-made quiches, smouldering waffles and the occasional bargain Chinese tracksuit.

A sign warns visitors not to feed the ducks, white geese, doves and pigeons that populate the lake as there is a risk of botulism, and you're not supposed to climb over the low railings on to the grassy slope leading down to the water – though many do, especially in summer. It's packed with sunbathers, lunching office-workers and grannies defying the bird-feeding ban. Close to the southern end of the ponds is the hands-on **Musée des Enfants** (*see p172*).

East of here is the bilingual university, the French side being the ULB and the Flemish the VUB. They are both enclosed by boulevard du Triomphe, within a pleasant campus. This is a lively area, with a sweep of bars and restaurants along the chaussée de Boondael, between the university and the **Abbaye de la Cambre**. This beautiful group of buildings, with custard-yellow walls surrounding a white church, contains the National Geographic Institute and an art school. The formal French garden is a peaceful place for a stroll, dotted with conical yew bushes and gravelled terraces to swish one's crinoline along.

On the east side of Bois de la Cambre, Ixelles runs way down almost to the end of the wood, past the communal **Cimetière d'Ixelles**, where architect Victor Horta is buried.

Sights & Museums

Cimetière d'Ixelles.
See p138.

FREE **Abbaye de la Cambre**
11 avenue Emile Duray (02 648 11 21). Tram 93, 94. **Open** 9am-noon, 3-6pm Mon-Fri, Sun; 3-6pm Sat. **Admission** free. **Map** p136 H5 ❶
Founded in the 12th century by the noble Gisèle for the Cîteaux Order, the Abbaye de la Cambre was badly damaged during the Wars of Religion and later rebuilt, in both the 16th and 18th centuries,

EXPLORE

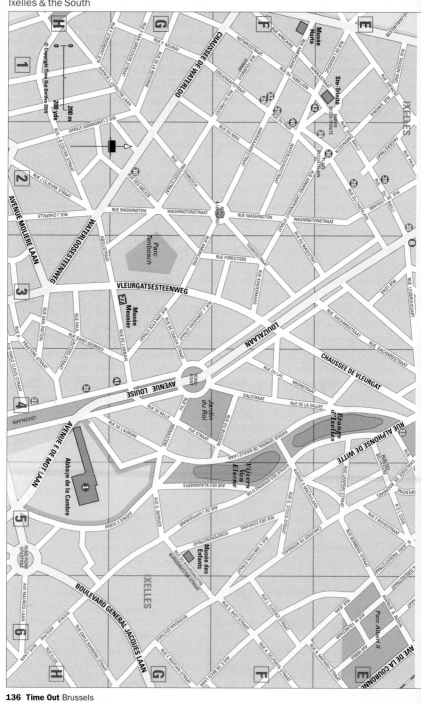

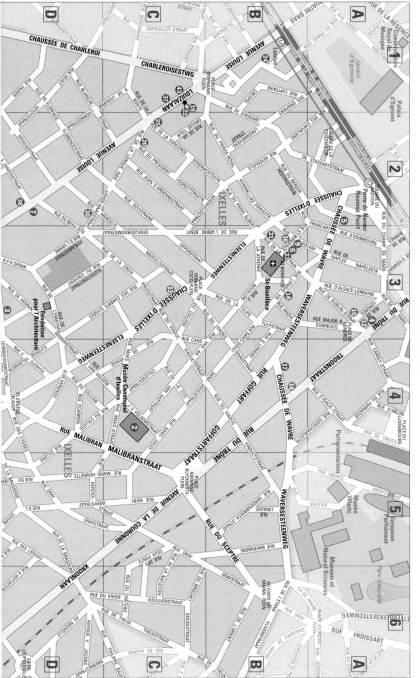

EXPLORE

although the 14th-century church attached to the abbey survives. It's all set in elegant French gardens, alongside the National Geographical Institute and the renowned National School for Visual Arts.

FREE Cimetière d'Ixelles

478 chaussée de Boondael (02 515 66 91, www. ixelles.irisnet.be). Bus 71, 72, 95. **Open** *May-Sept* 8am-6pm daily. *Oct-Apr* 8am-4.30pm Mon, Tue, Thur-Sun; 8am-6pm Wed. **Admission** free.

With all the ongoing memorials between now and 2018, it's probably as good a time as any to head to the most atmospheric cemetery in Brussels and the Pelouse d'Honneur in Block A. Here, you'll find the graves of soldiers from Britain, Belgium, France, Italy and Russia, guarded by a row of military statues created by Brussels-born sculptor Charles Samuel. Elsewhere are the resting places of Belgians as prominent as Victor Horta, industrialist Ernest Solvay and painter Antoine Wiertz. *Photo p135.*

Musée Communal d'Ixelles.

★ Musée Communal d'Ixelles

71 rue Van Volsem (02 515 64 21, www.museum ofixelles.irisnet.be). Bus 38, 60, 71. **Open** 9.30am-5pm Tue-Sun. **Admission** €8; €5 reductions. **Map** p137 C4 ❷

This excellent little museum, founded in 1892, is justifiably well known for its exhibitions of mainly modern art. Its permanent collection features works by local artists such as Magritte, Delvaux, Spilliaert and Van Rysselberghe, along with original posters by Toulouse-Lautrec. Two wings blend perfectly for a well-lit and interesting space.

Restaurants

AMI

13 rue Lesbroussart (02 646 88 41). Tram 81, or bus 71. **Open** noon-3pm Mon-Wed; noon-3pm, 6-9pm Thur-Sat. **Main courses** €4-€5.50. **Map** p137 D3 ❸ **Vegetarian**
See p140 **The Burgers of Brussels**.

★ L'Ancienne Poissonnerie

65 rue du Trône (02 502 75 05, www.ancienne poissonnerie.be). Métro Trône. **Open** noon-3pm, 7-11pm Mon-Fri; 7-11pm Sat. **Main courses** €14.50-€26.50. **Map** p137 A3 ❹ **Italian**

The art nouveau Poissonnerie began life as a baker's, then became a fish and seafood emporium. It is now a listed monument, so, mercifully, neither its exterior nor its interior tiled wall can be changed. In its third reincarnation, owner Nicola Piscopo has created a rather beautiful Italian restaurant in a white and bleached wood setting, an imaginative and harmonious mix of old and new. Classic meat, fish and own-made pasta dishes are served from a white-tiled open kitchen; the food is Italian, but with a nod to French and other world influences. It attracts the suits at lunchtime and the well-heeled in the evening, but the AP remains a bastion of democratic eating.

Cose Cosi

16 chaussée de Wavre (02 512 11 71, www. cose-cosi.be). Métro Porte de Namur. **Open** noon-2.30pm, 6-11.30pm daily. **Main courses** €8-€24. **Map** p137 A2 ❺ **Italian**

From the outside, Cosi looks just a bit smarter than your average Italiano. Inside, the first surprise is the size of the place and how many diners it manages to pack in. Then you notice the antelope heads, animal skins, Zulu spears, faux shuttered windows, tropical plants; you could be in a safari lodge, except there's a baby grand piano – which staff step up to for a quick song. As bizarre as it may sound, it hangs together surprisingly well, with a lively atmosphere and generous plates of finely prepared Italian staples and grilled meats and fish. Staff are exceedingly friendly and efficient, the wine flows and the chatter is loud.

Le Deuxième Element

7 rue St-Boniface (02 502 00 28, www.2eme element.be). Métro Porte de Namur. **Open** noon-2.30pm, 7-11pm Mon-Fri; 7-11.30pm Sat, Sun. **Main courses** €12.50-€15. **Map** p137 B3 ❻ **Thai**

Instead of bamboo and Buddhas, you'll find chic minimalist, with wooden café tables and stylish modern art. The food is authentic Thai, though, with no meddling with time-honoured flavours; plenty of ginger, lemongrass and fresh Thai basil ensure a perfect red curry. Lunchtime shoppers and business people refuelling with a plat du jour make way for large groups of loud friends in the evening. Le Deuxième gets mobbed every mealtime, so it's always best to book.

Manhattn's

164 avenue Louise (02 502 00 28, www. manhattns.com). Métro Louise, or tram 93, 94. **Open** noon-3pm, 6.30-10.30pm Mon-Fri; noon-10.30pm Sat, Sun. **Main courses** €8-€13. **Map** p137 D2 **7** Burgers
See p140 **The Burgers of Brussels**.

Rouge Tomate

190 avenue Louise (02 647 70 44, www.rouge tomate.be). Tram 81, 93, 94. **Open** noon-2.30pm, 7-10.30pm Mon-Fri; 7-10.30pm Sat. **Main courses** €25-€36. **Map** p136 E3 **8**
Modern European
What a location this is, a real urban retreat. A beautiful 1883 townhouse, it includes a wood-lined library room and an utterly contemporary dining room leading down to a garden and decked terrace. The well-heeled of Louise come to dine here, but there's little snobbery or attitude. It's on the expensive side, but then this is the Bond Street of Brussels and there will always be a sense of occasion. Dress smartly, have room on your credit card and you'll fit right in.

Saint Boniface

9 rue St-Boniface (02 511 53 66, www.saint boniface.be). Métro Porte de Namur, or bus 71. **Open** noon-2.30pm, 7-10pm Tue-Thur; noon-2.30pm, 7-10.30pm Fri; 7-10.30pm Sat. **Main courses** €20-€28. **Map** p137 B3 **9** French
The Saint Boniface looks as if it has been standing on its little plot forever, beamed up from a distant Dordogne village. It cares not a jot for its trendier neighbours, its red-and-white checked tablecloths and cottage feel providing a warm, traditional glow. Old posters and oil lamps stand guard over a menu of rich and hearty Périgordine classics: tuck into the likes of duck, puy lentils, foie gras, lamb studded with garlic, and sliced potatoes soaked in goose fat. Notices pinned to the wall warn that mobile phones are not welcome, which is all well and good – you shouldn't be distracted from the authentic eating in this time-warp joint.

★ De la Vigne à l'Assiette

51 rue de la Longue Haie (02 647 68 03, http:// sites.resto.com/delavignealassiette). Métro Louise, or tram 93, 94. **Open** noon-2pm, 7-10pm Tue-Fri; 7-10pm Sat. **Set menu** lunch €19, dinner €50. **Map** p137 D2 **10** Modern European

Eddy Dandrimont, joint owner of this tiny brasserie, is an award-winning sommelier. His stunning yet reasonably priced wine list is the perfect match for the food: dishes that are French-based but make quirky use of spices, herbs and subtle infusions. Much care is taken with the vegetables and salads. The room is rustic in feel, with globe lamps and scrubbed walls, while the youngish Ixelles clientele adds to the atmosphere.

Pubs & Bars

★ Café Belga

18 place Flagey (02 640 35 08). Tram 81, or bus 59, 71. **Open** 24hrs daily. **Map** p136 E4 **11**
The shop window of the prestigious Flagey arts complex, the Café Belga spreads itself over the ground floor of this former broadcasting house, its zinc-and-chrome 1950s look another attractive design from leisure guru Frédéric Nicolay. It's sleek, certainly, and spacious, definitely, but not without charm – and always, always busy. Unless you're having food (soups, salads, sandwiches, recommendable breakfasts), it's counter-service only. And not cheap, but that doesn't stop a constant flow of young arty types through its rather grandiose doors. The outdoor terrace comes into its own in summer, when the occasionally terse staff work their braces off.

El Café

463 avenue de la Couronne (02 640 07 79, www.elcafe.be). Tram 94, or bus 95. **Open** noon-late daily.
Formerly called Couleur Pourpre, this remains a stylish haunt in the busy university quarter in the far south of Ixelles, by the cemetery. It's always stood out from the student crowd, offering strong cocktails and a huge selection of whiskies, as well as disco lighting and DJ sounds. But in the changeover, El Café tried to keep away the more raucous members of the learnéd fraternity. Prices went up, bouncers came in. Then income went down... so, now you'll find €10 weekday lunch deals, happy hour daily (7-9pm) and a friendlier vibe. They could still do with turning the music down a notch or two.

★ Golden Stones

12 place de Londres (02 502 92 88, www. facebook.com/goldenstonespublichouse.be). Métro Trône, or bus 34, 38. **Open** noon-2am daily. **Map** p137 A3 **12**
Any growing pains at this sports bar and grill kitchen are eased by a warm welcome and radiant staff. The Fenerbahce football memorabilia hints at the owner's Turkish origins, but he's come to this pleasant little square by way of Cheltenham. Big-screen Premier League action can be accompanied with quality burgers and ribs, all-day Irish breakfasts and lashings of Guinness. It's on the pricey side, but this can be offset by late-afternoon happy hours all week long.

EXPLORE

THE BURGERS OF BRUSSELS

Manhattan has come to Belgium in the form of prime grilled meat in a bun.

The history of the Brussels burger is, frankly, a limp one. For years, homegrown hamburger chain Quick dominated the streets, even keeping the golden arches out of town. But now, change is in the air: burgers are appearing on many a trendy menu and some new outlets serve very little else.

The first sign was when a prime site on the Grand'Place seemed to morph overnight into a **Hard Rock Café** (see p50). There were local tuts, but in fairness the exterior is not too in-yer-face. However, there are alternatives to the big international brands.

Many head for avenue Louise and **Manhattn's** (see p139). Opened in 2014, this NYC-style eatery and takeaway has earned praise for the grass-fed, matured beef used in its Gatsby, Gotham and Rockefeller burgers, and for its own-made sauces and accompaniments – though its ordering service is somewhat confusing. It's very much a grab-a-bite-before-a-show kind of place.

Nearby **Cool Bun** (see p126) has also made its mark. Its strapline, 'Burgers & Wine', fits the Brussels psyche perfectly. Most of the flame-grilled meat is onglet (hanger steak), a flavoursome cut that must be cooked quickly to rare or medium to avoid toughness. Its second branch in the EU Quarter is already doing a brisk trade with the white-collar crowd.

Brussels' vegetarian options have grown considerably too, and new vegetarian/organic restaurant **AMI** (see p138) by the Ixelles Ponds sells mini burgers. Even the buns are vegetable-based and therefore gluten-free. They're pretty small, though, so it's best to order a couple or choose the soup-and-burger combo.

In Ste-Catherine, **Ellis Gourmet Burger** (see p83) is part of a small independent chain with restaurants in Belgium, Rotterdam and Amsterdam. Ellis takes its burgers seriously; its top offer is made with West Flanders red beef bred by Belgian farmer Hendrik Dierendonck. Around the corner, **Chicago Eet Café** (see p83) offers only three types of burger – beef, chicken, veggie – but ingredients, including Vieux Bruges and smoked mozzarella cheeses, are first-rate. Also in the Lower Town, check out **Houtsiplou** (see p57), a wacky, friendly and often full bistro-style place serving beef, fish, veggie and even duck burgers with foie gras.

For a burger on the go, check out the street-food trail (see p61 **Trucking On**) – especially **Urban Cook** (www.urbancook.be). This is the outlet for Mathieu Vandenbussche, who has given up cheffing at some of Brussels' top restaurants to develop chin-dripping gourmet burgers made with organic beef.

Finally, there's the make-your-own option. If you have access to a kitchen or want to vacuum-pack a treat to take home, pop into butcher **Jack O'Shea** (see p84) and pick up his prime Aberdeen Angus burgers. Some days he even has wagyu, if you really want to push out that burger boat.

Manhattn's.

★ De Haus

183 chaussée d'Ixelles (02 503 21 95, www.
dehaus.be). Bus 54, 71. **Open** 6pm-2am Tue-
Thur; 6pm-5am Fri-Sat. **Map** p137 C3 ⑱

This excellent and irreverent venue close to place
Fernand Cocq, calling itself a 'gin and tonic bar', is,
in fact, a lively and intelligently conceived nightspot.
Opened in 2014, it gained a crowd almost immediately, attracted by happy hours, a savvy music policy, retro touches to the decor and, most of all, plenty
of atmosphere amid the framed old photos and
wooden interior. It's the kind of place you come to for
a damn fine night, whether it's on gin, the local Taras
Boulba ale or the Cointreau fizz.

L'Horloge du Sud

141 rue du Trône (02 512 18 64, www.horloge
dusud.be). Métro Trône, or bus 34, 38, 95. **Open**
11am-3pm, 6pm-midnight Mon-Fri; 6pm-midnight
Sat. **Map** p137 B4 ⑭

Near the vibrant heart of the Matongé, spacious
and comfortable L'Horloge du Sud is a far cry from
the tacky, lurid and almost perpetually crowded
bars of nearby rue de Longue Vie. There's a loose
collection of old tables and chairs, plants, warrior
statues, musical instruments and a massive mirror,
all of which merge woozily as the drum rhythms and
plentiful selection of Caribbean rums and cocktails
kick in. African and Belgian food is on offer, as well
as occasional live music, regular DJ sets and a vibe
of a totally mixed clientele having barrels of fun.
Praiseworthy and unique.

★ London Calling

46 rue de Dublin (02 852 36 17, www.facebook.
com/londoncallingdublin). Métro Trône, or bus
34, 38. **Open** 4pm-midnight Mon-Fri; 7pm-4am
Sat. **Map** p137 A3 ⑮

A great little spot this, halfway between the Matongé
and the EU Quarter, a real musos' destination that
appeals to an international crowd. Affordable
drinks, DJs most nights, occasional live funk or jazz
other parts of the week – what's not to like? Twofers
on cocktails during the week, but people don't start
filling the place until after 9pm.

Ultime Atome

14 rue St-Boniface (02 513 48 84, www.ultime
atome.be). Métro Porte de Namur, or bus 54, 71.
Open 8am-12.30am Mon-Thur; 8am-1am Fri;
9am-1am Sat; 10am-12.30am Sun. **Map** p137 B3 ⑯

For more than two decades, this tasteful brasserie
has been serving a huge choice of sought-out beers
and superior pub grills. Actually, the Grimbergen-
style *carbonade de boeuf* and *entrecôte irlandaise*
here would put a lot of restaurants to shame, but
that's not why you've come. You're here to do the 92,
or at least give the 15 dozen-plus beers a good seeing-
to. Of special interest are the artisanal varieties;
Piraat Blonde from Ertvelde, Oerbier from Esen and
Quintine Blonde from Ellezelles. *Photo p142.*

De Haus.

Shops & Services

Beer Mania

174-178 chaussée de Wavre (02 512 17 88,
www.beermania.be). Métro Porte de Namur.
Open 11am-9pm Mon-Sat; 1-6pm Sun. **Map**
p137 B4 ⑰ **Food & drink**

Beer Mania boasts over 400 beers, along with matching glasses, gift packages, accessories and books.
There's even a bar, so that you can sit down and sample the beers in comfort.

★ Belgikïe

36 rue Longue Vie (02 512 54 12, www.belgikie.be).
Métro Porte de Namur, or bus 54, 71. **Open** 11am-
6pm Tue-Sat. **Map** p137 B3 ⑱ **Gifts & souvenirs**

Ultime Atome. See p141.

Original knick-knacks, unusual accessories and off-beat souvenirs fill this little shop near the Matongé. All have been created by Belgian hand: the reversible mittens by Valérie, the coffee mugs of Brussels street scenes by Sil and the delicate porcelain designs by Eve Vaucheret. Many of the 40-plus producers are trained interior designers or architects.

Francis Ferent

60 avenue Louise (02 545 78 30, www.ferent.be). Métro Louise. **Open** 10am-6.30pm Mon-Sat. **Map** p137 C1 ⑲ **Fashion**

The flagship store of a small empire of boutiques stocking international labels for men, women and children. Brands include DKNY, Dolce & Gabbana, Sonia Rykiel, Miu Miu, Marc Jacobs, Helmut Lang and Prada. You might get an icy reception, though – the assistants seem to think they own the place.

Isabelle Baines

4 rue de la Longue Haie (no phone, www.isabelle baines.com). Métro Louise. **Open** 10.30am-6.30pm Tue-Sat. **Map** p137 C2 ⑳ **Fashion**

Local designer Baines opened her first boutique in Brussels in 1986, selling her machine-knitted/hand-finished jumpers, cardigans and gilets. Expect top-quality, long-lasting classic pieces with a modern twist; the winter collection is made from wool and cashmere, the summer one from cotton.

IN THE KNOW
TAX-FREE SHOPPING

Prices include a sales tax of up to 21 per cent. In many shops, non-EU residents can request a Tax-Free Cheque on purchases of more than €145, which can be cashed at customs when leaving the EU to reclaim VAT. Shops in the scheme have a 'Tax-Free Shopping' sticker on their door.

★ Look 50

10 rue de la Paix (02 512 24 18). Métro Porte de Namur, or bus 71. **Open** 10.30am-6.30pm Mon-Sat. **No credit cards. Map** p137 B3 ㉑ **Fashion**

Look 50 is vintage at its most raw. No glam, no horrifying price tags, no pretence. Here, customers dig through the tightly packed mess of clothes to find the item that suits them best. The key era is the 1970s, with leather jackets, polyester dresses, funky vibrant shirts and fun hats. The jukebox in the entrance is not for sale.

Nicolas Woit

60 avenue Louise (02 545 78 30, www.facebook.com/nicolaswoit). Métro Louise. **Open** 10am-6pm Mon-Sat. **Map** p137 C1 ㉒ **Fashion & accessories**

Woit studied fashion in Paris before opening in Brussels in 1998. Leaving downtown Antoine Dansaert for the bright lights of avenue Louise, Woit uses luxurious materials to create garments with a bold, girlie and lightheartedly glamorous feel. Accessories – hats, scarves, bags and jewellery adorned with semi-precious stones – are integral to the overall look.

Nina Meert

1-5 rue St-Boniface (02 514 22 63, www.nina meert.be). Métro Porte de Namur, or bus 71. **Open** 11am-7pm Tue-Sat. **Map** p137 B3 ㉓ **Fashion**

Nina Meert was born into a family of painters and worked at Pucci in Florence and Cacharel in Paris before opening her own shop in Brussels in 1979. Isabelle Adjani and Meryl Streep are among the famous names who have worn her creations, which are simple, comfortable and made from natural fibres such as wool and silk. Her top-notch knitwear collection is also very successful.

Y-Enzo

27 Galerie Espace Louise (02 514 65 68, www.y-enzo.be). Métro Louise. **Open** 10am-6.30pm Mon-Sat. **Map** p137 B1 ㉔ **Accessories**

Ultra-upmarket footwear by Yves Saint Laurent, Gucci, Stephane Kélian and Dirk Bikkembergs, among others, plus a limited number of designer bags and clothes.

Zadig & Voltaire

92 avenue Louise (02 514 24 40, www.zadig-et-voltaire.com). Métro Louise, or tram 93, 94.
Open 10am-6.30pm Mon-Fri; 10.30am-7pm Sat.
Map p137 C2 ㉕ **Fashion & accessories**
High-quality, ready-to-wear tops, cardigans and footwear from this sassy if pricey Paris boutique (look out for occasional price cuts). There's men's, women's and children's wear at no.92, and a more select choice for women and children at no.80. Over on Antoine Dansaert, it's for women only.
Other locations 80 avenue Louise, Ixelles (02 502 54 93); 73 rue Antoine Dansaert, St-Géry (02 514 05 24).

WEST OF AVENUE LOUISE

By far the best way to experience avenue Louise is to catch a tram – the 93 or 94 – which run from place Louise and glide the length of the boulevard to the Bois de la Cambre. This is where foreign money and Belgian inheritances are spent in the big-name boutiques that line each side of the city's own Fifth Avenue. In recent years, though, steep rents have forced many of the best-known Belgian names off this prize square on the Monopoly board. Alarm bells rang when Olivier Strelli, a long-established clothes designer of Italian and Congolese provenance whose scarves have adorned Mick Jagger and Brigitte Bardot, shut up shop. Like Strelli, other Belgian companies have opted for a web-only enterprise, and the larger Italian, French and Spanish chains have duly moved in. Many local designers have helped create a new buzz around place Brugmann, in the far south-west corner of Ixelles, near where the commune meets St-Gilles and Forest.

Halfway along avenue Louise, running west, is rue du Bailli. Here, and on the surrounding streets that converge around place du Châtelain, you'll find gift shops, clothing and shoe boutiques, and hip but affordable restaurants. The area has a neighbourhood feel despite throngs of bright young things drawn by its buzzy nightlife; the great food market on Châtelain every Wednesday afternoon helps engender the communal vibe. Several art galleries, particularly from France, have set up around here and Sablon; one such is **La Maison Particulière**.

Rue du Page, which runs south-west off place du Châtelain, is home to some of Brussels' most enduring restaurants, while the small square of parvis de la Trinité, to the north-west, is an assemblage of graceful houses around a lovely church, which looks as if it might well belong somewhere in Latin America.

Further south on avenue Louise, near the Abbaye, look out for an unusual bust in the wide grassy space between the dual-lane highway. It's a likeness of a heroic Belgian pilot, looking towards the innocuous-looking apartment building at 453 avenue Louise. In World War II, this was a Gestapo base for surveillance and detention. Jean-Michel de Selys Longchamp, returning to Kent on a mission with the RAF, went solo and diverted to Brussels. Flying his Typhoon in low, he destroyed great lumps of the façade, killing a top Gestapo officer. Selys Longchamp was both demoted and awarded the Distinguished Flying Cross, in recognition of his insubordination and his bravery. Seven months later, he was killed over Ostend.

Avenue Louise then makes a slight swing to the right; one block westward on rue de l'Abbaye is the **Musée Meunier**, which displays just over a quarter of the artist's prolific output. Once you reach the Bois de la Cambre, you're at the city's green belt, which stretches as far as Flanders.

EXPLORE

Belgikie.
See p141.

Sights & Museums

★ Maison Particulière
49 rue du Châtelain (02 649 81 78, www.maison particuliere.be). Tram 93, 94. **Open** 11am-6pm Tue-Sun. **Admission** €10; free under-26s. **Map** p136 E2

A private art centre thrown open to the public by its founders, Myriam and Amaury de Solages, the Maison Particulière typifies Brussels' thriving gallery scene. The pair renovated a graceful townhouse dating from 1880 to create a striking, three-storey space for regular shows by contemporary Belgian artists, and set up their own non-profit organisation for the outside world to appreciate them. Nothing is for sale – here, exposure is the key, and the discovery of a relaxing, inspirational space .

FREE Musée Meunier
59 rue de l'Abbaye (02 648 44 49, www.fine-arts-museum.be). Tram 93, 94, or bus 38. **Open** 10am-noon, 12.45-5pm Tue-Fri. **Admission** free. **Map** p136 G3 ⑰

The house and studio of the renowned 19th-century Belgian artist is home to more than 170 of his sculptures and 120 of his paintings; the best known are his bronze figures of workers. Meunier began painting religious scenes, but turned to sculpture inspired by social realism: farmers, miners and workers heroically labour in grim surroundings.

Restaurants

CO2
46 rue du Page (02 537 80 47, www.restaurant-co2.be). Tram 81, or bus 54. **Open** noon-2.30pm Mon; noon-2.30pm, 7-11pm Tue-Fri; 7-11pm Sat. **Main courses** €16-€25. **Map** p136 F1 ⑳ **Modern European**

CO2 – named after patrons Christian and Oliver – is very much part of the trendy Châtelain set where locals drop in for a drink and some mixed tapas, or brasserie-style food such as beef tartare, steak or scallops. What hits you first is the burst of colour, either from the red-orange seating and walls or the light effects hitting the walls. In the evening, they have access to the car showroom next door and set up another fairy-lit bar area. It's fun and funky without taking itself too seriously.

★ Le Fils de Jules
35 rue du Page (02 534 00 57, www.filsdejules.be). Tram 81, or bus 54. **Open** 7-11pm Mon-Thur; 7pm-midnight Fri, Sat; noon-11pm Sun. **Main courses** €21-€27. **Map** p136 F1 ㉙ **French**

Jules is an integral part of Châtelain, pulling in classy urbanites hungry for its authentic French foodie experience. The difference here is that the menu is firmly based in the Landais and Basque region, with dripping duck products, chunks of fish, thick lentils and salardaise potatoes drenched in

Maison Particulière.

garlic. The wine list is a discovery too, with its illegible local-language labels. The decor blends New York art deco and 1970s copper, but the punters add the real colour; the set Sunday evening menu (€29.50) ensures a full house.

Kamo
550A chaussée de Waterloo (02 264 78 48).
Tram 93, 94, or bus 60. **Open** 7-10pm Mon; noon-2pm, 7-10pm Tue-Sat. **Set menu** €50-€85. **Map** p136 G2  **Japanese**

Kamo moved to new premises in 2014 and is looking slickly light and airy with its bleached woods and Zen-like simplicity. Something extraordinary happens here – the ever-packed restaurant serves the best sashimi, sushi and kaisendon in town. It's why Michelin awarded it a star. Down a glass or two of *umeshu* (a sweet and sour plum wine) and Brussels becomes a little more like Tokyo with every passing moment.

La Porte des Indes
455 avenue Louise (02 647 86 51, www.laporte desindes.com). Tram 93, 94. **Open** noon-2.30pm, 7-10.30pm Mon-Thur; noon-2.30pm, 7-11pm Fri, Sat; 7-10.30pm Sun. **Main courses** €22. **Map** p136 H4 **Indian**

Not for the curry-and-pint-of-Kingfisher crowd, this. La Porte is refined and expensive, hushed and cushioned, decorated in Maharajah baroque with vast palms and over-the-top lighting and artefacts. It's the perfect backdrop for the top-notch southern Indian food (with nods to the north). A dish from the royal court of Hyderabad – lamb cutlets soaked in garam masala, ginger and lemon – is an example of the finesse and careful balance achieved in the kitchen. Dress well and expect to spend liberally.

La Quincaillerie
45 rue du Page (02 533 98 33, www.quincaillerie. be). Tram 81, or bus 54. **Open** noon-2pm, 7pm-midnight Mon-Sat; 7pm-midnight Sun. **Main courses** €13-€38. **Map** p136 F1 **Brasserie**

The name means ironmonger, but this isn't any old theme restaurant. The fine interior is largely untouched, the tables set with the original wooden drawers for holding nails, screws and widgets. A cast-iron gallery circles the ensemble, overlooked by a giant clock. The seafood bar, piled with crustaceans, is considered one of the best in the city, and the restaurant attracts a wealthy set. It's puzzling that the service is often abrupt, even rude, although that doesn't seem to scare anyone off – you'll need to book for any night of the week.

Pubs & Bars

Café de la Presse
493 avenue Louise (02 644 48 03, www.cafedela presse.be). Tram 93, 94. **Open** 7.30am-8pm Mon-Fri; 8.30am-8pm Sat, Sun. **Map** p136 H4

Winery. See p146.

On the corner of avenue Louise and rue Émile Claus, this café was opened in 2011 by François Lafontaine, who has since become something of a local coffee guru. Among his several other venues proffering high-quality joe is the Café du Sablon (*see p111*) in the Upper Town. The formula was first, and most successfully, tried at this café, thanks to its large size, high turnover and young, chattering clientele. Those between jobs spend entire afternoons here, caning the Wi-Fi, sipping slowly from a mug of Costa Rica's finest and maybe indulging in a board game or two.

Le Châtelain
17 place du Châtelain (02 538 67 94). Tram 81, or bus 54. **Open** 11am-1am Mon-Fri; 5pm-1am Sat. **No credit cards. Map** p136 E2

A real locals' place right on place du Châtelain, but a world away from the surrounding trendy eateries and boutiques. Out front, it's a bar, with regulars holding court of a late afternoon under the gaze of stage and screen stars; note the large painted portrait of Jacques Brel and original theatre handbills. At the back, it's a restaurant, serving solid local dishes, should the need arise. In its entirety, Le Châtelain pretends to be nothing more than it is – a refreshing attitude in this part of town.

Michael Collins
1 rue du Bailli (02 644 61 21, www.michael collins.eu). Tram 93, 94. **Open** 10am-3am daily. **Map** p136 E2

Occupying an old residential building on a prominent corner of avenue Louise, this Irish pub and restaurant is more upscale than its Celtic counterparts in town – but perfectly approachable for a Premier League Sunday afternoon. Equally, the pub grub is a notch above (Irish striploin steak with sautéed mushrooms or spicy bloody mary pasta, for example), and there's a full range of bottled Belgian

EXPLORE

beers (Tripel Karmeliet, Westmalle Tripel) to complement the draught Kilkenny and Guinness. Pub quizzes and live music fill the agenda on Mondays and Fridays respectively, and the back courtyard is handy when it's three-deep at the bar during big game nights.

★ Winery
18 place Brugmann (02 345 47 17, www. winery.be). Bus 60. **Open** *11am-8pm Mon-Sat.*
This is a clever little venture, attached to a wine shop in the shadows of the old church on the square. Wine bars aren't that prevalent in Brussels, but this place has attracted a goodly local crowd who appreciate its unpretentious decor and prices. In fact, it doesn't look like a wine bar at all, with its black and white tiled floor and tall, pale wood tables. *Photo p145.*
► *Winery has another branch in the EU Quarter, at rue 17 Justes Lipse (02 231 69 89).*

Shops & Services

Châtelain Market
5 place du Châtelain (no phone). Tram 81, or bus 54. **Open** *2-7pm Wed.* **No credit cards.** **Map** p136 E2 ⑳ **Market**
Wednesday afternoons bring flowers, organic fruit and veg, Italian sausage and burrata, wild mushrooms and artisanal goats' cheese to place du Châtelain. There are also home-made quiches, thai wok dishes and an impressive rôtisserie slowly roasting chicken, ribs and belly pork. There's even a traditional Belgian butcher with sides of beef, veal

chops, pigs' trotters, tongue and brain. It's not cheap – but this is something that doesn't exist anywhere else in Brussels in quite the same way.

Crossword
79 avenue Louise (02 537 42 26, www.crossword-brussels.be). Métro Louise, or tram 93, 94. **Open** *10am-6.30pm Mon-Sat.* **Map** p137 C1 ㊲ **Fashion**
Sophistication itself, Crossword is where the modern gentleman should go for classic jackets, silk ties, brand-name shirts and even cufflinks, by the likes of Ravazzolo, Raffaele Caruso and Mazzarelli. Two other branches nearby provide the full kit and caboodle for every occasion.
Other locations Crossword – Casual Attitude, Galerie de la Toison d'Or, Ixelles (02 511 03 54). Crossword – Shirt & Shoes, Galerie Espace Louise 13-14, Ixelles (02 512 58 92).

Les Enfants d'Edouard
175-177 avenue Louise (02 640 42 45, www. lesenfantsdedouard.net). Tram 93, 94. **Open** *10am-6.30pm Mon-Sat.* **Map** p137 D2 ㊳ **Fashion**
Edouard's Children sells second-hand designer labels and end-of-line stock. It's all in excellent condition, and as a result prices can lean towards the expensive. Brands include Guess, Balmain, Charles Jourdan and Ferragamo.

Eva Luna
41 rue du Bailli (02 647 46 45, www.evaluna.be). Tram 92, 94. **Open** *1-6.30pm Mon; 11am-2pm, 2.30-6.30pm Tue-Sat.* **Map** p136 E2 ㊴ **Accessories**

Maison Degand.

Eva Luna describes itself as a love shop rather than a lingerie retailer, and sells not only romantic, sexy and sassy underwear, but also the fragrant massage oils and cheeky sex toys to go with them. Designed primarily for women, the shop is soft and sensual.

Librarie Nijinski

15-17 rue du Page (02 539 20 29). Tram 81, or bus 54. **Open** 11am-7pm Mon-Sat. **No credit cards. Map** p136 F1 ⑩ **Books & music**
This large second-hand store sells books in many languages, including English. A play area has toys and children's books in English too. Staff are relaxed and friendly, and prices are reasonable.

★ Maison Degand

415 avenue Louise (02 649 00 73, www.degand.be). Tram 93, 94. **Open** 10am-6.30pm Mon-Sat. **Map** p136 G4 ⑪ **Fashion & accessories**
Maison Degand, housed in a grand fin-de-siècle mansion with most of the original interior preserved, sells luxury clothes for men and women, including made-to-measure suits and cashmere sweaters. It also stocks accessories, such as cufflinks, ties, cravats, cigar cutters and hip flasks. The annex sells more casual weekend wear.

Rose

56-58 rue de l'Aqueduc (02 534 98 08, www.rose shop.be). Tram 81, or bus 54. **Open** 10.30am-6pm Mon; 10.30am-6.30pm Tue-Sat. **Map** p136 F1 ⑫ **Accessories**
Rose was established in 2003 by Elodie Gleis, who gave up a job in advertising to open this temple to all things girlie. She sells a mix of decorative objects for the home, fashion accessories and small gifts, which she sources from different parts of Europe.

Serneels

69 avenue Louise (02 538 30 66, www.serneels.be). Métro Louise. **Open** 9.30am-6.30pm Mon-Fri. **Map** p137 C1 ⑬ **Toys**
Just about every toy a little heart could desire is stocked at this deluxe store – at high-flying prices. There are modern electronic favourites, as well as beautiful traditional toys and puzzles.

THE SOUTH

Beyond Ixelles spreads a vast swathe of greenery. Not too long ago it was the Forêt de Soignes, the hunting ground of the Dukes of Brabant. The forest's northern tip is the **Bois de la Cambre** (Apr-Sept 6am-10pm daily; Oct-Mar 7am-9pm daily), located at the end of avenue Louise some four kilometres (2.4 miles) from the city centre. One of Brussels' biggest open spaces, it was first formally laid out in the then-popular English style in 1861, though the immense mature trees are testament to its earlier days. It's perfect for picnickers, joggers and cyclists – traffic does

pass through but is severely restricted at weekends, with certain roads closed altogether. In the middle is a lake, shaped like an apostrophe, with an island containing the **Châlet Robinson** restaurant, accessible only by boat.

During the 18th and 19th centuries, the forested area decreased considerably, and over 20,000 oaks were felled on Napoléon's orders to build the Boulogne flotilla. The English, meanwhile, were playing cricket. The Bois de la Cambre was where some of Wellington's troops

IN THE KNOW
PLACE BRUGMANN

With rents so high on avenue Louise and rue Antoine Dansaert in downtown, a cluster of Belgian designers decided to set up shop around place Brugmann, as far southwest as you can go in Ixelles without being in St-Gilles. Eyebrows were already raised when Frédéric de Thibault set up **Winery** (*see p146*) here, in the shadow of the old church, in 2005. When Belgium's leading sommelier Eric Boschmann and star chef Christelle Verheyden began running a Saturday food and wine club at this trendy wine bar, Brugmann was on the map.

Then designers Sandrina Fasoli and Michael Marson (graduates of the National School of Visual Arts at Abbaye de la Cambre, also in south Ixelles) opened an outlet for their fashion label on Brugmann: **Sandrina Fasoli** (www.sandrinafasoli.com) specialises in fresh, refined womenswear with a slight touch of nostalgia. In 2010, they were joined by **Wouters & Hendrix** (www.wouters-hendrix.com), fashionable jewellers from Antwerp's Royal Academy of Fine Arts, whose pieces adorn the shelves of Liberty and La Garçonne. Fellow jeweller Pili Collado, creator of **Les Précieuses**, now has shops on both Antoine Dansaert (*see p80*) and Brugmann. *Parfumière* Anne Pascale Mathy-Devalck has a gorgeous store (created by architect Olivier Hannaert and designer Michel Penneman) for her personalised scents at **L'Antichambre** (www.l-antichambre.com).

In the vicinity, you'll also find desirable accessories at **Graphie Sud** (www.graphie sud.com), pre-owned fashion by Chanel, Dior and Balenciaga at **Pièce Unique** (www.piece-unique.com) and on-trend eatiere **Brasserie Plasch** (www.plasch.be). It's not all chic, however – vintners and designers love taking their offspring to **Le Balmoral** (www.lebalmoral.be), a family-friendly, US-style milk bar.

EXPLORE

EXPLORE

gathered before what would be the Battle of Waterloo. A bronze plaque, laid 150 years afterwards, marks the spot where the game took place, a lawn now called the Pelouse des Anglais.

Hugging the west side of the Bois, the chaussée de Waterloo leads south to the famed village of the same name, although the battlefield itself is closer to nearby Braine-l'Alleud – *see p150* **Battle Stations**. The victorious Wellington had the right to give it a name; he chose Waterloo as he had spent the previous night there. His Prussian ally, Gebhard von Blücher, whose decisive action turned the battle, wanted to call it La Belle Alliance, the inn where the two commanders had met afterwards. Wellington, as ever, won the day.

South-east of Bois de la Cambre, villages such as **Watermael-Boitsfort** (www.watermael-boitsfort.be) make for fine afternoons out by virtue of their bucolic setting. With 24,000 inhabitants, W-B hits the spot between city and country. Expats love the village feel, large houses and the huge International School here. Watermael and Boitsfort were entirely separate entities until Napoleon combined them by imperial decree in 1811. They still have separate railway stations; Watermael's is a pretty little design from 1844.

Watermael-Boitsfort's three main squares are Bischofsheim, Gilson and Wiener, a good place to get off the no.94 tram from town. The Sunday morning market provides the focus for village life, with spice stalls, authentic Spanish food, Thai goodies and a farm dairy selling cheese, fresh milk and cream. Boitsfort is known for its parks and sculpture gardens. Up in Watermael, the attractive little church of St-Clément (50 rue du Loutrier, 02 672 52 29) has a tower dating from the tenth century. From here it's only a short walk to café-lined place Keym.

Moving further east along the green belt, well-to-do **Woluwe-St-Pierre** is a suitable setting for the two-star Michelin restaurant, **Bon-Bon**.

One of the many wealthy foreign residents who settled in the quieter climes of south Brussels was Dutch banker David van Buuren. In 1928, he built an art deco house at 41 avenue Léo Errera (on the west side of the Bois de la Cambre). Later opened as the **Musée David et Alice van Buuren**, it combines art, architecture and landscaping to stunning effect. Beyond the museum extends plenty of verdant greenery – perhaps the most charming example being the expansive **Parc de Wolvendael**, owned by successive royals through the centuries.

Elsewhere, the forest is divided between the leafy southern and eastern communes. In Forest and Uccle, green patches such as the **Parc de Forest** and **Parc Duden** were set aside for urban use in the 19th century. The houses are notably less elegant and the shops notably cheaper. Further south stretch the sedate, suburban streets of the city's largest commune, **Uccle**, a quaint

area filling up fast with *nouveaux riches* eager for green surrounds near town. Cutting right through the area, the lengthy chaussée d'Alsemberg is dotted with spots such as **Bar du Matin**. Further on, the **Bistro Dikkenek**, opposite Calevoet train stop, takes its name and its theme from the 2006 movie that was partly filmed here.

Sights & Museums

★ Musée David et Alice van Buuren
41 avenue Léo Errera (02 343 48 51, www. museumvanbuuren.com). Tram 3, 7. **Open** *Museum & garden* 2-5.30pm Mon, Wed-Sun. **Admission** *Museum* €10; €5-€8 reductions. *Garden* €5. **No credit cards**.
Every object here – even the custom-made piano – conforms to the highly polished lines of the art deco movement favoured by its pre-war owner, David van Buuren. His large art collection, spanning five centuries, is remarkable; there's a version of Bruegel's *Landscape with the Fall of Icarus*, as well as works by Ensor, Wouters and Van de Woestijne (a friend of the Van Buurens), plus a Braque, and a Van Gogh sketch of *The Potato Eaters*. A framed letter from David Ben Gurion shows the Van Buurens' dedication to the Zionist cause. Outside, the garden is laid out in a maze designed by René Pechère.

Restaurants

Les 2 Frères
2 avenue Vanderaey, Uccle (02 376 76 06, www. les2freres.be). Tram 92, 97. **Open** noon-2.30pm, 7-11pm Mon-Fri; 7-11pm Sat. **Main courses** €17-€27. Belgian
Ex-maths teacher Patrick Roth has created an unusual equation between rustic and urban in this classy French brasserie. The clubby feel and two impressive terraces make you feel you're living the high life. There's no messing with the food; what you see is what you get, but the straightforward dishes of meat, fish and seafood are cooked to perfection. When the kitchen closes, the 2 Frères turns into a bar.

★ Bon-Bon
453 avenue de Tervuren, Woluwe-St-Pierre (02 346 66 15, www.bon-bon.be). Tram 44. **Open** 7-9.30pm Mon; 12.30-1.30pm, 7.30-9pm Tue-Fri. **Set menu** lunch €80, dinner €155-€220. French
Grey upholstery and dark natural wood contrast nicely with crisp white linen in this classy restaurant. Young chef Christophe Hardiquest honed his skills at some of Brussels' top establishments, including Sea Grill, La Villa Lorraine and the Conrad Brussels hotel. He and his team are pure artisans, crafting each day's menu from the best seasonal ingredients. It might be fish in a salt crust or gazpacho of white pearl oysters, but you won't know until you get there. Flavours come with a strong Med influence and – naturally for its two-Michelin-star status – top-whack prices.

Les Brasseries Georges

259 avenue Winston Churchill, Uccle (02 347 21 00, www.brasseriesgeorges.be). Tram 7, 38. **Open** noon-12.30am Mon-Thur, Sun; noon-1am Fri, Sat. **Main courses** €15-€48. Brasserie

Here, the feel of a fin-de-siècle Parisian brasserie is generated to perfection by the twisting copper and brass, the vast stained-glass windows, potted palms and statuettes of classical muses, all revealed as you pass the obligatory red curtain. The speciality is crustacea: perhaps a starter of oysters or whelks, or a vast plateau de fruits de mer.

★ Châlet Robinson

1 sentier de l'Embarcadère, Bois de la Cambre (02 372 92 92, www.chaletrobinson.be). Tram 25, 94. **Open** noon-2.30pm, 7-11pm Mon-Sat; noon-10pm Sun. Closed Mon, Tue Nov-Mar. **Main courses** €16-€28. Belgian

Set on an island in the middle of a lake (acesss is by a small electric ferry), the Châlet Robinson has been in operation since 1877 – though the original was destroyed by fire in 1991. Reopened in 2006, it remains a favourite spot for lunch. The massive cedar building has terraces down to the lake. There are classic Belgian dishes, but you can also just have an ice-cream or cocktail under umbrellas at the waterside. It's a lovely experience by day or night, as is the park itself.

Pubs & Bars

Bon-Bon.

★ Bar du Matin

172 chaussée d'Alsemberg, Forest (02 537 71 59, http://bardumatin.blogspot.be). Tram 3, 4, or bus 54. **Open** 8am-1am Mon-Wed, Sun; 8am-2am Thur-Sat.

This is the *bar du jour*, just inside the border where Forest meets St-Gilles meets Ixelles, where DJ Kwak spins tunes and savvy creatives converge for apéritifs of a late afternoon. It's another Frédéric Nicolay production, all urban chic and large bay windows, but the verdant location means he's breaking new ground, location-wise.

Bistro Dikkenek

2 Dieweg, Uccle (02 374 47 19, www.facebook.com/ bistrodikkenek). Train Uccle-Calevoet, or bus 60. **Open** 10.30am-10pm Tue-Wed, Sun; 10.30am-midnight Thur-Fri; 4pm-midnight Sat.

Wine bar, gastropub and billiard hall, Bistro Dikkenek is named and themed after the 2006 film *Dikkenek*, typified by its dark, bar-stool humour. Every table bears the name of one of the characters. What saves a cult classic from being a flop, bar-wise, is the pub itself, its huge windows observing the steady coming and going of trains from its quiet corner location. Time stands still amid the authentic old-fashioned decor, as old locals chug back the Chouffes while trendier, younger types sip pinot grigio and wonder what all the fuss is about.

EXPLORE

BATTLE STATIONS

It's 200 years since the Battle of Waterloo.

On 19 June 2015, Napoleon met his Waterloo. Again. Dressed in crisp replica uniforms, 5,000 men gathered in the fields south of Waterloo to re-enact the battle that determined the future of Europe. A French lawyer played the part of Napoleon, while a New Zealand events consultant stood in for the Duke of Wellington. They faced each other across rolling fields, 11 miles south of Brussels, to recreate one of the most significant battles in human history.

Two hundred years may have passed since Waterloo was fought, but this one-day encounter is still remembered all over the world. It has given its name to dozens of towns in the United States, Canada and Australia, as well as a London railway station, an Amsterdam square and a song by Abba. Even now, commemoration of the battle can spark off international tension, as the Belgian mint discovered in early 2015 when it was forced by France to scrap a €2 coin minted to mark the bicentenary.

Not long after the battle was fought, curious tourists travelled from Brussels to look at the fields where Napoleon's dreams of empire were finally crushed and a new European order was shaped by the British, German and Dutch victors. It soon became a popular subject for novelists and poets, including Tolstoy, Hugo, Thackeray and Byron. By the early 20th century, the Belgian government realised that it needed to preserve the battlefield from developers. It classified the site as a protected monument in 1914, just a few months before other Belgian fields were turned once more into muddy battlegrounds.

Yet the local authorities have failed to make Waterloo into a world-class historical site. It doesn't help that the battlefield itself lies on the border of several communes or that the main road from Brussels to Charleroi crosses the site. Key historic spots are also scattered, making it difficult to track down the hidden farmhouses, sunken lanes and roadside inns that shaped the outcome of the battle.

But things are improving at last. The Walloon government – now responsible for the site – recently launched an ambitious €40 million plan to improve the battlefield area. Several ugly buildings were demolished, including a dilapidated waxworks museum, and the sprawling car park was discreetly hidden from sight.

The main attraction for visitors has always been the Lion Mound, a 40-metre (130-foot) earth pyramid, built in the 1820s by migrant women from Liège, on the spot where the Prince of Orange was wounded as he led his Dutch troops. A steep flight of steps climbs to the summit, from where you can look down on the entire battlefield. At the foot, a circular neoclassical building contains the Panorama, a fascinating circular fresco of the battle painted to commemorate its first centenary. It's so huge – 110 metres (360 feet) long, 12 metres (40 feet) high – that it's a highly immersive experience viewing it. One of

EXPLORE

the last remaining such pictures in the world, it was created in 1912 by a French artist who patriotically depicted a moment when the French had the upper hand.

The dull visitor centre next to the Panorama was replaced in 2015 by a new underground complex. Here, visitors are plunged into a high-tech battlefield experience complete with pounding rain and lightning flashes.

But to understand the battle properly you need to tramp across the open fields. You can take a rough trail across the battlefield, beginning on the windswept ridge where Wellington positioned his troops, following the sunken lanes where French horses tumbled to the ground and ending up on the distant ridge where Napoleon watched in the late afternoon as his battle plan fell apart.

Hidden from sight is Hougoumont, an old walled farm where British troops held back repeated French assaults. Still visible today are the bullet holes in the farmhouse walls and the bare trees blasted to death by cannon fire. The abandoned buildings were restored in 2015 by the UK's Landmark Trust, which now rents out the former gardener's cottage as a holiday home.

There is still more to see scattered around the edge of the battlefield, including the modest country inn where Napoleon spent his last night as a military leader. A few miles to the north, in Waterloo town, is a larger inn where Wellington slept on the eve of battle (and Lord Uxbridge had his leg amputated the next day). The old inn now contains the excellent Wellington Museum (chaussée de Bruxelles 147,

02 357 28 60, www.museewellington.be) with various mementoes of the battle.

Across the road, the town's neoclassical church is filled with memorials to dead British officers. Other monuments – French, British and Prussian – can be found scattered across the site. But the largest monument of all, a bronze statue of Britannia surrounded by three lions, erected in 1890, stands almost forgotten in a corner of Brussels municipal cemetery close to the NATO headquarters.

The Walloon government wants to turn Waterloo into a battlefield site to match Gettysburg in the US. But it might turn out to be a long battle.

Waterloo Battlefield

www.waterloo1815.be. **Open** *Apr-Sept* 9.30am-6.30pm daily. *Oct-Mar* 10am-5pm daily. **Admission** €7-€13.50; €4.50-€8 reductions.

Access to the battlefield is free and unrestricted, but you have to pay to visit the Lion Mound, Panorama, Napoleon's headquarters and visitor centre.

The easiest way to reach Waterloo from Brussels is by bus – the W or less frequent 365 – from Midi station operated by TEC (www.infotec.be). The journey takes 50 minutes to the centre of Waterloo town, where you can visit the Wellington Museum, then another ten minutes to the battlefield site. A one-day ticket covers all travel. You can also catch a train from Midi to Waterloo (journey time 17 minutes), walk ten minutes into the town centre, and then catch a bus to the battlefield.

EXPLORE

St-Gilles

The atmospheric residential area of St-Gilles is an easy tram hop from Gare du Midi. The sprawl of this hilly, multicultural commune covers the estuary of rail tracks around the station, but its heart is the parvis de St-Gilles. A pedestrianised main square with a constant daytime bustle, the parvis hosts a produce market five days a week and several excellent bars. It's crossed by the chaussée de Waterloo, the main road that starts at the northern tip of St-Gilles, guarded by the vast Porte de Hal, a medieval city gate that was revamped in neo-Gothic style in the 19th century and is now a museum. The chaussée continues southwards to the urban hub of the Barrière de St-Gilles, then on to the district's imposing Hôtel de Ville. Between the two is the transport stop of Horta, named after St-Gilles' favourite son, art nouveau architect Victor, who was responsible for many of the strikingly beautiful houses that dot the streets between here and Ixelles. One of which is his own house, now a museum and the main reason to visit here.

Brasserie de l'Union.

Don't Miss

1 Musée Horta Discover Horta's home (p154).

2 Parvis de St-Gilles Bars aplenty and a food market too (p154).

3 Porte de Hal Medieval city gate, now a museum with views (p154).

4 Midi Market Piles of olives and bunches of bright flowers (p156).

5 Brasserie de l'Union A fine bar, home to fans of the revered Union St-Gilloise football team (p157).

AROUND ST-GILLES

A good starting point for any exploration of St-Gilles is the imposing landmark of **Porte de Hal**, originally a 14th-century gatehouse, now a museum. A tunnel redirects local traffic underground, so the building sits in relatively peaceful gardens. On the corner opposite are **Botkamp** (*see p170*), a new video-game hangout for teenagers, and DJ bar **Potemkine**, both recent arrivals.

St-Gilles is built on a hill that climbs roughly north to south – as the altitude increases, the changes are subtle but significant. Terraces of rooming houses and tacky shops give way to row upon row of well-groomed, middle-class townhouses, culminating in the magnificent belle époque and art nouveau mansions located around avenue Brugmann. Running south from the Porte is chaussée de Waterloo. Its northern end is generally uninspiring, dotted with the occasional ethnic restaurant. For the real St-Gilles, you need to head uphill towards the main square, the **parvis de St-Gilles**, where a market proffers fine cheeses, sausages and other local produce on Tuesdays, Wednesdays, Fridays and weekends. Overlooking the square are the keynote bars of **Barvis** and the **Brasseries de l'Union** and **Verschueren**.

Further up the hill, beyond the charming little square of Barrière de St-Gilles, where several large avenues converge, the richer St-Gilles appears; the houses are truly monumental, although the traffic and trams cutting through their midst do detract somewhat from the grandeur. Clearly visible to the south of the Barrière, occupying a commanding position at the head of avenue Dejaer, is the local **Hôtel de Ville**, an impressive 19th-century building in French Renaissance style. Designed by Albert Dumont in 1900-04, the building's most visually arresting features are the frescoes on the ceiling above the main staircase and adorning the Marriage Room.

The Hôtel de Ville was created during the commune's golden age; when a few wealthy men commissioned fabulous art nouveau residences. With their swirling, daring lines and elaborate friezes, these houses appear both flamboyant and insouciant beside their more stalwart neighbours. The majority can be found in the area south of the Barrière and to the east of the immense Prison de St-Gilles. Most are closed to the public, but one striking exception is architect Victor Horta's own house, the **Musée Horta**.

The prison, the place where heroic World War I nurse Edith Cavell was incarcerated for ten weeks, two in solitary confinement, is in keeping with its genteel surrounds, bisected by pleasant avenue de la Jonction. At the head of the avenue is the art nouveau Hôtel Hannon, built in 1902

by Jules Brunfaut. The building is currently closed for long-term renovation; the **Contretype** photography gallery it formerly housed has moved to near Porte de Hal.

To the west of the prison extends the accessible greenery of the **Parc de Forest** and **Parc Duden**. Here is where you'll find the **Stade Joseph Marien**, rural home ground of local football team Union St-Gilloise (www.rusg.be). Belgium's most successful side before World War II, they still engender local support – hence the touches of yellow and blue in bars such as the Brasserie de l'Union.

Sights & Museums

FREE Contretype

4A Cité Fontainas (02 538 42 20, www.contretype. org). Métro/pré-métro Porte de Hal. **Open** noon-6pm Wed-Fri; 1-6pm Sat, Sun. **Admission** free. **Map** p155 A3 ❶

Having moved out of the Hôtel Hannon, this gallery of contemporary photography, set up by Jean-Louis Godefroid in 1978, hosts regular exhibitions by local and European artists.

★ Musée Horta

25 rue Américaine (02 543 04 90, www.horta museum.be). Tram 81, 91, 92, 97, or bus 54. **Open** 2-5.30pm Tue-Sun. **Admission** €8; €4 reductions; €2.50 6-18s. **No credit cards.** **Map** p155 D6 ❷

Victor Horta built this house in 1899-1901 as his home and studio. The exterior is plain enough, and is nothing compared to the Paul Hankar-designed house round the corner in rue Defacqz. This external reticence is fairly typical of an architect who was Belgian enough to want to keep his delights hidden away indoors. The interior is astonishingly light, graceful and harmonious. It was clearly designed as a place to live in; there's no attempt to dazzle or disturb. The attention to detail is astonishing, with every functional element, even the door handles, designed in the fluid, sensuous architectural style Horta helped to create. The staircase and stairwell are particularly breathtaking: an extravaganza of wrought iron, mirrors and floral designs, topped by a stained-glass canopy. A word of warning: the museum is often very crowded and even Horta's wonderful staircase loses its appeal when you have to queue to climb it.

▶ *For more on art nouveau, see pp256-260.*

Porte de Hal

150 boulevard de Midi (02 533 34 50, www. kmkg.be). Métro/pré-métro Porte de Hal. **Open** 9.30am-5pm Tue-Fri; 10am-5pm Sat, Sun. **Admission** €5; €1.50-€4 reductions; free under-6s. **No credit cards. Map** p155 A3 ❸

At the junction where St-Gilles meets the Petit Ring, this is the sole surviving medieval gate of the

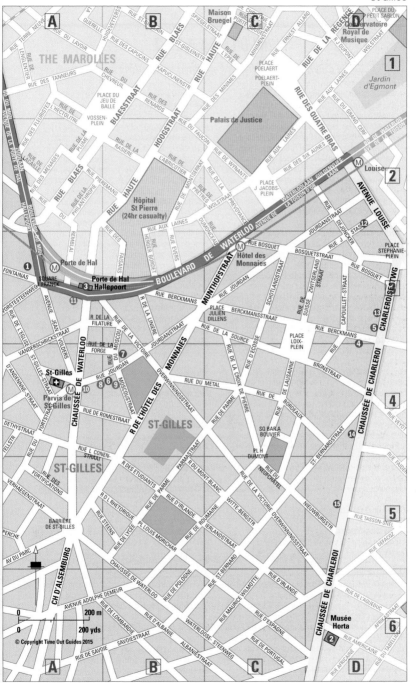

EXPLORE

EXPLORE

MIDI MARKET

Get down to Gare du Midi for a bargain-hunting bonanza.

The new development around and under the Gare du Midi is a real urban travesty, bleak by day and barren at night. Yet come here on a Sunday morning (7am-1pm) and you'll find one of Europe's biggest and brightest markets in full swing – the brilliant **Midi Market**.

One of the greatest frustrations of visiting markets when you're abroad is that you can't buy much of the stuff you want: the cheese will be too smelly, and that cheap crate of avocados won't last the journey. Of the 450 stalls at Midi, though, around half are non-comestibles. The clothing section alone is vast; you'll need to develop a strong sense of what is tat and what is not (though the €3 price tags on the bras give a good indication). Better value and quality are the kids' clothes, and basics such as T-shirts and socks.

Do take in the food, even if you can't take it home. Most of the stallholders are North African, and peddle their wares with all the catcalling vim and vigour of downtown Marrakech. Fruit and veg comes in a wave

of towering primary colours and is sold individually, in boxes or by the bag (you'll be given a plastic carrier to fill yourself). Bunches of fragrant herbs are stacked high, but it's the olive stalls that truly impress, with every colour, size, marinade and sauce imaginable – if you're not sure, one will be thrust at you to taste. These stalls are also excellent for nuts, dried fruit, dates and figs.

Another highlight is the flower and plant section. Imagine a whole street brimming with cut roses, tulips and bargain mixed bunches. You'll also be near-blinded by the fluorescent sweep of bedding plants; Belgians have a weakness for bright red geraniums and begonias.

So what else can you get your hands on? Well, what do you want? Coffeepots, toys, phone covers, tablecloths, foam rubber offcuts, shoes, purses, handbags, tools, mops and bin bags; it's all there. And through it all comes the thumping of the latest Arabic disco music – available to buy on CD, of course.

many that once studded the old city walls. Over the centuries the gate has been used as a prison, a toll booth and a grain store; it was given this somewhat Disneyesque neo-Gothic touch by Henri Beyaert in the late 1860s. A spiral staircase connects its six levels, from the panoramic views atop its battlements to the entrance passageway on its own green island surrounded by rushing traffic. In between are displays relating to the role of the guilds, the history of the city's fortifications and fearsome-looking examples of weaponry and armoury. There's a temporary exhibition space too, just below the battlements.

Restaurants

Café des Spores

103 chaussée d'Alsemberg (02 534 13 03, www.cafedesspores.be). Tram 4, 51, 92. **Open** 7.30-10.30pm Tue-Sat. **Set menu** €25-€35. Modern European

Anyone for mushrooms? If not, you're better off elsewhere. At the Café des Spores, earthy fungi feature in every dish. Cartoonist-cum-chef Pierre Lefèvre has fallen in love with the humble mushroom, forever experimenting with its possibilities and describing his culinary endeavours as 'cuisine ruled by nature'. People travel from afar to try his imaginative menus, which change daily according to his mood and what's available.

▶ *Just opposite, La Buvette (www.la-buvette.be) is Pierre Lefèvre's original venture – an old horse butcher's shop transformed into a place for pre-dinner drinks.*

Cool Bun

34 rue Berckmans (02 537 80 02, www.cool-bun.be). Métro Louise, or tram 93, 94, 97. **Open** noon-3.30pm, 6.30-11pm Mon-Sat. **Main courses** €14-€28. **Map** p155 D3 ❹ Burgers *See p140* **The Burgers of Brussels**. ▶ *There's another branch of Cool Bun in the EU Quarter; see p126.*

Ma Folle de Soeur

53 chaussée de Charleroi (02 538 22 39, www. mafolledesoeur.be). Métro Louise, or tram 93, 94, 97. **Open** noon-2.30pm, 6.30-10.30pm Mon-Fri; 6.30-10.30pm Sat. **Main courses** €13-€22.50. **Map** p155 D3 ❺ Belgian/French

Run by two sisters, this small restaurant has a huge picture window facing the street and a mellow dining room, its wooden bar and tables softened by yellow walls and soft candlelight in the evening. The menu has plenty of flair and a touch of adventure – it's Belgian in nature, with French bistro influences. Office workers give way to young lovers and groups of friends in the evening. There's a back garden for summer evenings.

Brasserie de l'Union.

Maison du Peuple
*39 parvis de St-Gilles (02 850 09 08, www.
maison-du-peuple.be). Pré-métro Parvis de
St-Gilles.* **Open** 8.30am-1am Mon-Thur, Sun;
8.30am-3am Fri, Sat. **Main courses** €7-€15.
Map p155 B4 ❻ **Café**
Situated on the ground floor of a wonderful turn-of-the-century building, MdP offers a vibrant blend
of café culture, live music and art. Exhibitions and
parties are attended by an ever-so-cool but friendly
crowd, and there's an early-evening happy hour.
Breakfast is available first thing, then the kitchen
turns its attention to well-made antipasti, croque
monsieurs, quiches and panini.

Aux Mille et Une Nuits
*7 rue de Moscou (02 537 41 27, www.milleetune
nuits.be). Pré-métro Parvis de St-Gilles.* **Open**
6-11.30pm Tue-Sat. **Main courses** €11-€17.50.
Map p155 B4 ❼ **North African**
You might think twice before walking into this pink-painted Tunisian restaurant, but its full-on lighting
and kitsch decor give it an edge in an area full of
North African restaurants. It resembles a modern
Bedouin tent, with oriental rugs on the walls and
thousands of tiny lights sparkling brightly above
like stars. And the food? Out of this world. For start-ers, try the harira chickpea soup or honey-soaked
chicken in crisp pastry. And you can't go far wrong

with the caramelised lamb couscous or the chicken
tagine with grapes and honey. Service is impeccable.

Pubs & Bars

Barvis
*35 parvis de St-Gilles (no phone, www.facebook.
com/barvisdiskobar). Pré-métro Parvis de
St-Gilles.* **Open** noon-2am daily. **No credit
cards. Map** p155 A4 ❽
Convivial though St-Gilles and its parvis may be, the
word 'party' is rarely used in association with the
commune and its main square. Barvis 'Diskobar' is
at least attempting to give it some late-night welly,
though this friendly little beerhall is just as pleasant
by day. True, after dark it cranks up the volume, hav-ing provided an hour of happy drinks from 8pm and
offering a little live music – something a bit under-ground, maybe, or danceable, at least.

★ Brasserie de l'Union
*55 parvis de St-Gilles (02 538 15 79). Pré-
métro Parvis de St-Gilles.* **Open** 8am-1am
daily. **No credit cards. Map** p155 B4 ❾
A tatty-round-the-edges bohemian bar, happy to
serve the local community at large – some befriended
solely by spaniels, and deep in one-way conversa-tions – the Union consists of one large, busy room
propping up a corner of the square. Sunday morning

market browsing is accompanied by an accordionist squeezing out tunes – though nothing can quite drown out the din of children running amok. After they depart, along with the spaniels, the squeezeboxer and the senile, the night is claimed by characters from the covers of pulp-fiction novels.

★ Brasserie Verschueren

11-13 parvis de St-Gilles (02 539 40 68). Pré-métro Parvis de St-Gilles. **Open** 8am-2am Mon-Fri; 9am-2am Sat, Sun. **No credit cards. Map** p155 A4 ❿

The classier of the corner bars serving the parvis, the Verschueren twinkles with art deco touches. Three rows of tables and banquettes are waited on by rather erratic staff, safe in the knowledge that few of the boho-intellectual regulars are paying much attention; the Verschueren is simply their natural habitat, drink or no drink. If they cared to look up, they'd find a more than adequate selection of beers – including bottled rarities such as Pecheresse. Rather incongruous alongside the classic station clock and window panelling, a vast league ladder of football club names from the lower local divisions occupies the back wall, each team name delineated in bright Subbuteo colours. The bar has a Facebook page.

Chez Moeder Lambic

68 rue de Savoie (02 544 16 99, www.moeder lambic.eu). Pré-métro Horta or Albert, tram 81, 97. **Open** 4pm-3am daily. **No credit cards.**

Happy to collect dust in its own little corner, the collectors' cavern of Chez Moeder Lambic hides from the soaring St-Gilles town hall behind beer-labelled windows. Inside, it's a dark hive, with three long shelves of obscure bottles framing the bar counter and wooden tables. It would take a lifetime to sample every cobwebbed variety here – some of shabby ilk are still trying – but to pass the time, racks of comic books line one wall. Outsiders can only guesstimate the number of brews, daring to stab at 300.

▶ *Sister establishment Chez Moeder Lambic Fontainas (8 place Fontainas, 02 503 60 68) is sleek and funky, with some 40 beers on tap.*

★ Oeno TK

29-31 rue Africaine (02 534 64 34, www. facebook.com/fineworldwines). Tram 81, or bus 54. **Open** 3-8pm Mon, Tue; 1-10.30pm Wed-Sat; 3-10.30pm Thur, Fri.

Oeno is so cool, it should be kept in an ice bucket along with its vast selection of wines. Sleekly designed, with exposed brick and statement lighting, it's a place to discover and be discovered. A central table with bar seats provides a place for the glamorous people to mix and mingle. A blackboard lists special wines, most of which are available by the glass or bottle. There's also charcuterie, cheese plates and tasty little snacks such as grilled artichokes. It's also a shop, so you can taste first, then tuck a bottle in your bag for later.

EXPLORE

Potemkine Bar

2 avenue de la Porte de Hal (0486 72 26 24 mobile, www.lepotemkine.be). Métro/pré-métro Porte de Hal. **Open** 24hrs daily. **Map** p155 A3 ⓫

Rumours of the closure of this multipurpose bar have been greatly exaggerated. In the shadow of the Porte de Hal and beneath an incongruous and somewhat forlorn faux whale skeleton hanging from the ceiling, Potemkine is a wide, airy space suited to both brunch and beery evenings. The seemingly random agenda of live music and assorted performances is very hit-and-miss, and the generous opening hours have enraged local residents and politicians – but, like that pram hurtling down the Odessa steps, Potemkine keeps on going, a sound choice for a convivial drink in this no-man's-land before St-Gilles becomes St-Gilles.

Shops & Services

Dille & Kamille

16 rue Jean Stas (02 538 81 25, www.dille-kamille. be). Métro Louise. **Open** 9.30am-6.30pm Mon-Sat. **Map** p155 D2 ⓬ **Homewares**

Dille & Kamille is a chichi garden and home store. Plants and decorative baskets are at the front, while foodstuffs (olive oils, mustards, herbs, teas) are towards the back. The middle section features lots of household basics, kitchen gadgets, cookbooks and traditional wooden toys. Great for browsing.

Mig's World Wines

43 chaussée de Charleroi (02 534 77 03, www.migsworldwines.be). Métro Louise, or tram 92, 97. **Open** 11am-7pm Mon-Sat. **Map** p155 D3 ⓭ **Food & drink**

Best known for its Australian wines (owner Miguel Saelens stocks around 100 varieties), this shop also sells wines from around 30 other regions and countries. Go on a Saturday for wine tasting.

★ Mmmmh!

92 chaussée de Charleroi (02 534 23 40, www. mmmmh.be). Tram 92, 97. **Open** 10am-7pm Tue-Sat; 10am-6pm Sun. **Map** p155 D4 ⓮ **Food & drink/Homewares**

This is the city's largest one-stop shop for culinary supplies and kitchenware, stocking some 8,000 products. As well as selling oils, sauces, pans and juice extractors, Mmmmh! runs workshops and invites chefs and food writers to give talks.

Schleiper

149-151 chaussée de Charleroi (02 541 05 41, www.schleiper.com). Tram 92, 97. **Open** 10am-6.30pm Mon-Sat. **Map** p155 D5 ⓯ **Art supplies**

An excellent choice of all types of art (and some office) supplies, as well as framed artworks for sale and an efficient framing service.

Other locations 63 & 75 rue de l'Étang, Etterbeek (02 541 05 12, 02 643 39 00).

EXPLORE

Brasserie Verschueren.

The West & Laeken

The west of Brussels is a mystery even to those who have visited the Belgian capital a few times. With St-Géry and Ste-Catherine full of bars, shops and restaurants, why cross the canal? On the other side, Anderlecht, Koekelberg, Molenbeek and Jette are unlikely to feature on most visitors' lists of must-sees. Although ex-industrial, largely grey and uninspired, they are nevertheless home to a couple of appealingly offbeat attractions, including the bizarre Basilica in Koekelberg and the René Magritte Museum, set in the artist's former home in Jette. Football fans will want to make a beeline for Anderlecht – the stadium is about a ten-minute ride from downtown De Brouckère. The metro also runs to the national stadium, which is being rebuilt for Euro 2020. It forms part of the recreation zone that includes the Atomium, Bruparck and the verdant royal estate of Laeken.

EXPLORE

René Magritte Museum.

Don't Miss

1 Atomium Symbol of Brussels (p165).

2 René Magritte Museum Where the great man lived and worked (p164).

3 Serres Royales Open for just three weeks a year, but well worth a visit (p167).

4 Basilique du Sacré-Coeur Overblown mix of neo-Gothic and art deco, with a superb view (p164).

5 Église Notre-Dame de Laeken Resting place of many Belgian royals (p167).

ANDERLECHT

Type the word 'Anderlecht' into an internet search engine and the first entries refer you to RSC Anderlecht (www.rsca.be), Belgium's biggest football club. Match nights bring the football bars that stretch all the way along avenue Théo Verbeek to life. This all may change when the new national arena is built at Heysel for Euro 2020 – plans call for 'Les Mauves' to move in afterwards.

Anderlecht is a rough translation of 'love of Erasmus', after the great humanist who lived here for only five months, but whose influence on the Low Countries can still be felt to this day. The house where he stayed, **Maison d'Erasmus** (31 rue de Chapitre, 02 521 13 83, www.erasmus house.museum; open 10am-6pm Tue-Sun), is a sanctuary amid city life, where the atmosphere seems little changed over the centuries.

Like the current stadium, the majority of sights in Anderlecht are near St-Guidon métro station: the beautiful Gothic **Collégiale des Sts Pierre et Guidon** (place de la Vaillance, 02 523 02 20; open 9am-noon, 2-5pm daily) and, behind it, the 17th-century **Béguinage de l'Anderlecht**, now a museum (8 rue du Chapelain, 02 521 13 83; open 10am-noon,

2-5pm Tue-Sun). The *béguinages* were groups of lay sisterhoods whose members lived in religious communities, unbound by vows. Their charity work was prevalent across the Low Countries.

Back towards town, off rue Emile Carpentier, stands the moving **Monument aux Martyrs Juifs**; etched into its side are the names of 23,838 men, women and children taken from the Nazi collection point in Mechelen and sent to concentration camps. Not one of those listed survived. Nearby, the **Musée de la Résistance** (14 rue van Lint, 02 522 40 41; open 9am-noon, 1-4pm Mon-Tue, Thur-Fri) examines some of the secrets of Belgium's World War II experience.

Finally, close to the Petit Ring, the **Musée Bruxellois de la Gueuze** (56 rue Gheude, 02 521 49 28, www.cantillon.be; open 8.30am-5pm Mon-Fri; 10am-5pm Sat) offers a tasting tour of the city's last working brewer of Gueuze, the unusual beer that ferments naturally in Anderlecht's gloomy climate.

Restaurants

La Paix 1892
49 rue Ropsy-Chaudron (02 523 09 58, www.lapaix1892.com). Métro Clemenceau.

EXPLORE

Anderlecht.

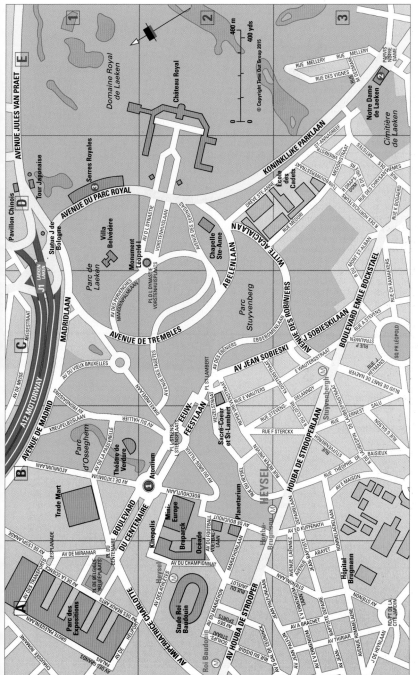

Open noon-1.45pm Mon-Thur; noon-1.45pm, 7-9pm Fri. **Main courses** €35-€46. French
La Paix is so wonderfully Brussels. There's been a restaurant here for 120 years: it originated as a place for workers in the abattoir and market opposite. Over the years it became a popular brasserie despite – or because of – its defiantly untrendy location in deepest Anderlecht. Now it's run by TV celebrity chef David Martin (he also owns the Bozar Brasserie; *see p108*) and holds a Michelin star. This doesn't mean the spirit has gone. The room of 30 tables still has its soaring ceiling, its metal pillars and wooden bar, and punters come from across the city for lunch or to fight for a place on its one evening opening.

JETTE & KOEKELBERG

The large, anonymous commune of Jette is set between the western canal districts and Laeken. Its very anonymity made it the perfect home for that most respectable and bourgeois of surrealists, René Magritte. The equally anonymous house where he lived with his wife and muse, Georgette, between 1930 and 1954 opened as the **René Magritte Museum** in 1999 – it's an essential stop for anyone with more than a passing interest in Surrealism.

The tiny border commune of Koekelberg is home to Brussels' most bizarre and overblown church, the **Basilique du Sacré Coeur**, along with a tempting recent addition, the **Belgian Chocolate Village**.

Sights & Museums

★ Basilique du Sacré-Coeur
1 parvis de la Basilique, Koekelberg (02 421 16 67, www.basilicakoekelberg.be). Métro Simonis. **Open** *Church* Summer 8am-6pm daily. Winter 10am-5pm daily. *Dome* Summer 9am-5pm daily. Winter 10am-4pm daily. **Admission** *Church* free. *Dome* €5. **No credit cards.**
Commissioned by Léopold II in 1905, this vast structure, an extraordinary mix of neo-Gothic and art deco with an illuminated cherry-coloured crucifix on top, took seven decades to finish. A climb to the gallery right under the dome allows a view as far as Mechelen Cathedral on clear days.

Belgian Chocolate Village
20 rue de Neck, Koekelberg (02 420 70 76, www.belgianchocolatevillage.be). Métro Simonis. **Open** *Term time* 9am-6pm Tue-Fri; 10am-6pm Sat, Sun. *School hols* 9am-6pm Mon-Fri; 10am-6pm Sat, Sun. **Admission** €8; €7 reductions; €5 6-18s; free under-6s.
Opened in autumn 2014, in the former Victoria biscuit factory, the Belgian Chocolate Village covers various aspects of the industry, including a tropical greenhouse and its cocoa trees, a demonstration workshop and a tasting salon. Each visit is timed

Basilique du Sacré-Coeur.

at an hour long and comes with an audio-guide – although you can probably see what there is to see in half that time.

★ René Magritte Museum
135 rue Esseghem (02 428 26 26, www.magritte museum.be). Métro Belgica then tram 51, or tram 63, 93. **Open** 10am-6pm Wed-Sun. **Admission** €7.50; €6 reductions. **No credit cards.**
Magritte's house is a fittingly bizarre monument to the artist. The window and fireplace in the front room may be familiar – they appear in numerous Magritte paintings – but perhaps the most surprising discovery is the tiny back room where he executed hundreds of his works. The Magrittes lived on the ground floor and also used the garret. The first and second floors were occupied by others, but have since been restored to as authentic a condition as possible. The Magrittes led quiet lives; the artist painted some of his masterpieces from his Renoir and Vache periods in a suit and bow tie. Visitors can see original works, documents, letters and photos, and 17 of the 19 rooms are open to the public.
▶ *Another must-see is the Musée Magritte (see p106), part of the arts complex in the Royal Quarter, which contains more than 200 of his works. See also pp261-263 Surrealism.*

LAEKEN

Some distance north of the centre, Laeken stretches over a huge green area, divided into a royal estate and residence, and the public leisure complex of Heysel. Each of its main sights is worth a visit; they just make unlikely neighbours. It's easy to reach by métro and the sights are all situated within walking distance of one another.

Much will change when construction starts in 2016 on the national stadium for the Euro 2020 football championships – *see p166* **2020 Vision**. Until then, there's the **Parc des Expositions** (aka Brussels Expo, www.bruexpo.be), originally 11 palaces built to mark a century of Belgian independence, now the host of regular trade fairs; and the **Bruparck** (*see p170*), a family-friendly complex containing the Mini-Europe model park of iconic buildings, the Océade water park and the Kinepolis multiplex cinema. Rising above it all is the iconic **Atomium**, built for Expo 1958 and not part of the Euro 2020 overhaul.

For something more tranquil, walk south to glorious **Parc du Laeken**. Its centrepiece is the Château Royal, the residence of the Belgian royal family. Built in 1782-84 for the Austrian governor-general, it was taken over by Napoléon,

who planned the catastrophic invasion of Russia here. Eventually, he did a deal with Josephine and swapped Laeken for the Elysée Palace in Paris. Now it is very much a private residence and, unlike the Palais Royal (*see p108*) in the Upper Town, not, sadly, open to the public. However, the magnificent **Serres Royales** – the Royal Greenhouses – are open at certain times each year. Try to visit at night when they're lit up by spotlights.

Also in the park are a couple of royal follies, whims of Léopold II after he visited the 1900 Paris Exhibition and saw two oriental buildings he wanted in his own back garden. The **Tour Japonaise** is a five-level red tower used for temporary exhibitions. Across avenue Jules van Praet, the **Pavillon Chinois** is yet another curiosity offering oriental ceramics. Currently, both are closed indefinitely for safety reasons; more information on www.kmkg-mrah.be. Ten minutes' walk from the Château Royal is the church of **Notre-Dame de Laeken**.

Sights & Museums

★ Atomium

Boulevard du Centenaire (02 475 47 77, www.atomium.be). Métro Heysel. **Open** 10am-6pm daily.

2020 VISION

The new national stadium will change the face of Heysel.

When Brussels was announced as one of 13 cities to host football's European Championships in 2020, thoughts turned to Heysel, synonymous with the tragic European Cup Final of 1985. Both the name of the area and the stadium at its centre, Heysel also refers to the disaster in which 39 mostly Juventus fans lost their lives when hooliganism, poor crowd control and a crumbling infrastructure combined to cause horrific scenes before the match.

After a decade of recriminations, legal processes and the long-term banning of English teams from playing in Europe, Belgium's national stadium was rebuilt as the Stade Roi Baudouin. It was welcomed back into the international fold with the staging of the opening match of Euro 2000.

The venue also formed part of Belgium's bid to co-host Euro 2020. But in 2016, when builders begin on the site, it won't be to renovate or revamp the Stade Roi Baudouin, but to create an entirely new venue: Eurostadium Brussels. Set on a parking lot of the Brussels Expo complex, the project will create a 62,000-capacity national stadium, plus a shopping centre, conference hall and theatre. This will affect not only Brussels Expo, but the adjoining Bruparck leisure complex (*see p170*), specifically the Mini-Europe theme park and Océade water park, which will be forced to move. Uccle has been mooted as Bruparck's new location.

Other consequences of the new construction will be the removal of the athletics track (where so many world records have been set as part of the Van Damme Memorial meet in September), and the uprooting of the city's flagship football club, Anderlecht, after more than a century in south-west Brussels. It's not yet clear what will happen to the track and field event – or to Anderlecht's current home stadium after the team's move into the new Eurostadium.

What will remain will be the memorial to the 39 victims of the 1985 tragedy, a sundial and the words of WH Auden's 'Funeral Blues': 'Stop all the clocks…'.

Serres Royales.

Admission €11; €6-€8 reductions. Combined ticket to Bruparck; see website. **Map** p163 B2 ❶
Designed by André Waterkeyn for the 1958 World Fair, this iconic structure never fails to impress with its sheer size and scale: a crystal molecule of metal magnified 165 billion times. After years of neglect, dynamic curator Diane Hennebert secured €24 million to renovate the iconic molecule, which reopened in 2005. Now it features interactive exhibitions, a new visitors' centre and restaurant, and a panoramic viewing point on level seven.

FREE Église Notre-Dame de Laeken

Parvis Notre-Dame (02 478 20 05, www.ndlaeken-olvlaken.be). Métro Bockstael, or tram 94, or bus 53. **Open** *Church* Jan-Nov 2-5pm Tue-Sun. *Royal Crypt* Jan-Nov 2-5pm Sun. **Admission** free. **Map** p163 E3 ❷
Although opening is limited, with no admission in December, this huge, neo-Gothic church is worth a wander. Designed by Joseph Poelaert, it was commissioned by King Léopold I in memory of his wife, Queen Louise-Marie, but not completed until 60 years after her death. The Royal Crypt holds the tombs of Léopolds I, II and III, Albert I, Baudouin, various wives and princes – and Louise-Marie herself, who died in Ostend at the age of 38.

★ Serres Royales

61 avenue du Parc Royal (02 551 20 20, www.monarchie.be/palace-and-heritage/greenhouses-laeken). Métro Heysel. **Open** *Apr, May* Tue-Sun. **Admission** €2.50; free under-18s. **No credit cards. Map** p163 D1 ❸
Open to the public only for three weeks in spring, this sequence of 11 linked greenhouses was built on the orders of Léopold II by Alphonse Balat in the 1870s. They are soaring edifices, forming an iron and glass cathedral to botany. Léopold moved into one on his deathbed, and other royals have, in the past, set up writing desks and seating areas in others.

IN THE KNOW
GETTING ABOUT BY BOAT

Launched in 2013, the **Waterbus** (www.waterbus.eu) runs the ten-kilometre (6.2-mile) length of the Zenne Canal from Sainctelette-Beco (between Yser and Ribaucourt métro stations), past Laeken, all the way up to Vilvoorde, a journey of just under an hour that costs €3 (under-12s travel half-price). During the five-week Bruxelles les Bains (www.bruxellesles bains.be), the city beach near Sainctelette that opens from early July to early August, the service runs every day except Monday. Either side, from 1 May to 30 October, it operates Tuesdays to Thursdays. The plan is to extend the service in the future.

Arts & Entertainment

Children

Brussels is fun, safe and entertaining. The city of chocolate and Tintin, festooned with cartoon murals, is fringed with large parks and extensive woodlands. Skateboard parks and bowling alleys complement the family-friendly leisure destination of Laeken, where you'll find a planetarium, a water park, a European (what else?) theme park and, of course, the Atomium. Films are shown in their original language, and there are plenty of children's theatre and puppet shows. On top of all that, Belgium is small and reasonably affordable to get around by train from three stations in the capital – theme parks, wildlife centres and a sandy coastline are within easy reach of town. More long-term visitors will soon find that Brussels is geared up for providing expat residents with reliable childcare. If you time your trip around December, an ice rink, a Christmas market, merry-go-rounds and a big wheel fill the main square and several downtown streets.

ATTRACTIONS

The city's only permanent circus, the Cirque Royal, has long been a venue for pop singers rather than acrobats. Belgian circus companies such as **Alexandre Bouglione** (www.bouglione.be) make regular visits to Brussels, setting up at various venues around town, though suitable sites are fewer and fewer. The annual **Hopla!** (www.hopla-cirk.be) festival of circus arts takes place in April at more than a dozen squares, streets and parks across the city. For better or worse, Brussels has no zoo to speak of – although **Pairi Daiza** is just over an hour away by train.

The city's main family-friendly destination, the **Bruparck**, has been under threat of closure for some years, as its fate is tied in with the demolition of the adjacent national football stadium and the various solutions to its rebuilding (*see p166* **2020 Vision**). At present, its two main attractions, the Océade water park and Mini-Europe theme park, have been given a reprieve until at least 2016, when construction starts on the new stadium. For the time being, the Bruparck's other features are tacky food

and beverage outlet the Village and multiplex cinema **Kinepolis** (*see p178*). All is spread beneath the iconic structure of the **Atomium** (*see p167*), which can also be factored in on a day out, as can the nearby **Planétarium**.

FREE Botkamp

1 avenue de la Porte de Hal, St-Gilles (no phone, www.botkamp.com). Métro/pré-métro Porte de Hal. **Open** 9am-midnight Mon-Thur, Sun; 9am-6am Fri, Sat. **Admission** free. **No credit cards. Map** p304 B8.

Opened in 2014, this is the city's first centre for video and trading card games, a veritable paradise for teenagers. Comfortable, safe and well run, it organises regular weekend tournaments in Mario Kart, the latest versions of FIFA and League of Legends. The venue also acts as a centre for training and workshops in the latest gaming technologies.

★ Bruparck

1 avenue du Football, Laeken (02 474 83 83, www.bruparck.com). Métro Heysel.
Mini-Europe *02 478 05 50, www.minieurope. com.* **Open** *July, Aug* 9.30am-8pm daily. *Mid Mar-June, Sept* 9.30am-6pm daily. *Oct-early Jan*

10am-6pm daily. **Admission** €14.50;
€10.80 under-12s; free children up to 1.2m.
Océade *02 478 43 20, www.oceade.be.* **Open**
July, Aug, school hols 10am-9pm daily. *Apr-June*
10am-6pm Tue-Fri; 10am-9pm Sat, Sun. *Sept-
Mar* 10am-6pm Wed-Fri; 10am-9pm Sat, Sun.
Admission €20; children 1.15m-1.30m €17;
free children under 1.15m.

Its future will be in question after work starts on the
national stadium complex in 2016, but for now the
Bruparck and its surrounding attractions provide
an easy family day out, a short stroll from Heysel
métro station. All the EU landmarks have been recreated down to the smallest detail for the outdoor
model park of Mini-Europe, including St Mark's
Church in Zagreb, Croatia, the EU's newest member.
Some of the models even move: the Eiffel Tower and
Big Ben (listen out for its sonorous chimes) might
stand still, but Vesuvius erupts and the Berlin Wall
crumbles. Features are occasionally added – such as
a World War I commemorative walk – to encourage
repeat custom from locals.

There's probably no need to persuade the kids
to visit the Océade water park with its Barracuda
flume, Salto Angel slides and Hurricane toboggan
run; there's also the Aquafunhouse for smaller ones
and a sauna for the grown-ups.

▶ *Joint tickets for Mini-Europe, the Océade, the
Atomium and the Planetarium – or a combination
thereof – are available and offer considerable
savings on the individual admission charges.
Check websites for details.*

Planétarium

*10 avenue de Bouchout, Laeken (02 474 70 50,
www.planetarium.be). Métro Heysel.* **Shows**
times vary. **Admission** €7; €5 reductions.
Right beside the Bruparck, the Planétarium covers
various aspects of the cosmos in 40-minute bursts.
The schedule is divided into term time and school
holidays, with programmes for smaller ones starting
at 10.30am. Later shows, such as 'Violent Universe',
with colliding galaxies and crashing meteorites, suit
older visitors. Nearly all shows are given in three languages, but do ask first.

Public Aquarium of Brussels

*27 avenue Émile Bossaert, Koekelberg (02 414
02 09, www.aquariologie.be). Tram 19, or bus
49.* **Open** *Term time* noon-6pm Tue-Fri; 10am-
6pm Sat, Sun. *School hols* 10am-6pm Tue-Sun.
Admission €8.50; €5 reductions; free children
under 1m.
The audio guide recommends a visit of one hour and
15 minutes – but only the most fascinated of fish
fans could stretch any stroll around here for more
than an hour. True, there are 48 tanks and 250 types
of marine creature, and the general message of food-
chain fragility is an important one. However, those
trekking all the way up to Koekelberg shouldn't
expect vast pools of gliding manta rays.

MUSEUMS

Brussels has a few museums that may appeal to
kids, though the standout, hands-on Scientastic,
in Bourse pré-métro station, was forced to close
by the city's transport authority in 2012. Almost
every child is fascinated by the huge iguanadon
dinosaur skeletons displayed in the **Museum of
Natural Sciences** (*see p126*), while the **Musée
des Instruments de Musique** (*see p106*) is
likely to entertain younger ones, mainly because
they get to don cool headphones and listen to the
various musical instruments. At the **Centre
Belge de la Bande Dessinée** (*see p63*),
children can find out how animated films work
and step inside full-size replicas of comic book
scenes, though it's not a place where they can
run wild. Cartoon murals sprinkle the city
streets (*see p28*). Also of multi-generational

IN THE KNOW
THE BELGIAN COAST

The 14 resorts along the 65-kilometre
(40-mile) Belgian coastline offer wide
sandy beaches and a solid infrastructure
of pools, bowling alleys, mini-golf courses,
cinemas and ice-cream shops. They
also lay on busy summer programmes
featuring kite-flying festivals, Flemish Pop
Idol contests and beach races. Kids will
also insist that you rent one of the little
go-karts that are found in every resort.
They come in every imaginable design.

Ostend (see *p232*), the biggest resort,
may be the most fun for adults, but it's the
least suited to children. Busy **Blankenberge**
has more for kids to do, with its modern
Sea Life centre (050 42 43 00, www.
sealifeeurope.com/blankenberge) allowing
intimate contact with sharks. **Knokke-Heist**
is more elegant, and has a butterfly park
and bird sanctuary. Elsewhere, there are
fishing boats to watch in **Nieuwpoort**,
and a former Russian submarine moored
at the Seafront centre (050 55 14 15,
www.seafront.be) in **Zeebrugge**.

Young children might be equally as
happy muddling around with Belgian
families in quieter resorts. **Oostduinkerke**,
for example, has shrimp fishermen on
horseback and a fishing museum, while
De Haan has, well, nothing much except
for picturesque fin-de-siècle architecture.

All the resorts are linked by a coastal
tram that runs from De Panne to Knokke-
Heist. The Brussels tourist office (see
p289) can provide further practical
information to help you plan.

ARTS & ENTERTAINMENT

appeal are the **Belgian Chocolate Village** (*see p164*) and **Autoworld** (*see p128*), situated at opposite ends of the city.

★ Musée des Enfants

15 rue du Bourgmestre, Ixelles (02 640 01 07, www.museedesenfants.be). Tram 25, 94, or bus 71. **Open** *Term time* 2.30-5pm Wed, Sat, Sun. *School hols* Jan-June, Aug-Dec 2.30-5pm daily. July 2.30-5pm Mon-Fri. **Admission** €8.50; free under-3s. **No credit cards. Map** p311 H12.

A rambling townhouse in Ixelles has been turned into a superb children's museum, with rooms for theatre, dressing-up, giant interactive puzzles, educational games, painting and clay modelling. There's a kitchen where kids are taught baking, a domestic animal enclosure and an adventure playground. Not surprisingly, it can get mobbed.

Musée du Jouet

24 rue de l'Association, Upper Town (02 219 61 68, www.museedujouet.eu). Tram 92, 93. **Open** 10am-1pm, 2-6pm daily. **Admission** €6.50; €5.50 reductions. **No credit cards. Map** p303 F3.

This cluttered private museum is run by an enthusiastic toy collector. It displays gaily painted train sets and tin cars, fantastic clockwork toys (including a jumping zebra), puzzles, teddies and dolls' houses. Check the website for details of special events.

PARKS

The cobbled streets, crowded trams and confusing métro stations of Brussels aren't exactly made for pushchairs, so you may find yourself spending a lot of time in the various parks. Close to the city centre, the **Parc de Bruxelles** has a decent playground and a café selling ice-cream. In Ixelles, the **Bois de la Cambre** at the end of avenue Louise (entrances on chaussée de Waterloo and avenues Louise and Roosevelt) is a landscaped park with a lake, lawns, horse-riding trails and woodland rambles. There are also two cafés, one with a playground and the other facing a rollerskating rink. Several main roads through the park are closed to traffic at weekends, creating a huge loop that's popular with cyclists, in-line skaters and kids learning to ride bikes. Also in

---

IN THE KNOW BABYSITTING

The leading francophone resource for families in Belgium, **La Ligue des Familles** (www.laligue.be) matches those looking for a babysitter with those offering to provide help. Its website has an English-language function too. The French-only Office de la Naissance et de l'Enfance, or **ONE** (www.one.be), deals with all aspects of childcare. The nationwide **Baby-Sitters** (www.baby-sitters.be) runs small ads for potential babysitters. Many upmarket hotels in Brussels provide a babysitting service for guests.

Technopolis. *See p174.*

Ixelles, the small **Parc Tenbosch** (entrances on chaussée de Vleurgat and place Tenbosch) has a safe playground with well-maintained wooden equipment, a sandpit, football pitch and pond complete with lazy terrapins.

Some wilder retreats are found in Uccle, the city's leafy southern commune, including the **Parc de la Sauvagère** nature reserve (entrance on avenue de la Chênaie), which has an outdoor playground ideal for young children, a picnic area, basketball court, duck pond and farm animals in enclosures. There's also the lovely **Parc de Wolvendael** (entrances on avenues de Fré and Paul Stroobant), with an outdoor café, mini-golf and a playground. It's located on a sloping hill that makes a perfect place to ski or sledge in winter. Further west, the **Little Steam Train of Forest** (323B chaussée de Neerstalle, 02 376 69 96, www.ptvf.fte2.org; open mid Apr-June 2-6pm Sat, Sun; July-Sept 2-6pm Sun) is run by local enthusiasts and chuffs on a little circuit through the park. It's more a model train than heritage vehicle, but should keep little ones happy. The **Parc de Woluwe** (entrance on avenue de Tervuren) is another popular spot for sledging.

The **Rouge Cloître** park on the edge of the Forêt de Soignes has two playgrounds with good climbing equipment. Further out, the **Park van Tervuren** (entrance on Leuvensesteenweg) has woodland rambles and cycle trails. Tram 44 runs from Montgomery through the forest, though the African Museum at the southern terminus is closed for long-term renovation.

DAY TRIPS

It's fairly easy to get out of Brussels for a day at the beach or a canoe trip in the Ardennes. This small country has an expansive network of motorways, but there's also a good, cheap train service that runs to most places of interest. Belgian Railways (www.sncb.be) publishes a free brochure listing special excursions, many of them suited to kids. Under-12s travel free if travelling with an older ticketholder.

★ Kayak Ansiaux
Kayak Ansiaux, 15 rue du Vélodrome, Anseremme (082 22 43 97, www.dinant-evasion.be). Train to Anseremme. **Open** May-mid Sept daily. **Admission** €15-€20.
The biggest of the many kayaking centres in the Ardennes, based at Anseremme on the River Lesse, near Dinant. From the station, a minibus takes you to the start point a few kilometres upstream. There are two courses: a long one of 21km/13 miles (five hours) starting from Houyet at 12.30pm, and a shorter one of 12km/7.5 miles (2hr 30min) starting from Gendron at 2.30pm. Prices depend on type of kayak, and there are all-in packages with transport too.

★ Pairi Daiza
Domaine de Cambron, Brugelette (068 25 08 50, www.pairidaiza.eu). Train to Cambron-Casteau. **Open** *July, Aug* 10am-7pm daily. *Easter-June, Sept-mid Nov* 10am-6pm daily. **Admission** €28.50; €23.50 3-11s; free under 3s.

The grounds of an old abbey near Ath have been turned into an exotic bird sanctuary. The main attractions for kids are the giant walk-through aviary for birds of paradise, as well as the giant tortoise and an Antarctic section. There's also an adventure playground, a petting farm and a restaurant.

Parc d'Aventures Scientifiques (Pass)

3 rue de Mons, Frameries (070 22 22 52, www.pass. be). Train to Mons then bus 1, 2. **Open** *July, Aug* 10am-6pm daily. *Feb-Apr* 9am-4pm Mon, Tue, Thur, Fri; 10am-6pm Sat, Sun. *Mid-end Jan, May, June, Oct, Nov* 9am-4pm Mon, Tue, Thur, Fri. **Admission** €12.50; €11 15-25s; €9.50 6-14s; free under-6s.

Belgium's interactive science centre is located in a former coalmine near Mons, restyled by French architect Jean Nouvel. The centre hosts hands-on exhibitions that are both innovative and educational. Opening hours are byzantine; the place is closed during September, December and the first half of January.

Planckendael

582 Leuvensesteenweg, Muizen, near Mechelen (03 224 89 10, www.planckendael.be). Train to Muizen, or Mechelen then Planckendael Express bus (Apr-Sept every 20min, 10min journey time). **Open** *July, Aug* 10am-7pm daily. *May, June, Sept* 10am-6pm daily. *Mar, Apr, Oct* 10am-5.30pm daily. *Jan, Feb, Nov, Dec* 10am-4.45pm daily. **Admission** €25; €17.50 reductions; free under-3s.

The wide open spaces of Planckendael wildlife park provide an ideal habitat for rhinos, deer, antelope, wolves, birds and cranes. Founded by Antwerp Zoo as a breeding park, the estate also has a restaurant, adventure playgrounds and rope bridges.

★ Technopolis

Technologielaan, Mechelen (015 34 20 00, www. technopolis.be). Train to Mechelen then bus 282, 682. **Open** 9.30am-5pm daily. Closed 1st wk Sept. **Admission** €16; €12.50 3-11s; free under-3s.

One of the best science museums in Europe. Kids can ride a bike along a high wire, try out a flight simulator, lie on a bed of nails or print banknotes with their own face on. The Xplora Zone ties technology in with its practical uses in later life – you can learn how to sort out a tiger's dental problems, make an animated film, or create clothes in 2D then see them in 3D. Staff are friendly and well informed. *Photos p172.*

Walibi Belgium & Aqualibi

100 boulevard de l'Europe, Wavre (010 42 15 00, www.walibi.be). Train to Walibi-Bierges. **Walibi Open** *Apr-Oct* 10am-6/8/11pm daily. **Admission** €35; €30 reductions; free children up to 1m.

Aqualibi Open *Jan* 4-10pm Fri; 10am-8pm Sat, Sun. *Feb-Apr, Sept-Dec* 2-8pm Wed; 10am-8pm Thur, Sat, Sun; 4-10pm Fri. *May-June* 2-8pm Wed; 10am-6pm Thur; 10am-10pm Fri; 10am-8pm Sat, Sun. *July, Aug* 10am-8pm Mon-Thur, Sat, Sun; 10am-10pm Fri. **Admission** €19; €15 reductions; €5 children 1-1.2m.

The biggest and oldest theme park in Belgium, Walibi involves some 40 rides, with daunting names such as Calamity Mine and Vampire. There are gentler ones for younger children and a 4D cinema. Aqualibi is a big waterpark with chutes, wave machines and four toboggans. Both Walibi and Aqualibi have a complex schedule of opening times and ticket prices – check the main Walibi website for full details.

Walibi Belgium.

Film

Brussels took to cinema right from the get-go. It was here, at the Galeries St-Hubert in 1896, that the Lumière brothers gave their first public screening outside Paris of the new *cinématographe*. Primitive versions of this new machine had been created earlier by a Belgian physicist, Joseph Plateau – whose name is on the annual prize given to the domestic filmmaker who best propagates the reputation of Belgian cinema abroad. In recent years, directors such as Ixelles-born Jaco Van Dormael, the Dardenne brothers and Michaël R Roskam have gained awards at Cannes and/ or been nominated for Best Foreign Language Oscars. In Brussels, the filmgoer will find plenty of original-language offerings, reasonably priced tickets, and festivals and special events galore. There's a healthy mix of big-budget blockbusters and less mainstream arthouse flicks. If you want to catch a major new release at the weekend, though, you'll have to book seats in advance – you're not the only cinephile in town.

WHERE TO GO

Local screens fall into two main categories: the UGC and Kinepolis circuit, which mainly shows blockbusters and takes the lion's share of the audience; and an arthouse circuit, showing films in repertory, as well as world and Belgian cinema. In the past, various councils have had to come up with extra grants to keep arthouse cinemas and local culture clubs alive.

The multiplexes march onward. The UGC network offers UGC Unlimited, a ticket system whereby a monthly fee of less than €20 allows unlimited access to the company's screens in Brussels and Antwerp. Kinepolis was the world's first multiplex and continues to forge ahead with technological advances.

At the other end of the scale, little **Styx** in Ixelles has weathered every storm to remain open as a rare, truly local cinema – no matter how modest its sound quality. Sadly, the legendary art deco picture house in the Galeries St-Hubert, the Arenberg, was forced to close its doors on New Year's Eve 2011. A month later, it reopened

under new management as the **Cinéma Galeries**. The **Arenberg**, meanwhile, laudably continues its passionate celluloid activities at other venues across town, staging mini-series and films of educational value to schoolchildren and young filmmakers. Other age-old local cinemas, such as the much-loved Movy, have not survived the download revolution.

TIMINGS & TICKETS

Film schedules can be found in English at www.cinenews.be and http://cinebel.dhnet.be. These give a full programme, plus details of new releases and previews. You can also search by genre. You can't purchase tickets from these sites, though – this has to be done via the individual or cinema-chain websites.

Average ticket prices are in the region of €10. Films are categorised as 'VO st Bil' for original version with bilingual subtitles, 'VO st NL' for original version with Dutch subtitles and 'VO st FR' for original version with French subtitles. Dubbing is rare.

FESTIVALS & SPECIAL EVENTS

The **Brussels Film Festival** (*see p32*) has been given a new lease of life since moving to Flagey, focusing on European filmmakers who are just starting out. Held in June, the festival guarantees fresh talent; this, along with parallel screenings from better-known European names, means that it rarely disappoints. The festival bar is also good value, and usually staffed by a director or a well-known actor.

One event not to miss is the **Be Film Festival** (www.befilmfestival.be), a look back at the previous year in Belgian film with famous key guests and a relaxed, holiday atmosphere. Run in the days between Christmas and New Year, it's co-hosted at the Bozar and the nearby and newly revamped Cinematek (the former Musée du Cinéma). There, it's also worth looking out for various mini-seasons and special events, most notably visiting guest directors personally presenting their own work.

Horror flick fans can sink their teeth into the gory **Brussels International Festival of Fantastic Film** (*see p31*) in spring, more than three decades old and now based at the Bozar. It takes in a vampires' ball, a body-painting contest and late-night screenings of seriously weird cinema.

IN THE KNOW BELGIAN BERT'S GREAT INVENTION

Who created the first multiplex? A Texan tycoon? A canny French entrepreneur? No. Albert Bert from Harelbeke. Here, in this modest community near Kortrijk, Albert Bert's father once ran the Majestiek Cinema, Harelbeke's only thriving source of entertainment – until TV came along. To help his father's dwindling income, young Albert installed another theatre under the same roof. Duplex begat Trioscoop, that begat Pentascoop in Kortrijk. Later came the Decascoop, off the motorway outside Ghent. Keeping prices low and sound quality and seat comfort high, Bert had hit upon a new trend: the multiplex. In 1988, allied with his sister-in-law, Bert-Claeys, Bert created the first real megaplex: **Kinepolis** (see p178). Set alongside the Bruparck leisure complex, Kinepolis became part of the family weekend. Today, while the 24-screen Brussels flagship continues to embrace each and every technological development, the Kinepolis group oversees a total of 35 cinemas across Europe, comprising nearly 400 screening rooms and 100,000 seats.

Also based at Flagey, **Anima** (www.anima festival.be) is a long-running festival of animation; in 2015, it attracted nearly 40,000 visitors for the ten-day event. Staged in February, it showcases animators from around the world – prizes most recently went to Sweden's Niki Lindroth von Bahr and Tokyo-based Sarina Nihel. November in St-Gilles sees the Independent Film Festival give an outlet to young directors. Known for 40 years as the Fifi, in 2015 it became the **Brussels Independent Film Festival** (*see p35*), aka FIFB, and runs for five days. Shortly afterwards, in December, is the **Festival of Mediterranean Film** (www.cinemamed.be) at the Botanique. In 2014, it featured works from countries as diverse as Montenegro, Malta and Tunisia.

Many new Belgian and French films are also featured at the **Francophone Film Festival** (www.fiff.be) in Namur in October, which celebrated its 30th birthday in 2105. Flemish films are screened at the **Flanders Film Festival** (www.filmfestival.be), also in October, in Ghent, an occasion renowned for its movie soundtrack awards. Bruges also hosts its own **Flanders Film Festival**, a rebranded version of the former Razor Reel (www.rrfff.be) inaugurated in 2008. Ten days of full-length features, animated films, talks and workshops are held in November.

On Fridays and Saturdays in July and August, the **Nova** cinema goes walkabout, providing free open-air screenings at sundown (PleinOpenAir), showing offbeat movies in unlikely settings. The carnival atmosphere is supplemented with free concerts and finger food.

CINEMAS

Actor's Studio

16 petite rue des Bouchers & 19 rue de la Fourche, Grand'Place & Around (02 503 31 45, www.facebook.com/actorsstudiobxl). Métro/pré-métro De Brouckère. **No credit cards.** **Map** p301 D4.
It might take a bit of finding the first time – it's tucked into a hotel basement among the busy restaurants near the Grand'Place – but this two-screen studio is one of Brussels' little gems. If your taste leans towards Korean horror rather than the Hollywood variety, or you want to see Finnish films by the Kaurismaki brothers in VO, the Actor's is for you.

Arenberg

02 511 65 15, www.arenberg.be.
In 1896, at what would become the Arenberg in the prestigious Galeries St-Hubert, the Lumières' first-ever film show was screened outside Paris. In 1939, it became a gorgeous art deco cinema. Commendably sticking to an independent, eclectic and arthouse agenda, in modern times Arenberg bravely swam against the multiplex tide, receiving ever more subsidies until it was forced to close in 2011. A petition of 36,000 signatures wasn't enough to save it.

Brussels Film Festival.

While incoming management created the Cinéma Galeries (*see below*) in January 2012 at the Arenberg's former premises, a new concept was being launched: *cinémas nomades*. Setting up at venues such as the Nova, Aventure Ciné Confort and Université Populaire (www.universitepopulaire.be), the Arenberg still puts on special seasons and educational films for schoolchildren and students. It also hopes to reignite its formerly popular Écran Total, an annual summer bash devoted to well-known arthouse directors and sundry nostalgia. Even without a permanent home, the Arenberg still has a major role to play in the city's cinema scene.

Aventure Ciné Confort

Galerie du Centre Bloc II, 57 rue des Fripiers, Grand'Place & Around (02 219 9202, www. cinema-aventure.be). Métro/pre-métro De Brouckère. **No credit cards. Map** p301 D4.
If you miss a big film on its first run, your best chance of catching it is to head for this rather rundown picture house, located in a shopping mall. Sound and picture quality on the two screens aren't great, but you can't fault the number of films on offer. Turn up on time – screenings start within three minutes of the scheduled slot.

★ Cinéma Galeries

26 galerie de la Reine, Grand'Place & Around (02 514 74 98, www.galeries.be). Métro Gare Centrale. **No credit cards. Map** p301 D4.
Occupying the sumptuous former space of the Arenberg (*see p176*), the Cinéma Galeries presents works by mainly contemporary directors on its three screens, as well as retrospectives and documentaries. It also makes use of a large hall to host exhibitions of a cinematic nature and generally ensures that the filmic tradition at this heritage art deco building goes on unbowed.

★ Cinematek

Palais des Beaux-Arts, 9 rue Baron Horta, Upper Town (02 551 19 00, www.cinematek.be). Métro Gare Centrale or Parc, or tram 92, 93. **Map** p303 E5.
This revered institution, a little cinema, archive and museum, became the Cinematek after an overhaul in 2009. Its programming draws on the 50,000 reels in its vaults, including silent films with live piano accompaniment: the Film Museum is the closest you'll get to cinema heaven. Each month, three or four movie cycles focus on a director or a theme – anything from ethnographic shorts from the silent period to Dirty Harry-era Clint Eastwood. Tickets are cheap but the cinema is tiny, so book ahead.
▶ *The on-site museum displays early cinema equipment and vintage film magazines; see p105.*

Flagey

Place Ste-Croix, next to place Flagey, Ixelles (02 641 10 20, www.flagey.be). Tram 81 or bus 59, 71. **Map** p308 G10.
This in-vogue cinema at the fashionable arts centre seats little more than 100 people, but the comfort is second to none. Programming is planned jointly with the Cinematek, and blends classics with more adventurous international modern fare.
▶ *After the film, repair to Café Belga – open until 2am and popular with the arty crowd.*

ARTS & ENTERTAINMENT

Kinepolis

20 boulevard du Centenaire, Laeken (02 474 26 00, www.kinepolis.com). Métro Heysel.
Kinepolis, located way up in Laeken, is state of the art. With its giant screens (24 of them in all) and futuristic sound systems, this multiplex is total cinema, Flemish-style. Cutting-edge technology also includes one of the few servers powerful enough to download entire movies by satellite for the big screen.

Nova

3 rue d'Arenberg, Grand'Place & Around (02 511 24 77, www.nova-cinema.com). Métro Gare Centrale. **No credit cards. Map** p301 D4.
Creaky seats, trash-aesthetic decor and adventurous programming ensure that the Nova regularly appears on lists of the best alternative cinemas in Europe. A gem that has miraculously survived on meagre means for years, this is also a major venue for the Brussels International Festival of Fantastic Film (*see p31*). The monthly Open Screens, which allow budding filmmakers to showcase their efforts, are popular, raucous affairs.

★ Styx

72 rue de l'Arbre Bénit, Ixelles (02 512 21 02, www.cinema-styx.wikeo.be). Métro Porte de Namur or bus 54, 71. **No credit cards. Map** p305 E8.
Stylishly approaching its 50th year, the Styx is Brussels' most adorable fleapit. The sound quality may be less than perfect, but the programming is irresistible – from Truffaut retrospectives and *Amores Perros* to modern Belgian classics in the making.

UGC De Brouckère

38 place De Brouckère, St-Géry & Ste-Catherine (078 154 321, www.ugc.be). Métro/pré-métro De Brouckère. **Map** p301 C3.
A midtown mecca for multiplex fans. It's not all popcorn and blockbusters, though: you can order a beer in the bar, sink back into the bucket-shaped armchairs and marvel at the gold-leaf surroundings in one of the city's biggest auditoriums. Look out for American Movie Day on 4 July, with fireworks in the streets and up to a dozen pre-release films from the US. Luckily, it's all done with style.

UGC Toison d'Or

8 avenue de la Toison d'Or, Ixelles (078 154 321, www.ugc.be). Métro Porte de Namur. **Map** p305 E7.
With 15 screens (rather confusingly, at two not-quite-adjacent locations), the UGC Toison d'Or is the only serious competition to Kinepolis – and its more adventurous programming often carries the day. First-class sound and fabulous picture quality make this the best address to randomly turn up at without knowing what you want to see. On the whole, tickets aren't cheap – though the lunchtime shows are.

Vendôme

18 chaussée de Wavre, Ixelles (02 502 37 00, www.cinema-vendome.be). Métro Porte de Namur. **No credit cards. Map** p305 E7.
Round the corner from the Toison d'Or, this five-screen independent is a treasure, and has smartened itself up. The films are mainly European and US indie releases, but the cinema is also a regular on the local festival circuit.

UGC De Brouckère.

ESSENTIAL BELGIAN FILMS

From Tintin to the Dardennes brothers.

Rosetta.

LE CRABE AUX PINCES D'OR
CLAUDE MISONNE (1947)
Though set in Karaboudjan, this film is significant: it was the first full-length animated version of a Tintin strip cartoon. It was only screened twice before the producer fled to South America in a cloud of debt. The only copy is stored in the Cinematek archive. A DVD version came out in 2008.

LE BANQUET DES FRAUDEURS
HENRI STORCK (1952)
The first Belgian film to be entered for Cannes, *The Smugglers' Banquet* was also the first major work by Henri Storck. The greatest Belgian filmmaker of the pre- and immediate post-war era, Storck sets this tense crime drama at the crossroads of Belgium, Germany and the Netherlands, anticipating the cross-border undercurrents yet to come.

LE FAR WEST
JACQUES BREL (1973)
Brel's ninth film, and his second in the director's chair, follows the main character, Jacques, on a journey from Brussels to a faraway land. Belgium's most renowned singer-songwriter made the movie soon after finding out his cancer was terminal – he would soon set off himself on a series of ocean voyages before dying in 1978.

BRUSSELS BY NIGHT
MARC DIDDEN (1983)
Didden's story concerns a suicidal hitman as he trawls the low-life bars and back alleys of the Belgian capital. A prize winner at the 1984 London Film Festival, this grim tale was co-written by Didden and Dominique Deruddere, who would soon be creating his own dark, off-the-wall works, such as *Crazy Love*.

TOTO LE HÉROS
JACO VAN DORMAEL (1991)
The film that launched the career of Jaco Van Dormael, and was the first of several collaborations with his musician-composer brother Pierre, *Toto le Héros* is an engaging fantasy told by an old man as half-remembered dreams. Its flexible structure and blurring of reality set the tone for a decade of globally acclaimed Belgian cinema.

ROSETTA
THE DARDENNE BROTHERS (1999)
Rosetta put the Dardenne brothers, Jean-Pierre and Luc, on the global map, with a sensational debut by Émilie Dequenne in the lead role. Alcoholism, underpaid employment, alienation: all the ills of Belgian society are laid bare in this multi-layered masterpiece that walked away with the Palme d'Or at Cannes.

Gay & Lesbian

I n keeping with the Belgian life philosophy of *laissez-faire*, Brussels is a free and easy place for gays and lesbians to lead their lives. Belgium was the second country in the world (after the Netherlands) to introduce marriage equality in 2003, followed by full adoption rights in 2006. Public support has been consistently supportive – a 2013 poll by IFOP, a leading market research company, found that 71 per cent of Belgians supported equal marriage and adoption rights.

The gay quarter is located right in the heart of the city in the medieval streets close to Grand'Place. There's a bar-hopping approach to nightlife and in summer the drinking spills out on to the streets, particularly around rue du Marché au Charbon. Closing times are often open-ended, depending on business, time of year or mood of the patron. In general, though, this is a late-night city.

ARTS & ENTERTAINMENT

The political and social centre of gay and lesbian life in Brussels is the non-profit organisation **Tels Quels** (02 512 45 87, www.telsquels.be). It runs its own cultural/political festival in March, organises other events, maintains a documents archive and provides educational resources. A useful general site for the Brussels gay scene is www.patroc.com/brussels, and www.sillylilly.net is an excellent resource and blog for lesbian Brussels. And if you're looking for somewhere gay-friendly to stay, check out the 120-plus Brussels listings on www.misterbnb.com.

BARS

Le Baroque

44 rue du Marché au Charbon, Grand'Place & Around (no phone, www.barlebaroque.be). Pré-métro Bourse. **Open** 5pm-late daily. **Map** p301 C5.
The fancy-sounding Baroque is the Brussels bear cave, where beards and bellies come together in a lively and extra-friendly atmosphere.

★ Le Belgica

32 rue du Marché au Charbon, Grand'Place & Around (no phone, www.lebelgica.be). Pré-métro Bourse. **Open** 8pm-3am Thur-Sun. **Map** p301 C5.

The Belgica is now one of the grand-daddies of the gay scene, though it still appeals to all generations of party types. Nothing much happens before 11pm, but then the place packs out and the house music starts to ramp up. Try the eponymous vodka-based shot glass poured from a jug and you'll feel right at home. Keep an eye out for Léopold II; he looks on most disapprovingly.

Le Boys Boudoir

25 rue du Marché au Charbon, Grand'Place & Around (02 614 58 38, www.leboysboudoir.be). Pré-métro Bourse. **Open** 7.30pm-late daily. **Map** p301 C5.
As the name suggests, the Boudoir attracts the younger set in a full-on party atmosphere. Sunday evenings offer that formidable pick-me-up mix of drag and karaoke.

★ Chez Maman

7 rue des Grandes Carmes, Grand'Place & Around (no phone, www.chezmaman.be). Pré-métro Bourse. Open 11pm-late Fri, Sat. **Map** p301 C5.
If you like playing sardines, pack yourself into CM and be part of the package-holiday disco and 1970s-style drag. Maman herself remains the star attraction, though the likes of Jean Biche and Loulou

BE PROUD OF BEPRIDE

The city's main gay event gets bigger every year.

In an age when it's de rigueur to say that everything must be bigger and better than ever before, **Brussels Pride** (*see p31*) can sit back smugly and say that it's true. The 2014 Pride Parade drew 100,000 people on to the streets of the city, doubling the 2012 gathering of 50,000; not bad for an event that started in the mid 1990s with only 2,000 people turning out. Now, in a city where sexual orientation takes a back seat to hedonism, the tangled streets of the Lower Town become everyone's party central.

As Pride's got bigger and – presumably – better, its construct has become more complex. The Pride Festival itself lasts the first two weeks of May and kick-starts the European Pride calendar. This is when the more measured countrywide programme of events, talks and exhibitions take place, bringing together the political and philosophical themes of the festival. Then, across the second weekend of May, the party poppers are pulled in an explosion of camp, leather, nuns (there are always nuns) and plenty of glitz. The Pride Village sets out its stalls on the streets, parties erupt across the city and the culminating Pride Parade – BePride, or Pride4every1 in text-speak – starts off on its glorious procession along boulevard Anspach. For a small city, Brussels certainly pulls out all the stops. By day, it's a family affair from toddlers in buggies to the *troisième âge* revelling in balloons and pinkness. By night, the streets thump with music as the crowds club-hop across town from one free party to the next.

And the real mark of success? In 2015, the Commission Consultative de Manneken-Pis approved a new Pride costume for the peeing boy. Respect.

ARTS & ENTERTAINMENT

ARTS & ENTERTAINMENT

Velvet vie to steal her stiletto glory. Be prepared to queue later in the evening; what with all that hairspray, fire regs are strict on numbers.

Le Club

45 rue des Pierres, Grand'Place & Around (no phone, www.barclub.eu). Pré-métro Bourse. **Open** 8pm-late Tue-Sun. **Map** p301 C4.
Le Club is a classy but well-priced cocktail bar with a mixed clientele. It's the perfect spot for tête-a-têtes or pre-party gatherings.

★ Dolores Bar

40 rue du Marché au Charbon, Grand'Place & Around (02 324 91 40, www.facebook.com/ledolores). Pré-métro Bourse. **Open** 6pm-1am Tue-Thur, Sun; 6pm-4am Fri, Sat. **Map** p301 C5.
The new kid on the Charbon block, Dolores throws its doors open to a mixed crowd that appreciates cool music, the occasional singalong and a rare (for this part of town) terrace area.

★ L'Homo Erectus

57 rue des Pierres, Grand'Place & Around (0477 923 596, www.lhomoerectus.com). Pré-métro Bourse. **Open** 4pm-dawn daily. **Map** p301 C4.
The pun, of course, is fully intended. Barely half a minute's walk from Grand'Place, you can't miss this tiny bar with its Darwin-like window of apes slowly evolving into upright macho man. But you don't need to worry about being square-jawed; this scene favourite has evolved into a house of fun.
▶ *Much of the same can be found round the corner at little brother L'Homo Erectus Classicus, 5 rue du Marché au Charbon.*

La Réserve

2A petite rue au Beurre, Grand'Place & Around (02 511 66 06, www.facebook.com/lareserve brussels). Pré-métro Bourse. **Open** 3-11pm Mon, Tue; 3pm-late Wed-Sun. **Map** p301 C4.
Every city has its stalwart and La Réserve is the oldest gay bar in town. Set in an ancient house near Grand'Place, it lulls you into thinking you've stumbled into an Agatha Christie film. But there's no mystery to its charming and fun-loving ways. It attracts a 40-plus crowd, but this doesn't stop the younger fellas dropping in to make sure they're not missing out on anything.

★ Stamm Bar

114 rue Marché au Charbon, Grand'Place & Around (0471 80 14 39, www.stammbar.be). Pré-métro Bourse. **Open** 3-7pm, 9pm-late Sun; 9pm-late Mon-Sat. **Map** p301 C4.
The Brussels scene was bereft when Gérard decided to retire from old cruise bar the Duq in 2015. But all is fair in love and scoring, and the Stamm Bar is now the place to head for late-night cruising to a soundtrack of thumping music. Certainly no suits and certainly men only.

CLUBS

★ La Démence

Fuse, 208 rue Blaes, Marolles (02 511 97 89, www.lademence.com). Métro/pré-métro Porte de Hal, or bus 27, 48. **Open** 10pm-noon monthly. **Admission** €25-€30; €20-€25 under-26s. **Map** p304 B8.
La Démence is still up there with the big hitters of the European party scene and the boys pile in from London, Amsterdam, Paris and Cologne to swell the ranks of locals. It's a wild night on three levels with two dance floors. Muscles pump to techno and house and there's a chill-out area to rest those twinkle toes. Check the website for exact dates and to book advance tickets.

Flash Tea Dance @ Le You

Le You, 18 rue Duquesnoy, Grand'Place & Around (02 639 14 00, www.facebook.com/flashgayteadance). Métro Gare Centrale. **Open** 10.30pm-5am Sun. **Admission** free before midnight. **Map** p301 D5.
The Sunday tea dance has become an institution on the Brussels scene. A young, good-looking and friendly crowd struts its stuff to live DJ sets until the early hours. A nod to holiday spirit comes with novelty items such as the Ball Pit and Catch the Money Balloon. Just go with the flow, everyone else does.

SAUNAS & GYMS

La Griffe

41-43 rue de Dinant, Grand'Place & Around (02 512 62 51, www.saunalagriffe.eu). Bus 95.

La Démence

Open 11.30am-10pm Mon-Fri; 1-10pm Sat, Sun. **Admission** €12-€17. **Map** p301 C6.
Small, clean and cosy in a 1970s airport lounge sort of way, the Griffe has all the usual facilities including a proper hammam. Mainly for the more mature man and his admirers.

Macho II
106 rue du Marché au Charbon, Grand'Place & Around (02 513 56 67, www.machosauna.be). Pré-métro Anneessens. **Open** noon-midnight Mon-Sat; 8am-midnight Sun after La Démence. **Admission** Mon-Wed, Fri-Sun €19; Thur €13; free-€13 reductions. **Map** p301 C5.
The Macho is well known for its serious saunas and decently equipped fitness room. It's a big, well-kept establishment and the staff are attentive. Expect to find a youngish crowd, particularly later on in the night. A ticket allows repeat entry on the same day.

Oasis
10 rue van Orley, Upper Town (02 218 08 00, www. oasis-sauna.be). Métro Madou. **Open** 11.30am-midnight daily. **Admission** €12-€18. **Map** p303 F3.
Oasis is set in a vast townhouse and the bar area is still very much a *grande salle*, with a marble fireplace and corniced ceilings. Some parts are seedier, but they're meant to be. It's clean, it's popular and it has all the facilities, including a stylish whirlpool area. The old servants' stairs at the back of the house challenge even the most nimble-footed.

Spades4
23-25 rue Bodeghem, St-Géry & Ste-Catherine (02 502 07 72, www.saunaspades4.be).

Pré-métro Anneessens. **Open** noon-midnight daily. **Admission** €12-€16; €10-€12 reductions. **Map** p302 B5.
Brussels' biggest and most exclusive sauna is spread over six sizeable floors. It's tastefully designed, has an excellent bar and good food, and the staff are friendly and helpful. Facilities include legitimate massage, an SM labyrinth and a cinema, as well as masses of private rooms. There is also a well-equipped fitness room and a roof terrace.

SEX SHOPS

Argos
13 rue des Riches Claires, St-Géry & Ste-Catherine (02 502 92 49, www.argosvideo.be). Pré-métro Bourse. **Open** 10am-10pm Mon-Sat; 2-8pm Sun. **Map** p301 C4.
Just looking in the window of this fetish shop sparks wonder and awe. No smoky glass or artfully arranged blinds, just in-yer-face devices for all tastes. It also has an extensive DVD library.

Rob Brussels @ Man to Man
11 rue des Riches Claires, St-Géry & Ste-Catherine (02 514 02 96). Pré-métro Bourse. **Open** 10am-6.30pm Tue-Fri; 10am-6pm Sat. **Map** p301 C4.
Fetish superstore Rob adds Brussels to its international franchise, bringing with it a vast range of rubber and leather clothing and accessories, all in a stylish setting. The Man to Man moniker reminds us of a time when the emphasis was on hairdressing, with the fetish as a sideline. But now that things have reversed, how long will it be before the barber's chair is used as a prop rather than a seat for a crop?

Nightlife

For a small city, Brussels punches well above its weight with a confident but relaxed music and clubbing scene. It may not be up there with the likes of London or Berlin, but it simply doesn't care about the comparison. This is a dedicated party town where a good night out can start in a cosy blues or jazz bar and finish the next morning in one of the iconic dance clubs or a smooth electro lounge. It's resolutely Belgian in style: no nonsense, no attitude, go with the flow. But this is not a parochial scene; the city plays to its international strengths with the world's top DJs adding to the mix of hard-hitting, home-grown talent. Determined and devoted nighthawks will most certainly be well rewarded.

CLUBS

Belgium takes its clubbing very seriously, arguing that it was the birthplace of European techno, thanks to the work of just one man, the legendary DJ Pierre, who placed Brussels' most enduring club, **Fuse**, firmly on the world dance map. It also lays claim to the invention of the mega-club, such as **La Rocca** in Lier. The club scene is surprisingly varied, from smooth and chic to heady and hedonistic. Some reliably solid venues have been around for years; others open and close with alarming regularity. The clubbing scene is generally relaxed, though the new clutch of smarter places are not fond of large groups of men turning up unless it's gay night.

The best place to start looking for information is www.noctis.com, Belgium's most detailed party website. Most clubs have an online presence, either with a website or a MySpace or Facebook page. Flyers are ubiquitous in the entrances of most leading bars and clubs in Brussels. Admission prices to clubs are generally reasonable, often with reductions for early entry. Drinks bills are also bearable, but note that credit cards are rarely accepted.

Bazaar Brussels
63 rue des Capucins, Marolles (02 511 26 00, www.bazaarbrussels.be). Bus 27. **Open** 11pm-late Wed-Sun. **Admission** €5-€15. **Map** p304 C7.

A regularly heaving party space, set in the cellar of the old Capucin monastery. It gets packed with beautiful people and boasts some glorious special nights, such as the fetishy Karnage.

★ Bloody Louis
32 avenue Louise, Ixelles (0477 444 444 mobile, www.bloodylouis.be). Métro Louise. **Open** 11pm-6am Fri, Sat. **Admission** €10. **Map** p305 D8.

Newish kid on the beat, Bloody Louis considers itself the biggest club in town – and with space for 1,600 people on the dancefloor, it would be churlish to argue. You'll find international DJs, massive club nights and, every second Sunday of the month, the gay party Fly.

Catclub
Various venues (no phone, www.catclub.be).
When Brussels-based Lady Jane decided to invite a few friends to a one-off party in 2002, she couldn't have known that Catclub would become such a highly regarded night. Events take place every month or so on an ever-changing circuit of venues; see the website for details and also check out www.facebook.com/catclubbrussels.

FREE Club Clandestin
0471 501 876 mobile, www.clubclandestin.be. Bus 95. **Open** 10.30pm-5am Thur-Sat. **Admission** free. **No credit cards**.

The Clandestine is just that, a micro club with a secret address in the Sablon district. You'll need to ask them to text or mail you from the website. If you want to hang out with the beautiful people, this is the place to be. Plus that little bit of mystery.

Club La Vilaine
10 rue de la Vierge Noir, St-Géry & Ste-Catherine (0485 864 060 mobile, www.clublavilaine.be). Metro Ste-Catherine. **Open** 10pm-4am Wed-Sat. **Admission** free-€8. **Map** p302 C3.
Opened in 2015, La Vilaine is another addition to the burgeoning second life of the Ste-Catherine area. Its speciality is old-school electronic music, with resident and guest DJs looking to the 1980s, '90s and '00s for their inspiration.

FREE Le Coaster
28 rue des Riches Claires, St-Géry & Ste-Catherine (02 512 08 47, www.facebook.com/coasterbrussels). Pré-métro Bourse. **Open** 8pm-5am Mon-Thur; 8pm-7am Fri, Sat. **Admission** free. **No credit cards. Map** p301 B4.
Not a club per se, the Coaster is a wild blip in the regularised St-Géry bar scene. Two rooms crammed into a 17th-century house fill up with young guys and gals out for a night of danceable music without the rigmarole of a nightclub. There's even table football. Reasonable drinks prices, an easy-going crowd and dancing on the tables when there's no more space make Le Coaster soar like a rocket.

★ Fuse
208 rue Blaes, Marolles (02 511 97 89, www.fuse. be). Métro/pré-métro Porte de Hal, or bus 27, 48. **Open** 11pm-7am Thur-Sat. **Admission** €8-€14. **Map** p304 B8.
Fuse is the only club in Brussels with a truly international reputation and draws crowds from all over Benelux, France and Germany. It also hosts La Démence (*see p182*), the biggest and brightest gay night in Belgium. Don't come expecting a sleek superclub: Fuse is more like a disused Spanish hacienda with two floors of 2,000 people cranked to the max. It can also open midweek or on Sundays; see the website and www.facebook.com/fusebrussels.

FREE Havana
4 rue de l'Epée, Marolles (02 502 12 24, http:// havana-brussels.com). Tram 92, 94. **Open** 7pm-2am Thur; 7pm-5am Fri; 7pm-7am Sat. **Admission** free. **Map** p304 C7.
In the shadow of the Palais de Justice, Havana is a classy joint carved out of an old Marollien house, attracting an international, professional crowd. You can eat, drink (three bars) or dance to Latin-based live acts, with the place degenerating into a popular free-for-all as the evening moves into the wee hours. A nice summer terrace too.

★ Madame Moustache
5-7 quai au Bois à Brûler, St-Géry & Ste-Catherine (0489 739 912 mobile,

Fuse.

ARTS & ENTERTAINMENT

www.madamemoustache.be). Métro Ste-Catherine.
Open 7pm-4am Tue-Sat. **Admission** €8-€10.
No credit cards. Map p302 C3.
Madame M has brought a splash of light and life
to Ste-Catherine, slap bang in the middle of the
fish restaurant area. A colourful, hedonistic place,
it attracts a good-looking crowd out for a mix of
garage rock, retro disco and electronic club nights.
Occasional live concerts add texture to one of downtown's coolest spots.

★ Mirano Continental

*38 chaussée de Louvain, St-Josse (02 217 30 08,
www.mirano.be). Métro Madou.* **Open** 11pm-late
Fri, Sat. **Admission** members €10; non-members
€15. **No credit cards** (except bar). **Map** p306 G4.
This old 1950s cinema has been raising the roof for
years with its full-on house, minimal and electro parties for a super-cool Euro crowd. The doormen will
make sure you're dressed on the right side of respectable, so smarten up to ensure entry. Once in, you're
in one of Brussels' biggest spaces, where the sounds
and style are pumped to the max.

Recyclart

*Gare de Bruxelles-Chapelle, 25 rue des Ursulines,
Marolles (02 502 57 34, www.recyclart.be). Métro
Gare Centrale, or pré-métro Anneessens, or bus
27, 48, 95.* **Open** varies. **Admission** free-€7.
No credit cards. Map p301 C6.
Part of an urban regeneration project under the old
Chapelle railway station, Recyclart is a hotbed of
discovery. An agenda of electro sounds gives the

young crowd something to funk about, as new talent
gets a chance to showcase its spin-doctoring. Varied,
inventive and always throbbing. Occasional exhibitions are also held.

Le You

*18 rue Duquesnoy, Grand' Place & Around (02
639 14 00, www.leyou.be). Métro Gare Centrale.*
Open 11.30pm-5am Thur; 11.30pm-6am Fri, Sat.
Admission €10. **No credit cards. Map** p301 D5.
Le You is party central. Progressive house, breaks
and trance anthems are the order of the day, with a
good-looking, well-dressed crowd – although any
attempt at sophistication fades once lasers start hitting mirror balls. It's also famed for its Sunday gay
tea dance (*see p182*), which has nothing whatsoever
to do with tea.

Further afield

Cherry Moon

*144 Gentsesteenweg, Lokeren (09 349 0138,
www.cherrymoon.com). Train to Zele then bus
36 to Groenlaan.* **Open** 10pm-7am Fri, Sat,
nights before public hols. **Admission** €7-€15.
No credit cards.
One of Belgium's biggest (capacity 2,000) and longest-
serving nightclubs, Cherry Moon has been playing
hard trance and techno since 1991.

La Rocca

*384 Antwerpsesteenweg, Lier (03 489 1767,
www.larocca.be). Train to Lier or Mortsel then*

Madame Moustache. See p185.

ARTS & ENTERTAINMENT

MUSIC

For a city of only one million inhabitants, Brussels has an impressive and wide-ranging array of music on offer. There's a full schedule every night of the week, often going on until the small hours. Whether you're dancing to indie hipsters at the Botanique or nodding along to avant-garde acts at the Jazz Station, there's something to suit most music lovers.

Rock & pop

At the top end of the scale, major international artists have a range of venues to choose from. Led Zeppelin and Madonna have played at the city's biggest indoor venue, the **Forest National**, while Paul Weller, Franz Ferdinand and Brian Ferry have favoured the far more intimate setting of the **Ancienne Belgique**, a renovated theatre that's a short stroll from the Grand'Place. The other medium-sized venue, **Botanique**, is a spectacular greenhouse with three superb concert spaces.

★ Ancienne Belgique

110 boulevard Anspach, Grand' Place & Around (02 548 24 24, www.abconcerts.be). Pré-métro Bourse. **Open** *Box office* 10am-6pm Mon-Fri. **Admission** €15-€33. **Map** p301 C4.

The Ancienne Belgique used to be old, down-at-heel and terrific – Jacques Brel put in many an electrifying performance on its stage. It's now classy, shiny and, more importantly, still terrific. Its main hall can hold 2,000, mostly standing. There's also an intimate club room (capacity 280) for up-and-coming acts, as well as Huis 23, used for album launches and film screenings.

Les Ateliers Claus

15 rue Crickx, St-Gilles (02 534 51 03, www.lesateliersdaus.com). Bus 48, or tram 81. **Open** around 8.30pm, days vary. **Admission** €8-€15. **Map** p304 A10.

The tiny Ateliers – it holds around 150 people max – is worth the trip to St-Gilles if you're looking for somewhere friendly and in the know. The experimental programme is eclectic and non-scene, mixing guitar duos with proto-rock vocals. It all feels more New York than Brussels.

Beursschouwburg

20-28 rue Auguste Orts, St-Géry & Ste-Catherine (02 550 03 50, www.beursschouwburg.be). Pré-métro Bourse. **Open** *Box office* 10am-6pm Mon-Fri & 1hr before performance. **Admission** varies. **No credit cards. Map** p301 C4.

As well as being one of Brussels' major theatre venues (*see p197*), the Beurs has a strong programme of rock and world music, whether in its performance spaces, the rooftop bar or on the street.

bus 90 to Lier Duwyckstraat. **Open** 11.30pm-7.30am Fri-Sun. **Admission** €10. **No credit cards.**
Located between Antwerp and Mechelen, La Rocca enjoys a venerated position in Belgium's clubbing history, all-hallowed and treated with the greatest respect. No trackies or trainers.

COMEDY

As well as a lively and long-established culture of home-grown political irony, there's a burgeoning English-language comedy scene on display at the following venues. *See also p189* **Stand-Up Brussels**.

Black Sheep

8 Chaussée de Boondael, Ixelles (02 644 38 03, www.facebook.com/theblacksheepbrussels). Tram 81, or bus 59, 71. **Open** 5pm-1am daily. *Show* 8pm. **Admission** advance €16; door €20. **Map** p308 G10.

Kings of Comedy Club

489 Chaussée de Boondael, Ixelles (02 649 99 30, www.kocc.be). Métro Delta, or tram 25, 94. **Open** 6pm-3am daily. *Show* 8.30pm, days vary. **Admission** €5-€10. **No credit cards. Map** p311 J13.

Théâtre 140

140 avenue Plasky, Schaerbeek (02 733 97 08, www.theatre140.be). Pré-métro Diamant, or bus 29, 63. **Open** every 4-6 weeks. *Show* 8.30pm. **Admission** €26; Indian buffet €12. **Map** p307 L3.

★ Botanique

*236 rue Royale, St-Josse (02 226 12 11,
reservations 02 218 37 32, www.botanique.be).
Métro Botanique.* **Open** *Box office* 10am-6pm
daily. **Admission** €7-€20. **Map** p306 F2.
The unmissable 'Le Bota' is managed by the French-
speaking cultural community. The main corridor is
lined with luxuriant foliage and ponds, a reminder
of the period before the war when the building was
the centre of a vast botanical garden. The best of
the three separate venues here is the mid-sized
La Rotonde (capacity 350), where the audience
stands on steep steps and everyone gets a great
view of the band.

FREE Café Central

*14 Borgval, St-Géry & Ste-Catherine (no phone,
www.lecafecentral.com). Pré-métro Bourse.* **Open**
3pm-4am daily. **Admission** free. **Map** p301 C4.
Café Central has become one of the capital's most
fashionable venues, and an epicentre of cool. There
is a constant stream of gigs here, along with DJ
nights and cult-film screenings. The Central is also a
venue for various music festivals, including the legendary Jazz Marathon (*see p31*).

Cirque Royale

*81 rue de l'Enseignement, Upper Town (02 218
20 15, www.cirque-royal.org). Métro Madou.*
Open *Box office* 10.30am-6pm Mon-Fri &
1hr before performance. **Admission** varies.
Map p303 F4.
This is the nearest thing Brussels has to the Royal
Albert Hall. Plush and spherical, with great acoustics, it tends to draw the grand old men of rock
– Johnny Hallyday is among those to have been
subjected to calls for almost endless encores on its
stage. There's no dancing, though – in keeping with
its other role as a classical venue, you're expected to
sit down and look enraptured. Even talking to your
neighbour can draw disapproving glances.

Forest National

*208 avenue Victor Rousseau, Forest (0900 69
500, www.forestnational.be; tickets 070 69 11
11 premium line, www.sherpa.be). Tram 18, 52,
or bus 48, 54.* **Open** 1hr before performance
starts. **Admission** varies.
The biggest indoor venue in Brussels, this huge concrete and metal shed south of St-Gilles can accommodate 8,000 and can be cavernous or surprisingly
intimate depending on configuration. The big world
tour stars come here, as do the arena musicals.

FREE Grain d'Orge

*142 chaussée de Wavre, Ixelles (02 511 26 47).
Métro Porte de Namur.* **Open** 11am-3am Fri.
Concerts 9.30pm. **Admission** free. **Map** p305 F7.
The spit-and-sawdust Grain d'Orge has hosted gigs
every Friday night since 1983. Most of the acts tend
towards American-style rock, blues or country.

It's an easy place with an easy style and, this being
Belgium, a certain knowing sense of irony is all part
of the general fun.

FREE Kultuurkaffee

*Vrije Universiteit Brussel (Flemish University),
boulevard de la Plaine 2, Ixelles (02 629 23 25,
www.vub.ac.be/cultuur). Tram 23, 90.* **Open**
Concerts 8pm/8.30pm Thur. **Admission** free.
No credit cards. Map p311 J14.
A good place to sample the rather hidden, but often
quite adventurous, culture of the Flemish student
community, akin to their British counterparts when
it comes to liking late nights and a good drink. The
Kultuurkaffee, with support from radio station
Studio Brussel, puts on rock acts, electronica, world
music and the occasional Flemish oddity.

Magasin 4

*51B avenue du Port, Molenbeek (02 223 34 74,
www.magasin4.be). Métro Yser.* **Open** 7pm/8pm on
gig nights. **Admission** €8-€10. **No credit cards.**
This version of Magasin 4 opened its doors in 2010 in
an old industrial building on the canal in Molenbeek.
It's not as dilapidated as its predecessor, but it's still
sweaty and wonderful. Run by an association with
charity status, M4 remains one of the city's wilder
venues, with rock and indie bands alternated with
dubstep, drum 'n' bass and DJ nights. Check the
website for gig start times, as well as an occasional
10pm entry curfew.

Recyclart

*Gare de Bruxelles-Chapelle, 25 rue des Ursulines,
Marolles (02 502 57 34, www.recyclart.be). Métro
Gare Centrale, or pré-métro Anneessens, or bus
27, 48, 95.* **Open** *Concerts* around 10pm Fri, Sat,
last Sun of mth. **Admission** free-€8. **No credit
cards. Map** p301 C6.
This alternative venue, occupying several parts of
a now little-used train station, is well worth a visit
for the concerts, club nights (*see p186*) and other
events hosted here, from kids' puppet shows to
philosophical debates. It might look as if it has
been squatted by anarchists but, in fact, the non-
profit association that runs it has the full backing
of the city, and the place was set up with a grant
from the European Commission. Expect the likes
of indie, rock, dub, electronica and DJ sets. Every
last Thursday of the month, there's a free concert in
the buzzy bar (8pm-1am).

Jazz, folk & blues

Brussels has a great jazz tradition, embodied
in the wonderful Toots Thielemans. Jazz
continues to thrive here: stars to look out for
include saxophonist Steve Houben and his
trumpeter son Gregory, double bassist Philippe
Aerts, and Jef Neve the internationally renowned
pianist and composer. The Brussels Jazz

STAND-UP BRUSSELS

You're having a laugh.

Belgian humour can be pretty dark and excruciatingly to the point, often poking fun at politicians, language politics and themselves. But its main outlets are not so much in front of a microphone as in comic strip, film and on-stage revue, such as those at the **Théâtre de la Toison d'Or** (*see p199*). The established comedy circuit is more fractured, but – not so surprising for this multinational city – English comedy has arrived and is doing rather well for itself.

Stand Up World (www.standupworld.com) set itself up at **Théâtre 140** (*see p187*) in 2002 and has presented some of the world's top English-speaking comedians, including Al Murray, Jimmy Carr, Nina Conti, Sarah Millican and Omid Djalili. There's a big audience for the big names, so reserve a ticket (and optional Indian buffet) online and pay on the night.

Over in Ixelles, the **Black Sheep** (*see p187*) burger restaurant is home to **English Comedy Brussels** (www.englishcomedybrussels.com), which organises either solo stand-up shows or comedy nights with up to four international comedians, all performing in English. **International Comedians** (www.internationalcomedians.com), a European touring outfit, also plays here with a line-up of comedians from around the continent. Check the website for English-language nights.

If you want to check out the wacky world of Belgian comedy, sometimes with a bit of magic thrown in, **Kings of Comedy** (*see p187; pictured*) is a French-speaking comedy club that offers scratch events and up-and-coming talent as well as more established acts. It also shows comedy from around the French-speaking world, including African countries.

Finally, 2015 saw the launch of the **Kermezzo(o)** festival (www.kermezzoo.be) in mid April . The three-week festival at Parc du Cinquantenaire includes stand-up, cabaret, burlesque, circus and even comedy for kids. Starting in the daytime, it stretches late into the night – it's all a bit international, all a bit wild and all very much Brussels.

ARTS & ENTERTAINMENT

ARTS & ENTERTAINMENT

ESSENTIAL BRUSSELS MUSIC

Sounds of the city.

LOOKING FOR ST TROPEZ
TELEX (1979)

This debut by the ground-breaking electronic band from Brussels included big hit 'Moskow Diskow'. Part synth-pop, part disco, Telex remained anonymous, but worked with the likes of Sparks and the Pet Shop Boys. The band broke up after the death of driving force Marc Moulin in 2008.

CARPE DIEM
LARA FABIAN (1994)

Fabian, the biggest-selling female Belgian artist of all time, shot to fame with this 13-track breakthrough. Her childhood was spent between Etterbeek and Catania, and she wrote and sang catchy pop-dance tunes with true global appeal. She has since produced albums in French, Italian, English and Russian.

TOOTS 90 TOOTS
THIELEMANS (2012)

This 'best of' includes the greatest work – 'Bluesette', 'Midnight Cowboy' – of this legendary jazzster. Brussels-born harmonica player, guitarist and whistler Toots played with Charlie Parker and Miles Davis in Paris, then Ella Fitzgerald and Quincy Jones in the US. Oh, and on the theme to *Sesame Street*.

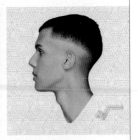

TC MATIC
TC MATIC (1981)

Founded in Brussels, TC Matic married new wave with French *chanson* and spawned successful careers for singer Arno Hintjens and guitarist/producer Jean-Marie Aerts. Fêted by the big UK names of the day, TC Matic only survived four albums but helped bring Belgian music to the international foreground.

BOÎTE À BONBONS
JACQUES BREL (2003)

They're all here, in this 16-CD box set, every gem penned by the bard of Schaerbeek, Jacques Brel. Released on the 25th anniversary of the death of Belgium's greatest singer-songwriter, it comprises three decades of honest, poignant songs, later covered by everyone from David Bowie to Nina Simone.

RACINE CARRÉE
STROMAE (2013)

Square Root was a global smash for this Etterbeek-raised singer-songwriter, who moves effortlessly through rap, hip hop and electronic genres. Originally inspired by Jacques Brel and Cuban and Congolese rhythms, Stromae brings his own background to the party – his father was lost in the Rwandan genocide.

Orchestra became only the second Belgian act – after Toots – to play at the New York Blue Note Jazz Club. Popular and often packed venues such as **Music Village** testify to locals' continuing enthusiasm for jazz, as do the number of jazz acts appearing at larger, more rock-oriented venues. The annual **Brussels Jazz Marathon** (*see p31*) in May is one of the city's biggest music events. For comprehensive gig listings, check out www.jazzinbelgium.com.

Brussels also stages some of the best world music around, much of it home-grown: award-winning a cappella outfit Zap Mama grew out of an African vocal workshop in Brussels. For visits from some of Africa's biggest stars, keep an eye out for fly posters around Matongé, the African quarter in Ixelles.

Couleur Café (*see p32*), one of the biggest world music festivals in Europe, is held in late June/early July at Tour et Taxis. This vast former customs warehouse (parts of the site are still under renovation) has space for four stages, a crafts village, workshops and food stalls. The festival continues its search for a permanent home, as Tour et Taxis becomes more of a corporate expo venue.

★ FREE L'Archiduc

6 rue Antoine Dansaert, St-Géry & Ste-Catherine (02 512 06 52, www.archiduc.be). Pré-métro Bourse. **Open** 4pm-5am daily. **Admission** free. **Map** p301 C4.

Built in the 1930s when it was opened by Madame Alice, this little art deco jewel was once an after-hours club for jazz fans. Nat King Cole used to drop by for an après-gig drink and to tinkle the ivories – the original 1929 piano is still in use. Brel was a regular. Bands at the Ancienne Belgique (*see p187*) tend to finish the night here, and Lady Gaga arrived on the arm of Tony Bennett after their album launch. Ring the doorbell to enter.

▶ *L'Archiduc is also one of the city's finest bars. See p75 for a review.*

Bonnefooi

8 rue des Pierres, Grand' Place & Around (02 513 53 93, www.bonnefooi.be). Pré-métro Bourse. **Open** 4pm-8am daily. **Admission** free-€5. **No credit cards. Map** p301 C4.

Bonnefooi sees itself as a place that you come across by chance, which is exactly what the word means in Brussels dialect. Early-evening jazz segues neatly into DJ sets as the night progresses – from lounge bar to disco in one easy sweep. Unusually for Brussels, there's a security guard on the door, so smile sweetly.

Bravo

7-11 rue de l'Alost, St-Géry & Ste-Catherine (no phone, www.bravobxl.com). Métro Ste-Catherine or Comte de Flandre. **Open** 9am-late Mon-Fri; 10.30am-late Sat, Sun. **Admission** free-€5. **Map** p302 B3.

Live music venue by night, relaxed bar by day, Bravo is the latest and, arguably, bravest venture from Brussels entertainment entrepreneur Frédéric Nicolay. No easy retro themes here, as typical of his earlier creations, such as the Roi des Belges (*see p77*) in the heart of St-Géry; Bravo is stripped back, bare in feel, industrial in style and ready for action. It is also tucked down a grey side street set in from the canal, at the other end from the nightlife vortex and its constant passing trade. Own-made drinks, both soft and alcoholic, complement an extensive beer selection and a menu of superior snacks, charcuterie platters and healthy soups. Downstairs, regular live music currently includes jazz sessions on Wednesdays and soul-tinged !Groove jams on Fridays, interspersed with one-off shows and CD releases under the ballpark category of world music.

Brussels Folk Club

La Porte Noire, 67 rue des Alexiens, Grand' Place & Around (no phone, www.theblackdoor.be). Bus 48, 95. **Open** 6.30pm 2nd Sun of mth. *Concerts* 7pm. **No credit cards. Map** p301 C6.

Once a month, the Brussels Folk Club moves into the Black Door, an evocative, arched cellar that was once the kitchen for the nuns of a 16th-century Alexien convent. Wimples aside, this has become a fixture on the Brussels folk scene, with contemporary and traditional international music reflecting the diversity of the city. Artisanal Belgian beers and quality food only add to the cosmopolitan – and usually packed to the brickwork – vibe.

FREE Café Bizon

7 rue Pont de la Carpe, St-Géry & Ste-Catherine (02 502 46 99, www.cafebizon.com). Pré-métro Bourse. **Open** 4pm-2am Mon-Fri; 6pm-2am Sat, Sun. *Concerts* 9.30pm/10pm. **Admission** free. **Map** p301 C4.

This small, friendly and authentic bar has a mid-west America feel with its brickwork, bar stools and comfortable grunge. The live blues acts set up on the floor and manage to transport you far away from the surrounding Chinatown neighbourhood. A tiny mezzanine level gives you a view of the proceedings in the often packed bar. Blues, booze and a bison's head, what more do you need?

Espace Senghor

366 chaussée de Wavre, EU Quarter (02 230 31 40, www.senghor.be). Métro Maelbeek or Schuman. **Open** varies. **Admission** €8-€20. **No credit cards. Map** p308 F5.

The French-speaking community restored and now runs this venue adjacent to the EU Quarter. It has an imaginative and popular programme of jazz and world music concerts, usually three or four times a month. It's not the place for a riotous night out, but the musical line-up is usually excellent in a beautiful little theatre spot.

ARTS & ENTERTAINMENT

Jazz Station

193A chaussée de Louvain, St-Josse (02 733 13 78, www.jazzstation.be). Bus 29, 63. **Open** 11am-7pm Wed-Sat. *Concerts* varies. **Admission** €6-€10. **No credit cards. Map** p307 J3.

Jazz Station is set in a lovely old building and has real artistic flair. As well as jazz concerts, it offers an experimental space for new and emerging bands; during the day, jazz outfits hold open rehearsals so that serious fans can see how it's all put together. With low entry fees, a swinging bar and an exhibition space, Jazz Station is a superbly creative venue.

★ Music Village

50 rue des Pierres, Grand' Place & Around (02 513 13 45, www.themusicvillage.com). Pré-métro Bourse. **Open** 7pm-late Wed-Sat. *Concerts* 8.30pm Wed, Thur; 9pm Fri, Sat. **Admission** €7.50-€20. **Map** p301 C4.

The Music Village occupies two 17th-century buildings near the Grand'Place. The club provides a home for more traditional jazz styles, as well as the occasional avant-garde act (booking online advisable). Weekdays attract a lot of business visitors, but Fridays and Saturdays are reserved for performers sufficiently well known to fill the place with jazz aficionados. Dinner is optional.

Sounds Jazz Club

28 rue de la Tulipe, Ixelles (02 512 92 50 after 6pm, www.soundsjazzclub.be). Métro Porte de Namur, or bus 54, 71. **Open** 8pm-4am Mon-Sat. *Concerts* 10pm. **Admission** free-€15. **No credit cards. Map** p305 F8.

Sounds continues to be a compulsory port of call for local jazz fans. Far enough out of town to discourage tourists (though only 15 minutes by bus), it attracts expats and eurocrats who like to swap their dull grey suits for glad rags. It favours modern-ish jazz, but there is also the odd big band night; Wednesdays usually bring Latino concerts. It's open until very late, even midweek.

La Soupape

26 rue Alphonse de Witte, Ixelles (02 649 58 88, www. lasoupape.be). Tram 81, 82, or bus 38, 59, 60, 71. **Open** 8.30pm-midnight on gig nights. **Admission** €7-€9. **No credit cards. Map** p311 G10.

Set in a side street in the ever more lively area near place Flagey and the Ixelles lakes, this intimate, fun venue specialises in *chanson française* – it holds heats for a national competition. La Soupape is a great place for discovering new talent, with many acts destined to be seen later by far more than the 50 people squeezed around its rickety tables. Because of this, it's always best to reserve.

La Tentation

28 rue de Laeken, St-Géry & Ste-Catherine (02 223 22 75, www.centrogalego.be). Métro/pré-métro De Brouckère. **Open** 7pm-1am Fri, Sat & event nights. **Admission** €5-€30. **Map** p302 C3.

This fine building, with its Horta staircase, was saved by the Centro Gallego, run by Brussels' Galician community. It has a commendably eclectic approach in its world music concerts, held twice monthly. As well as traditional Galician music, it puts on flamenco, salsa and even Flemish folk (flamenco, the Spanish for 'Flemish', was originally a pejorative catch-all for undesirables, not least Gypsies and Flemish representatives at the Spanish court). The centre also runs courses in belly dancing and the Galician bagpipes.

Théâtre Marni

23-25 rue de Vergnies, Ixelles (02 639 09 82, www.theatremarni.com). Tram 81, 82, or bus 71. **Open** 8pm-2am Tue-Sat. *Concerts* 8.30pm. **Admission** €14. **Map** p308 G9.

This renovated theatre, a former bowling alley near place Flagey, has a wonderfully varied programme of quality music and world music from Belgium and beyond. Gigs take place in the large and comfortable main theatre or in the entrance hall, and often include a meal and drink in the ticket price. The Marni also has a splendid bar attached.

Music Village.

ARTS & ENTERTAINMENT

Performing Arts

The performing arts in Belgium are seen as an essential part of the nation's cultural life. The avant-garde sits comfortably alongside the traditionally staged play, grand opera meets low-brow revue and leaping over it all is the dance scene for which Belgium is so renowned. A national and international mix of performances and productions happens everywhere, from the stone edifices of national institutions to pocket theatres and even the street. The season runs from September to June; venues are usually closed in summer, which is when the performing arts festivals take over. Traditionally, healthy subsidies meant that ticket prices were reasonable, but recent cuts to the arts budget, particularly in Flanders and at federal level, have brought an atmosphere of unease and, in some cases, absolute outrage. There may need to be some fancy footwork to ensure that the show goes on.

INFORMATION & TICKETS

Useful listings site www.agenda.be covers classical music, dance and theatre. Tickets are usually booked direct with the venue, so it's worth checking venue websites for an online booking option. Some will charge a small booking fee. There is a culture of turning up on the door, but it's always worth checking ahead that seats are available. Classical concerts and opera tend to sell out, so these should be booked well in advance. Most venues offload unsold tickets with **Arsène 50** (BIP, 2-4 rue Royale, Upper Town, www.arsene50.be; open 12.30-5pm Tue-Sat), which sells them at half price plus a €1 booking fee. All available performances are updated on the website daily. If you go to the office in person, you'll receive a voucher to exchange at the theatre, or you can book online from 2pm.

CLASSICAL MUSIC & OPERA

The operatic jewel in the crown is **Théâtre de la Monnaie**, which holds a special place in Belgian hearts: it was an opera performance held here in 1830 that precipitated the events that led to

Belgium's emergence as an independent state (*see p249*). The **Bozar** (as the **Palais des Beaux-Arts** is commonly called) is the centre for classical concerts, along with the **Conservatoire Royal** and **Flagey** – but the cathedral and city churches have also proven themselves to be worthy, atmospheric venues.

Cathédrale des Sts Michel et Gudule

Place Ste-Gudule, Upper Town (02 217 83 45, www.cathedralisbruxellensis.be). Métro Gare Centrale or Parc, or tram 92, 93. **Open & tickets** varies. **Map** p303 E4.
Brussels' most grandiose church (*see p100*) isn't the greatest for acoustics with its ten-second echo. However, there are some impressive organ recitals and the Sunday 12.30pm mass (10am in summer) features special concerts most of the year round. Evening ones are more rare.

Conservatoire Royal de Bruxelles

30 rue de la Régence, Upper Town (02 511 04 27, www.conservatoire.be). Tram 92, 94, or bus 95. **Open** Box office 1hr before performance or 10 days in advance from the Bozar. **Tickets** from €5. **Map** p305 D6.

Théâtre de la Monnaie.

ARTS & ENTERTAINMENT

The Conservatory's fine hall is a little too narrow for full-size symphonic orchestras, but it's perfect for chamber formations and solo recitals. It is here that the preliminary rounds of the famous Queen Elisabeth competition (*see p32*) are held. The venue also organises lunchtime concerts at the Musée des Instruments de Musique (*see p106*) and hosts the imaginative Midi-Minimes festival (www.midis-minimes.be) in summer.

Flagey

Place Ste-Croix, next to place Flagey, Ixelles (02 641 10 20, www.flagey.be). Tram 81, or bus 59, 71. **Open** *Box office* 11am-10pm Tue-Sat & 1hr before performance. **Tickets** varies. **Map** p308 G10.

Flagey, former home of the National Radio Orchestra, folded in the 1990s, then reopened after a great deal of lengthy and very expensive renovation work. In its heyday, the main studio was acoustically one of Europe's finest, and hosted some truly memorable world premières. Now it presents a range of contemporary and classical concerts as well as being a venue for festivals.

★ Palais des Beaux-Arts (Bozar)

23 rue Ravenstein, Upper Town (02 507 82 00, www.bozar.be). Métro Gare Centrale or Parc, or tram 92, 93. **Open** *Box office* In person 11am-7pm Tue-Sat & 1hr before performance. By phone 11am-6pm Mon-Fri; 1-7pm Sat. **Tickets** €11-€75; €9.50-€52 reductions. **Map** p303 E5.

See p195 **Bozar for All**.

★ Théâtre de la Monnaie

Place de la Monnaie/4 rue Léopold, Grand'Place & Around (070 23 39 39, www.lamonnaie.be). Métro/pré-métro De Brouckère. **Open** *Box office* (23 rue Léopold) 11am-6pm Tue-Sat & 1hr before performance. **Tickets** €12-€197. **Map** p301 D4.

The national opera house soaks up the lion's share of federal arts subsidies, though it will be taking a massive funding hit in the coming years (*see p199* **In the Know**). Its repertoire balances contemporary work and sturdy productions of the classics with an impressive programme of recitals in its smaller spaces.

DANCE

Brussels has no resident classical ballet company. That honour goes to Antwerp-based Royal Ballet of Flanders (https://operaballet.be), which produces ballet and musical theatre of outstanding quality. It was announced in 2015 that internationally renowned choreographer Sidi Larbi Cherakoui is to be the company's new artistic director, while continuing to be involved with his own group, Eastman (www.east-man.be). Anne Teresa de Keersmaeker, director of Rosas (www.rosas.be), continues to be at the top of her game, along with Wim Vandekeybus and his company Ultima Vez (www.ultimavez.com). Alain Platel's celebrated collective Les Ballets C de la B (www.lesballetscdelab.be) is a global success and Charleroi Danses/Plan K (www.charleroi-danses.be), led by a quartet of artistic directors, is ever-influential.

BOZAR FOR ALL

Proactive, inclusive and an art deco masterpiece.

When Victor Horta's art nouveau masterpiece the Maison du Peuple was unceremoniously demolished in 1965 (see p260), the folk of Brussels felt they had lost a true people's palace. What they didn't realise was that there was another building ready to take on the mantle, though it would be a few more decades before it fully emerged.

In most European capitals, a Centre for Fine Arts would be just that – a staid, stately institution filled with little but paintings. Not in Brussels. Here, it takes many names: Palais des Beaux-Arts (see p106) in French, Paleis Voor Schone Kunsten in Dutch, shortened to Bozar or PSK, respectively. But it's the Bozar moniker that has become the snappy, recognisable brand name throughout the city.

Horta was given a major task in designing the building into the side of a hill between the Lower and Upper Towns. He also had to keep it low-level, so as not to spoil the king's view from the palace above. The result is a sturdy art deco arts centre on eight levels. For much of its life, the Beaux-Arts was a temple of high art attracting a middle-class, moneyed set. Oh, how things can change.

When current director Paul Dujardin took over in 2002, he wanted to reinstate the Bozar as a place where anyone could enjoy the arts and, in his first four years, he doubled the visitor footprint to one million a year. Now it's home to the National Orchestra of Belgium, who can play to a 2,200 crowd in the main Henry Le Boeuf hall. In this semicircular space stands the grand organ, the only musical instrument Horta designed, though it hasn't been played since 1967. Its restoration should be finished by the end of 2015. Other rooms offer performance spaces for chamber music, theatre and dance, while above them are the vast exhibition halls for visual art as well as cinema spaces (the Bozar hosts the annual International Festival of Fantastic Film; see p176).

What makes the Bozar a real people's palace is that no one feels excluded and, with its shop, restaurant (Bozar Brasserie; see p108) and bars, no one feels intimidated. It still rightly gives space to higher art – it hosts the final stages of the prestigious Concours Musical International Reine Elisabeth de Belgique (Queen Elisabeth Music Competition; see p32) for example – but its mixed programming also represents multicultural classical music, dance and theatre from around the world. It attracts audiences of all ages and runs engaging participation programmes. Bringing artists and audiences together is one of the city's great cultural achievements of recent years. Horta would be proud.

ARTS & ENTERTAINMENT

ARTS & ENTERTAINMENT

IN THE KNOW EVENTS PASS

In an effort to reduce car usage, many of the bigger cultural institutions are using an Events Pass. Included in the ticket price is a return journey on public transport (bus, tram or métro). You'll find a code printed on the ticket that you need to enter at one of STIB's ticket machines to retrieve the pass. Details at www.stib-mivb.be.

Les Brigittines

1 petite rue des Brigittines, Marolles (02 506 43 00, www.brigittines.be). Bus 27, 48, 95. **Open** *Box office* 10am-1pm, 2-6pm Mon-Fri & 1hr before performance. **Tickets** €12-€14; €5-€10 reductions. **No credit cards. Map** p301 C6.

Les Brigittines, by the abandoned railway station of Bruxelles-Chapelle, is an extraordinary multimedia space: a decommissioned church taken back to its bare arches and pillars with a modern glass extension. Known primarily as a dance venue and as the centre of a summer dance festival, it is also used for theatre and art installations.

Cirque Royal

81 rue de l'Enseignement, Upper Town (02 218 20 15, www.cirque-royal.org). Métro Madou. **Open** *Box office* 10.30am-6pm Mon-Fri & 1hr before start of performance. **Tickets** varies. **Map** p303 F4.

This vast theatre space hosts the big international tours. Come here if you want to see the St Petersburg Ballet or the Chippendales.

Halles de Schaerbeek

22B rue Royale Ste-Marie, Schaerbeek (02 218 21 07, www.halles.be). Tram 25, 92, 94. **Open** *Box office* 1-6pm Tue-Fri; 1-6pm if performance Sat. **Tickets** €15-€18; €12-€15 reductions. **Map** p306 F1.

This magnificent former agricultural hall has become a key venue for art forms across the board. An important cultural centre for the local community, it features a full programme of dance, hip hop, circus and theatre.

★ Kaaitheaterstudio's

81 rue du Notre-Dame du Sommeil, St-Géry & Ste-Catherine (02 201 59 59, www.kaaitheater.be). Métro Ste-Catherine. **Open** *Box office* 11am-6pm Mon-Fri & 1hr before performance. **Tickets** €10-€16; €8 under-26s. **Map** p302 A3.

The renowned studio complex of its bigger sister, Kaaitheater (*see p197*), Kaaitheaterstudio's stages smaller theatre productions, as well as the more esoteric dance companies, in an intimate setting. Two internationally renowned Belgian companies are based here: Meg Stuart's Damaged Goods (www.damagedgoods.be) and Thomas Hauert's Cie Zoo (www.zoo-thomashauert.be).

Les Brigittines.

Koninklijke Vlaamse Schouwburg. See p198.

★ Théâtre les Tanneurs

75 rue des Tanneurs, Marolles (02 512 17 84, www.lestanneurs.be). Métro/pré-métro Porte de Hal, or bus 20, 48. **Open** Box office 1hr before performance. **Tickets** €12; €5-€8 reductions. **No credit cards. Map** p304 B7.

Les Tanneurs has won the support of a loyal local crowd, thanks to its radical approach to theatre and dance, and its community-focused workshops and projects. A little powerhouse.

THEATRE

Two of Belgium's largest arts subsidies go to the **Koninklijke Vlaamse Schouwburg** (Royal Flemish Theatre) and the **Théâtre National**. Each is resolutely representative of its language community, though there is a healthy sharing of ideas and projects. The other big Flemish (and international) players are the **Kaaitheater** and **Beursschouwburg**. The more political, fringe scene tends to be French-language, such as **Théâtre 140** and the tiny **Théâtre de Poche**. In summer, festivals take over the city, offering wide-ranging programmes of theatre and dance. The one truly international festival is **Kunstenfestivaldesarts** (*see p31*), which dives deep into the unknown.

There are numerous English-language amateur theatre groups in Brussels: American Theatre Company, the English Comedy Club, the Brussels Light Opera Company, the Brussels Shakespeare Society, European Theatre Club and the Irish Theatre Group. There's also Green Parrot Productions (www.greenparrot.eu), an amateur theatre company for children and adults that specialises in popular musicals. Three of the theatre groups clubbed together to buy their own premises and are based at the Warehouse Studio (73 rue Waelhem, Schaerbeek, no phone). Details of all these groups can be found at the English Language Theatre in Brussels portal: http://theatreinbrussels.com.

Beursschouwburg

20-28 rue Auguste Orts, St-Géry & Ste-Catherine (02 550 03 50, www.beursschouwburg.be). Pré-métro Bourse. **Open** Box office 10am-6pm Mon-Fri & 1hr before performance. **Tickets** varies. **No credit cards. Map** p301 C4.

The Beurs is a centre of excellence for modern cross-form art and performance. Its overall aesthetic is industrial and minimalist, providing an understated backdrop to its innovative and highly international programme. In 2015, it celebrated its 50th birthday with the banner 'under construction, unpredictable, unpronounceable, since 1965'.

★ Kaaitheater

20 square Sainctelette, Schaerbeek (02 201 59 59, www.kaaitheater.be). Métro Yser. **Open** Box office 11am-6pm Tue-Fri & 1hr before performance. **Tickets** varies; €8 under-26s. **Map** p302 C1.

The art deco Kaai is one of Brussels' most invigorating performance spaces, and stands at the forefront of the avant-garde. Visiting theatre and dance companies include Forced Entertainment (UK), the Wooster Group (USA) and Toneelgroep (NL).

Koninklijke Vlaamse Schouwburg

9 quai aux Pierres de Taille, St-Géry & Ste-Catherine (02 210 11 12, www.kvs.be). Métro Yser. **Open** *Box office* noon-7pm Tue-Fri &1hr before performance. **Tickets** €17-€20; €9-€17 reductions. **Map** p302 C2. Known as the KVS, the Royal Flemish Theatre is one of the big subsidised houses providing serious theatre in Dutch. Productions range from weirdly modern to firmly classical, with a sprinkling of guest productions from Belgium and Europe. There is a more experimental black box studio next door, the KVS Box. *Photo p197.*

Rideau de Bruxelles

7A rue Goffart, Ixelles (02 737 16 01, www. rideaudebruxelles.be). **Open** *Box office* 2-6pm Tue-Fri; 2-6pm if performance Sat. **Tickets** €20; €10-€15 reductions. **Map** p308 F8. Since leaving the Bozar in 2014, the Rideau has set up home in Ixelles where it seems to have taken a new lease of life. Concentrating on new French writing, the work is fresh and relevant.

★ Théâtre 140

140 avenue Plasky, Schaerbeek (02 733 97 08, www.theatre140.be). Pré-métro Diamant, or bus 29, 63. **Open** *Box office* noon-6pm Mon-Fri; 3-7pm if performance Sat; from 7.30pm on performance days (cash only). **Tickets** €18; €8-€16 reductions. **Map** p307 L3.

Jo Dekmine runs the 140, as he has done for decades; the 2015 season is the theatre's 53rd. Forever seeking out the new and exciting, the programme is all about innovative theatre from home and abroad. The after-show bar is worth a visit in itself. All in all, a marvellous place.

Théâtre des Martyrs

22 place des Martyrs, Grand'Place & Around (02 223 32 08, www.theatredesmartyrs.be). Metro/pré-métro De Brouckère or Rogier. **Open** *Box office* 11am-6pm Tue-Fri; 2-6pm Sat. **Tickets** €14.50-€16.50; €9-€14 reductions. **Map** p301 D3. The fresh, modern interior in a classic townhouse is representative of the Martyrs, one of the city's most exciting theatre spaces by a long chalk, and home to three resident companies. The production style is modern and resolutely French, with an emphasis on new takes on classic playwrights: Shakespeare, Chekhov, Molière and Duras. The studio space receives smaller visiting companies.

Théâtre National

111-115 boulevard Emile Jacqmain, St-Géry & Ste-Catherine (02 203 53 03, www.theatre national.be). Métro/pré-métro De Brouckère. **Open** *Box office* 11am-6pm Tue-Sat &1hr before performance. **Tickets** €19; €8-€15 reductions. **Map** p303 D2.

Théâtre du Toone.

It's important to remember that this isn't truly a national theatre as such, being that it serves only the French-speaking community. Nonetheless, this is one of Belgium's most important producing houses, and one of its most heavily subsidised. The National has found great success with a mix of classical, modern, satirical and youth theatre – all played out in the most beautiful performance spaces.

Théâtre de Poche

1A chemin de Gymnase, Ixelles (02 649 17 27, www.poche.be). Tram 23, 90, 93, 94. **Open** *Box office* 10am-5.30pm Mon-Sat. **Tickets** €18; Wed €8; €12-€15 reductions. **No credit cards. Map** p310 G14.

The little Pocket Theatre was founded by Roger Domani in 1951 and was originally located on the chaussée d'Ixelles, until it was demolished to make way for a shopping gallery. Since then, it has sat in a small building in the Bois de la Cambre, which has been the making of it. The work is demanding and hard-hitting and always pushes limits, taking world politics as its starting point.

Théâtre Royal des Galeries

32 galerie de la Roi, Grand'Place & Around (02 512 04 07, www.theatredesgaleries.be). Métro Gare Centrale. **Open** *Box office* 11am-6pm Tue-Sat. **Tickets** €12-€29; €10-€23 reductions. **Map** p301 D4.

This gem's claim to fame is that Magritte painted a fresco on the ceiling, though the powers-that-be couldn't cope with his strange spherical bells flying through the clouds, so they placed a vast glass-balled chandelier there instead. Today, the theatre is perhaps best known for its New Year revue.

Théâtre Royal du Parc

3 rue de la Loi, Upper Town (02 505 30 30, www.theatreduparc.be). Métro Arts-Loi or Parc. **Open** *Box office* noon-7pm Tue-Sat. **Tickets** €5-€31; €5-€14 reductions. **Map** p303 F5.

This stunner was built as a playhouse for the rich in 1782 and has managed to hang on to a mixed-age, mixed-interest audience ever since. The programme is a combination of traditional and contemporary.

Théâtre de la Toison d'Or

396 galeries de la Toison d'Or, Ixelles (02 510 05 10, www.ttotheatre.com). Métro Porte de Namur. **Open** *Box office* 10am-4pm Mon; 10am-6pm Tue-Fri; 2-6pm Sat. **Tickets** €16-€22; €8-€20 reductions. **Map** p305 E7.

A magnet for camp, madcap comedy and revue – offbeat takes on Eurovision, piss-takes of the sci-fi genre, irreverent stand-up comedy and café-theatre.

★ Théâtre du Toone

21 petite rue des Bouchers, Grand'Place & Around (02 511 71 37, www.toone.be). Métro/pré-métro De Brouckère. **Open** *Box office*

IN THE KNOW
LOWERING THE BARRE

In December 2014, Peter de Caluwe, artistic director of La Monnaie (*see p194*), caused a major stir in cultural circles when he announced the withdrawal of all dance programming at the Opera House. With a new government came new arts cuts, and the federally funded Monnaie is faced with a reduction of 16.28 per cent to its budget over the next five years, totalling €6.5 million. Add in previous cuts and de Caluwe reckons on a 30 per cent funding slash over ten years. He calls it a 'cultural blackout'.

La Monnaie has a long history of dance, dating from when Maurice Béjart headed a company there in the 1960s. More recently, Anne Teresa de Keersmaeker made it home for her company Rosas, and it has long attracted world-class choreographers such as Belgian supremo Sidi Larbi Cherkaoui. But with de Caluwe also losing 16 staff, he says something has to give – now the international dance community is waiting to see how the government will react.

1pm-midnight Tue-Sun. **Tickets** €12; €9 reductions. **No credit cards. Map** p301 D4.

This tiny place has been going for generations. It is a world-famous, world-class marionette theatre with productions in Bruxellois dialect. It's essential to book tickets in advance (you can send a form direct from the website).

Théâtre Varia

78 rue du Sceptre, Ixelles (02 640 35 50, www.varia.be). Bus 38, 60, 95, 96. **Open** *Box office* 1-7pm Tue-Fri. **Tickets** €18-€20; €6-€15 reductions. **Map** p308 H8.

Firmly French in nature, the Varia mixes up a programme of new writing (Belgian and Moroccan) with modern takes on Shakespeare in translation and a varied dance programme. This is an edgy space that addresses social issues and life stories in a no-nonsense way.

Wolubilis

251 avenue Paul Hymans, Woluwe-St-Lambert (02 761 60 30, www.wolubilis.be). Métro Roodebeek, or bus 29, 45. **Open** *Box office* 10am-5pm Mon-Fri; from 7.30pm on performance nights. **Tickets** €15-€50; €9-€45 reductions.

Wolubilis is an impressively modern arts centre featuring stylish design and a 486-seat theatre with a convertible stage – well suited to its broad remit of drama, music, dance, film and rock concerts. You can eat there, too, so it makes the short trip from the centre of town worthwhile.

ARTS & ENTERTAINMENT

Escapes & Excursions

Antwerp

Antwerp has been a key player on the European stage for hundreds of years, including being a major trading centre (specialising in diamonds) and an artistic powerhouse in the 16th century and becoming one of the world's most important ports in the 19th. Today, it is a world-class, world heritage city. It remains the global hub for the uncut diamond industry, has attracted new technology and knowledge-based investment and still boasts one of Europe's biggest ports. Its rich artistic and cultural heritage is evident in the historic centre and numerous museums. Another bonus is that this is a city made for walking – no hills, streetloads of pedestrianised areas and the air ringing with the sound of bicycle bells.

Antwerp developed as a significant trading port in the 12th century. As the rival harbour of Bruges slowly silted up and the Flemish textile industry flourished, so Antwerp boomed. By the mid 16th century, it was the leading trading centre in Europe, with a population of 100,000 and a large diamond industry – set up by Jews escaping Portugal – bringing magnificent wealth. It was a time of great cultural prestige, with new architecture reflecting the city's new status; a raft of artists made it their home, Peter Paul Rubens and Anthony van Dyck among them.

This era of prosperity came to a savage end with the Reformation and subsequent religious riots and repression. By 1589, the population had shrunk to 42,000; the death blow was dealt by the Treaty of Munster in 1648, closing off the River Scheldt to shipping. The Industrial Revolution saw Antwerp again prosper, to the extent that it ranked as the world's third largest port at the end of the 19th century. The hosting of World Fairs in 1885, 1894 and 1930, as well as the Olympic Games in 1920, confirmed the city's global status. Although Antwerp suffered badly during the two world wars and the interim slump, it started to recover in the 1990s.

GETTING THERE & INFORMATION

Antwerp makes a perfect day trip from Brussels, with regular trains taking around 40 minutes.

You arrive at the cathedral-like Antwerpen Centraal station, from where it's a short walk to the compact and manageable old town.

Toerisme Antwerpen

13 Grote Markt (03 232 01 03, www. visitantwerpen.be). **Open** 9am-5.45pm Mon-Sat; 9am-4.45pm Sun & bank holidays. **Map** p205 A3 Another branch of the tourist office can be found at level 0 at Centraal Station.

SIGHTS & MUSEUMS
Grote Markt & around

The best way to get your bearings is to head along the Meir, the pedestrianised street that leads from the station to the city centre, towards the cathedral spire and the **Grote Markt** with its charmingly ornate guildhouses and 16th-century **Stadhuis** (Town Hall), along with the 19th-century statue of Brabo, symbol of the city. The stunning 14th-century **Onze Lieve Vrouwekathedraal** (Cathedral of Our Lady), the largest Gothic church in the Low Countries, is just off the square. From here, a walk along Vleeshouwersstraat brings you to the **Vleeshuis** (Butcher's Hall). Literally meaning 'flesh house', it was built as a guildhouse and meat market.

Across Jordaenskaai, you'll come to the river Scheldt and the **Steen**, a bulky castle that once defended the river. The Steen is almost as old as Antwerp itself and has become a noted symbol of the city. Built in 1200, it was part of the fortifications; later it served as a prison, and then housed the National Maritime Museum until the collection was moved to the new MAS museum in 2011. It's still worth walking around the exterior and enjoying the river terraces – don't miss the statue of Lange Wapper, a giant of legend who was said to terrorise the locals in medieval times.

South of the Steen, in St Jansvliet, you'll find the entrance to the 600-metre (1,969-foot) **St Anna pedestrian tunnel**, which connects the right and left banks of the river. Wooden escalators take you underground from the art deco bulkhead, then it's a ten-minute walk to the other side and a great view of the city skyline. Antwerp was built mainly on the right bank of the Scheldt and consequently the left bank isn't too lively. Nevertheless, it can claim the only beach in Antwerp, the **St Anna Strand**, a good 15-minute walk from the tunnel – keep the river to your right.

The narrow knot of streets behind the cathedral emerge at the baroque church of **St Carolus Borromeuskerk** on Hendrik Conscienceplein, one of the city's prettiest

**IN THE KNOW
CHURCH KNOW-HOW**

The diocese of Antwerp runs a website that presents the cultural and historic aspects of its churches specifically for tourists. TOPA (Antwerp, Churches & Tourism) also lays on guided tours to five of its churches. For details, see www.topa.be.

squares. Close by is the lovely **Rockoxhuis Museum**. Mayor Nicolaas Rockox was a friend of Rubens and his 17th-century townhouse is filled with period furnishings. Further north is the classical **Koninklijke Academie voor Schone Kunsten** (Royal Academy of Fine Arts). While it's very much a place of learning, the building and its extensive library are well worth a visit. On Lange Nieuwstraat is the extravagantly baroque **St Jacobskerk**. This was Rubens' parish church and is where he's buried.

Not far south of the church is one of the city's major tourist draws, the **Rubenshuis**, home to the artist for most of his life. He bought it in 1611, following his return from Italy. It's wise to come early to avoid the large tour parties; speed through the ugly modern ticket office outside the house and plunge into the wonderful interior.

ESCAPES & EXCURSIONS

St Anna pedestrian tunnel.

Rockoxhuis Museum.

ESCAPES & EXCURSIONS

FREE Koninklijke Academie voor Schone Kunsten

31 Mutsaardstraat (03 213 71 00, www.artesis.be/academie). **Open** *Library* 10am-5pm Mon-Wed, Fri; 10am-6pm Thur. **Admission** free. **Map** p205 B2 ❶
One of the oldest art schools in the world, founded in 1663. The Academy's fashion department formed the driving force behind the avant-garde Antwerp Six, who famously took London Fashion Week by storm in 1987. *See p215* **Six and Up.**

★ Onze Lieve Vrouwekathedraal

Handschoenmarkt (03 213 99 51, www.de kathedraal.be). **Open** 10am-5pm Mon-Fri; 10am-3pm Sat; 1-4pm Sun. **Admission** €6; free under-12s. **No credit cards**. **Map** p205 B3 ❷
The cathedral has an impressive collection of paintings and sculpture, the most celebrated of which

are four works by Rubens: *The Resurrection, The Assumption, The Raising of the Cross* and – the one that's considered a masterpiece – *The Descent from the Cross.* Outside, the single spire rises 123m (404ft) and would have been flanked by a twin had the money not dried up. *See p206* **Finishing Touches.**

Rockoxhuis Museum

10-12 Keizerstraat (03 201 92 50, www.rockoxhuis. be). **Open** 10am-5pm Tue-Sun. **Admission** €8; €1-€6 reductions; free under-19s. **No credit cards**. **Map** p205 B2 ❸
This is more a gallery than a recreated home, but it gives an authentic idea of how the wealthy would have lived in 17th-century Antwerp. The focus is the small but perfectly formed art collection, which includes works by Matsys, Van Dyck and local boys Joachim Beuckelaer and Frans Snyders.

★ Rubenshuis

9-11 Wapper (03 201 15 55, www.rubenshuis.be). **Open** 10am-5pm Tue-Sun. **Admission** €8; €6 reductions; free under-12s & last Wed of mth. **No credit cards**. **Map** p205 C3 ❹
This is one of the most notable baroque buildings in Antwerp. The house passed through several owners before the City of Antwerp bought it; it has since been completely renovated and the garden entirely reconstructed. Much of the furniture dates from the 17th century, but was not originally in the house. Highlights include the semicircular gallery where

IN THE KNOW BACK IN 2018

The **Koninklijk Museum voor Schone Kunsten** (Royal Museum of Fine Arts, www.kmska.be) is closed for renovations until 2018. Until then, the museum's Flemish art collection and temporary exhibitions are hosted in alternative spaces around Antwerp. Check the website for the latest news.

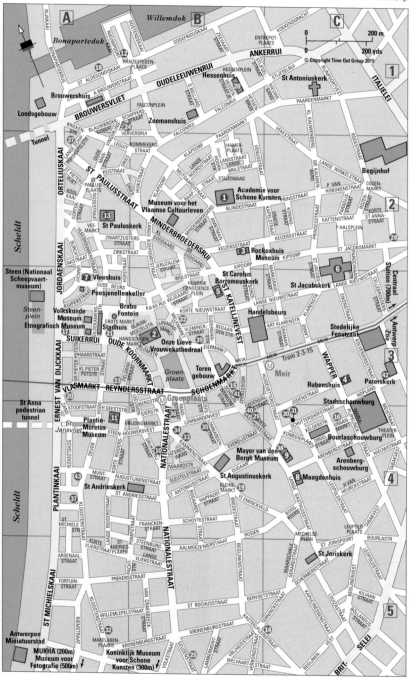

Rubens displayed his vast collection of classical sculpture, and his spacious studio, overlooked by a mezzanine, where his own work could be admired by potential buyers. Not many of his paintings are on display, though do look out for an endearing self-portrait (c1630) and a later, more anxious-looking one of him in the studio.

St Carolus Borromeuskerk

Hendrik Conscienceplein (03 664 33 08, www.top. carolusborromeus.com). **Open** *Church* See website or notice on door. *Side room* 10am-noon, 2-4pm Wed. **Admission** *Church* free. *Side room* €2. *Concerts* €10-€15. **No credit cards. Map** p205 B3 ❺
Built for the Jesuits in the early 17th century, St Carolus is an exuberant, frothy monument to

baroque excess. Rubens produced 39 widely praised ceiling paintings and three altarpieces for the church, only for the lot to go up in smoke during a fire in 1718. Now it's a beautifully restored church with a small exhibition of artifacts in the *kantkamer* ('side room') and occasional concerts.

St Jacobskerk

73-75 Lange Nieuwstraat (03 232 10 32, www. topa.be). **Open** *Apr-Oct* 2-5pm daily. *Nov-Mar* 9am-noon Mon-Sat. **Admission** €2; €1.50 reductions; free under-12s. **No credit cards. Map** p205 C2/3 ❻
Reopened in 2014 after major renovations, this late Gothic church has 23 altars and an extensive art collection. It is best known as Rubens' burial place. The artist painted the work that hangs over his tomb,

FINISHING TOUCHES

Antwerp's refurbished cathedral is finally ready after 50 years.

Back in 1965, a programme of works started on **Onze Lieve Vrouwekathedraal** (*see p204*), Antwerp's landmark cathedral. This wasn't just about tinkering around with plaster, it was a complete renovation both outside and in. Important monuments of a certain age are in constant need of repair, and the cathedral required some serious love and attention. Just as in medieval times, a team of skilled craftspeople and expert surveyors and restorers had to work through the repairs bit by little bit.

Fifty years on, and the city can finally celebrate the fact that the scaffolding is down. In those five decades, there was always at least one part of the building that was inaccessible or covered in white sheeting. Now, the whole place is open again – and it looks magnificent, with artworks back in place (some by Rubens, of course) and the full sweep of the cathedral open to view.

The total cost, around €52 million, was paid for by the province of Antwerp. Apart from the tower, that is – the city council had to pick up that bill thanks to Napoleon, who assigned cathedral bell towers to city authorities to use as watchtowers. There was also a major glitch in summer 2014; a massive hailstorm hit Antwerp and damaged the cathedral's roof and windows, adding another €1 million of repairs.

On the plus side, a temporary exhibition in the cathedral, Reunion (10am-5pm daily), has been extended until the end of 2017 or into 2018, when the Fine Arts Museum will reopen after its own major renovations. The exhibition brings together works of art and

eight altarpieces that lived in the cathedral until French revolutionaries sacked the place in 1794.

Of course, renovations on this scale never really end. The organ won't be popped back into place until 2016 and the roof will eventually need replacing. But De Kathedraal, as it's known locally, has not looked this glorious in years.

Our Lady Surrounded by Saints, specifically for this purpose. In the painting, St George is believed to be a self-portrait, the Virgin a portrait of Isabella Brant, Rubens' first wife, and Mary Magdalene a portrait of Hélène Fourment, his second wife.

Vleeshuis

38-40 Vleeshouwersstraat (03 292 61 00, www.museumvleeshuis.be). **Open** 10am-5pm Thur-Sun. **Admission** €5; €3 reductions; free under-12s. **No credit cards. Map** p205 A3 ❼
Built by the Butchers' Guild in 1503, the Vleeshuis is a puzzling construction, in late Gothic style with little turrets and walls that alternate red brick with white stone. Today, the hall is used as a museum of musical instruments, representing 600 years of Antwerp's musical history. It also holds concerts of early music.

South of the Grote Markt

The south side of Antwerp is both home to the city's older residential districts and many of its best museums. A few minutes' walk south of the Grote Markt is the **Vrijdagmarkt**; each Friday, bailiffs come here to auction off debtors' seized goods. That aside, the square is lined with idiosyncratic cafés as well as the **Museum Plantin-Moretus**, home of printing pioneer Christophe Plantin. The business he was to build in this immense 16th-century house became the single largest printing and publishing concern in the Low Countries (with 22 presses), as well as a magnet for intellectuals. It was here that Plantin printed many of the greatest works of his day.

Equally enjoyable is the idiosyncratic **Mayer van den Bergh Museum**. A five-minute walk south-east from the centre, this thoroughly engaging display of the private art collection of Fritz Mayer van den Bergh is housed in a recreated 16th-century townhouse. Further on, the **Maagdenhuis** is an old foundling hospital containing a collection of art and artefacts from the city's social welfare centres. The city's major museums are a short walk further south to the area known as 't Zuid (or catch tram no.8 from Groenplaats). The **Koninklijk Museum voor Schone Kunsten** (Royal Museum of Fine Arts) is the focal point of southern Antwerp, but is closed for renovations until 2018 (*see p204* **In the Know**).

Antwerp has a brash, optimistic attitude towards encouraging new artistic talent. The high-profile contemporary art museum **MUHKA** (Museum voor Hedendaagse Kunst van Antwerpen) displays works from the 1970s onwards. Fashion followers will adore **MoMu**, the design museum, located in the beautiful late 19th-century ModeNatie complex (www.modenatie.com). The building is also home to the Flanders Fashion Institute and the fashion

---

IN THE KNOW GALLERIES

Antwerp's thriving contemporary art scene is conveniently central, located near the Waalsekaai, between the Royal Museum of Fine Arts and the MUHKA. Galleries worth investigating include **Micheline Szwajcer** (14 Verlatstraat, 03 237 11 27, www.gms.be), **Stella Lohaus** (47 Vlaamsekaai, 03 248 08 71, www.stellalohausgallery.com) and **Zeno X** (16 Leopold de Waelplaats, 03 216 16 26, www.zeno-x.com).

---

department of the Royal Academy of Fine Arts, as well as a trendy café, library and workshops.

Photography buffs, meanwhile, should head to the **Museum voor Fotografie**. The wing designed by architect Georges Baines contains large exhibition halls and also houses the Antwerp Film Museum.

Maagdenhuis

33 Lange Gasthuisstraat (03 338 26 20). **Open** 10am-5pm Mon, Wed-Fri; 1-5pm Sat, Sun. **Admission** €7; €1 reductions; free under-12s. **No credit cards. Map** p205 C4 ❽
This beautiful old house with its inner courtyard and chapel makes for a fine visit. The collection is modest but includes pieces by Rubens, Van Dyck and Jordaens, as well as sculptures and small items of social history.

Mayer van den Bergh Museum

19 Lange Gasthuisstraat (03 338 81 88, www.museummayervandenbergh.be). **Open** 10am-5pm Tue-Sun. **Admission** €8; €6 reductions; free under-12s. **Map** p205 C4 ❾
Purpose-built in 1904 by Mayer van den Bergh's mother after the early death of her son at 33, this immensely charming place boasts as its most prized exhibit Pieter Bruegel the Elder's astonishing *Dulle Griet* ('Mad Meg'), a Bosch-like allegory of a world turned upside down. Look out also for a hugely powerful crucifixion triptych by Quentin Matsys, plus some beautiful 15th-century carved wooden angels.

★ MoMu

28 Nationalestraat (03 470 27 70, www.momu.be, www.fashioninantwerp.be). **Open** 10am-6pm Tue-Sun; 10am-9pm 1st Thur mth. Admission €8; €3 reductions; free under-18s. **No credit cards. Map** p205 B4 ❿
Contemporary fashion and a historic costume and lace collection are the Mode Museum's highlights. The overall aim is to make the museum a living space, where processes are as important as the finished product, and where fashion and design are put into a social context.

ESCAPES & EXCURSIONS

Museum Aan de Stroom (MAS).

MUHKA

*16-30 Leuvenstraat (03 260 99 99, www.muhka.
be).* **Open** 11am-6pm Tue, Wed, Fri-Sun; 11am-
9pm Thur. **Admission** €8; €1-€4 reductions;
free under-13s.

The contemporary art focus here is firmly on temporary exhibitions, and the strength of the museum
lies in the way in which space is used in the light-
flooded, mostly white-painted rooms.

Museum voor Fotografie

*47 Waalsekaai (03 242 93 00, www.foto
museum.be).* **Open** 10am-6pm Tue-Sun.
Admission €8; €3-€6 reductions; free under-
18s. **No credit cards.**

The museum's photography collection is one of
Europe's most important, taking an interactive
approach with workshops, temporary exhibitions,
films and lectures – plus there's a great café.

★ Museum Plantin-Moretus

*22 Vrijdagmarkt (03 221 14 50, www.museum
plantinmoretus.be).* **Open** 10am-5pm Tue-Sun.
Admission €8; €1-€6 reductions; free under-18s.
No credit cards. Map p205 A4 ⓫

At the Museum Plantin-Moretus you can discover
all the intricacies of printing, with tours of the
huge presses, a beautiful proofreading room and
a foundry. There are also maps by Mercator (the
famous cartographer, a contemporary of Plantin's,
was born in nearby Rupelmonde), Plantin's Biblia
Regia, one of the rare Gutenberg Bibles and other
invaluable manuscripts.

North of the Grote Markt & Napoleon Dock

Between the Vleeshuis and the Napoleon Dock,
near Verversrui, is what remains of the red-light
district. Perhaps because it is so close to the
historic centre, many prostitutes have been
persuaded to move elsewhere. This seems a little
harsh, especially seeing as many women working
in the red-light district helped save rare paintings
when fire broke out in 1968 in **St Pauluskerk**, a
flamboyant Gothic-style church crowned with a
late 17th-century baroque bell tower.

Head further north and you'll come to the
docks, built under Napoleon in the early 1800s
and now an upmarket area with inner-city loft
living. It's well worth exploring – look out for
the noted **Kattendijksluis**, the old sluice gate
linking the dock to the river. The shiniest new
addition to the area, though, has to be the
monumental **Museum Aan de Stroom**. This
striking red-clad building, standing 60 metres
(197 feet) high, with nine floors, is the new pride
of Antwerp, a museum for the people, connecting
the city to the sea and to the rest of the world.

★ Museum Aan de Stroom (MAS)

1 Hanzestedenplaats (03 338 44 00, www.mas.be).
Open *Galleries* Apr-Oct 10am-5pm Tue-Fri;
10am-6pm Sat, Sun. Nov-Mar 10am-5pm Tue-
Sun. *Panorama & boulevard* Apr-Oct 9.30am-
midnight Tue-Sun. Nov-Mar 9.30am-10pm
Tue-Sun. **Admission** *Galleries* €5-€10; €3-€8

ESCAPES & EXCURSIONS

reductions; free under-12s & last Wed of mth. *Panorama & boulevard* free. **Map** p205 A1 ⑫
MAS is a stunning example of how a historic city such as Antwerp can be cutting-edge, contemporary and creative. The permanent collection comprises four themes: Display of Power, Metropolis, World Port, and Life & Death. All in all, the museum houses around 470,000 items with 180,000 of them in the Viewable Storage space, a great idea for seeing objects not displayed in the main galleries. A series of superbly curated temporary exhibitions enhance the experience. Note that you can enter the building and head to the roof deck to see the city panorama for free – and it's open until late at night.

★ FREE St Pauluskerk
22 Sint-Paulusstraat (03 232 32 67). **Open** *Apr-Oct* 2-5pm daily. **Admission** free. **Map** p205 A2 ⑬
The baroque interior of this impressive church contains more than 50 paintings by Flemish masters (Rubens, Jordaens, Van Dyck) and carved wood panelling; there are also 200 sculptures and a treasure room. On the outside, on the corner of Veermarkt, is a carved 18th-century Calvary with 60 life-size figures. The church also hosts monthly concerts; details at www.muziekinsintpaulus.be.

Centraal Station & the Meir

Built in 1905 by Louis Delacenserie, **Centraal Station** is built in iron and glass, and features an impressive dome, majestic stairs and lashings of lavish gold decoration. It's a surprising and splendidly ostentatious construction. Inside, it is a monument to classic and contemporary design as you descend deeply from the lofty old to the sleekly new of the section designed for inter-city trains and high-speed international connections.

Next to the station is Antwerp's extensive **Zoo**, one of Europe's oldest. West of Centraal Station is the diamond district, a predominantly Jewish area. To find out more about Antwerp's diamond industry, visit the special pavilion at MAS.

South of the station is the area known as **Zurenborg**, or the Cogels Osylei quarter, named after that street, Waterloostraat and Transvaalstraat. This is the golden triangle of art nouveau, with perfectly preserved houses lining the streets. If you prefer to hop on a tram, take the 11 to Draakplaats, which will drop you in the middle of it all. The tourist office (*see p202*) also offers a guided tour of the area.

The **Meir**, Antwerp's main shopping street, takes you from the station to the historic centre. At ground level are chain-shop window displays, but look up at some of the impressive buildings, such as the art deco **Boerentoren**, the first skyscraper in Europe.

Antwerp Zoo
26 Koningin Astridplein (03 202 45 40, www.zoo antwerpen.be). **Open** *July, Aug* 10am-7pm daily. *May, June, Sept* 10am-6pm Mon-Sat; 10am-7pm Sun. *Mar, Apr, Oct* 10am-5.30pm Mon-Fri; 10am-6pm Sat; 10am-7pm Sun. *Jan, Feb, Nov, Dec* 10am-4.45pm daily. **Admission** €22.50; free under-3s.
The zoo is the biggest in Belgium and one of Europe's oldest (opened in 1843). The original architecture, needless to say, is more impressive than the animals' living quarters.

Further afield

★ FREE Openlucht Museum voor Beeldhouwkunst Middelheim
61 Middelheimlaan (03 288 33 60, www. middelheimmuseum.be). **Open** *June, July* 10am-9pm Tue-Sun. *May, Aug* 10am-8pm Tue-Sun. *Apr, Sept* 10am-7pm Tue-Sun. *Oct-Mar* 10am-5pm Tue-Sun. **Admission** free.
This open-air sculpture museum is in a beautiful park about five kilometres (three miles) south of the city centre. There are 215 works to discover, many by famous artists such as Auguste Rodin, Rik Wouters and Henry Moore. Well worth the trip on a sunny day.

HOTELS

Price categories for a standard double room are: **Deluxe** (€250 or over), **Expensive** (€150-€249), **Moderate** (€90-€149) and **Budget** (under €90).

Deluxe

De Witte Lelie
16-18 Keizerstraat, 2000 Antwerp (03 226 19 66, www.dewittelelie.be). **Rooms** 10. **Map** p205 B2.
The building may be 17th century, but the interior is utterly contemporary. Expect good-sized rooms, lashings of low-key luxury and a generous breakfast.

Expensive

Hilton Antwerp Old Town
Groenplaats, 2000 Antwerp (03 204 12 12, www.placeshilton.com/antwerp). **Rooms** 210. **Map** 205 B3.
The Hilton offers the usual facilities and a range of extras, but in a stylish building with more charm than you might expect. Bang in the middle of town.

Hotel Prinse
63 Keizerstraat, 2000 Antwerp (03 226 40 50, www.hotelprinse.be). **Rooms** 34. **Map** 205 C2.
A 16th-century private house with a striking modern interior, lovely courtyard and 34 ensuite rooms.

Hotel Rubens Grote Markt
29 Oude Beurs, 2000 Antwerp (03 222 48 48, www. hotelrubensantwerp.be). **Rooms** 36. **Map** 205 B3.

ESCAPES & EXCURSIONS

IN THE KNOW THE BIG A

In 2015, the city council introduced a new marketing slogan to promote Antwerp around the world. Using the existing and well-known 'A' badge, it introduced the word *Atypisch* ('Atypical') to describe this historical and creative city on the river. As the locals say: 'Antwerp is the city, the rest is parking'.

Centrally located, just a short walk from the square and cathedral, the Rubens is a comfortable, traditionally styled hotel. There's a lovely garden and breakfast terrace for fine days.

Radisson Blu Astrid Hotel

7 Koningin Astridplein, 2018 Antwerp (03 203 12 34, www.radissonblu.com/astridhotel-antwerp). **Rooms** 24.

Directly opposite Centraal Station, the Astrid may appear to be made from Lego, but its interior is designed by US architect Michael Graves. Facilities include a pool, sauna and gym.

'T Sandt

17 Zand, 2000 Antwerp (03 232 93 90, www.hotelsandt.be). **Rooms** 29. **Map** p205 A3.

All rooms in this 19th-century building by the Scheldt are suites and very spacious; each is decorated in a different style. An Italianate garden and rooftop terrace bar are further attractions.

Moderate

Maison d'Anvers

7 Blauwmoezelstraat, 2000 Antwerp (03 231 75 75, www.maisondanvers.be). **Rooms** 6. **Map** p205 B3.

Centrally located in an old Antwerp house, this small hotel has been tastefully modernised. Rooms are simple with clean lines. It's on a pedestrianised street, so be aware of parking restrictions.

Miller's Dream

35 Molenstraat, 2018 Antwerp (03 259 1590, www.millers-dream.com). **Rooms** 3.

This beautiful colonial-style house is near the park, south of Britselei. Three stunning, spacious, ensuite studio rooms are decorated with modern art.

Budget

Alias Youth Hostel

256 Provinciestraat, 2018 Antwerp (03 230 05 22, www.aliasyouthhostel.com). **Beds** 116. **No credit cards.**

A classy, clean youth hostel with sleeping options ranging from singles to dorms for eight people.

There's free tea, coffee and fruit in the morning, and gratis Wi-Fi too. Some rooms are ensuite.

Hotel Postiljon

6 Blauwmoezelstraat, 2000 Antwerp (03 231 75 75, www.hotelpostiljon.be). **Rooms** 21. **Map** p205 B3

This sister of the Maison d'Anvers (they're next to each other) is more basic, though that is reflected in the bargain prices. Some rooms look directly on to the cathedral – what more can you ask?

RESTAURANTS

De Broers van Julienne

45-47 Kasteelpleinstraat (03 232 02 03, www.debroersvanjulienne.be). **Open** noon-9pm Mon-Thur; noon-10pm Fri, Sat; 5.30-9pm Sun. **Main courses** €13-€18. **Map** p205 C5 ⓮
Vegetarian

There's a certain hush about this charming meat-free restaurant. It's all to do with the calm, colonial style and reading-room atmosphere, with a pretty garden under shady trees in summer. The kitchen prides itself on using natural and organic ingredients. The shop and bakery at the front are equally classy.

★ Ciro's

6 Amerikalei (03 238 11 47, www.ciros.be). **Open** 11am-11pm Tue-Sun. **Main courses** €16.50-€29. Belgian

Ciro's first opened in 1962 and gives an essential glimpse of retro Antwerp. The crowds come for the steak and chips, regarded as the best in Antwerp. Nothing much changes here – which is what everyone wants.

★ Désiré de Lille

14-18 Schrijnwerkerstraat (03 232 62 26, www.desiredelille.be). **Open** 9am-8pm Mon-Thur, Sun; 9am-10pm Fri, Sat. **Main courses** €4-€12. **No credit cards. Map** p205 B3 ⓯ Café
Désiré started off as a funfair stand, selling freshly made waffles, fruit-filled doughnuts and *laquemants*, a kind of baked pancake. It occupies a genteel 1930s restaurant, with banquettes, railway carriage lights and big windows opening on to the street. A glass pergola at the back gives a conservatory feel and leads to a magnificent garden.

★ Graanmarkt 13

13 Graanmarkt (03 337 79 91, www.graanmarkt13.be). **Open** noon-2.30pm, 6.30-10pm Tue-Sat. **Set menu** lunch €29; dinner €39. **Map** p205 C4 ⓰
Modern European

This is a light, fresh and utterly modern emporium that changes its menus regularly depending on what's available in the market. The menus can be adapted for vegetarians, vegans or special diets. It's not just a restaurant; there's also a concept store, a gallery and even an apartment to rent.

Het Pomphuis.

Hippodroom

*10 Leopold de Waelplaats (03 248 52 52, www.
hippodroom.be).* **Open** noon-2.30pm, 6-11pm
Tue-Sat. **Main courses** €19-€34. **International**
Hippodroom's long, slender dining room – complete
with massive works of art and minimally set tables –
contrasts perfectly with its turn-of-the-century exterior. Its confident aesthetic style extends to the menu:
Iranian caviar, sushi, French-inspired fillet of lamb
with truffle risotto, and vegetarian options.

Izumi

*14 Beeldhouwersstraat (03 216 13 79, www.
izumi.be).* **Open** noon-2pm, 6.30-10.30pm Tue-
Sat. **Set menu** €48-€65. **Japanese**
Nestling in an old Antwerp townhouse since 1978,
Izumi has an unassailable reputation as the best
Japanese restaurant in the city. This is pure Japanese
culinary art, prepared in the time-honoured fashion
and heavy on the fish and seafood: tuna belly, fried
eel with cucumber, squid, octopus, urchin and full
spreads of sushi, sashimi and teriyaki.

Lucy Chang

*16-17 Marnixplaats (03 248 95 60, www.lucy
chang.be).* **Open** noon-11pm Mon-Sat. **Main
courses** €10-€20. **No credit cards**. **Pan-Asian**
The first thing you see is an oriental market stall,
with a long, low bar to its right. This is for people
who just want to pop in for a small plate of dim
sum or a bowl of noodle soup. Food is from Laos,
Vietnam, Thailand, Malaysia and China, and comes
as one-dish meals, where everything arrives at once
and can be shared.

Maritime

4 Suikerrui (03 233 07 58, www.maritime.be).
Open noon-2.30pm, 6-9.30pm Mon, Tue, Fri;
noon-3.30pm, 6-9.30pm Sat, Sun. **Main courses**
€25-€38. **Map** p205 A3 ⓱ **Fish & seafood**
Maritime looks classically Belgian with its wooden
beams, chi-chi chairs and red tablecloths. The food
is equally classic, with the focus on eels and mussels.
And not just eels in green sauce – you can try them in
cream or fried in butter, or have mussels in a Madras
curry sauce. Lobster is popular too. The perfect spot
for a fishy treat.

Món

*30 St-Aldegondiskaai (03 345 67 89, www.mon
antwerp.com).* **Open** noon-2.30pm, 6-10pm Mon-
Sat; noon-10pm Sun. **Main courses** €17-€32.
Map p205 A1 ⓳ **Steakhouse**
Light and airy with a glass-fronted kitchen in
the centre of the dining space, Món gives a nod to
Barcelona, the source of its famed charcoal oven.
It's used to cook slabs of Limousin beef from cattle
reared on a farm in Stabroek, just outside Antwerp.
Also, look out for delights such as caramelised pork
belly, zapped in the Josper oven.

Het Pomphuis

*Droogdok, 7 Siberiastraat (03 770 86 25, www.
hetpomphuis.be).* **Open** 11am-2.30pm; 6-11pm
Mon-Fri; 11am-11pm Sat, Sun. **Main courses**
€20-€33. **Modern European**
This magnificent old building, the pumphouse for
the dry dock, was converted a decade ago into an
equally magnificent restaurant. Massive arched

windows and lofty ceilings surround crisply laid tables. The menu is unusual for Antwerp, with dishes such as goat's cheese salad with dates, apple and beetroot syrup.

★ Vridagvisdag

75 Lange Elzenstraat (0495 10 80 08 mobile, www.vrijdagvisdag.be). **Open** noon-2pm, 6-10pm Thur, Fri; 6.30-10pm Sat; 5.30-9.30pm Sun. **Main courses** €20-€70. **Fish & seafood**
Friday is fish day, according to the name of this rocking restaurant to the south of the city centre. This is truly authentic; *Antwerpenaar* in style and nature, and designed for locals who come for the plates of seafood, the oysters and the Marseille bouillabaisse.

BARS & NIGHTLIFE

Bars

Berlin

1-3 Kleine Markt (03 227 11 01). **Open** 8.30am-late Mon-Fri; 10am-late Sat, Sun. **Map** p205 B4 ⑲
Dark and broody, but tasteful, Berlin has become something of an institution for singles, couples and families – a big play area at the back, with tables for mum and dad to knock back the drinks, has made sure of that. Brasserie-style food is served throughout the day. Evenings and weekend afternoons can be a bit of a scrum.

★ Café Beveren

2 Vlasmarkt (03 231 22 25). **Open** 3pm-late Mon, Thur-Sun. **No credit cards. Map** p205 A3 ⑳
This is your actual dockside Antwerp, the kind of spot you might find in Rotterdam or Hamburg, where age-mellowed regulars fumble with their reading glasses before another round of cards. The red-lined banquettes encase the café in a lost era – note also the fully working De Cap fairground organ and old Rowe Ami jukebox, and watch out for spontaneous outbreaks of old-time dancing.

★ Den Engel

5 Grote Markt (03 233 12 52, www.cafedenengel. be). **Open** 9am-late daily. **No credit cards. Map** p205 A3 ㉑
Antwerp's bar of all bars. It isn't fab or fashionable, and whatever edges it once cut blunted long ago; it is simply an institution, ramshackle relief from the official goings-on next door at the Town Hall. Councillors clink glasses with nervous fiancés, journalists accept drinks and gossip from politicians, while locals of all ages provide a cheery backdrop. Next door's Den Bengel (the Miscreant) copes with the overflow from Den Engel (the Angel).

ESCAPES & EXCURSIONS

Red & Blue. *See p214.*

★ Entrepôt du Congo

42 Vlaamsekaai (0475 52 82 15 mobile,
www.entrepotducongo.com). **Open** 8am-1am
Mon-Thur, Sun; 8am-2am Fri, Sat. **No credit**
cards.

This pioneering enterprise began the regeneration
of the southern quaysides into the trendy quarter of
galleries and designer bars it is today. A century ago,
Congo boats would dock here, unloading crates of
colonial plunder into this grand corner edifice. Now
it's a classy bar, with a bare wood-and-tile interior,
serving notably good food (sandwiches, pasta, omelettes and a long list of salads).

De Pelikaan

14 Melkmarkt (03 227 23 51). **Open** 9am-late
daily. **No credit cards. Map** p205 B3 ㉒

The downtown and ever downbeat Pelican has
been dragging writers, designers and musicians
through its doors and keeping them glued to its bar
counter for longer than most care to remember. Set
in the shadow of the cathedral, it makes no effort to
appeal to curious passers-by, leaving the dressing
up to tackier venues nearby. It isn't even dressed
down: it's just got out of bed and put on whatever
it could find on the bedroom floor, invariably the
same as what it found there yesterday. Enter, drink,
swap stories, get drunk, go home. Perfect.

De Vagant

25 Reyndersstraat (03 233 15 38, www.devagant.
be). **Open** 11am-late Mon-Sat; noon-late Sun.
No credit cards. Map p205 A3 ㉓

Genever was to Antwerp what gin was to London,
the opiate of historic port cities drowned in a sea of
cheap alcohol. Prohibition arrived in 1919 and wasn't
repealed until 1984. This bar opened a year later,
with 200 types of once-forbidden genever in myriad strengths and flavours, accompanied by small
chunks of cheese and deft slices of meat. Sipped
and not slammed, genever boasts a proud history
– detailed on the drinks menu and celebrated in an
exquisite interior of old flagons and pre-prohibition
posters. Upstairs, a restaurant serves dishes concocted from the stuff.

Clubs

Also try **Red & Blue** (*see p214*) on a Friday.

★ Café d'Anvers

15 Verversrui (03 226 38 70, www.cafe-d-anvers.
com). **Open** 11pm-6am Thur; 11pm-7.30am Fri,
Sat. **Admission** €7-€14. **No credit cards.**
Map p205 A/B1 ㉔

The C d'A has been around since 1989 and still draws
in the crowds (up to 630) in two rooms. Set smack in
the middle of town, this old brickwork/industrial
combo is louched up with ironwork chandeliers and
Louis XV armchairs. Party central.

Petrol

25 d'Herbouvillekaai (03 226 49 63, www.petrol
club.be). **Open** 11pm-late Fri, Sat. **Admission**
€8-€20. **No credit cards.**

Beside the river and south of the city centre, Petrol
is a large converted warehouse that takes in around
800 people on its weekend party nights. DJs play the
whole gamut of electro dance from deep house to
hard techno. Antwerp hedonism at its best.

Gay & lesbian

See www.patroc.com/antwerp for information.

Atthis

27 Geuzenstraat (03 216 37 37, www.atthis.be).
Open 8.30pm-2am Fri, Sat. **No credit cards.**
Map p205 B5 ㉕

A women-only private club that's a little more
refined than most in Belgium. There's a video library
and a lesbian centre under the same name.

Boots

22 Van Aerdstraat (03 233 21 36, www.the-boots.
com). **Open** 10.30pm-4am Fri; 10.30pm-5am Sat;
5-10pm Sun. **Admission** €8 weekend membership.
No credit cards.

The great-granddaddy of Belgium's cruisy bars
and probably the sleaziest too. Stairs lead up and

ESCAPES & EXCURSIONS

up through a dark bar area into an even darker play area, where anything that can happen is likely to happen. There is a strict dress code, but you can change on the premises. You'll also need ID to secure the temporary membership.

Hessenhuis
53 Falconrui (03 231 13 56, www.hessenhuis.com). **Open** 11am-late Tue-Fri; 5pm-late Sat; 6pm-late Sun. **No credit cards. Map** p205 B1 ②
The old Hessenhuis in the dock area is a popular pre-club destination, attracting townie gays and their female friends. The interior is a combination of modern and rustic, though the clientele is full-on chic, ready to enjoy the live entertainment or theme nights. By day, it's a quieter café and lunch spot.

★ Red & Blue
11-13 Lange Schipperskapelstraat (03 213 05 55, www.redandblue.be). **Open** 11pm-7am Sat. **Admission** €12 plus €2 membership. **Map** p205 A2 ②
The name comes from the club's location in the old red-light district. The girls may have moved on, but the boys have arrived and plan to stay. Friday night is mixed and everyone's made to feel wildy welcome; Saturday is men-only. *Photo p212.*

Theatre & dance

★ deSingel
25 Desguinlei (03 248 28 28, www.desingel.be). **Open** *Box office* 10am-6.30pm Mon, Tue; 4-6.30pm Sat. **Tickets** €10-€40.
Antwerp's modern equivalent to Brussels' Bozar, with cutting-edge dance and theatre in a massive concrete setting, and an intelligent agenda of events.

Vlaamse Opera
8 Van Ertbornstraat (03 202 10 11, box office 070 22 02 02, www.operaballet.be). **Open** *Box office* (3 Frankrijklei) 11am-5.45pm Tue-Sat. **Tickets** €4-€70.
Flemish Opera productions are divided between the opera house in Ghent and the old but acoustically splendid Antwerp Hall.

SHOPS & SERVICES

Antwerp's role as one of the world's most celebrated fashion hubs has made it a clothes shopper's paradise. The main commercial drag, containing all the international chains, is the Meir, the pedestrianised stretch between the station and the city centre. Huidevettersstraat to the south is more upbeat, with some one-off boutiques, and things start to get really interesting around Schutterhofstraat, home to chic bathroom shops, contemporary jewellers and various understated designer clothing stores. The avant-garde core is the warren of streets known as the

Wilde Zee ('Wild Sea'): head to Kammenstraat for upbeat streetwear and retro shops; St Antoniusstraat is where Walter van Beirendonck hangs out; and Nationalestraat is home to Dries van Noten's temple of fashion.

Antwerp also has a well-deserved reputation for its fine antiques and charming bric-à-brac shops, most of which can be found in the district of St Andries: head for Lombardenvest, Steenhouwersvest and Kloosterstraat.

Books

★ Mekanik Strip
73 St Jacobsmarkt (03 234 23 47, www.mekanik-strip.be). **Open** 10am-6.30pm Tue-Fri; 10am-6pm Sat. **Map** p205 C2 ②
A huge selection of English, French and Dutch comics, plus magazines, books, videos, posters, Tintin collectibles and its own gallery.

Fashion & accessories

For some background on the Antwerp Six, *see p215* **Six and Up.**

Ann Demeulemeester
Leopold de Waelplaats (03 216 01 33, www.ann demeulemeester.be). **Open** 11am-7pm Mon-Sat.
Demeulemeester, the star member of the Antwerp Six, designs clothes that are slick yet sensual, soft with edgy attitude and perfectly on trend. Her minimalist shop is in a different part of Antwerp from any of her contemporaries' shops but, fittingly, located opposite the Fine Arts Museum.

Closing Date
15 Korte Gasthuisstraat (03 232 87 22, www. dosingdate.be). **Open** 11am-6.30pm Mon-Sat. **Map** p205 B4 ②
Clubbers with cash and eccentrics with panache gather here to pore over racks of clothes by the likes of McQueen, Dsquared2 and Amaya Arzuaga.

Coccodrillo
9A/B Schuttershofstraat (03 233 20 93, www. coccodrillo.be). **Open** 10am-6pm Mon-Sat. **Map** p205 C4 ③
Prada, Patrick Cox, Jil Sander, Ann Demeulemeester, Dries van Noten and Helmut Lang are among those represented at this full-on fashion footwear mecca.

★ DVS
1st floor, 9 Schuttershofstraat (0488 49 28 14 mobile, www.waltervanbeirendonck.com). **Open** 10am-6pm Wed-Sat. **Map** p205 C4 ③
Walter van Beirendonck's city shop looks like a gallery as much as it does a showcase for top Antwerp designers (Walter included). Look out for pieces by the likes of Veronique Branquinho, Dirk van Saene and Frieda Degeyter.

ESCAPES & EXCURSIONS

SIX AND UP

The Antwerp design wave of 1987 – and their followers.

The Antwerp Six designers, who all studied at the Royal Academy and came to global prominence in 1987 when they took London Fashion Week by storm, still live or work in the city. Well documented in the city's fashion museum **MoMu** (see p207), which showcases textile and costume collections from the 16th century to the present day, they remain at the cutting edge of Belgian fashion – which in turn leads the way in Europe.

Ann Demeulemeester lives in Antwerp with her photographer husband Patrick Robyn, and runs a shop (see p214) near the Fine Arts Museum in which her romantic, unashamedly sensuous designs speak for themselves. **Walter van Beirendonck**, now bald, bearded and looking more like an ageing member of ZZ Top than an enfant terrible of design, creates clothes inspired by nature and technology, and teaches at the Royal Academy. To showcase his own work and that of another Sixer, **Dirk van Saene**, and other friends, he runs the shop DVS (see p214). **Dries van Noten** sells his designs at Het Modepaleis (see p216).

The other members are **Dirk Bikkembergs** and **Marina Yee**, while **Martin Margiela**, who actually graduated a year earlier than the Six, could almost be thought of as Antwerp's number seven. The media-shy but always daring designer now works mostly in Paris.

After these pioneers came a strong second wave of Belgian designers. **Lieve van Gorp** started her own label in the 1990s with a leather accessories collection of bags and belts. **Olivier Theyskens** (who studied in Brussels) is the glamorous dark prince of Belgian goth fashion; he has dressed Madonna for the red carpet and spruced up the middle-aged Rochas fashion house in Paris. **Veronique Branquinho** is still based in Antwerp, but her shows take place in Paris. **Raf Simons** started out as a furniture designer and turned to fashion after van Beirendonck took him to Paris Fashion Week, where he saw Margiela's all-white show. He launched his own menswear label in 1995 and is currently creative director at Dior.

Bruno Pieters, one of Antwerp's star graduates in 1999, has worked for the likes of Martin Margiela, Josephus Thimister and Christian Lacroix. Now, he's set out on his own, with shoes, handbags, jewellery and a menswear collection.

As for the future, that looks bright too. Antwerp-born **Niels Peeraer**, who graduated from the Royal Academy in 2011, won acclaim designing bags for Delvaux and has an eponymous brand based in Paris. Other names include are **Alexandra Verschueren**, who creates exquisitely detailed outfits that resemble origami; and **Léa Dickely**, who has made an impact with soft silhouettes and sheer, draped fabrics in greys and smokes. One thing's for sure, Antwerp is still turning out the catwalk stars of the future.

ESCAPES & EXCURSIONS

MoMu.

Erotische Verbeelding

165 Kloosterstraat (03 226 89 50, www.erotische verbeelding.com). **Open** 11am-6pm Mon-Sat. **Map** p205 A5 ❷

This women-only store stocks sex aids, tasteful-looking dildos, a smattering of S&M and slinky lingerie in a safe and sophisticated environment.

★ Fish & Chips

36-38 Kammenstraat (03 227 08 24, www. fishandchips.be). **Open** 10am-6.30pm Mon-Sat. **Map** p205 B4 ❸

Antwerp's chaotic temple to cool. On Saturdays, DJs spin in a booth overhanging the ground floor, which boasts skater gear and raver labels.

Huis A Boon

4 Lombardenvest (03 232 33 87, www.gloves boon.be). **Open** *Mid Sept-mid Feb* 10am-6pm Mon-Sat. *Mid Feb-mid Sept* 11am-6pm Mon-Sat. **Map** p205 B4 ❹

Huis A Boon is a wonderfully evocative time capsule of a glove shop, with hundreds of different pairs (for men and women) displayed on dark shelves and in little drawers. Take a seat in a leather armchair and go back in time.

★ Louis

2 Lombardenstraat (03 232 98 72). **Open** 10am-6.30pm Mon-Sat. **Map** p205 B4 ❺

This was one of the first boutiques to champion Belgian fashion and is now a shrine for the fashion-conscious, both men and women. Martin Margiela, Veronique Branquinho, Rick Owens and Raf Simons are staple labels.

★ Het Modepaleis

16 Nationalestraat (03 470 25 10, www.dries vannoten.be). **Open** 10am-6.30pm Mon-Sat. **Map** p205 B4 ❻

Welcome to the fashion temple of Antwerp. Dries van Noten sells his own collections in this landmark building dating from 1881. Both the men's and women's floors offer top-level flair.

★ Nadine Wijnants

26 Kloosterstraat (0484 643 303, www.nadine wijnants.be). **Open** 11am-6pm Fri, Sat or by appointment. **Map** p205 A4 ❼

One of the top jewellery designers in Belgium, Wijnants creates charming, affordable pieces with semi-precious stones, silver, bronze and gold plate.

Verso

11 Lange Gasthuisstraat (03 226 92 92, www. verso.be). **Open** 10am-6pm Mon-Fri; 10am-6.30pm Sat. **Map** p205 C4 ❽

Set in an old bank, Verso is a temple to cutting-edge design. Fashionistas examine styles from the likes of Helmut Lang, Miu Miu, YSL, Armani and Versace. So exclusive it hurts.

XSO

13-15 Eiermarkt (03 231 87 49, www.xso.be). **Open** 10am-6pm Mon-Fri; 10am-6.30pm Sat. **Map** p205 B3 ❾

Set in a quiet courtyard in the centre of town, this shop mixes Japanese purity (white walls, slate floors) with Italian flair. Labels include Issey Miyake, Kenzo and Giorgio Armani.

Food & confectionery

★ Chocolatier Goossens

6 Isabellalei (03 239 13 10, www.goossens-chocolatier.com). **Open** 9am-6pm Mon-Sat. **No credit cards**.

Perfect gifts include teddy bears, chocolate lips and even Kama Sutra reliefs made from 100% cocoa butter.

★ Chocolate Line

50 Paleis op de Meir (03 206 20 30, www.the chocolateline.be). **Open** 10.30am-6.30pm Mon, Sun; 9.30am-6.30pm Tue-Sat.

The palace on the Meir used to be home to Napoléon and Léopold II. Now it's home to Dominique Persoone, who makes and sells extraordinary chocolate in these palatial surrounds. Among the usual truffles can be found chocolate oddities such as lipstick and, the star of the show, the chocolate shooter. Yep, you get a good snort of pure cocoa. Gives full meaning to the name of the place.

Philip's Biscuits

11 Korte Gasthuisstraat (03 231 26 60, www. philipsbiscuits.be). **Open** 10am-6pm Mon-Sat. **No credit cards. Map** p205 B4 ❿

The place for macaroons, *speculoos* (ginger biscuits) and hand-shaped butter biscuits.

Vervloet Kaashandel

28 Wiegstraat (03 233 37 29). **Open** 9am-6pm Mon-Sat. **No credit cards. Map** p205 B3 ⓫

Luc Wouters specialises in cheeses from Belgium, including his own variety of hard goat's cheese.

Homewares

Donum

47 Hopland (03 231 39 18, www.donum.be). **Open** 10am-6pm Mon-Fri; 10am-6.30pm Sat. **Map** p205 C3 ⓬

This place, set in a former school building, is seriously cool. Italian design is the order of the day.

'T Koetshuis (Chelsea)

10 Kloosterstraat (03 248 33 42). **Open** noon-6pm Tue-Sat; 1-6pm Sun. **No credit cards. Map** p205 A4 ⓭

Its official name is Chelsea, but 'T Koetshuis ('Coach House') is what you'll find written over the door. The art deco and art nouveau furnishings are chosen with care, so don't expect any bargains.

ESCAPES & EXCURSIONS

Bruges

B ruges, with its modest population of barely 120,000, is mobbed by three million tourists every year, many from Britain. Despite large crowds, it's a romantic, atmospheric and historical city that invites gentle exploration of its squares, alleyways and quays. By far the easiest and most enjoyable way to visit the city is on foot: it's compact, largely traffic-free and always easy to get around – and anything has to be better than one of those horse-drawn carriages. On the downside, Bruges still has far too many touristy chocolate shops and lace emporia, its boat trips are a let-down and there are too few modern art galleries and new-style cafés. It's best approached *à deux* on a winter break. Wander by the canals, take in a couple of sights, enjoy a Flemish beer – and maybe then the city will begin to work its spell.

Bruges used its year in the limelight as European City of Culture in 2002 to embark on major projects designed to change its twee image. It finally abandoned its love affair with Gothic (both real and fake) and the city planning department approved the construction of the brutally modern, controversial red hulk of the **Concertgebouw** (www.concertgebouw.be), a concert hall seating 1,200 with a gallery attached. Two bridges were built in the south of the city, including Jürg Conzett's sleek design spanning the Coupure canal, and a daring pavilion was added to the Burg by the Japanese architect Toyo Ito. Museums were also given a radical makeover: the **Memling Museum** was redesigned and a spectacular Gothic loft opened to the public, while the **Groeninge Museum** was given a new look that downgrades the world-famous Van Eycks from their star position.

The admission fee to many churches and historic buildings is nominal. For heavyweight cultural attractions, such as the Groeninge Museum, it costs around €8. Therefore, it's up to you whether it's worth investing in a **Bruges City Card** (www.bruggecitycard.be; €46/48hrs, €49/72hrs) or not. Note that the Gruuthuse Museum is closed for restoration until the end of 2017.

GETTING THERE & INFORMATION

From Brussels, there are two trains an hour (journey time 50 minutes). From the station, it's a 15-minute walk to the centre, or you can take a taxi (such as Taxi Snel, 050 36 36 49, www.taxisnel.be) or bus.

Several shops rent out bicycles by the hour, the day (€5-€10) or the week; options include **'t Koffieboontje** (4 Hallestraat, 050 33 80 27, www.hotel-koffieboontje.be) or **Eric Popelier** (14 Hallestraat, 050 34 32 62, www.fietsen popelier.be). For details of guided bike tours, contact **Quasimundo** (050 33 07 75, www.quasimundo.com).

Toerisme Brugge
050 44 46 46, www.brugge.be.
Bruges railway station Open 10am-5pm Mon-Fri; 10am-2pm Sat, Sun. **Map** p219 A5.
Concertgebouw *34 't Zand.* **Open** 10am-6pm daily. **Map** p219 A1.

SIGHTS & MUSEUMS

The traditional starting point for any visit is the main square, the **Markt**. Its most striking monuments are the **Halle** (Cloth Hall) and the **Belfort** (Belfry; open 9.30am-5pm daily). Both the belfry and square are symbols of the civic pride and great mercantile power of medieval Bruges; the view from the top of the 80-metre (263-foot) belfry makes the climb – all 366 steps – worth the effort. The city's carillonneur climbs up every Sunday to play at 2.15pm, also giving ringings on the stroke of 9pm on Mondays, Wednesdays and Saturdays in summer.

Most buildings on the square are modern reconstructions, including **Craenenburg**, built on the site of the same house where Emperor Maximilian was held prisoner by local citizens. The building contains a popular pub (of the same name) with a typical Old Flemish interior.

The statues at the centre of the square are of Jan Breydel and Pieter de Coninck, who inspired locals to slaughter several thousand French citizens at the start of the 14th century, an early example of ethnic cleansing known as the Brugse Metten. The statues were unveiled by King Léopold II, who is said to have spoken Dutch for the first time during the ceremony.

From here, it's a very short walk to the **Burg**. This beautiful square was the place chosen by Baldwin I to build a castle in the ninth century. These days, it's occupied by the **Stadhuis** (Town Hall; open 9.30am-5pm daily), built in splendid Gothic style in the 14th century. The lavish Gothic Hall on the first floor features a spectacular ceiling, while the walls are painted with scenes relating the history of the city, often with more verve than accuracy. The paintings date from the early 20th century.

On one corner of the Burg stands the **Paleis van het Brugse Vrije** (open 9.30am-12.30pm, 1.30-5pm daily), constructed in the 16th century and renovated in the 18th. The façade overlooking the canal is all that remains of the original structure; the rest is neoclassical in style. Only one room inside the palace can be visited; an impressive chimneypiece of black marble and oak, built by Lanceloot Blondeel in 1528, runs almost the whole length of one wall.

The oldest building on the Burg, tucked away in a corner next to the Stadhuis, is the easily missed **Heiligbloed Basiliek** (Basilica of the Holy Blood; open Apr-Sept 9.30am-noon, 2-6pm Tue-Sun; Oct-Mar 10am-noon, 2-4pm Tue, Thur-Sun; 10am-noon Wed). The bizarre interior is well worth a look. The Lower Chapel was built in the 12th century in honour of St Basil and is pure Romanesque in style. Its refined sobriety is in surprising contrast to the generous interior of the Upper Chapel, which was built in the 12th century in Romanesque style, then rebuilt in Gothic style and finally heavily altered in the 19th century. It's in this chapel that the crystal phial containing two drops of holy blood, stored in a silver tabernacle, is exhibited every Friday. This is one of the holiest relics of medieval Europe. The phial is supposed to have been given to Thierry d'Alsace by the

Patri of Jerusalem during the second Crusade. Legend has it that the blood liquefied every Friday, but the miracle is said to have stopped working in the 15th century.

The relic is carried through the streets every year on Ascension Day. The Procession of the Holy Blood, a major event in Bruges, dates from the early Middle Ages and still involves thousands of participants dressed in rich costumes, plus musicians and even animals.

From the Burg, head south to the **Vismarkt** (Fish Market – every morning from Tuesday to Saturday), taking the narrow Blinde Ezelstraat ('Blind Donkey Street'). The walk east from here follows the **Groenerei** canal, one of the most attractive waterways in Bruges. The water, trees and gabled houses – especially the Pelican House at no.8 – make it a favourite romantic spot. It can be noisy during the day, so come back after dark, when most tourists have gone, to look at the beautiful floodlit bridges.

Just west of Vismarkt is Huidevettersplaats ('Tanners' Square'), which in turn leads to the **Rozenhoedkaai**. The grand view of the canal, bordered by ancient buildings and trees, has captivated photographers since the mid 19th century, but it can get a bit too crowded. The quay leads to another picturesque canal, the **Dijver**. The main attractions here are the **Groeninge Museum**, the most prestigious museum in Bruges, covering 600 years of Flemish art, and the nearby **Brangwyn Museum-Arentshuis**. A small stone bridge leads from Arentspark to the **Onze Lieve Vrouwkerk** (Church of Our Lady), an imposing brick structure with a massive tower, best seen from the garden. The bridge is constantly blocked as tourists snap photos, though few realise the bridge was built as recently as 1910.

Directly opposite the church is the medieval **St Janshospitaal**, still in use in the early 20th century. The street outside was raised in the 19th century, so that the entrance to the building (like that of the Onze Lieve Vrouwkerk) now lies below ground level. The former hospital wards, with their vast oak ceilings, are now occupied by an interesting museum of local history and medicine. Exhibits include old photographs, paintings and a rather grim collection of surgical instruments. Within the hospital's ancient chapel is the **Memling Museum**, containing a small, remarkable collection of the 15th-century painter Hans Memling, who was born in Frankfurt but lived and studied in Bruges.

From St Janshospitaal, turn right on Katelijnestraat and you find the **Begijnhof**, one of most charming locations in Bruges. Founded by Margaret of Constantinople in 1245, it features rows of modest whitewashed houses around an inner lawn, covered with daffodils in spring. The atmosphere is calm and serene, far removed from

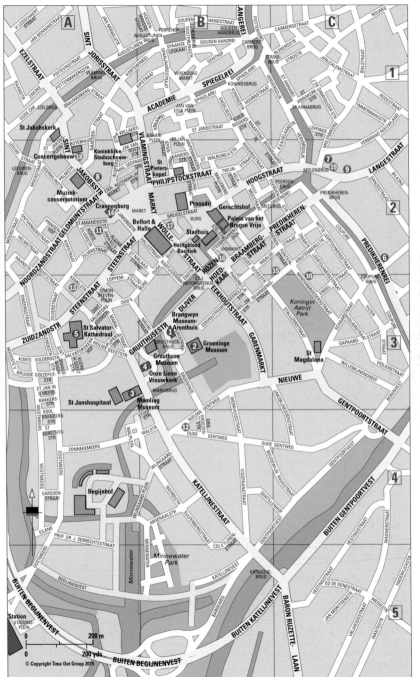

ESCAPES & EXCURSIONS

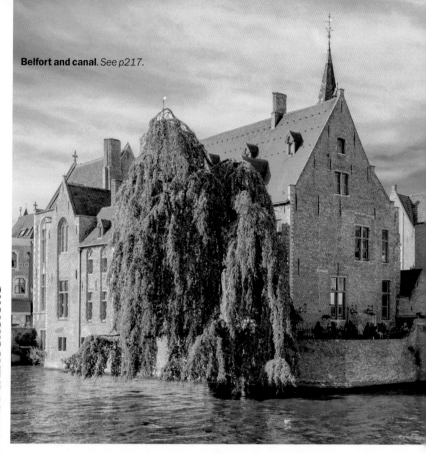

Belfort and canal. *See p217.*

the crowded streets around. There are no longer any *béguines* (lay sisters) here (the last ones died in the 1930s); the women you see walking around the Begijnhof today are Benedictine nuns. It is possible to visit the church, and one of the houses is also open to visitors.

At the Begijnhof's southern entrance is the picturesque **Minnewater Park**, with swans, lawns and small houses. Before the River Zwin silted up, barges and ships would penetrate this far into the city. Walking back towards the Markt, you see the huge **St Salvator-kathedraal**, Bruge's cathedral, surrounded by old trees.

Brangwyn Museum-Arentshuis

16 Dijver (050 44 87 43, https://bezoekers. brugge.be/en). **Open** 9.30am-5pm Tue-Sun. **Admission** €4; €3 reductions; free under-12s. **Map** p219 B3 ❶

Set in an 18th-century townhouse in the intimate Arentspark, this small museum displays works by the Bruges-born British painter and engraver Frank Brangwyn (1867-1956).

★ Groeninge Museum

12 Dijver (050 44 87 43, https://bezoekers. brugge.be/en). **Open** 9.30am-5pm Tue-Sun. **Admission** €8; €6 reductions; free under-12s. **Map** p219 B3 ❷

Pride of place at this must-visit museum goes to its outstanding collection of Flemish primitives. No master illustrates the concept of 15th-century painting better than Van Eyck, who created the illusion of texture and detail by inventing a technique of applying oil and varnish in painstaking layers. The colours are not only longer lasting, but also the malleability of the paints enabled him to achieve a wonderful subtlety of clarity and hue. His virtuosity and strict attention to detail were such that many artists travelled to Flanders to learn his secrets. His most striking work is the *Madonna with Canon George van der Paele*. Also keep an eye out for pieces by the likes of Memling, Rogier van der Weyden, Hieronymus Bosch and Gerard David. There are fine examples of Belgian Surrealism – Ensor, Magritte, Delvaux – in the later rooms.

★ Onze Lieve Vrouwekerk

Mariastraat (050 44 87 11, https://bezoekers.brugge.be/en). **Open** 9.30am-5pm daily. **Admission** Until 2017 €3; after 2017 €6; free under-12s. **No credit cards. Map** p219 B3 ❹

Currently undergoing major restoration, with the chancel, tombs and major artworks out of bounds until 2017, the Onze Lieve Vrouwekerk is still worth a visit, even just to walk around what is the second tallest brick structure in the world. Once it has reopened, you'll be able to admire the main attractions: Michelangelo's *Madonna and Child* and the burial tombs of Charles the Bold and his daughter, Mary of Burgundy.

FREE St Salvator-kathedraal

St Salvatorskerkhof (050 33 68 41, www.sintsalvator.be). **Open** *Church* 10am-1pm, 2-5.30pm Mon-Fri; 10am-1pm, 2-3.30pm Sat; 11.30am-noon, 2-5pm Sun. *Treasury* 2-5pm Mon-Fri, Sun. **Admission** *Church* free. *Treasury* €3. **No credit cards. Map** p219 A3 ❺

Work on the cathedral began in the tenth century, but after four fires and the Iconoclastic Riots, nothing of that period has survived except the base of the tower. This troubled history is also largely responsible for the varied and eclectic style of the interior. The choir dates from the 14th century, although part of an even older 13th-century construction still survives. The painted columns (similar to those in the Upper Chapel of the Heiligbloed Basiliek) are a relatively recent addition, as are the stained-glass windows. There are several paintings by Bernard van Orley in the right transept, but the lighting is bad and they're difficult to see. However, the treasury has been restored and relit, allowing visitors to admire a spectacular painting by Dirk Bouts known as the *Hippolytus Altarpiece*.

HOTELS

Bruges has more than 100 hotels, plus an ever growing number of small B&Bs (*gastenkamers*) that are often located in lovingly restored houses in the old quarters (and are a serious challenge to the hotels). Many hotels close in January and early February. For details, check www.discoverbruges.com. The tourist information office (*see p217*) runs a free accommodation booking service.

Price categories below are for a standard double room: **Expensive** (€150-€249), **Moderate** (€90-€149) and **B&B** (under €90).

Expensive

Best Western Hotel Acacia

3A-5 Korte Zilverstraat, 8000 Bruges (050 34 44 11, www.hotel-acacia.com). **Rooms** 59. **Map** p219 A2.

There has been a hotel on this site since the 1430s. The original building was demolished in the 1960s;

Memling Museum

38 Mariastraat (050 44 87 43, https://bezoekers.brugge.be/en). **Admission** €8; €6 reductions; free under-12s. **Map** p219 A3 ❸

Within the old chapel of St John's Hospital are works by artist Hans Memling (c1430-94). Memling undertook many commissions for the English aristocrat John Donne and the Italian banker Portinari. His talent as a portrait artist and his hunger for detail are quite astonishing. Like all the Flemish Primitives, Memling believed that the material world was a product of divine creation and that it was necessary to reproduce God's work as faithfully as possible. His use of colours is always brilliant. He ended his days as a patient of the hospital and carried out several commissions for the institution. *The Mystical Marriage of St Catherine* is one of several similar works by Memling (another is in New York's Metropolitan Museum). In the central panel, Jesus, sitting on Mary's lap, is sliding a ring on to St Catherine's finger. Also on display is a shrine made by Memling in 1489, which contains the relic of St Ursula.

it's now part of the Best Western chain. All rooms are en-suite, and there's also an indoor swimming pool, sauna and jacuzzi.

Golden Tulip Hotel de' Medici

15 Potterierei, 8000 Bruges (050 33 98 33, www. hoteldemedici.com). **Rooms** 101. **Map** p219 B1.
A modern four-star hotel in a pleasant canalside location near the historic centre. The interior is clinically efficient, but rooms are spacious and comfortable. There's a sauna, steam bath and gym.

★ Hotel De Orangerie

10 Kartuizerinnenstraat, 8000 Bruges (050 34 16 49, www.hotelorangerie.be). **Rooms** 20. **Map** p219 B2/3.
The rooms in this 15th-century convent, by a canal, are all individually decorated by Antwerp designer Pieter Porters. He is also responsible for decor in De Tuilerieën (7 Dijver, 8000 Bruges, 050 34 36 91, www. hoteltuilerieeen.com), a 15th-century mansion under the same hotel ownership.

★ Hotel Die Swaene

1 Steenhouwersdijk, 8000 Bruges (050 34 27 98, www.dieswaene.be). **Rooms** 30. **Map** p219 B2.

Right in the city centre, this canalside 15th-century mansion is wonderfully romantic. Each room is individually decorated; some have four-poster beds. There's a candlelit restaurant, and a pool and sauna.

Pand Hotel

16 Pandreitje, 8000 Bruges (050 34 06 66, www. pandhotel.com). **Rooms** 26. **Map** p219 B3.
This charming hotel in a leafy corner of Bruges occupies an 18th-century carriage house. Expect a friendly welcome.

Moderate

Hotel Adornes

26 St Annarei, 8000 Bruges (050 34 13 36, www.adornes.be). **Rooms** 20. **Map** p219 B1.
This friendly family hotel in a canalside location near St Annakerk is ideal for exploring the historic centre and the quiet Guido Gezelle quarter to the east. Rooms are comfortable and stylish.
► *The hotel also offers free bicycle use.*

Hotel Aragon

22 Naaldenstraat, 8000 Bruges (050 33 35 33, www.aragon.be). **Rooms** 42. **Map** p219 A1.

Pand Hotel.

The Aragon is an appealing hotel situated right in the heart of the historic merchant quarter, opposite a palace once owned by a Medici banker. The rooms are done out in a comfortable English style and the location is quiet.

Hotel Ter Reien

1 Langestraat, 8000 Bruges (050 34 91 00, www.hotelterreien.be). **Rooms** *26.* **Map** p219 C2.
A pleasant and affordable canalside hotel with a seductive inner courtyard, close to the centre. Rooms are bright and comfortable. The house was the birthplace of Fernand Khnopff, the Symbolist artist who painted views of deserted Bruges quays.

B&Bs

Absoluut Verhulst

1 Verbrand Nieuwland, 8000 Bruges (050 33 45 15, www.b-bverhulst.com). **Rooms** *3.* **No credit cards. Map** p219 C2.
This 17th-century house with creaking floorboards has three light, stylish rooms, including a duplex and a loft that can sleep up to five. Bikes can be rented for the day. A two-night minimum stay applies to weekend bookings.

★ Baert – Bed & Breakfast

28 Westmeers, 8000 Bruges (050 33 05 30, www.bedandbreakfastbrugge.be). **Rooms** *2.* **No credit cards. Map** p219 A3.
Huub Baert and Jeannine Robberecht run a stylish B&B in a restored stable building that belonged to a convent. Each of the two bright rooms have private canalside terraces that catch the sun. Born and bred in Bruges, Huub is an expert on local history.

Inne's Bed & Breakfast

9 Riddersstraat, 8000 Bruges (050 33 56 27, www.bb-bruges.be). **Rooms** *3.* **No credit cards. Map** p219 B2.
This exquisitely decorated townhouse, just a couple of minutes from the Burg, has three second-floor guest rooms on the second floor. All are decorated in a classy, pared-down style and hung with prints by Flemish Masters. Breakfasts are notable. The Gheeraerts also rent out self-catering holiday flats.

★ Koen & Annemie Dieltiens-Debruyne

40 Waalsestraat, 8000 Bruges (050 33 42 94, www.bedandbreakfastbruges.be). **Rooms** *3.* **No credit cards. Map** p219 C2.
A very stylish option in a beautiful 18th-century mansion in the heart of Bruges. A studio apartment is also available in a 17th-century house nearby.

RESTAURANTS

Bistro De Schaar

2 Hooistraat (050 33 59 79, www.bistrodeschaar. be). **Open** *noon-2pm, 6-9pm Mon, Tue, Fri-Sun.* **Main courses** €20-€32. **Map** p219 C2 ❻ Belgian
Located away from the tourist centre, just off Predikherenrei, this cracking little bistro offers a modern take on cosy rusticity. Grills are popular, as are less traditional dishes such as prawns in garlic or cheese-filled ravioli.

★ Bistro Refter

2 Molenmeers (050 44 99 00, www.bistrorefter. com). **Open** *noon-2pm, 7-10pm Tue-Sat.* **Set menu** lunch €17, dinner €37. **Map** p219 C2 ❼ Belgian
A superb bistro from Geert van Hecke of De Karmeliet (*see p224*) fame. It's called Refter because it occupies the refectory of an old Carmelite building, though the decor is now ultra-sleek and modern. It's much more affordable than its three-star sister, and is a set menu-only establishment, which makes everything that little bit easier.

In Den Wittenkop

14 St Jacobstraat (050 33 20 59, www.inden wittenkop.be). **Open** *noon-2pm, 6-10pm Mon-Sat.* **Main courses** €22-€39. **Map** p219 A2 ❽ Belgian
Despite being close to the tourist centre, this elderly café offers an authentic Bruges experience, along with classic steak frites and eels cooked in a variety of ways.

ESCAPES & EXCURSIONS

★ De Karmeliet

*19 Langestraat (050 33 82 59, www.dekarmeliet.
be).* **Open** 7-10pm Tue; noon-2pm, 7-10pm Wed-
Sat. **Main courses** €75-€130. **Map** p219 C2
❾ **Belgian**

At the three Michelin-starred De Karmeliet, chef
Geert van Hecke's staples include rabbit, local
breeds of chicken, truffles and scallops. Special
menus cover such themes as 'the flat country'. The
decor is airy and modern, and you can see Geert at
work at the back of the dining room. This is a cathedral to high dining, so expect to pay for it.

Parkrestaurant

*1 Minderbroedersstraat (0497 801 872, www.
parkrestaurant.be).* **Open** 11.30am-10pm Tue,
Wed, Fri-Sun. **Main courses** €25-€31. **Set menu**
€45-€75. **Map** p219 C3 ❿ **Belgian**

An elegant, welcoming restaurant located in a
patrician mansion facing the city's main park. The
kitchen produces some truly wonderful dishes
using Ardennes beef, fresh salmon, Ostend sole and
Sisteron lamb. The garden is an idyllic spot for a
summer meal.

★ De Stove

*4 Kleine St Amandstraat (050 33 78 35, www.
restaurantdestove.be).* **Open** 7-10pm Mon, Tue,
Fri; noon-2pm, 7-10pm Sat, Sun. Closed 2wks June.
Set menu €49-€66. **Map** p219 A2 ⓫ **Belgian**

A beguiling little restaurant, just off one of the main
shopping streets, serving a variety of hearty meat
and fish dishes. The interior is traditional Flemish
with an ancient iron stove and chimney.

Tanuki

1 Oude Gentweg (050 34 75 12, www.tanuki.be).
Open noon-2pm, 6.30-9.30pm Wed-Sun. **Main
courses** €34-€36. **Set menu** €80. **Map** p219 B4
⓬ **Japanese**

Tanuki's oriental minimalism offers a truly striking
contrast to the mostly Flemish restaurants in the
neighbourhood. Sushi and sashimi are a speciality,
always fresh and reliably tasty.

PUBS & BARS

★ Brugs Beertje

*5 Kemelstraat (050 33 96 16, www.brugsbeertje.
be).* **Open** 4pm-midnight Mon, Thur, Sun; 4pm-
1am Fri, Sat. **Map** p219 A3 ⓭

Drinkers rave about this traditional brown pub that
sells no less than 300 different beers. Set up by 'beer
professor' Jan De Bruyne, it's now mainly run by
his wife Daisy, who takes a more lenient line when
asked for 'a lager'.

Craenenburg

16 Markt (050 33 34 02, www.craenenburg.be).
Open 7am-midnight daily. **No credit cards.**
Map p219 A2 ⓮

Set on the site of the house where Maximilian of
Austria was held captive, this is a typical Bruges
tavern with yellowed walls, wooden tables and elaborate stained glass.

'T Estaminet

5 Park (050 33 09 16). **Open** 11.30am-3am Mon-
Wed, Sun; 4pm-3am Thur; 11.30am-6am, Fri, Sat.
Map p219 C2 ⓯

An old Bruges inn facing Astrid Park in a district
seldom reached by tourists. The owner has built up
what is undoubtedly one of the best jazz collections
in Bruges, attracting writers, politicians and women
with dogs.

★ Est Wijnbar

*7 Braambergstraat (050 33 38 39, www.wijnbar
est.be).* **Open** 4pm-midnight daily. **No credit
cards.** **Map** p219 B2 ⓰

A beautiful wine bar where you can sample 90 different wines in a classy setting. It hosts intimate (and
free) jazz concerts every Sunday from 8pm.

De Garre

1 De Garre (050 34 10 29, www.degarre.be).
Open noon-midnight Mon-Thur, Sun; noon-
1am Fri; 11am-1am Sat. **No credit cards.**
Map p219 B2 ⓱

At the end of the shortest blind alley in Bruges
(off Breidelstraat), this bar sells 130 different beers.
It's set in a 16th-century house with wooden beams,
brick walls and an authentic Bruges atmosphere.

De Republiek

36 St Jacobsstraat (0499 48 94 84). **Open**
11am-midnight daily. **No credit cards.**
Map p219 A2 ⓲

This candlelit café attached to an arts complex is a
decent place to pick up word-of-mouth tips on jazz,
films and dance events.

De Versteende Nacht

11 Langestraat (050 33 36 66). **Open** 5pm-late
Mon-Sat. **Map** p219 C2 ⓳

The manager of this jazz café is a huge fan of comic
strips, so it's no surprise that his bar is filled with
comic books, and its walls covered with cartoons.
There are regular jazz sessions.

SHOPS & SERVICES

The main shopping street is Steenstraat,
which runs from the Markt to 't Zand and has
the usual international chains. Geldmunt and
Noordzandstraat are home to fashion boutiques.
Wollestraat has its share of lace shops, plus
some smaller specialised stores. One long-
established lace store is **'t Apostelientje** (11
Balstraat, 050 33 78 80, www.apostelientje.be;
open 1-5pm Tue; 9.30am-12.15pm, 1.15-5pm
Wed-Sat; 9.30am-1pm Sun).

ESCAPES & EXCURSIONS

Ghent

Pretty Ghent comprises a compact, traffic-free centre cut through with canals and little trip-trap bridges. It has more listed buildings than the rest of Belgium put together, an ancient castle and a cathedral holding some of the world's most important works of art. But as crucial as Ghent's history is to its identity, it doesn't allow the past to hinder its present. These days, it is a thriving port, university city and the nerve centre of Belgium's digital industries. Apart from ten days of festival madness in July, the annual De Gentse Feesten, the city remains quietly unassuming and tends not to scream its riches from the rooftops. The locals seem to prefer it that way, perhaps aware they could have another Bruges on their hands if they don't watch out. Ghent has the pedigree of a wealthy city-state and it's not interested in cross-breeding.

Ghent's history is rich and erratic, combining periods of great glory and wealth with suffering and persecution. In the Middle Ages, when it was the centre of the cloth and wool trade, it was the largest town in western Europe and the university was considered one of the most scholarly. This provided rich pickings for Martin Luther and his followers, which led Ghent into a nightmare scenario of heretic bonfires and the infamous Iconoclastic Riots of 1566, when no church, monastery or convent remained undamaged.

In 1540, Ghent-born Emperor Charles V returned to the city in a rage after its citizens refused to pay higher taxes. He ordered the execution of the rebellion's ringleaders and then forced 50 of the city's elders, dressed only in white shirts and with nooses tied around their necks, to beg for mercy. Local residents became known as *stropdragers*, or noose-wearers.

Known as Gent to the Flemings and Gand to the Walloons, the capital of East Flanders lies on the banks of two rivers, the Leie and the Ketel, and offers a handful of must-see attractions.

GETTING THERE & INFORMATION

Ghent is just half an hour by train from the centre of Brussels. Four fast trains an hour shuttle between the two cities. From Gent St Pieters station, take the no.1 tram into town (pay at the platform machines). If you arrive by car, follow the signs reading 'P-route'; this will take you through streets where you are allowed to park and, eventually, to a multistorey car park.

City of Ghent Tourist Office

Oude Vismijn, Sint-Veerleplein 5 (09 266 56 60, www.visitgent.be). **Open** *Apr-Oct* 9.30am-6.30pm daily. *Nov-Mar* 9.30am-4.30pm daily. **Map** p227 A2.

SIGHTS & MUSEUMS

Stadhuis & around

St Michielsbrug is a good place to start any tour. One of the best views of the cathedral is from this bridge over the Leie, which overlooks the Graslei (Herb Quay) and Korenlei (Corn Quay). Both are lined with beautiful houses, most built during the Flemish Renaissance but some dating back as far as 1000. Just south of the bridge is **St Michielskerk**, standing alongside the former Dominican monastery Het Pand, which is part of the University of Ghent – the public are free to wander around. On the other side of the water is **St Niklaaskerk**, an outstanding piece of Scheldt Gothic architecture built in the 13th century.

ESCAPES & EXCURSIONS

Next door stands the **Stadhuis** (Town Hall), designed to be the largest town hall in Europe. Building began in 1518, but was halted because of religious strife and diminishing funds. Work resumed at the end of the 16th century, and the result of this staggered process is clearly visible. One part, decorated with countless statues, is in an ornate Gothic style, while the more sober section of the façade reflects post-Reformation taste. Across the Botermarkt from the Stadhuis soars the lofty **Belfort** (Belfry), dating from 1313.

Ghent's first cathedral was founded as St Peter's by St Bavo in the seventh century. Built over six centuries, the current **St Baafskathedraal** (also known as St Bavo's) is remarkable as much for its high and late Gothic style as for the art it contains. South and west of the cathedral are Ghent's shopping streets, busy Veldstraat and the more attractive Magaleinstraat and Koestraat.

Belfort

St Baafsplein (09 375 31 61 07 72, www.belfort gent.be). **Open** 10am-6pm daily. **Admission** €6; €4.50 reductions; €2 19-26s; free under-19s. **No credit cards. Map** p227 B3 ❶

Built in the 14th century and later heavily restored, the Belfort is one of three medieval towers that dominate the centre of Ghent. Its interior – containing both a carillon and a bell museum – is worth the entrance fee for the view over the city once you climb the tower.

IN THE KNOW GHENT GOES WILD

De Gentse Feesten (www.gentsefeesten. gent) is a home-grown bash with centuries of history, aimed firmly at locals but attracting more and more visitors every year as news of its good-natured vibe spreads. For ten days from mid July, the normally quiet cobbled streets resound with rock music, jazz bands and street theatre. The festival got under way in its current form in 1970, when local folk singer Walter De Buck decided to get people on to the streets for some popular culture, while giving artists an opportunity to promote themselves to a wider audience. He organised a programme of entertainment on the little square by St Jacob's Church; once the city council sat up and got involved, it started to snowball.

The event is organised around several sub-festivals – **Miramiro** (www.miramiro. be), for example, focuses on circus and street culture – though the internationally renowned 10 Days Off techno festival partied for the last time in 2014. Leading up to the Feesten is the **Gent Jazz Festival** (www.gentjazz.com), a sort of taster of things to come.

★ St Baafskathedraal

St Baafsplein (09 225 49 85, www.sintbaafs kathedraal.be). **Open** *Apr-Oct* 8.30am-6pm Mon-Sat; 1-6pm Sun. *Nov-Mar* 8.30am-5pm Mon-Sat; 1-5pm Sun. **Admission** free. *Chapel* (The Adoration of the Mystic Lamb) €4; €1 audio guide. **No credit cards. Map** p227 C4 ❷

Laurent Delvaux's elaborate rococo pulpit, in oak and marble, is the first thing you see on entering St Bavo's, while Peter Paul Rubens' *Entry of St Bavo into the Monastery* is displayed in the north transept. The cathedral's undisputed masterpiece, however, is *The Adoration of the Mystic Lamb* by Hubert and Jan van Eyck. The altarpiece is on display in the De Villa Chapel, which gets packed in high season but it is worth the wait. The picture depicts a scene from the Apocalypse according to St John, the colours so bright and glistening that the painting lights up the whole chapel. Created in a series of panels, it is being restored piece by piece in the Fine Arts Museum until 2017– though the greater part of the work still remains here. The 12th-century crypt is the oldest part of the cathedral. Although it contains tombs and the usual religious paraphernalia, it's actually most notable for its frescoes and for Justus van Gent's painting *The Calvary Scene*.

Gravensteen castle & around

Surrounded by water on the north-west edge of the centre is **Gravensteen castle**, formerly a fortress, a mint, a mill and now a modest museum. Next door, on St Veerleplein, a bas-relief Neptune towers over the entrance to the **Vismarkt** (Fish Market), while across the water is the **Museum voor Sierkunst en Vormgeving** (Museum of Decorative Arts & Design), with its worthwhile collection of furnishings over the centuries.

Just east of the castle on the Kraanlei is the quirky **Museum voor Volkskunde** (Folklore Museum), also called Het Huis van Alijn. Patershol, the tangle of streets north of here, is packed with fine restaurants and bars. Over the Leie, **Vrijdagmarkt** is a vast square that used to be the focal point of political life in the Middle Ages, and is still a marketplace; restaurants and bars line its sides. There are market stalls on many squares in Ghent, and markets most days of the week, as well as a decent fruit and vegetable market in Groentenmarkt every morning.

★ Gravensteen

St Veerleplein (09 269 87 50, www.gravensteen. stad.gent). **Open** *Apr-Sept* 10am-6pm daily. *Oct-Mar* 9am-5pm daily. **Admission** €10; €7.50 reductions; €6 19-26s; free under-19s. **No credit cards. Map** p227 A2 ❸

Built in 1180 by Philippe of Alsace, Count of Flanders, on the site of the first count's original stronghold, this is the only medieval fortress in Flanders. The arrestingly grim structure lost its military function

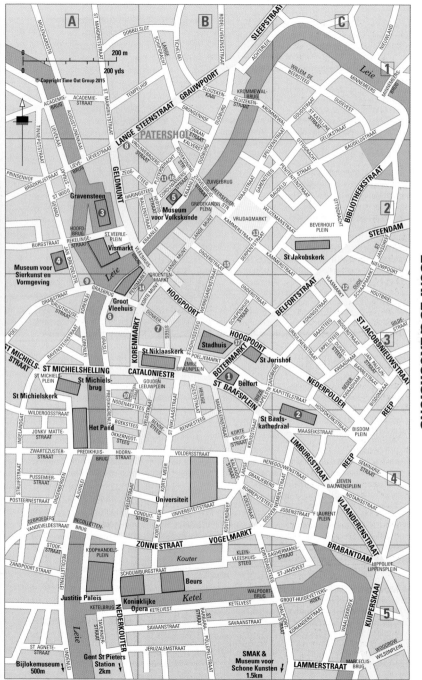

ESCAPES & EXCURSIONS

centuries ago – it was subsequently used as a mint, a court of justice and even a cotton mill. It has a small collection of torture instruments.

Museum voor Sierkunst en Vormgeving
5 Jan Breydelstraat (09 267 99 99, www.design museumgent.be). **Open** 10am-6pm Tue-Sun. **Admission** €8; €6 reductions; €2 19-26s; free under-19s. **Map** p227 A2 ❹
Located in an 18th-century house, this superb collection includes royal portraits alongside crystal chandeliers, silk wall coverings and ornate tapestries. The furniture, most of it French, includes baroque, rococo and Louis XVI pieces. A more modern extension houses exhibitions. There is also a stunning display of modern design, including art nouveau pieces by Victor Horta, Paul Hankar and Henry van de Velde.

Museum voor Volkskunde
65 Kraanlei (09 269 23 50, www.huisvanalijn.be). **Open** 11am-5.30pm Tue-Sat; 10am-5.30pm Sun. **Admission** €6; €4.50 reductions; €2 19-26s; free under-19s. **No credit cards. Map** p227 B2 ❺
Set inside 18 almshouses, with a garden and chapel, this museum is aimed at children, but parents will also enjoy it. It aims to show life in Ghent in the 19th century, and has candlestick-makers, cloth-makers, reconstructed sweet shops, pubs and a chemist.

South of St Pieters station

The area between St Pieters train station and the city centre is home to three intriguing museums. Along the west side of the River Leie is the former Abdij van de Bijloke. The red-brick abbey was founded in the early 13th century and maintained its religious function until it was closed down by invading French revolutionaries in 1797. It now houses **STAM** (Museum of the City of Ghent).

South of here, across the river (a five-minute walk from the train station; 25 minutes from the centre) is Citadelpark, laid out in the 1870s on the site of a Habsburg castle. Here is where you'll find the outstanding **SMAK** (Stedelijk Museum voor Actuele Kunst – Museum of Contemporary Art), considered the finest collection of modern art in Flanders. Facing SMAK is **Museum voor Schone Kunsten** (Museum of Fine Arts). One of the three most prestigious museums in the country for Flemish art, along with the Musées Royaux des Beaux-Arts in Brussels and the Groeninge Museum in Bruges.

★ Museum voor Schone Kunsten
1 Fernand Scribedreef, Citadelpark (09 240 07 00, www.mskgent.be). **Open** 10am-6pm Tue-Sun. **Admission** €8; €6 reductions; €2 19-26s; free under-19s. **No credit cards.**
The Museum of Fine Arts contains a huge permanent collection of Flemish Art from the 1400s to the mid 1900s. Highlights include *Christ Carrying the*

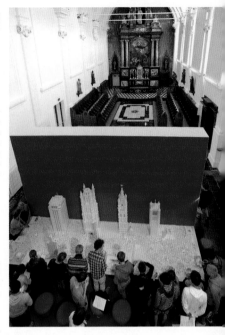

Cross by Hieronymus Bosch, *Jupiter and Antiope* by Anthony van Dyck and *Man of Sorrows* by Maerten Van Heemskerck. Also look out for the piece-by-piece restoration work of *The Adoration of the Mystic Lamb* by van Eyck, usually on display in its entirety in St Baafskathedraal. Here, the public can see restorers painstakingly going about their jobs behind glass. Complementing all this is a regular agenda of thought-provoking temporary exhibitions – in 2015, themes ranged from the mid 19th-century photography of Julia Margaret Cameron to the Gorod Ustinov artists' collective from Russia.

★ SMAK (Stedelijk Museum voor Actuele Kunst)
1 Jan Hoetplein (09 240 76 01, www.smak.be). **Open** 10am-6pm Tue-Sun. **Admission** €8; €4 reductions; €2 19-26s; free under-19s. **No credit cards.**
The Municipal Museum of Contemporary Art contains first-rate works by Francis Bacon, Joseph Beuys and David Hockney. There's also a good spread of minimal and conceptual art, and the 1960s are well represented with pieces by Christo, Warhol and Marcel Broodthaers.

STAM (Museum of the City of Ghent)
2 Godshuizenlaan (09 269 14 00, www.stamgent. be). **Open** 10am-6pm Tue-Sun. **Admission** €8; €4 reductions; €2 19-26s; free under-19s. **No credit cards.**

STAM.

Six rooms presented chronologically tell the history of Ghent by means of 300 artefacts, multimedia applications, listening benches and large-format photos. The last section, 'City of Tomorrow', is updated with development plans. Alongside, temporary exhibitions run for three or four months each – in early 2016, 'The Lost Kingdom' focuses on the short-lived unity of the Netherlands and what would become Belgium between 1815 and 1830.

HOTELS

In recent years, all the main chains have moved in, including NH, Novotel and Holiday Inn. During the Gentse Feesten from mid July, book at least a month ahead. See www.gent-hotels.eu. The Guild of Guesthouses (www.bedandbreakfast-gent.be) has a database of local B&B accommodation, from a room in a cosy private home to a self-contained suite in a 17th-century cloister. For hotels, price categories below are for a standard double room: **Deluxe** (€250 or over), **Expensive** (€150-€249) and **Moderate** (€90-€149).

Deluxe

★ Sandton Grand Hotel Reylof
36 Hoogstraat, 9000 Ghent (09 235 40 70, www.sandton.eu/sandton-grand-hotel-reylof). **Rooms** 158.

Ghent's premier hotel, the Sandton, is supremely luxurious, set in an 18th-century property and its former carriage house in the historic centre. A spa centre, gym, courtyard garden and top-notch French restaurant Lof are its main attractions – the Sandton also offers long-stay apartments with a full hotel service on hand.

Expensive

Ghent Marriott Hotel
10 Korenlei, 9000 Ghent (09 233 93 93, www.marriott.com). **Rooms** 140. **Map** p227 A3.

The most prominent of the chain hotels to have set up in Ghent in the last few years, the business-friendly Marriott enjoys a prime location on the banks of the Leie. Within walking distance of all the main sights, it has a gym, cycle rental, upscale local fare at the Coeur d'Artichaut restaurant and a cellar bar.

Moderate

Boatel
44 Voorhoutkaai, 9000 Ghent (09 267 10 30, www.theboatel.com). **Rooms** 5.

This former transport boat moored near Dampoort train station, ten minutes' walk from the centre of town, has been converted into a five-room hotel, complete with original woodwork and portholes. Known for serving a good breakfast.

ESCAPES & EXCURSIONS

Cour St-Georges

2 Botermarkt, 9000 Ghent (09 224 24 24, www. courstgeorges.be). **Rooms** 31. **Map** p227 B3.
Facing the Stadhuis and by the Belfort, the Cour dates from 1228 – Charles V and Napoleon were guests. The smallish rooms aren't as characterful as they might be, but have all the mod cons.

Erasmus

25 Poel, 9000 Ghent (09 224 21 95, www. erasmushotel.be). **Rooms** 11. **Map** p227 A3.
A cosy hotel five minutes' walk from the centre. The owners have preserved the authentic character of the 16th-century building while providing the well-furnished rooms with every modern comfort.

★ Hotel Gravensteen

35 Jan Breydelstraat, 9000 Ghent (09 225 11 50, www.gravensteen.be). **Rooms** 49. **Map** p227 A2.
A beautiful hotel in a 19th-century *hôtel particulier*. The Second Empire style is imposing and impeccable; the elegant rooms are equipped with modern facilities. The hotel has a bar and car park.

Hotel Harmony

37 Kraanlei, 9000 Ghent (09 324 26 80, www. hotel-harmony.be). **Rooms** 25. **Map** p227 B2.
The Harmony is an excellent mid-range choice. It comprises two historic buildings with a pretty garden in between, providing convenience and tranquillity in the heart of town.

RESTAURANTS

Belga Queen

10 Graslei (09 280 01 00, www.belgaqueen.be). **Open** noon-2.30pm, 6.30-11pm Mon-Thur, Sun; noon-2.30pm, 6.30pm-midnight Fri, Sat. **Main courses** €21-€34.50. **Set menu** €18-€22. **Map** p227 A3 ❻ **Belgian**
This fancy restaurant-cum-cocktail lounge, set on the town's most beautiful quayside, attracts hordes of *nouveaux riches* from the suburbs. The food is haute Belgian with excellent seafood. All this under the 13th-century beams of an imposing old grain store.

Georges IV

23 Donkersteeg (09 225 19 18, www.georgesseafood. be). **Open** noon-2.15pm, 6.30-10pm Wed-Fri; 6.30-10pm Sat; noon-2.15pm, 6.30-9.15pm Sun. **Main courses** €19-€35. **Map** p227 B3 ❼ **Fish & seafood**
This father-and-son fish restaurant has been in the same family since 1924. The prices are a tad steep, but the fish is expertly cooked. Bouillabaisse with North Sea fish is a local take on the Marseille classic. The scrupulously clean fishmonger's next door, with its tanks of lobsters, is under the same ownership and a good advert for the restaurant.

★ J-e-f

10 Lange Steenstraat (09 336 80 58, www. j-e-f.be). **Open** noon-11pm Tue-Fri; 6-11pm Sat. **Main courses** €23-€29. **Set menu** €28. **Map** p227 A2 ❽ **Belgian**
On the fringe of the Patershol quarter, J-e-f stands for Jason Blanckaert and Famke, who run the place, creating (Jason) and serving (Famke) contemporary Belgian cuisine in trendy, natural surroundings.

Korenlei Twee

2 Korenlei (09 224 00 73, www.korenleitwee.be). **Open** noon-2.30pm, 6-10.30pm Tue-Sat; noon-3pm Sun. **Set menu** lunch €21.50, dinner €60-€75. **Map** p227 A3 ❾ **Belgian**

Pakhuis.

Its large terrace overlooking the confluence of the Leie and Lieve rivers, Korenlei Twee is a relaxing, modern spot in an 18th-century building. You can opt for an affordable, convivial lunch or splash out on Zeeland oysters or Dover sole, priced by the day, if you go à la carte. There's a separate lobster menu – and also one for children.

Pakhuis

4 Schuurkenstraat (09 223 55 55, www.pakhuis.be).
Open noon-2.30pm, 6.30-11pm Mon-Thur; noon-2.30pm, 6.30pm-midnight Fri, Sat. **Main courses** €17-€39.50. **Map** p227 A3 ⑩ **Belgian/European**
This large renovated storage depot is worth visiting as much for its architecture as its Belgo-European food: the cast-iron pillars, wrought-iron balustrades, parquet floor and impressive oak bar are the main features of a classic interior. You can gawp with just a drink if you don't fancy eating.

★ Publiek

39 Ham (09 330 04 86, www.publiekgent.be). **Open** noon-2pm, 7-9pm Tue-Fri; 7-9pm Sat. **Set menu** lunch €27, dinner €57. **Belgian/contemporary**
Opened by top Flemish chef Olly Ceulenaere in 2014 in the former site of De Avonden near Dampoort, Publiek offers set meals, featuring fresh seasonal produce, to a discerning clientele. There's an à la carte menu of sorts, usually featuring three choices, but you're here to splash out in a one-star Michelin joint.

Vier Tafels

6 Plotersgracht (09 225 05 25, www.viertafels.be). **Open** 6-10.30pm Mon; noon-2pm, 6-10.30pm Tue-Sun. **Main courses** €21-€27. **Set menu** €12. **Map** p227 B2 ⑪ **Belgian/global**
One of the most popular restaurants in Patershol. It's not as expensive as other places nearby, but the food is every bit as good with top-notch global favourites and Ghent specialities. Crocodile, ostrich and Congolese chicken with palm-nut sauce – almost every continent gets a look-in on the menu. It also features a bar, Virus, for a pre-meal tipple.

PUBS & BARS

★ Café Charlatan

6 Vlasmarkt (09 224 24 57, www.charlatan.be). **Open** 8pm-late Tue-Sun. **No credit cards.** **Map** p227 C3 ⑫
Describing it as a music café doesn't begin to tell the story – although there is live music most evenings at 10pm, with a live radio link-up. The back room opens at weekends from 1am for urban house, disco and other danceable tunes. All sorts of performances take place, but Charlatan is simply a damn good hangout for musicians, night owls and locals who refuse to go home. It's undoubtedly at its brilliant best during the awesome Gentse Feesten (*see p226* **In the Know**), when this is simply the place to be at eight in the morning.

De Dulle Griet

50 Vrijdagsmarkt (09 224 24 55, www.dullegriet.be). **Open** 4.30pm-1am Mon; noon-1am Tue-Sat; noon-7.30pm Sun. **No credit cards.** **Map** p227 B2 ⑬
De Dulle Griet was the first pub in Belgium to specialise in local Flanders beers, so it's not surprising that its dimly lit and curious interior has welcomed many a tourist. It's still a lot of fun, though, mainly because locals love it as well – some indulge in the bizarre house custom of exchanging their shoe for a beer, and have the waiter then winch it up in a basket. Go figure – it's Ghent, after all.

't Galgenhuisje

5 Groentenmarkt (09 233 42 51). **Open** 11am-late daily. **No credit cards.** **Map** p227 B3 ⑭
A working and highly popular pub since the late 17th century, 't Galgenhuisje means 'the gallows' – a reference to its rather grisly medieval function.
▶ *Downstairs, in the 14th-century cellar, a restaurant serves fish and grilled meats.*

Pink Flamingo's Lounge

55 Onderstraat (09 233 47 18, www.pink flamingos.be). **Open** 5pm-midnight Mon, Sun; noon-midnight Wed; noon-3pm Thur, Fri; 2pm-3am Sat. **Map** p227 B2 ⑮
'Kitsch lounge bar' is how the PFL describes itself and, to prove the point, it alternates its cornucopia of tat every three months. Whatever the choice, you're guaranteed to be sipping your cocktail amid dolls, records, cartoon books and religious figurines.

Rococo

57 Corduwaniersstraat (09 224 30 35). **Open** 9pm-late Tue-Sun. **No credit cards.** **Map** p227 B2 ⑯
Located in Patershol, Rococo is one of Ghent's moodier bars. Artists gather around candlelit tables and a piano sits in one corner, sometimes too tempting for the would-be *chanteur* who's had a few too many. There's also an outdoor café at the back.

★ Den Turk

3 Botermarkt (09 233 01 97, www.cafeden turk.be). **Open** 11am-late daily. **No credit cards.** **Map** p227 B3 ⑰
Dating all the way from 1340, Den Turk is the oldest pub in Ghent, although you wouldn't know it from its distinctly ordinary decor. It plays host to regular jazz (plus a dash of blues and flamenco) and you can munch on a sizeable choice of snacks.

SHOPS & SERVICES

Ghent's central shopping district is very compact, completely pedestrianised and generally free of overwhelming crowds. Veldstraat is the main drag, with the usual international chain stores. Bennesteeg has Ghent's most upscale fashion boutiques, while Volder, St Niklaas and Magelein feature more quirky addresses.

Ostend

The Belgians are justly proud of their 68 kilometres (42 miles) of coastline. Not only does it provide a punctuation mark to their territory, but its sands are some of the finest in northern Europe. At low tide the soft beaches can stretch for several hundred metres, providing a safe play area and a paddler's paradise. And despite the cold, grey North Sea, which can whip up a fair wind all year round, the stalwart Belgians arrive in droves. In summer it's shoulder-to-shoulder solid, while in winter it's full of retired folk and city types with second homes. Almost exactly halfway along the coast, Ostend is its prime resort, a holiday destination with royal connections. Known for its beaches and its casino, Ostend was the home of influential fin-de-siècle artist James Ensor.

ESCAPES & EXCURSIONS

This tourist invasion of the dunes has its downside; massive building projects along the coastline have left it overdeveloped in a mish-mash of styles, a sort of Benidorm *à la belge*, where apartment blocks, villas and commercial enterprises vie for the perfect sea view. But all is not lost: the coast is redeemed by its broad promenades, which separate sand from cement and provide a safe passage for hired bikes, tandems and pedal cars, as well as plenty of long, lazy strolling.

Another charming feature uneclipsed by the building work is the humble beach hut. These remain in rows all along the Belgian coast as a testament to the 19th century, when they were drawn by horse to the water's edge for modest mixed-sex bathing. ('Horror!' cried the English, but that didn't stop the young Victoria popping over for a dip.) Today, the huts are painted up a treat in ice-cream colours and can be hired or bought, although families tend to pass them down from generation to generation.

EXPLORING OSTEND

Thanks to its royal connections, Ostend is considered the queen of the Belgian seaside resorts. Léopold I built a house here, but it was Léopold II, master builder of Belgium,

who commissioned several villas and gave Ostend its royal character. Despite criticism that he was neglecting the capital, Léopold II spent much of his time here – partly because it provided the perfect hideaway for his numerous affairs. His association with the town meant it became an extremely fashionable resort in the late 19th and early 20th centuries; so fashionable, in fact, that it rivalled Monte Carlo for wealth, casinos and racecourses. World War II finally put paid to all that, and serious aerial bombardment destroyed much of the old fabric, including the original casino, resulting in the curious blend of imperialistic grandeur and 1960s and '70s blocks that you'll see today.

The atmosphere in Ostend is pretty typical seaside stuff, with the long, wide promenade and soft, flat sands giving the place a calm air. The *Mercator*, an old Belgian navy training ship from the '30s, still stands in the yacht harbour, while the **Spuikom** harbour is now used mainly for watersports.

A plethora of events takes place throughout the summer months, from sporting get-togethers (sailing, cycling, windsurfing) to artistic shindigs. TAZ (www.theateraanzee.be), Theatre by the Sea, takes place in late July and August – there's a special English-language programme too. One of the oddest events by far is September's shrimp-peeling competition in the **Visserskai**, the fishing harbour, which provides the wonderful sight of the daily catch coming in.

The wind can be biting in winter, but hardy Belgians use their holiday flats all year round, so Ostend is never really empty. During the Christmas and New Year period there is a skating rink and an atmospheric Christmas market, along with fireworks on the beach on 31 December, and the strange but spectacular communal ritual of burning Christmas trees on the beach after Twelfth Night.

A smattering of architectural gems from old Ostend remain. **Fort Napoleon**, built in 1812, is the only intact Napoleonic fortress in Europe, while over at the western end of the promenade, Léopold II's **Galeries Royales** comprise a stately colonnade crowned with a belle époque pavilion. Léopold's own former villa is now a luxurious hotel, the **Thermae Palace**. In the **Church of St Peter & St Paul** is a somewhat darker relic; the marble mausoleum housing the first Léopold's beloved wife, Louise-Marie, who died in Ostend in 1850. The twin-towered church also houses stained-glass depictions of the Belgian kings.

The crowning glory of the post-war period is **Ostend Casino** (*photo p234*), built in 1953 and the fourth to stand on the spot. The walls of the gaming room are decorated with frescoes by Paul Delvaux, although you have to take a place at the tables to see them. The casino is also used as a multi-purpose arts complex in summer.

Ostend's artistic reputation stems from its link to the Expressionist painter James Ensor (1860-1949), who lived, worked and died here. A trail of 15 panels reproducing his often macabre works are dotted around town, while his home and studio, the **Ensorhuis** (27 Vlaanderenstraat, 059 50 81 18), is open to the public. So small was its upstairs workshop that Ensor could never fully unfurl his ultimate masterpiece, *Christ's Entry into Brussels*. The house used to belong to his aunt, who sold seashells and other souvenirs, and the shop continues this tradition.

The West Flanders Museum for Modern Art joined forces with its Ostend counterpart in 2009, and was rebranded, perhaps somewhat like the Bozar in Bruxelles, as **Mu.ZEE** (Romestraat 11, 059 50 81 18, www.muzee.be).

It exhibits local modern art from the Expressionists to the present day and includes video art and installations by Panamarenko, the man with the flying machines. It also takes care of the Ensorhuis, with details of the permanent collection on its website.

Ostend Marina.

ESCAPES & EXCURSIONS

Ostend Casino. *See p233.*

HOTELS & RESTAURANTS

Hotels in Ostend tend to be smarter than those at most seaside resorts. At the top end, Léopold's old villa, the huge **Thermae Palace Hotel** (7 Koningin Astridlaan, 059 80 66 44, www. thermaepalace.be) is one of Ostend's finest. The modern, mid-range **Hotel Europe** (52 Kapucijnenstraat, 059 70 10 12, www.europe hotel.be) is only 50 metres from the promenade, and comfortable. A decent choice near the railway station, the art deco-style **Hotel Louisa** (8B Louisastraat, 059 50 96 77, www.hotellouisa.be) is in the same price bracket. For the price and location, you can't beat **Hotel De Hofkamers** (5 IJzerstraat, 059 70 63 49, www.hotel-de hofkamers.be). Rack rates in high season are over €100 for a double room, but you should be able to find a relative bargain on hotel-booking sites.

It's no surprise to learn that fish is the order of the day in Ostend. For a quick bite, go to the Visserskai, where small stands sell fishy finger food – prepared crab, mussels and fresh young herring (*maatjesharing*) – and, yes, you do eat them raw. Among the pick of the restaurants are **'T Vistrapje** (37 Visserskaai, 059 80 23 82, www.vistrapje.be) and the more contemporary **Bistro Mathilda** (1 Leopold II Laan, 059 51 06 70, www.bistromathilda.be), whose Menu Mathilda (€59) features the best of what's in season. Also currently on-trend is the evening-only **Restaurant Eclips** (85 Kapucijnenstraat, 059 43 34 53, www.eclips-at-sea.be, closed Mon, Thur), located by the Casino. It requires a €50 per head minimum spend (cash only) – but if you're fine with that, you can expect exquisite meat fondues and first-rate service.

Drinking haunts are found around Langestraat and Van Iseghemlaan. Irish pubs abound, but one bizarre place is the **Cosy Corner Inn** (76A Langestraat, 059 70 92 61), full of atmosphere and bonhomie. On the seafront, the **Taverne Floride** (81 Albert I Promenade, 059 50 10 53) is a great spot for honest drinking and big-screen footie.

GETTING THERE & AROUND

The motorways to the coast can be a nightmare, particularly at weekends and in the summer, and parking comes with its own problems. By far the best way to get to Ostend is to catch the inter-city train from Brussels; the journey takes just over an hour. Once you're here, the coastal tram (www.delijn.be/en/kusttram) runs the entire length of the Belgian waterfront.

Visit Oostende

2 Monacoplein, 8400 Oostende (059 70 11 99, www.visitoostende.be). **Open** *July, Aug* 9am-7pm daily. *Apr-June, Sept-mid Nov* 10am-6pm daily. *Jan-Mar, mid Nov-24 Dec* 10am-5.30pm daily.

SEASIDE HEALING

A new audio tour follows the path of soul legend Marvin Gaye.

Staid, regal Ostend seems a rather unlikely place for a coked-out soul music legend to find his mojo. Not only that, but to rebuild his career and come out with a multi-million selling hit, 'Sexual Healing'. Yet Marvin Gaye washed up on these shores in 1981, met the locals, drank in their bars and wandered around the house of artist James Ensor.

All in all, Gaye lived in Ostend for about 18 months. His stay here has now been adapted into a downloadable audio tour and documentary by the city's tourist office Visit Oostende (see *p234*). The **Marvin Gaye Midnight Love Tour** (www.marvingaye.be/en), a two-hour walk interspersed with original interviews, starts with Gaye stepping off the ferry with his son Bubby on Valentine's Day in 1981.

While in London, his career in freefall, Gaye had met Belgian promoter and soul-music fan Freddy Cousaert, who invited

him to his home town to recharge his batteries. Cousaert found Gaye an apartment overlooking the North Sea, the Résidence Jane at 77 Albert I Promenade. Gaye took to Ostend right away, jogging on the beach and hanging out in the fishermen's bars.

Belgian filmmaker Richard Olivier recorded some of Gaye's everyday life here, footage that was later used in a cult BBC documentary. Gaye also performed at the Ostend Casino and, inspired by the erotic images created by James Ensor, wrote a song called 'Sexual Healing'. Recorded at a small studio near Waterloo, it would go on to become a worldwide smash.

By the time it did, however, in late 1982, Gaye had already returned to the States after his mother, Alberta, was rushed into hospital with a kidney infection. She survived the ordeal, only to see her son shot dead by his father in 1984.

ESCAPES & EXCURSIONS

History

How a charcoal forest became Europe's capital.

TEXT: GARY HILLS

History offers little insight into how Brussels managed to flourish on such an unforgiving site, an inhospitable marsh fed by the River Senne, a tributary with little purpose except to flood. Located inland and with no obvious access to the sea, the area's saving grace was the vast charcoal forest that surrounded it. The Silva Carbonaria was a source of valuable fuel and iron ore. The Forêt de Soignes south-east of modern-day Brussels is the last remnant of this ancient forest, now a place to amble rather than scratch for survival. The area was also overlooked by what became known as the Coudenberg, a rare hill that offered drier, firmer ground.

The development of the city we know today was largely fashioned by ever-changing military and political intervention in a strategic buffer zone at the confluence of major language groups and vested interests. Thus the story of Brussels is one of power, high drama and changing fortunes; not bad for a city with such bog-standard beginnings.

IN CONTEXT

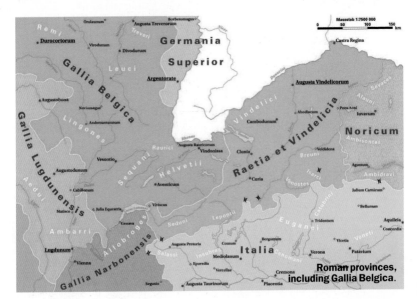

Roman provinces, including Gallia Belgica.

THE ROMANS

When Julius Caesar first arrived in what is now known as Belgium in 59 BC, he found Celtic and Germanic tribes who had been drifting into the region since 2000 BC. The Belgae, as the Romans then called them, were notoriously tough and resistant, but no match for the formidable Roman army, which settled comfortably into control of what it then called Gallia Belgica, a useful cushion between the Rhine and the provinces of Gaul. The Roman settlements, therefore, were largely in the south-east, though we know that they also used the coast for salt production, the south-west for quarrying and the region near Ghent for ironworks.

THE FRANKS

The Roman empire in Gallia Belgica first began to founder in the third century AD, when the Franks, a coalition of Germanic tribes, began attacking its northern borders. Constant flooding, an ongoing problem in the Low Countries, hardly helped the Roman cause and by the fifth century they were gone. From 350 onwards, the Franks began to settle into the more economically viable parts of the region, but Gallia Belgica remained volatile as waves of invaders passed through to continue attacking Roman armies in Gaul.

These invasions are now seen as the first stage in the process that would lead to the deep linguistic division that cuts across present-day Belgium. Northern areas became Germanic-speaking – to the south, Latin languages remained dominant.

The presence of the Franks in the Brussels region is largely unrecorded, although burial sites provide pretty solid evidence that they used the tributaries of the Senne as a trading post. The rest is largely conjecture, although it seems an early church was erected in the hamlet of Brosella, the first mention of today's Brussels. The first more reliably documented reference to Bruocsella ('Dwelling in the Marsh') dates from 695, when it was a stopover on the trade route from Cologne to Bruges and Ghent.

From 768, King Charlemagne built an empire from Denmark to southern Italy, and from the Atlantic to the Danube. When he died in 814, his sons and grandsons fought one another over the fine print of their respective royal inheritances. As a result, in 843 the Treaty of Verdun split the kingdom between his three grandsons: Louis the German received East Francia, which roughly corresponds to modern-day Germany; Charles the Bald was given control of West Francia, which equates more or less to France plus Flanders; and

Lothair received Middle Francia, or the Middle Kingdom. This was a thin strip of land between the River Scheldt and Germany in the north, stretching down to the Mediterranean.

In the ninth and tenth centuries, the old Frankish kingdoms were subjected to regular invasions by marauding Vikings, who took advantage of the power vacuum. Feudal domains, most notably Flanders, rose in importance. Theoretically ruled by the kings of France, the Flemish counts were virtually autonomous. Other fiefdoms were Liège, Hainaut, Namur, Luxembourg and Brabant.

Around 1000, a church dedicated to St Géry was erected on an island formed by the Senne. Île St-Géry, or Grand Ile, would become the heart of the city; it still exists today in the shape of place St-Géry, although the early fortifications have given way to an agricultural hall and trendy bars. Walk along the narrow street called Borgwal and you retrace the line of the original wooden palisades. Borgwal, therefore, can lay claim to being the oldest street in Brussels.

From 1020, Brosella started to be mentioned as a port and, in 1047, its ruler, Lambert II, Count of Louvain (Leuven), built a fort on Coudenberg Hill. The growing strategic and military importance of the Brussels settlement saw the erection of the original city walls over an 80-year period. Referred to as the *première enceinte*, or first enclosure, they constituted an impressive run of towers and gateways that kept the inhabitants in and the attackers out. All that is left today is a pair of isolated towers, including the Tour Noire, sandwiched between blandish modern buildings near place Ste-Catherine.

THE DUKES OF BRABANT

From 1106, the Counts of Louvain began to be known as the Dukes of Brabant, even though they continued to rule Brussels from the city of Louvain. They started to use the surrounding forests as hunting grounds and the city soon started to spread out from the marshy valley of the Senne into the hills and plateaux around it. The new city walls gave people confidence to build grand stone houses, today reflected in street names such as Plattesteen. Brussels became an important commercial centre for wool and cloth production, sold in France, Italy and England. An Anglo-Belgian trading partnership was established. In 1282,

there is the first recorded mention of the Drapers' Guild, something that indicated the importance of the cloth trade, and the future of Brussels itself.

The economic health of Flanders depended on Anglo-French relations, with Flanders often suffering from English reprisals against the French. Despite the fact that the Flemish counts were in the pockets of the French royals, the Flemish often remained hostile to the French. On 11 July 1302, at the Battle of the Golden Spurs, the French knights suffered a shock defeat, the victorious Flemish collecting 700 pairs of spurs from the fleeing French. It was a milestone in Flemish resistance and the victory became ingrained in the Flemish and Belgian consciousness – 11 July is still a public holiday across Flanders.

The balance of the England-France-Flanders triangle became even more fragile with the outbreak of the Hundred Years War in 1337. At the outset, a Flemish landowner called Jacob van Artevelde led a rebellion in Ghent against the pro-French counts of Flanders, who fled to France. Flanders had been officially neutral, but Van Artevelde actively allied it with the English.

During this time, Brussels continued to grow dramatically. While Louvain officially remained the capital of Brabant, the rulers were already receiving dignitaries in Brussels, and the city's jurisdiction widened to take in places such as Schaerbeek and Ixelles. But in 1356 there was a power struggle between the daughters of Duke John III, resulting in a deadly battle won by Count Louis de Malle of Flanders. For the first time in its history, Brussels was briefly ruled by the Flemish.

This brutal shock forced the city's elders to recognise the need for stronger defences and, in 1357, construction began on a new set of walls, the *seconde enceinte*, or second enclosure. It was these walls that gave the centre of Brussels its pentagonal shape and now provide the city with its inner ring road: le Petit Ring. The names of the gates are still with us: Porte de Namur, Porte d'Anderlecht and so on, but only the Porte de Hal remains, a lonely Cinderella castle on a traffic island.

THE DUKES OF BURGUNDY

A process of great cultural change began in the 1360s when Margaret of Malle, daughter of Count Louis, married Philip the Bold, Duke of Burgundy. When Louis died in 1384, Flanders and other provinces came together in a loose union under the authority of the Dukes of Burgundy. The key figure was Philip the Good (Philippe le Bon), grandson of Margaret and Philip the Bold. Having inherited Flanders, Burgundy, Artois and other provinces, he then acquired Brabant, Holland, Hainaut, Namur and Luxembourg through a combination of politics, purchase and military action.

Although the Dukes of Burgundy ruled for less than a century, the cultural changes during this period were significant. In addition to their ducal palace in Dijon, they had important residences in Lille, Bruges and Brussels. The court moved regularly between them, although from 1459 it became based mainly in Brussels. The Dukes initiated their own court culture in the Low Countries and were active patrons of the arts. Parades, tournaments, jousting and pageants were a major part of city and court life, a means of displaying power and wealth. This was also apparent in the great building works that now took place.

'Charles passed the Edict of Blood in 1550, which demanded the death penalty for those convicted of heresy.'

The first university in the Low Countries was founded in Leuven in 1425; work on Brussels' formidable Town Hall, still the dominant feature of the Grand'Place, started in 1402; the tower of Mechelen Cathedral was begun in 1452. In the arts, the best-known evidence of the Dukes' patronage was in 15th-century painting: the Brabant-born painter Jan van Eyck worked in Ghent and Bruges; Rogier van der Weyden worked in Brussels as the city's official painter; and German artist Hans Memling settled in Bruges in 1465.

Although the textile industries were swiftly declining in the 14th and 15th centuries, mainly as a result of cheaper competition from England, other industries were replacing them. Brussels was a centre for tapestry and goldsmiths, and its first printing works opened in 1475. The Coudenberg Palace ranked as one of Europe's finest courts.

With the death of Philip the Good in 1467, the end of the Dukes of Burgundy was in sight. Philip was succeeded by his son Charles the Rash (Charles le Téméraire), who disliked Brussels and moved his court to Mechelen. He was succeeded by his daughter Mary, whose death five years later left the Netherlands in disarray. Mary had married Maximilian von Habsburg of Austria, and their son Philip was only four when she died. The Low Countries were then ruled by Maximilian for ten years, making them part of the Habsburg empire.

THE SPANISH NETHERLANDS

Maximilian's son Philip married Juana, the daughter of King Ferdinand and Queen Isabella of Spain. Their son Charles was born in Ghent in 1500 and, after an extraordinary series of premature deaths and childless marriages among the ruling families of Europe, he had inherited most of Europe by the time he was 20. He became Lord of the Netherlands in 1506 and King of Spain in 1516, and was made Emperor Charles V of Germany when his grandfather Maximilian died in 1519. In this way, a native of Ghent found himself ruling the Netherlands, Austria, the Tyrol, Spain, Mexico, Peru, the Caribbean, Sicily, Naples and the German empire. Charles spent much of his earlier reign in Brussels and spoke both Dutch and French. While the connections with Spain were to prove quite disastrous in the future, Charles understood the Belgians and became a popular ruler. He returned great wealth and prosperity to Brussels, just as its medieval glories were fading.

Brussels had its new statement-piece Town Hall in place with its 90-metre (300-foot) tower and the palaces on the hill beamed prestigiously over the city. The first regular international mail service was set up in Brussels in 1520 by Jean-Baptiste de Tour et Taxis. Antwerp was even more prosperous than Brussels, the crossroads of the trading routes between Spain, Portugal, Russia and the Baltic.

Charles' reign saw the beginning of the Reformation, which would have devastating consequences for Europe. Lutherans from Germany extended their influence westwards

The abdication of Charles at the Coudenberg Palace.

into the Netherlands, while Calvinism spread northwards from Geneva. Although Charles was prepared to negotiate with Luther and his followers, he would also deal harshly with Protestants, whom many considered heretics. The first Lutheran martyrs were burned in Brussels in 1523, and in 1550 Charles passed the Edict of Blood, which demanded the death penalty for those convicted of heresy.

Charles abdicated in 1555, in an emotional ceremony at the Coudenberg Palace, and handed over the reins of the Netherlands to his son Philip, who became Philip II of Spain. Like his father, Philip inherited a collection of provinces in the Low Countries, rather than a nation. There was no common ancestry among the 17 provinces, and the French and Dutch language split was patently evident.

While Charles had remained popular in dealing with heavy taxation and the spread of Protestantism, Philip was never liked. Spanish by birth and sentiment, he spoke neither French nor Dutch. Aided by the Inquisition, he was also sterner in defending Catholicism. A poor citizen in Bruges who happened to trample on a consecrated wafer had his hand and foot wrenched off by red-hot irons and his tongue ripped out, before being slowly roasted over an open fire. The Grand'Place became a grisly home to executioners.

THE DUTCH REVOLT

Philip appointed his half-sister Margaret of Parma as regent, but power lay with two hated pro-Spanish councillors, Cardinal Granvelle and Count Berlaymont. Opposing Philip were Prince William of Orange, Count Egmont and Count Hoorn. In 1565, they helped form the Compromise of Nobles. Berlaymont referred to them disparagingly as 'ces gueux', beggars, and 'Vivent les gueux!' became their rallying cry. They objected to Philip's refusal to tolerate Protestantism, his attempt to centralise power, the heavy taxes imposed on the provinces, and the presence of Spanish troops in the Netherlands.

The spread of Protestantism burgeoned among the poor in the towns of Flanders, Brabant, Holland and Zeeland. In the 1560s, Calvinist preachers attracted huge crowds, railing against the wealth of the Catholic Church. In the Iconoclastic Riots of 1566,

IN CONTEXT

Calvinist mobs destroyed Catholic churches across the Netherlands. In Antwerp, crowds hacked up the Madonna, pulled down the statue of Christ at the altar, burned manuscripts and rubbed the sacred oil on their shoes.

Philip appointed the Duke of Alva as the new governor in the 17 provinces, and he arrived with an army of 10,000. One of his very first acts was to set up the 'Council of Blood'. On 4 January 1568 alone, he had 84 people executed on the scaffold. In March, there were 1,500 arrests, 800 of them in one day and, in June, Counts Egmont and Hoorn were beheaded on Grand'Place. Their deaths marked the start of a full-scale revolt in the Netherlands that would last 80 years.

In 1579, the ten southern provinces formed the Union of Arras, accepting the authority of Philip and of Catholicism. The north's response was the 1581 Union of Utrecht, which was essentially a declaration that the seven northern provinces no longer recognised Philip's authority. By the end of the century, the northern provinces had formed the Republic of the United Netherlands, also known as the United Provinces, while the southern provinces were known as the Spanish Netherlands, a split that became irreversible.

In 1598, Philip handed over his remaining territories in the Netherlands to his son-in-law, Archduke Albrecht of Austria. Philip hoped this might ease reconciliation between north and south. However, when Albrecht died without an heir in 1621, the provinces reverted to Spanish rule. Philip's daughter Isabella remained governor until her death in 1633. Isabella and Albrecht maintained a lavish court, with painter Peter Paul Rubens as its focal point.

They negotiated an uneasy truce with the Dutch in 1609, but it lasted just 12 years, the subsequent war continuing until 1648. During its last phase, the religious gap widened between the two sides, with the United Provinces becoming more firmly Calvinist and the Spanish Netherlands in the grip of the Catholic Counter-Reformation. The war ended with the Treaty of Munster, in which Spain recognised the independence of the north's United Provinces, with the agreed borders corresponding to those between Belgium and the Netherlands today.

The late 17th century brought a succession of gruelling wars: the War of Devolution, the Dutch War and the War of the Grand Alliance. In all, the Spanish Netherlands was either

Albrecht and Isabella.

attacked or occupied. The ensuing peace treaties led to the territory of the Spanish Netherlands being slowly whittled away, with France finally taking hold of both Artois and Ypres. It was at this time, in 1695, that Louis XIV, unable to enter Brussels to claim the Spanish Netherlands, ordered the pointless and barbaric bombardment of the city, destroying most of its medieval fabric.

THE AUSTRIAN NETHERLANDS

When Philip IV of Spain died in 1665, the Spanish throne passed directly to his sickly four-year-old son Charles. Despite two marriages, Charles II remained childless and for most of the 1690s he seemed to be teetering on the verge of death. Eager to fill a vacuum, the French, English, Dutch and Austrians began plotting over his successor. By the time Charles II died in 1700, there were two candidates: Archduke Charles of Austria and Philip of Anjou, grandson of Louis XIV of France. Charles favoured the Frenchman and in 1701 he entered Madrid as King of Spain. The French occupied Dutch-held barrier fortresses in the Spanish Netherlands, and the English and the Dutch declared war on France. The War of Spanish Succession lasted from 1701 to 1713, during which time the Spanish Netherlands was governed by the French and the English. Peace was made at the 1713 Treaty of Utrecht and the 1714 Treaty of Rastatt. Philip of Anjou kept the Spanish throne, but the Austrians came away with the Spanish Netherlands, henceforth known as the Austrian Netherlands.

Practically safe from French armies, the Austrian Netherlands lived in relative peace until Emperor Charles VI of Austria wanted his daughter Maria Theresa to inherit his empire. France invaded once more until the Treaty of Aix-La-Chapelle restored Austrian rule in 1748 and gave the throne to Maria Theresa's husband, Francis I. The real power, however, lay solely with Maria Theresa. Her rule, lasting until 1780, brought considerable economic renewal. While her governor, Charles of Lorraine, built roads and waterways, there were improvements in agricultural technology. The late 18th century was the only time in Belgium's history when it was self-sufficient in grain. There were also new glass, coal and cotton industries, independent of the powerful guilds.

Cultural life developed, censorship relaxed, French books circulated freely and bookshops were opened in the outlying towns. There was a growing printing industry. Rural culture still followed traditional values, however, with companies travelling the countryside performing medieval mystery plays.

In 1731, the Coudenberg Palace burnt down after a vat of boiling sugar started a fire in the royal kitchens. In 1740, work began on a new palace, the Palais du Roi, today the town residence of the Belgian royal family. The neoclassical place Royale and the Palais de la Nation, the seat of the Belgian parliament, were built in the 1770s and 1780s. In 1782, work started on the official residence of the Belgian royal family at Laeken.

In 1780, Maria Theresa's son, Joseph II, assumed the throne. He immediately attempted to modernise the country, closing monasteries and seminaries, taxing the Church and reforming both the judicial system and governmental administration. In 1781, he passed the Edict of Toleration, recognising religious freedoms.

More conservative Belgians saw their traditional privileges and vested interests threatened by Joseph II's wayward spate of reforms. The result was the Brabançon Revolution of 1789-90, which involved all the provinces except Luxembourg. The rebels, led by a Brussels lawyer, wrote a new constitution inspired by the US Articles of Confederation, and formed the Confederation of the United Belgian States. But the revolution collapsed into chaos as a result of the widening split between conservative and progressive rebels. Around 100,000 peasants, led by priests, marched en masse through the centre of Brussels to register their protest against the progressive. Many were subsequently forced to flee to France. Austrian authority was finally restored in 1791.

FRENCH REVOLUTIONARY RULE

In 1792, the French declared war on Austria and Prussia, occupying the Austrian Netherlands and independent Liège. The French armies were initially greeted as liberators, but the welcome quickly faded, and when the French temporarily withdrew from Brussels in 1793, citizens ransacked the houses of pro-French families. When France reoccupied the Austrian Netherlands

IN CONTEXT

Peasant uprising, Brabant.

in 1794, tens of thousands of Belgians emigrated. The French exacted strict war levies and military requisitions and set up an *agence de commerce* to take anything from cattle to art back to France. Among their booty was Jan van Eyck's religious painting *The Adoration of the Mystic Lamb*, now hanging in Ghent's cathedral. They also confiscated the palace at Laeken. In 1795, the French absorbed the former Austrian Netherlands and created nine new *départements*. Brussels became a departmental capital answering to Paris. Liège and the Netherlands were united for the first time, and the French referred to the region as Belgique.

From 1796, French law applied to Belgium. The Belgians accepted the occupation and annexation passively but unenthusiastically; French leaders complained of their apathy. Opposition came in 1798, with conscription. There were riots across Flanders and 10,000 peasants formed an army in Brabant. The uprising was soon crushed, brutally and bloodily, with hundreds executed. The last five years of the century saw industry in decline, the depopulation of towns, new taxes, economic hardship, and organised gangs of robbers roaming the highways.

Slowly, the French encouraged the growth of industries such as coal and cotton, which benefited from the new markets in France. The new industries were capitalist, funded by entrepreneurial nobles and traders who had bought former monastery lands cheaply. One of the most notable beneficiaries of the French occupation was Antwerp, where Napoléon constructed a new harbour and port, which he described as 'a pistol aimed at the heart of England'.

He also made his mark on Brussels, replacing its old walls with open boulevards. He bought the palace at Laeken as his official residence, but only used it occasionally before trading it for the Elysée Palace in Paris in a legal settlement with the Empress Joséphine. French rule came to a sharp end in 1814, when Napoléon was forced to abdicate as Emperor of France, following his defeat at the Battle of Leipzig. His opponents (Britain, Prussia, Russia, Austria) recaptured Brussels in February 1814 and appointed a council of conservatives to govern the city and work towards a return to Austrian rule. In 1814, the Congress of Vienna began its work to break up and redistribute Napoléon's empire.

WATERLOO

On his return from exile, Napoléon rounded up an army. The Congress of Vienna quickly condemned the landing and Europe prepared for war. The armies of the British, Spanish, Prussians, Austrians and Dutch numbered over one million men between them. Napoléon had gathered about 375,000 soldiers. The Duke of Wellington, commander-in-chief of the British, Hanoverians and Belgians, established his headquarters in Brussels. One of the legends is that Wellington was attending a ball hosted by the Duke and Duchess of Richmond in the rue de la Blanchisserie when he received news of Napoléon's approach.

His forces ill-trained and lines of command unclear, Wellington was dependent on the 120,000 Prussian troops under Field Marshal von Blücher. Napoléon's strategy was simple: to stop the armies of Wellington and von Blücher from joining up.

On 15 June 1815, Napoléon crossed the border, took Charleroi and moved towards Brussels. Wellington's army took up positions at the pre-planned spot of Mont St-Jean, 15 kilometres (nine miles) south of Brussels. The next day, Napoléon defeated von Blücher's forces at Ligny. Believing they were on the run, Napoléon crucially failed to follow his victory through. Napoléon continued towards Brussels. At Quatre-Bras, on the Brussels–Charleroi road, Napoléon formally challenged Wellington. Positions were taken closer to the village of Braine l'Alleud.

The night of 17 June teemed with rain. The waterlogged ground soon put paid to Napoléon's plan for an early attack the next day. Wellington's defenders held off at the fortified farm of Hougoumont, where 3,000 French corpses were piled up by late afternoon. Meanwhile, von Blücher's troops were closing in. The arrival of the Prussians swung the battle in Wellington's favour. Napoléon threw every resource into a last desperate attempt to snatch victory. His beloved Imperial Guard entered the fray but, bogged down in the heavy mud churned up by their own cavalry, they made easy targets.

With the arrival of von Blücher's entire army, Wellington urged his soldiers into a huge counter attack. Gradually, French confidence evaporated and their troops fled. The Battle of Waterloo was over.

At 9.30pm, Wellington and von Blücher embraced at the Belle Alliance inn just south of Waterloo. The victory dispatch was sent from the village and, following the convention of the time, Waterloo was the name given to the battle.

Napoleon escaped to Paris, where he abdicated and surrendered to the British. He was banished to the island of St Helena, where he died in 1821.

Brussels and nearby Waterloo soon became a destination for curious British visitors. Battle re-enactments later took place, culminating in the Bicentenary celebrations in June 2015. *See p150* **Battle Stations.**

UNITY AND REVOLUTION

The Congress of Vienna redrew the map of Europe after Napoléon. One main dilemma was the Netherlands. The north had existed as an independent state since 1648, but the former Spanish and Austrian Netherlands had no tradition of independence and Congress was reluctant to create one. Austria had no desire to recover these provinces, and there was no question of their going to France.

The Congress of Vienna decided to unite the Netherlands with the Austrian Netherlands and form the United Kingdom of the Netherlands, thereby creating a strong buffer between France and Prussia. It was a solution that only suited certain Belgian entrepreneurs, who realised that union with the Dutch might compensate for the loss of markets in France.

The United Kingdom of the Netherlands was created as a constitutional monarchy ruled by William of Orange. As well as its 17 provinces, the new kingdom had twin capitals, the Hague and Brussels. The southerners found many reasons to resent the new state. The wealthy south was already industrialised. Although Brussels was joint capital, the new country was governed by a Dutch king, Dutch ministers and Dutch civil servants. While being more numerous and prosperous, Belgians had little political power.

Many took refuge in memories of the earlier grandeur of Antwerp and Brussels, regarding the Dutch as upstarts. There was also fury at attempts to introduce Dutch as the national language. Belgium's Catholics were opposed to the new government as it had declared religious freedom and removed Catholic bias in the education system. Belgian liberals also opposed the new state, seeking freedom of the press and less autocracy. In 1828, the Catholics and liberals formed an unlikely alliance, demanding that the Belgians, not the Dutch, become the dominant force in the Netherlands. The government duly repealed the language decrees in the south and guaranteed freedom of education, but it would neither accept Belgian supremacy nor grant freedom of the press.

IN CONTEXT

THE GILDED GUILDS

What makes Grand'Place grand.

Grand'Place is the spiritual heart of Brussels, the main set-piece around which the tangle of medieval streets jostle for space. It began as a marketplace around the church of St Nicholas and was first paved over in the 12th century, a welcome change to the mud and marsh that preceded it. As the area became a focus, so it attracted traders who set up in streets such as rue des Harengs ('Herrings') and rue Chair et Pain ('Flesh and Bread').

As the economy grew, skilled craftspeople moved in and organised themselves economically and politically into the guilds, a powerful mix of union, local magistrate and charity. The guilds laid down the rules of the professions, concerning themselves with product quality, working hours and conditions, apprenticeships and masterships. The guilds became a powerful force across Europe and shaped cities such as Amsterdam, Ghent and London, whose livery companies exist today.

The power of the guilds should never be underestimated. Their wealthiest families were able to exert considerable influence on the authorities to further their own economic interests. This same lobbying function allowed them to provide a counterbalance to aristocratic taxes, levies and trade restrictions. The powerful textile guilds were the most troublesome to the authorities, followed by the smiths, brewers, butchers and then the carpenters. As the textile industry declined and new non-guild industries

developed, the guilds lost much of their influence. Towards the end of the 16th century their great era was on the wane.

Despite this loss of power, what you see today on Grand'Place is a result of the guilds' irrepressible wealth, which was still in place following the French bombardment of Brussels in 1695. Over three days and three nights, the French reduced medieval Brussels to rubble. Only the tower of the Hôtel de Ville survived as the aggressors used it as a target marker. It took the guilds five years to rebuild their lost houses in the Baroque style that to this day makes Grand'Place one of Europe's finest squares. As well as numbers, the houses were given names, something that provided them with the prestige they demanded. Mayor Charles Buls decided that the square should be returned to its former glory and, in 1883, the city agreed to be responsible for the upkeep of the façades.

In recent years, the buildings have been scrubbed to within an inch of their lives and gilded with gold leaf, gleaming above the square in an almost semi-religious way. Today, only one guild still occupies the same house that it built for itself – the magnificent Brewers' House at no.10 (officially L'Arbre d'Or, or the Golden Tree). The rest are occupied by bars, shops and restaurants, and filled with tourists – although nothing can take away from their overall splendour. Just look up, it's all there to see.

The winter of 1829-30 was severe. While farmers suffered, overproduction in the industries of the south had caused wage cuts, bankruptcies and unemployment. Workers in both sectors staged regular demonstrations in Brussels. On 25 August 1830, the banned revolutionary opera *La Muette de Portici* by Daniel Auber, was performed at the Théâtre de la Monnaie. During the aria 'L'Amour Sacré de la Patrie' ('Sacred Love of the Fatherland'), liberals and students in the theatre started rioting, then joined the workers protesting in the square outside.

This signalled the start of the Belgian Revolution. The Dutch government negotiated with its leaders and there seemed to be a possibility of administrative separation. But William I prevaricated and the impatient and disillusioned rebels decided to go for secession. At the end of September, William sent 10,000 troops into Brussels, insufficient to crush the revolution but enough to inflame the southern provinces into joining the uprising. Belgian soldiers deserted their regiments, and William's troops were soon driven out of Brussels.

A new government was rapidly assembled. On 4 October 1830, the rebels declared an independent state and provisional government; on 3 November, they held elections for a National Congress. It met on 10 November and comprised 200 people, mostly intellectuals, lawyers and journalists. There were very few representatives from industry or finance. On 22 November, the new Congress set out a constitution. Belgium would be a parliamentary monarchy and unitary state of nine provinces, with freedom of religion, education, assembly, press and language, and a separate church and state. On 3 March 1831, the Congress passed an electoral law defining the electorate, which consisted of about 46,000 men of the bourgeoisie. This meant that one out of every 95 inhabitants had the vote, a relatively high proportion – in France, it was one in 160.

The rest of the world soon recognised the new nation, and in January 1831 the Great Powers met in London to discuss the issue. Britain advocated creating a Belgian state, France and Germany agreed, and Belgium was recognised as an independent and neutral entity. Deciding on a new king was less easy, but eventually Léopold of Saxe-Coburg-Gotha

was selected. He was related to the major European royal households, most famously as uncle to both Victoria and Albert. He took an oath to the constitution on 21 July, now Belgium's National Day. Shortly afterwards, the Dutch invaded Belgium, and this helped prolong a sense of unity among the Catholics and liberals. The Dutch beat the Belgian rebels at Leuven and Hasselt, but retreated on hearing reports of an approaching French army of 50,000. They did not recognise the new country until 1839.

INDEPENDENT BELGIUM

It was more or less inevitable that the coalition between liberals and Catholics in the new state of Belgium would be neither harmonious nor long-lived. The political history of Belgium in the 19th century was of a tug of war between the two, the main bones of contention being the education system and the language split. Belgium's history as a nation state began with the Catholics and the French speakers in the ascendant. The new constitution allowed people to use whichever language they desired, but French was the language spoken in the courts, the education system (apart from some primary schools) and the administration. In the country as a whole, Flemish was more widely spoken, with 2.4 million Flemish speakers to 1.8 million French ones. The majority of Belgians were being governed in an alien language.

Intellectuals in both Antwerp and Ghent soon began to resent the predominance of French. In 1840, they organised a petition demanding the use of Flemish in the administration and law courts of Flemish-speaking provinces. To begin with, the Catholics were dominant at most levels. Membership of monasteries and convents more than doubled during the 1830s and 1840s, and in 1834 a new Catholic university was founded at Mechelen, moving to Leuven in 1835. The Catholic Church also controlled most secondary education. In 1846, the liberals held a congress in Brussels to clarify the points of their political programme and plan an election strategy. The Catholics did not start to organise themselves in anything like the same way until the 1860s. Charles Rogier first formed a liberal government in 1848 and the liberals governed, with a few gaps, until 1884.

IN CONTEXT

IN CONTEXT

Although Belgium lost the Dutch East Indies markets when it split from the Netherlands, there was industrial expansion from the 1830s, at a time when much of Europe had plummeting industrial prices. With its programme of railway construction and industrial investment, Belgium was the first country in mainland Europe to undergo the Industrial Revolution. In Brussels the canal system was extended with the new Canal de Charleroi and, with it, a whole new industrial complex was built on the western side of the city in Anderlecht, Forest and Molenbeek. It became known as Little Manchester. The king wished to maintain his capital as a prestigious centre of commerce, banking and luxury goods rather than a hub of manufacturing. There were also political reasons: with economic problems all across the country, an industrialised urban workforce was seen as dangerous. The Belgian Workers' Party was founded in 1885 and the Socialists would soon exert political influence.

Universal male suffrage was introduced in 1893 and in 1894 the Socialists gained their first parliamentary seats – but with the bulk of their support in Flanders, the Catholics retook power until 1917. There had already been concessions to Flemish speakers and the Catholics sped up the process. Language remained a big problem. Legislation had introduced bilingualism in Flanders and strengthened the Flemish position in law and education, but the Flemings were still governed and tried in French. In 1898, Flemish was given official equality with French, though the electorate (only taxpayers could vote) was almost entirely French-speaking.

EXPANSION AND EXPLORATION

Despite constant dispute over particular issues, the Belgians did demonstrate a sense of unity in some areas of public life. Independence led to a building spree in Brussels. Among the earliest additions were the Galeries St-Hubert in the 1840s. These were then followed by a spate of official buildings and commemorative projects as Belgium began celebrating its own existence, culminating in the construction of the Parc du Cinquantenaire for the National Exhibition in 1880 celebrating the 50th anniversary of independence. The Palais de Justice was completed in 1883 on Galgenberg Hill, the

site of the gallows in past times. The first railway station in Brussels opened in 1835, where Yser métro station now stands, with a line to Mechelen.

The major planning feat of the 19th century was the covering over of the Senne. The river had become a repository for industrial and agricultural waste, including effluent from breweries and textile industries that had deliberately set up shop on its banks. Periodic cholera outbreaks led to an epidemic in 1866, when 3,500 people died. Rather than develop civil engineering schemes to clean up the river, the authorities chose a more radical approach.

The idea was not just for sanitary reasons. Central Brussels was short of grand property in the 19th century, and its tangle of streets resembled Bruges more than a major European capital. The *voûtement* – the covering of the river – gave the opportunity for grand boulevards, big hotels and Parisian-style apartment blocks for the wealthy. Property developers jumped for joy at the idea. Above the *voûtement* appeared the new boulevards Anspach, Lemonnier and Adolphe Max, achieving the required design but never the social cachet. The city elders hadn't thought that wealthy residents would much rather buy grand houses in Ixelles and St-Gilles than live in close quarters to others.

The grand plans of Léopold II, who succeeded his father in 1865, weren't limited to Belgium. As crown prince, he had been looking around for potential new territories, considering British-run Borneo, the Philippines, South Africa and Mozambique. Finally, he decided to grab a piece of the 'magnificent African cake'. Much of Central Africa was still unexplored and in 1876 Léopold set up the Association Internationale Africaine with the help of explorer Henry Stanley. Although other European governments and the United States expressed qualms about Léopold's activities in Africa, he dismissed them sufficiently for the Berlin Declaration of 1885 to recognise the independent state of the Congo, with Léopold as its head of state. He referred to himself as its proprietor and ruled his new territory with absolute power and pure terror.

Léopold's colonial adventures were to cast a dark shadow on Belgium's reputation. From 1895, when he started exporting wild rubber, it generated huge revenue, much of which was passed back to Belgium and used for massive public works, such as the Musée Royal de l'Afrique Centrale at Tervuren. Local entrepreneurs, industrialists and engineers who grew rich on the Congo Free State built great houses in the extravagant art nouveau style, with little regard for the expense.

By the early 20th century, Léopold's policy of extracting maximum profit from the Congo, regardless of ecological and human cost, was exposing Belgium to international criticism, particularly from Britain. In 1908, the Belgian government forced Léopold to hand the country over to the nation, and it remained a Belgian colony until independence in 1960.

WORLD WAR I & AFTERMATH

On its creation in 1830, Belgium declared itself to be perpetually neutral. But in August 1914, Kaiser Wilhelm of Germany demanded free passage through Belgium in order to invade France. Brave Belgium rejected his ultimatum. German troops entered the country – and stayed there for four years. The consequences were dire – see p252 **The Rape of Belgium**.

The Germans had been pro-Flemish, and a small group of Flemish politicians had been keen collaborators. In 1916, the Germans had declared the University of Ghent Flemish-speaking. It reverted to French and did not adopt Flemish again until 1930. Having just recovered what they had lost after World War I, the Flemings made a series of language gains during the 1930s. In 1932, French and Flemish ceased to have equality in Flanders, where the official language became Flemish.

The period following World War I had been marked by brief political unity, as Catholics, liberals and Socialists worked together to rebuild the country. This unity soon dissipated, however, particularly after the introduction of proportional representation. The first universal male suffrage elections without multiple votes for the bourgeoisie were held in 1919 (women had to wait until 1949), and resulted in a series of coalition governments: between 1918 and 1940, Belgium had 18 different administrations. After a slight respite, the country slumped into depression in the 1930s, with unemployment, social unrest and a move to the right. In the 1936 elections, Flemish nationalist and right-wing parties in Wallonia and Brussels made big gains, blaming the economic depression on the weak parliament, lack of strong leadership and the unions. Also, the Soldier King, Albert I, had died under suspicious circumstances in a rock-climbing accident in 1934, and his son, Léopold III, lacked his charisma.

German soldiers billeted in Brussels, World War I.

IN CONTEXT

THE RAPE OF BELGIUM

A country remembers.

The killing fields of Flanders, the battles of Ypres, Somme and Verdun, the white lines of cemeteries – the story of World War I has been described many times in the century since its outbreak in Belgium. But the catastrophic effect on Belgium itself is an entirely different story. Here, the centenary of World War I has brought it all home.

On 2 August 1914, Kaiser Wilhelm of Germany demanded that neutral Belgium give his troops free passage on their way to invade France. Belgium had half a day to respond to the ultimatum, which it rejected. On 4 August, German troops entered the country and the government took refuge in Antwerp. Seven hours later, Britain declared war on Germany. By midnight, five different empires were involved in the war.

The invasion changed the political and social landscape of this then-neutral country forever. The Germans rolled into the country in a spirit of spite as the tiny Belgian army put a spoke in the works of the meticulous Schlieffen Plan to snatch Paris by the Belgian back door. Although the Kaiser's forces duly entered Brussels on 20 August, Belgium's delaying tactic allowed Britain and France to get their act together for the Battle of the Marne that September.

The knock-on effect of this German exasperation was to impose brutal marshal law and retaliation on Belgian civilians, something that has come to be known as the 'Rape of Belgium'. The term – and its connotations – were undoubtedly inflamed by British and US propaganda and stories of sexual depravity and Jack the Ripper-like killings. But the awful reality was that atrocities did take place as occupying forces smashed through Belgian communities with terrifying force.

At the village of Hervé, the Germans left only 19 of the 500 houses standing, the shattered village littered with corpses. Other massacres occurred elsewhere: 110 civilians shot at Andenne, 384 at Tamines. Tiny, sleepy Dinant was smashed by artillery

and 674 civilians were executed. Two days later, Leuven, 26 kilometres (16 miles) east of Brussels, took some dreadful punishment. Over five days in August 2014, Leuven was systematically destroyed, its university burned to the ground and its library of ancient manuscripts lost, amounting to some 300,000 volumes. The population was ordered to evacuate and 248 civilians lost their lives.

Compared to the east, Brussels got off relatively lightly in terms of bombardment and destruction. Instead the Germans moved in with ease and determination, a constant grey stream pouring relentlessly into the capital. Then the iron glove fell and civilian suffering began. German currency and ID cards were introduced, and clocks were changed to an hour ahead. Absolutely anything deemed useful to the war effort was requisitioned, including bicycles and raw materials, even woollens. There were severe food shortages and civilians struggled to feed themselves. But struggle they did, and contemporary documentation shows an incredible resilience to the invaders, not just in day-to-day survival but in the subversive satire that the Belgians relish to this day.

English nurse Edith Cavell, who had stayed on in Brussels and was later executed by the invaders, said that her conversations with the Germans revealed they were surprised to find themselves in Brussels, having believed they were marching on Paris. The situation in the capital was largely saved by the intervention of the Americans, who organised the Commission for Relief in Belgium and set up charitable aid. The US ambassador, Brand Whitlock, became something of a Belgian national hero as a direct result.

By the end of September, Antwerp was under siege; it fell on 10 October, despite the arrival of British troops, including the poet Rupert Brooke, in a fleet of London buses. Over half a million refugees left Antwerp, among them thousands who had fled there from across Belgium. Some 1.5 million

Memorial to Edith Cavell and Marie Depage.

had already left the country, although many would later return. The government went to Le Havre, while King Albert I, successor to his uncle Léopold II, took up position with the small Belgian army in the north-west of the country. Widely known as 'le Chevalier' (the Soldier King), he won acclaim from his people by fighting with his troops in the trenches alongside the French and British.

The four-year-long German occupation had terrible consequences. A total of 44,000 war dead might be dwarfed by the losses of Russia and France, but 700,000 Belgians were deported to Germany to work on farms and in factories, including the *burgomaster* (mayor of Brussels) Adolphe Max. The economy was devastated. Belgium had once depended on other countries to power its raw materials and for its export markets – it lost both. Much of its rail system was destroyed in an attempt to prevent the German invasion, agricultural production slumped and there was widespread poverty and hunger. It is estimated that the country's losses represented about a

fifth of the national assets in 1914, and by no means were all of them recovered in war reparations. The prevailing consideration of subsequent post-war governments was how to rebuild the country.

Belgium saw a major response to the centenary of the outbreak of World War I in 2014, particularly in remembrance of those first summer months when civilians were on the front line. Each major city created its own events and commemorations, many following the timeline through to the centenary of the Armistice in November 1918.

The City of Brussels Archive has created a fascinating website, Brussels at War 14-18 (www.14-18.bruxelles.be), showing everyday life in Brussels at the time of the invasion. Other events in the coming years will be posted here. Antwerp has created a similar site with Antwerpen 14-18 (www.antwerpen 14-18.be), while Liège has Liège Expo 1418 (www.liegeexpo14-18.be). Finally, 2014-18 The Great War Centenary (www.flanders fields.be) covers events in West Flanders.

WORLD WAR II

After allying with France, Belgium reasserted its neutrality following the German invasion of Poland in 1939. It did little good. Hitler attacked on 10 May 1940. Showing opposite traits to his father, Léopold III surrendered after just 18 days. Much of the population was in support of Léopold's action – but not their government. Believing that Belgium should commit itself to the Allies, it became a government-in-exile in Le Havre and then London. Despite having initially espoused a policy of normalisation, the Germans gradually became more authoritarian during the course of the war, creating greater resistance. Belgium suffered the same problems as it had in World War I: deportations, forced labour, poverty and food shortages. In Brussels, there was a Gestapo HQ in avenue Louise and the Résidence Palace in rue de la Loi was the Nazi administrative centre for Belgium. From 1 June 1942, Belgian Jews were required to wear the yellow Star of David.

IN CONTEXT

'After the elections of 2010, Belgium was left without an elected government for a world record 589 days.'

The Germans created a deportation centre in Mechelen and, between 1942 and 1944, sent 25,257 people to Auschwitz. Two-thirds of those died on arrival. Against all the odds, a network of Belgian resistance and opposition managed to save thousands from a similar fate. Concentrating on the children, Belgians from all backgrounds risked their own lives by taking Jewish children into their families and homes, creating new identities for them. In that respect, Belgium saved more Jews per capita than any other occupied country.

Belgium was finally liberated in September 1944, and one of the first tasks was to tackle the thorny issue of collaboration. The war tribunals considered 405,000 cases, reaching 58,000 guilty verdicts, of which 33,000 were within Flanders. Then there was the behaviour of Léopold III. In a non-binding referendum, only 57 per cent voted in favour of his return (72 per cent of those in Flanders and 42 per cent in Wallonia), and when he did come back there were serious disturbances. In 1951, Léopold stepped aside in favour of his son, Baudouin.

Even today, the issue of collaboration is an extremely sensitive one: up to 15,000 Belgians convicted of collaboration receive reduced pension and property rights as a direct result. In February 1996, a military court in Brussels reconsidered the case of one Irma Laplasse, a Flemish farmer's wife who had betrayed resistance fighters to the Nazis in 1944; she had been executed by a firing squad for her crime in 1948. The court upheld her conviction, but ruled that the death sentence should have been commuted to life in prison. The judgement was met by protests from both sides. Concentration camp survivors and former members of the resistance and the Belgian secret army were outraged at any moves to rehabilitate Nazi collaborators; for its own part, the far-right Flemish Vlaams Blok party controversially campaigned for an amnesty for all those accused of collaborating, insisting that the tribunals were an attempt to victimise and repress the Flemish people as a whole.

POST-WAR BELGIUM

World War II had made it clear that Belgium's traditional neutrality was untenable, and even before the war was over the government-in-exile set about rejecting the policy in favour of international alliances. It signed the Benelux Customs Union with Luxembourg and the Netherlands, thus abolishing customs tariffs and setting a common external tariff. Belgium became an enthusiastic participant in post-war international relations; as an export-driven economy, it needed to belong to the growing global relations superstructure. Belgium was one of the first signatories of the UN Charter in June 1945, joining the Organisation for European Economic Co-operation in 1948. It also became a member of the Council of Europe and the European Coal and Steel Community, as well as the headquarters of the European Economic Community (EEC) when it was set up in 1957.

Brussels' new integrated role in a European context saw major upheavals in the capital. First proposed in 1837, a rail link through the city – directly connecting the main stations – was not adopted until 1901, and not begun in earnest until 1911. The more pressing need for post-war reconstruction in 1919, and then again in 1945, stalled the project. In the meantime, a third station, Gare Centrale, was created, according to plans left by Victor Horta, one of the key architects of the city's art nouveau and art deco style. The line now had to run through three stations, and caused city planners to tear down thousands of buildings.

Building the entire 3.5-kilometre (two-mile) rail link involved removing one million cubic metres of earth and inserting 85 kilometres (53 miles) of reinforced concrete pillars. Some 1,200 homes were destroyed in the process. Brussels had lost its soul and gained a global reputation as an architectural nightmare. When a young King Baudouin opened the line in 1952, it set a dangerous precedent for how the city would shape up during the second half of the 20th century.

Brussels' hosting of the World's Fair of 1958 allowed for further rapid modernisation, the ring boulevards becoming a network of highways and tunnels. Brussels became the HQ of NATO in 1967, the same year that the EEC main offices of the Berlaymont building were opened. Its enormous structure typified the grandiose, impersonal quarter of steel and glass growing up around it, as the EEC took on yet more members.

The language barrier separating French-speaking Wallonia from Flemish-speaking Flanders was formally created in 1962, leaving Brussels with an officially bilingual status. In 1965, the political parties also split into Flemish and Walloon wings, exacerbated by economic developments. Successive Belgian governments then made a series of reforms, granting greater autonomy to each community and changing Belgium from a centralised to a federal state; the 1993 fourth state reform also split Brabant into Flemish Brabant and Walloon Brabant. In 2001, Guy Verhofstadt's government introduced a fifth state reform and transferred yet more powers to the communities and the regions, including agriculture, fisheries, foreign trade and the responsibility for running local elections – the first of which took place in 2006.

After the elections of 2010, Belgium earned notoriety for beating the world record for the time taken to form a coalition government. The complex negotiations, headlined mainly by separatist, partisan politics meant that Belgium was without an elected government for 589 days. This was seen as something that could only drive a bigger, deeper nail into national unity.

THE ROYALS

During the EEC era, King Baudouin was a highly respected monarch. A quiet, unassuming man, he is credited with preventing Belgium from splitting into two. He died childless in 1993, after which the crown passed to his brother, who became King Albert II.

Royal marriage united the country in 1999 when the then heir, Prince Philippe, married Mathilde, an ordinary Belgian citizen. This was followed in 2003 with the marriage of his younger brother, Prince Laurent, to Belgo-British Claire Combs. Laurent has not been without controversy. He made the headlines in 2007 for being the first senior royal to testify in open court concerning alleged embezzlement of funds from the Belgian Navy.

On 3 July 2013, the 79-year-old King Albert announced to the nation that he would abdicate and on 21 July – Belgian National Day – Prince Philippe was sworn in as King of the Belgians with his wife Queen Mathilde.

COUNTRY AMONG NATIONS

Belgium's history has always been allied to the history of other European countries and the new millennium continued the pattern. With the swift expansion of the European Union, Brussels saw a large influx of diplomats, officials and staff from new member countries, the latest being Croatia in 2013. In 2003, Belgium joined its European neighbours in opposing the Iraq War, supporting diplomacy through the UN – although, as part of its NATO commitment, it supported forces in Afghanistan with 560 personnel and six F-16 fighter planes. Similarly, in 2014, it joined the international coalition against Isis with Jordan-based personnel and fighter planes operating in Iraq. For Belgium, though, the most critical battle remains on home ground as successive, fragile coalition governments attempt to tackle the country's deep-rooted political and linguistic divisions.

IN CONTEXT

Art Nouveau

*Built in Brussels, exported
to the world.*

TEXT: DEREK BLYTH & GARY HILLS

Brussels' art nouveau architectural movement
was born in the south-eastern suburbs in 1893.
Two houses built almost simultaneously just a few
blocks apart provided the inspiration for a style that
then spread to Paris, Barcelona and Glasgow. For
two decades, until the outbreak of World War I, the
Belgian capital was the scene of an extraordinary
revolution in architecture.

Architects embraced the bold new style, which
used materials such as iron, stone and mosaic tiles
in combination with motifs adopted from the natural
world. Increasingly daring buildings were designed
by the likes of Henry van de Velde, Ernest Blérot,
Gustave Strauven and Octave van Rysselberghe.
Numerous masterpieces were demolished in the
1960s, but the capital of art nouveau still has an
abundance of architectural gems.

At the forefront of the movement was Victor
Horta, who lived and worked in St-Gilles. Many of
the art nouveau houses here still stand, including
his own, which is now a museum on rue Américaine.

Maison de St-Cyr.

ARTS AND CRAFTS

Most critics agree that art nouveau originated in England in the 1880s with the Arts and Crafts movement. This, in turn, derived from the Pre-Raphaelite Brotherhood, whose overall message was a rejection of industrial manufacture and a mechanistic approach to painting. Its home was Birmingham and its foremost thinker was William Morris, whose textiles, tapestries and wallpapers, created with natural dyes and focusing on the plants, trees and flowers found in nature, had resonance in Europe. Also influential were the sensual paintings of Dante Gabriel Rossetti and the prints of Tokyo-born Hokusai.

Belgian painter and designer Fernand Khnopff also fell under their spell, later becoming friends with Rossetti and his contemporaries. He co-founded the Brussels-based artists' group Les XX, which held exhibitions each year and later evolved into the less exclusive Libre Esthétique. Founded in 1893, Libre Esthétique became a platform for the kind of ideas and concepts being explored by the likes of Victor Horta. While studying at the Royal Academy of Fine Arts in rue du Midi (where he would later become director), Horta struck up a friendship with Paul Hankar – both were interested in the techniques of using forged iron in building.

'Such was the extent of Horta's painstaking creativity, he never grew rich from his labours.'

Horta was soon able to put these techniques to use when he was chosen by his professor, Alphonse Balat, to work with him on the **Serres Royales** (see p167), the Royal Greenhouses at Laeken. Designed with arabesque lines in the ironwork and lashings of natural light, this first project would have a great influence on Horta's later works.

IN CONTEXT

The style Horta and Hankar were creating, which came to be known as art nouveau, blended traditional craftsmanship with contemporary style. Appreciating the benefits of natural light, Horta and his fellow architects took the whole house as a reflection of the tastes of its owner, from the staircase and hallway to details such as doorknobs and windowpanes. The style is marked by sinuous lines, ornate cast ironwork, rounded windows, tiled floors, stained glass and winding staircases; many houses also incorporate elaborate sgraffito murals, in which the top layer of glaze or plaster is etched away to reveal the layer below.

A generation of entrepreneurs grown rich on Belgium's industrialisation and the growth of the railways, and the children of those rich entrepreneurs, wanted to break away from the old traditions and grandiose neoclassicism imposed on the Belgian capital by King Léopold II. The preferred medium of free-thinkers and liberals, art nouveau was now embraced by the emerging middle class. Horta, in particular, had the time and budget to lavish attention on every detail. Such was the extent of his painstaking creativity, though, he never grew rich from his labours. The house he designed for himself – now a museum on rue Américaine – is quite modest by comparison.

GOLDEN YEARS

Extensively displayed at the 1900 Paris Expo, Horta's style soon spread across Europe and beyond. It became known as Jugendstil in Germany, Modernista or Modernismo in Spain, Stile Floreale or Stile Liberty in Italy, Sezessionstil in Austria and Szecesszió in Hungary. In Brussels, many important art nouveau houses were built on the streets around avenue Louise, including Horta's debut **Hôtel Tassel** at 6 rue Paul Emile-Janson – this elegant townhouse was among the buildings that UNESCO would later describe as 'works of human creative genius'.

At the same time, Paul Hankar was working on **Maison Hankar** at 71 rue Defacqz, whose exquisite façade incorporates sgraffito tiles by Adolphe Crespin. On the same street, Hankar also built the art nouveau house at no.48 for the symbolist painter Albert Ciamberlani, easily recognisable from its two large north-facing windows and faded sgraffito decoration. The house next door was also

designed by Hankar, as were several shopfronts in the city centre – an example of which survives at 13 rue Royale.

The streets and squares of St-Gilles are also liberally dotted with houses built by Horta and his followers. The most important is the Hôtel Horta at 25-26 rue Américaine, the architect's light-filled home and office. Now the **Musée Horta** (see p154), its beautiful interior comprises mosaic floors, Asian tapestries and elaborate staircases – the hallway is always crowded with visitors stopping to admire the handrail. Also of note, at 224 avenue Louise, is the **Hôtel Solvay**, built by Horta in 1898.

The style also gained a hold in Schaerbeek after Mayor Louis Bertrand decreed it to be in favour. One of Horta's earliest works here was for wealthy lawyer Eugène Autrique at 266 chaussée de Haecht. Horta refused any payment, on condition that the money saved was devoted to the construction of the building's stylish white stone façade. In this spirit, the **Maison Autrique** (see p119) has been renovated and reopened, partly as a museum.

Horta's followers adapted the art nouveau style for less wealthy clients, who saved money by preserving a traditional Belgian interior. The **Maison de St-Cyr** on square Ambiorix was designed by 22-year-old Gustave Strauven in 1905. With its narrow façade, ironwork and round loggia at the top, it's one of the most striking buildings in the city. Unlike Horta's houses, though, this *maison* is all about surface decoration, with the interior divided up into conventional rooms.

DECLINE AND FALL

Gradually, the style faded in favour of the more geometrical architecture of early 20th-century Vienna and Glasgow – a shift already in evidence in Paul Cauchie's **Maison de Cauchie** on rue des Francs, built in 1905. Inside, it's richly decorated with gilded murals of beautiful women in long gowns, echoing the style of Gustav Klimt.

Klimt himself designed a magnificent frieze for the dining room of the **Palais Stoclet** on avenue de Tervuren. Built by Austrian architect Josef Hoffman between 1905 and 1911, it's considered the finest example of the Wiener Werkstätte style, the Arts and Crafts workshop that Hoffman co-founded as part of the Vienna Secession movement. The marble-clad exterior has art nouveau influences, but

IN CONTEXT

it's stripped of ostentation and gives a determined nod to modernism. Hoffman, like Horta, designed everything down to the last doorknob; sadly, though, the exterior is all you'll be able to admire.

Even Horta himself eventually abandoned art nouveau, adopting a modern, more linear style when he came to design the **Palais des Beaux-Arts** (see p106) and the **Gare Centrale** (see p100). Nonetheless, there are still hints of art nouveau in his final buildings.

In the 1960s, hundreds of exceptional art nouveau buildings were torn down by city planners, often to be replaced by uninspired office blocks. With alarming speed, the city lost most of its art nouveau shopfronts, almost all of Victor Horta's department stores and a beautiful private home once owned by Blérot.

The most scandalous demolition of all came in 1964, when Horta's **Maison du Peuple** was torn down to make way for a banal office building, despite vociferous protest. Considered Horta's finest work, the Maison was a stunning glass and cast-iron palace with an auditorium, café and shops; although its remains were numbered and stored, much of the ironwork was lost. Some balustrades are now displayed in Horta métro station, and part of the building has been incorporated into a café in Antwerp.

Now, after decades of indifference, the city has recognised its architectural heritage and art nouveau survivors are properly protected. Some have been put to imaginative new uses, such as the Old England department store – reincarnated as the **Musée des Instruments de Musique** (see p106). Meanwhile, Horta's last art nouveau work before his wartime exile in the US, the Waucquez fabric warehouse, has been restored as a home for the **Centre Belge de la Bande Dessinée** (see p63).

The demolition of the Maison du Peuple helped spark the creation of the **Atelier de Recherche et d'Action Urbaines**, or ARAU (02 219 33 45, www.arau.org), in 1969. The organisation set out to confront a city government callously neglecting its architectural heritage. The immediate aim was to save and renovate historic buildings, and fight against a policy that was turning large areas into barren office districts.

As well as campaigning, ARAU runs insightful guided tours. The most popular ones, covering the city's art nouveau and art deco architecture, are organised on Saturday mornings (walking tours €10-€18, bus tours €19) from May to December, and take visitors around many remarkable art nouveau interiors usually closed to the public. Other walking tours focus on particular districts or themes.

Musée des Instruments de Musique.

Surrealism

Magritte and his gang of subversives.

If Surrealism was a reaction to the horrors of World War I, then Brussels was perfectly placed to be receptive to this revolutionary movement. The key figures of the local scene – writers Clément Pansaers, Paul Nougé and Marcel Lecomte, painters ELT Mesens and, of course, René Magritte – had close connections with the original Surrealists in Paris; Magritte and his wife Georgette moved there shortly after the first Surrealist manifesto was published. But the Belgian take on Surrealism was different to that in France, where the interpretation of dreams and the immediate expression of subconscious thought took on prime importance. Here, Surrealism was more subversive, more surreal, in fact – perhaps personified by Magritte himself, who painted trains coming out of fireplaces while dressed in his suit and bow tie in his gloomy living room in the gloomy Brussels neighbourhood of Jette.

THE FIRST WAVE

Before Surrealism came Dadaism, created in Zurich during World War I. At the same time, a young student from Lessines, René Magritte, had enrolled at the Academy of Fine Arts in Brussels. Already active in the artistic life of the city was Clément Pansaers, Belgium's main exponent of Dadaism, a failed Egyptologist-cum-poet. Although he would die young, before the first Surrealist Manifesto, Pansaers was well thought of by the likes of André Breton, de facto head of the movement in Paris.

Pansaers also introduced Dadaism to the writer Marcel Lecomte, who co-founded a Brussels-based group with fellow writer Paul Nougé. Magritte's illustrations featured in several of Lecomte's books, while the influential Surrealist wordsmith Nougé

collaborated with many of his contemporary artists, including Magritte. It is thought that the line on one of Magritte's most famous paintings, '*Ceci n'est pas une pipe*', was penned by Nougé. He also wrote the preface pieces to Magritte's early exhibitions.

This Belgian Surrealist group was formed the same year as Breton published his first Surrealist Manifesto, in 1924. The group's own journal was *Correspondance*, which experimented with language and even parodied their French counterparts.

Once Magritte moved back to Brussels, in 1930, after a three-year stint in Paris, these Surrealists would meet at his salon in Jette at weekends. Other visitors included anarchist poet Louis Scutenaire, his wife Irène Hamoir and gallery owner ELT Mesens.

René Magritte Museum.

THE SECOND WAVE

Gradually, it was Magritte who gained international recognition, earning enough from his paintings for him and Georgette to move out of Jette in 1954 and into a bigger place in Schaerbeek. They had survived the lean years during and immediately after World War II by Magritte making fake Picassos and forging banknotes.

Helping him in this task was the youngest member of the loose artistic community, Marcel Mariën, a would-be painter and photographer. Mariën was, in essence, a prankster, whose most notorious trick was to set up a false Magritte exhibition in Knokke and offer his paintings at knockdown prices. Afterwards, the pair never spoke again.

It was Mariën who published the post-war Surrealist magazine Les Lèvres Nues, along with Christian Dotremont, co-founder of the Revolutionary Surrealist Group and cross-border avant-garde movement CoBrA. Although it placed emphasis on spontaneity, CoBrA did not openly embrace Surrealism but leaned more towards abstract expressionism. Its members, initially drawn from Copenhagen, Brussels and Amsterdam (hence the name), remained close even after the group disbanded in 1951. The other major figure of the post-war era was Marcel Broodthaers, born the same year as the Surrealist Manifesto, who tried to subvert the idea of art and commerce with a series of bizarre exhibitions across Europe. His gravestone, in Ixelles Cemetery, is also his own work. Ultimately, for decades of endeavour,

camaraderie and subversion among the Belgian Surrealist fraternity, there is precious little work to show for it, apart from Magritte's.

Both Magritte and Nougé died within a few months of each other, in 1967. Scutenaire died almost exactly 20 years after Magritte, while watching a TV show dedicated to the life and work of his great friend.

Musée Magritte.

IN CONTEXT

MUSEUMS IN BRUSSELS

Magritte's house where the Surrealists used to meet, in Jette, was later bought by two Belgians and restored during the 1990s as a homage to the artist. Called the **René Magritte Museum** (see p164), it's surprisingly large, divided into three separate apartments – René and Georgette rented the ground floor and attic. Visitors can see many elements of the building in his paintings: the blue walls and fireplace from *La Durée Poignardée* – although there's no steam locomotive puffing forth – and the sash windows, glass doors, staircase and other bourgeois elements that Magritte manipulated so effortlessly.

The Magrittes came to a compromise over the colour scheme: Georgette preferred brown for the doors, stairs and panelling, while René insisted on the clashing salmon pink dining room, electric blue lounge and lime green bedroom. René and Georgette led quiet lives; the artist painted some of his masterpieces from his Renoir and Vache periods in a suit and bow tie. Documents, letters and photos are also on display, and 17 of the 19 rooms are open to the public.

> '*The Magrittes came to a compromise over the colour scheme of their house in Jette: Georgette preferred brown, while René insisted on the salmon pink dining room and electric blue lounge.*'

These days, interest in Magritte is stronger than ever – hence the huge success of another, more recently established museum set alongside the Musées Royaux des Beaux-Arts in the Upper Town. Half a million people a year visit the **Musée Magritte** (see p106) to view more than 200 of the artist's works.

IN CONTEXT

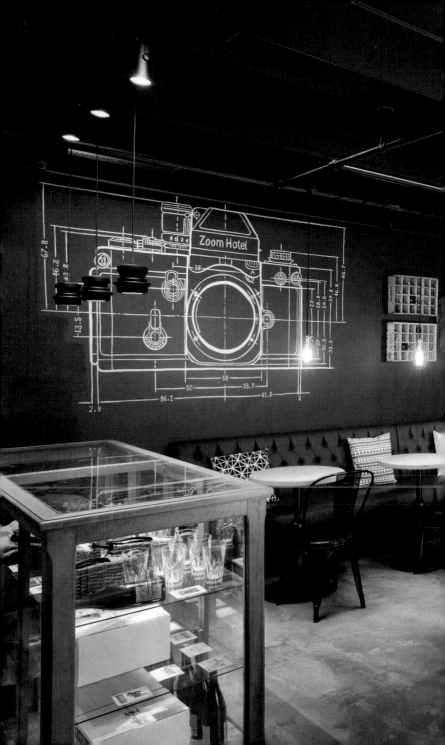

Hotels

Brussels has many more hotels than most other cities of its size. This is largely because of the EU and all the institutions that service it, along with the fact that multinationals set up base here to be close to the action. This means that significant numbers of visitors on expense accounts come to the three- to five-star category hotels and rates are geared towards their budgets. So you'll find the usual international chains, such as Hilton, Marriott and Sheraton, plus a scattering of charming independents, such as Le Plaza and Métropole, all trying to attract the big spenders. Ironically, this is advantageous for the leisure traveller, too, because hotels drop their rates considerably at weekends and in the summer months to avoid being empty. It's worth doing some research – availability and prices change on a daily basis – and experimenting with some of the quirkier independents; the Noga, Hotel Orts and Welcome, for example.

PRICES & CLASSIFICATION

In Belgium, hotel stars are awarded according to the quantity and type of services a hotel offers, rather than the innate quality of the property. As a result, a nondescript hotel with a slew of services will have more stars than one with character that doesn't see the need for trouser presses and 24-hour room service.

We have classified hotels according to their location, then by price category for a standard double room: **Deluxe** (€250 or over), **Expensive** (€150-€249), **Moderate** (€90-€149) and **Budget** (under €90). Note that at weekends, you can often find a double in a four- or even five-star for under €100 – but these are not standard rates. In addition, we have listed the best B&Bs and hostels. Most establishments can easily cope with enquiries in English.

Rooms tend to be of a decent size, but can vary dramatically, not only between hotels but also within the properties themselves. For the many hotels created out of townhouses, rooms are usually more compact, although their high ceilings give an impression of space, and period details often make up for the lack of elbow room.

GRAND'PLACE & AROUND

Deluxe

Crowne Plaza Brussels – Le Palace
3 rue Gineste, 1210 Brussels (02 203 62 00, www.ihg.com). Métro/pré-métro Rogier.
Rooms 354. **Map** p303 E2.
The Crowne Plaza Brussels dates from 1908 and is one of the city's landmark hotels. Major refurbishment has seen the faded 1930s updates replaced with an art nouveau look, all lines and curves, in keeping with the building's age. There's no stinting on modernity, though, with all the comforts you'd expect from a contemporary hotel. Single-sex saunas and a fully equipped gym open from 6am cater to healthier guests.
▶ *There's a jogging track right outside the hotel in the Botanical Gardens.*

★ Hotel Amigo
1-3 rue de l'Amigo, 1000 Brussels (02 547 47 47, www.roccofortehotels.com/hotels-and-resorts/hotel-amigo). Métro Gare Centrale or pré-métro Bourse. **Rooms** 173. **Map** p301 C5.
See p272 **Hotels with History**.

Hotel Métropole Brussels

31 place de Brouckère, 1000 Brussels (02 217 23 00, www.metropolehotel.com). Métro/pré-métro De Brouckère. **Rooms** 286. **Map** p301 D3.

The Métropole is the grande dame of the Brussels hotel scene (it opened in 1895) and displays the most stunning architecture in its public areas, including its renowned café (*see p65*). The French Renaissance main entrance leads into an Empire-style reception hall, with gilt flourishes, columns and stained-glass windows. An original cage lift conveys guests up to rooms in the main building, which are disappointing by comparison with the public spaces and lack the luxury touches of other top hotels. The 1925 extension at the back of the building has some delightful art deco fittings.

Le Plaza Brussels

118 boulevard Adolphe Max, 1000 Brussels (02 278 01 00, www.leplaza-brussels.be). Métro/pré-métro Rogier or De Brouckère. **Rooms** 187. **Map** p303 D2.

Like the Métropole, Le Plaza is an independent hotel owned by a well-known Belgian family. Dating from 1930, the building was the headquarters of the Nazis and later the Allied Forces in the war, so the (now listed) structure was largely spared bombing. The winter garden, which did suffer, was rebuilt and now houses the restaurant. The rest of the building, with original fittings (amethyst crystal chandeliers, Gobelins tapestry, marble bas-reliefs), has been restored to its former glory. The sumptuous rooms are decorated in shades of cream, beige and ochre, and an ornate Moorish-style theatre is used as a

IN THE KNOW BRUSSELS.BE

As well as the major hotel-booking sites, you can reserve rooms via the Brussels Tourist Office at www.visitbrussels.be/bitc/be_en/sleep/hotels.do. It has more than 100 hotels and 50 B&Bs on its database, as well as youth hostels.

function room. The only drawback is the surroundings – the boulevard has more than its fair share of sex shops.

Radisson SAS Royal Hotel

47 rue du Fossé aux Loups, 1000 Brussels (02 219 28 28, www.radissonblu.com/royalhotel-brussels). Métro/pré-métro De Brouckère. **Rooms** 281. **Map** p301 D4.

Behind the elaborate art deco façade of the Radisson SAS Royal lies a truly top-class business hotel with good leisure facilities and a well-deserved reputation for serving great food. Choose from four different styles of room (Maritime, Oriental, At Home and Business Class); all come with luxury fittings, Wi-Fi and tea/coffee-making facilities, but lovely little flourishes set each style apart – opt for a Maritime room if you prefer wooden rather than carpeted floors, for instance. You can indulge yourself at the fitness centre or at the Bar Dessiné, with Belgian cartoons on the walls and a superb selection of malt whiskies behind the bar. The hotel's executive chef is Yves Mattagne, who has earned two Michelin

Hotel Amigo.

stars for the in-house Sea Grill (*see p65*), so expect to eat very well, even if you have to pay handsomely for the pleasure.

Royal Windsor Hotel Grand Place

5 rue Duquesnoy, 1000 Brussels (02 505 55 55, www.warwickhotels.com/royal-windsor). Métro/pré-métro De Brouckère or métro Gare Centrale. **Rooms** 283. **Map** p301 D5.
Here, the big draw is the Grand Place suite, 250sq m (2,690sq ft) of Murano glass and marble, a private penthouse with its own lift, butler and, most dramatically, roof terrace with a near bird's-eye view of the Hôtel de Ville. And it's yours for just €7,500… At the other end of the scale, classic rooms are more than adequately comfortable. In between are varying levels of deluxe, premium and suite, with prices varying according to availability on the hotel's own website. Service is reliably old-school, furnishings too – though contemporary soundproofing may not go amiss on nights when the nearby Grand'Place is at its busiest.

Sheraton Brussels Hotel

3 place Rogier, 1210 Brussels (02 224 31 11, www.starwoodhotels.com). Métro/pré-métro Rogier. **Rooms** 511. **Map** p303 D2.
With 511 rooms, this is the biggest of all Brussels' hotels, boasting no fewer than 30 floors of spacious, elegant rooms with large beds and all the usual comforts and services you'd expect from this major American chain. Constant modernisation has resulted in a newly renovated lounge bar and 'smart rooms', an added perk for any high-powered business types staying on the exclusive top five

Le Dixseptième.

floors. Further draws include the panoramic views of the city from the upper-storey rooms and the top-floor heated indoor pool.
▶ *The Sheraton's in-house Crescendo (www.crescendo-restaurant.com) is a Belgian restaurant of some note, using locally sourced products – and guests will enjoy its laid-back weekend breakfast times of 6.30am-2pm.*

Expensive

9Hotel Central

10 rue des Colonies, 1000 Brussels (02 504 99 10, www.le9hotel.com). Métro Gare Centrale. **Rooms** 47. **Map** p301 D4.
See p277 **First Class.**

★ Le Dixseptième

25 rue de la Madeleine, 1000 Brussels (02 517 17 17, www.ledixseptieme.be). Métro Gare Centrale. **Rooms** 24. **Map** p301 D5.
See p272 **Hotels with History.**

★ Dominican Brussels

9 rue Léopold, 1000 Brussels (02 203 08 08, www.thedominican.be). Métro Gare Centrale. **Rooms** 150. **Map** p301 D4.
See p272 **Hotels with History.**

Floris Arlequin Grand Place

17-19 rue de la Fourche, 1000 Brussels (02 514 16 15, www.florishotels.com). Métro/pré-métro De Brouckère. **Rooms** 92. **Map** p301 D4.

IN THE KNOW PLACE ROGIER

Created as part of the construction of the North-South Connection in the 1950s when the Gare du Nord was moved back, place Rogier is a high-rise business quarter. As well as being home to the Rogier Tower (formerly Dexia, before the bank collapsed in 2011), it features a cluster of high-spec US chain hotels, a **Crowne Plaza** (see *p266*), a **Sheraton** (see above) and a **Hilton** (see *p269*). Despite the soulless, windy surroundings, guests are treated to prime views – the Sheraton's from a panoramic pool. First served by a pré-métro station and later a metro station, place Rogier is little more than five minutes' walk from the City 2 mall on the city centre's main shopping street of rue Neuve. Although officially part of the commune of St-Josse, place Rogier and its hotels have been categorised in this guide as 'Grand'Place & Around' for simplification purposes.

The contrast between this modern, 92-room hotel and the little cobbled street on which it stands could not be more stark. The rooms vary in size (but are uniformly comfortable, bright and clean), and three of them offer panoramic views over the rooftops, as does the top-floor breakfast room.

▶ *There are three other Floris hotels in town, including the Louise (59-61 rue de la Concorde, 02 515 00 60) and, near Midi station, the Ustel Midi (6-8 square de l'Aviation, 02 520 60 53).*

★ Hôtel des Galeries

38 rue des Bouchers, 1000 Brussels (02 213 74 70, www.hoteldesgaleries.be). Métro Gare Centrale or métro/pré-métro De Brouckère. **Rooms** 23. **Map** p301 D4.

Opened in 2014 and tucked behind a discreet doorway where rue des Bouchers meets the glitzy Galeries St-Hubert, this design-forward, contemporary boutique hotel makes an immediate impression on the first-time visitor. Designers Fleur Delesalle and Camille Flammarion have created 20 rooms and three suites of stark white furnishings contrasted with flashes of fire red and bottle green, offset by parquet flooring. Creaking floors, in fact, are probably the only minor gripe you'll have – staff and service are impeccable. *Photos p270.*

▶ *Round the corner, under the same umbrella and created by the same design team, Comptoir des Galeries (6 Galerie du Roi, 02 212 74 74, www.comptoirdesgaleries.be) features the contemporary, Michelin-starred cuisine of Julien Burlat.*

Hotel NH Atlanta Brussels

7 boulevard Adolphe Max, 1000 Brussels (02 217 01 20, www.nh-hotels.com/hotel/nh-atlanta-brussels). Métro/pré-métro De Brouckère. **Rooms** 241. **Map** p301 D3.

The Spanish NH Hoteles chain has been making huge inroads into Brussels and, at the last count, had seven properties in and around the city. The Atlanta is its flagship. Housed in an elegant early 20th-century building, the hotel boasts modern, bright and cheerful decor, thanks to the Mediterranean influence. A terrace attached to the breakfast room offers great rooftop views, a real bonus in summer. The highlight, though, of any stay at an NH hotel is the excellent attention to detail: for example, you can choose the type of pillow you want.

▶ *Equally impressive is the Atlanta Brussels' sister hotel, the four-star NH Brussels du Grand Sablon; see p273.*

Hilton Brussels City

20 place Rogier, 1210 Brussels (02 203 31 25, www.brussels-city.hilton.com). Métro/pré-métro Rogier. **Rooms** 284. **Map** p303 E2.

If you prefer smaller boutique hotels (and lower prices), then head for the four-star Hilton Brussels City. This stylish modern property, which is housed in three buildings dating from the 1930s and still retains some original features (such as the art deco lights in the restaurant), offers a more personalised service with the help of some of the best hotel staff in town. The rooms in the different buildings offer various configurations, but the decor, including pale wooden floors, remains the same. A modest gym, sauna and steam room, plus a decent buffet breakfast, make this a great place to stay.

Hilton Brussels Grand Place

3 carrefour de l'Europe, 1000 Brussels (02 548 40 80, www.placeshilton.com/brussels-grand-place). Métro Gare Centrale. **Rooms** 224. **Map** p303 E2.

The Hilton chain recently opened this new property right outside the main entrance to Gare Centrale. *See p277* **First Class**.

Le Quinze

15 Grand'Place, 1000 Brussels (02 511 09 56, www.hotel-le-quinze-grand-place.be). Métro Gare Centrale or pré-métro Bourse. **Rooms** 15. **Map** p301 D5.

Having changed its name from the Hotel Saint-Michel in spring 2015, Le Quinze is slowly rebranding itself – but don't expect anything too radical, given its prime historic location at the end of the Maison des Ducs de Brabant across one side of the Grand'Place. 'Quinze' refers to both its address, no.15, and the number of rooms available. If you want to wake up and look out over one of Europe's most beautiful squares, this is the place to do it – but if there's an event on in the main square, you might not get the earliest of nights.

Budget

A La Grande Cloche

10 place Rouppe, 1000 Brussels (02 512 61 40, www.hotelgrandecloche.com). Pré-métro Anneessens. **Rooms** 36. **Map** p301 B5.

This family-run hotel is located in a quiet square equidistant from Midi station and the Grand'Place. The rooms are clean and fairly comfy. Each has a queen bed: roomy for one, but a bit of a squeeze for two (the twin rooms avoid the problem and are usually spacious). The cheaper rooms tend to have a small shower box.

ST-GÉRY & STE-CATHERINE

Expensive

Atlas Hotel Brussels

30 rue du Vieux Marché aux Grains, 1000 Brussels (02 502 60 06, www.atlas-hotel.be). Pré-métro Bourse or métro Ste-Catherine. **Rooms** 89. **Map** p301 B4.

Behind the 18th-century façade of the Atlas lie acceptable rooms that teeter on the edge of sterility. Here, location scores highly over style. It's near the trendy shops of upmarket rue Antoine Dansaert and the bar vortex of St-Géry – if you're making a party of it, reserve one of the five split-level duplex rooms sleeping four. For an early night, book a back room overlooking the courtyard. A complimentary drink is served on weekday evenings.

Brussels Marriott Hotel Grand Place

3-7 rue Auguste Orts, 1000 Brussels (02 516 90 90, www.marriott.com/brudt). Pré-métro Bourse. **Rooms** 221. **Map** p301 C4.

While the façade of the Marriott is a beautifully restored remnant of the 19th century, most of the interior is completely new, creating a nice blend of original and modern. As you'd expect from an

Hôtel des Galeries. *See p269.*

American chain, the rooms come fitted to a high standard, and include large beds and adaptors for electronic devices. The room decor is bright, but the bathrooms – in muted shades of beige – are a tad more relaxing. A nice touch is the free tea and coffee served in the ground-floor bar before 9.30am.

Moderate

★ Brussels Welcome Hotel

23 quai au Bois à Brûler, 1000 Brussels (02 219 95 46, www.hotelwelcome.com). Métro Ste-Catherine. **Rooms** 17. **Map** p301 C3.

The typical 19th-century façade of the Welcome belies the exotic guest rooms inside: each one is unique and has been furnished with genuine antiques and artefacts to represent a different destination, among them Bali, India, Japan and Morocco. Other options include the Tibet room, which has a small terrace and is decorated in dramatic shades of red and black, or the Jules Verne room, which follows a round-the-world theme and boasts a large balcony. Factor in the friendliness of the owners, the Smeesters, and you've got a really great spot.

Hotel Orts

38-40 rue Auguste Orts, 1000 Brussels (02 450 22 00, www.hotelorts.com). Pré-métro Bourse. **Rooms** 14. **Map** p301 C4.

The Orts has injected a little affordable style into this previously lacklustre area. The architecture is grand fin-de-siècle Brussels and the building looks particularly stunning at night with its theatrical lighting. The individually colour-themed rooms are spacious and finished to a high standard. The corner rooms are more modest in size, but do offer a double vista. The location is perfect for sightseeing and nightlife – its street-level café (*see p75*) is a popular year-round terrace spot.

Noga Hotel

38 rue du Béguinage, 1000 Brussels (02 218 67 63, www.nogahotel.com). Métro Ste-Catherine. **Rooms** 19. **Map** p302 C3.

Noga means 'brightness' in Hebrew and this hotel lights up a charming and tranquil street in Ste-Catherine. The atmosphere is friendly and delightfully kitsch, with nautical-themed knick-knacks in the airy public areas jostling for space with pictures of royals and assorted bric-a-brac. The rooms, which have showers but no baths, are a tad more restrained, but each is individual in its design fittings. That said, you can pretty much guarantee they'll be spacious, comfortable – and bright.

THE MAROLLES

Budget

Hotel Galia

15-16 place du Jeu de Balle, 1000 Brussels (02 502 42 43, www.hotelgalia.com). Métro/pré-métro Porte de Hal or Gare du Midi. **Rooms** 40. **Map** p304 B7.

The Galia is a simple, family-run hotel that offers good-value accommodation and overlooks the square where the flea market is held, making it the ideal place for bargain hunters. It's decorated with images of Belgian comic strips and the cheerful rooms are basic but clean and pleasant, including fairly large triples and quads. The brighter front

HOTELS WITH HISTORY

Lay your head in an abbey, a jail or an ambassadorial residence.

Regularly cited as the finest hotel in Belgium, if not the Benelux, Rocco Forte's **Hotel Amigo** (*see p266; pictured*) was originally converted into an upscale lodging for the 1958 Expo. It has since accommodated everyone from pop stars to politicians, so it's strange to think that it started life as a prison – from 1522, according to the city records.

Although it's been razed to the ground twice since, the hotel's polished flagstones date from the middle of the last millennium. Equally impressive are the beautiful 18th-century Aubusson tapestries and paintings of the Flemish and Italian schools. The rest, however, is wonderfully contemporary, thanks to a €15-million refurbishment when the Rocco Forte group took over in 2000.

Sir Rocco's sister, designer Olga Polizzi, created 154 rooms and 19 suites, using the finest linens and leathers, and adding little touches of Belgium – an image of Tintin here, a Magritte print there. Nothing, however, reaches the heights of the Blaton Suite, named after the Belgian family who owned the hotel from 1957 to 2000.

Set on a quiet, wide, partly pedestrianised thoroughfare right behind the Opera House, the **Dominican Brussels** (*see p268*) was created on the site of a 15th-century abbey. It has been used as a lodging for quite a while since – Jacques-Louis David, painter of Marat and ally of Robespierre, resided here in exile until shortly before the Belgian revolution broke out next door.

There's nothing revolutionary about the Dominican these days. Opened in 2007, it combines high ceilings with the original stone floors and tranquil cloisters. A serene inner courtyard, which most rooms face, adds to the calm atmosphere. Rain showers, Nespresso machines and a pillow menu push the pamper factor, while the buffet breakfast can be taken in the courtyard or in cosy velvet chairs in the Grand Lounge restaurant.

Hidden on a slope leading to the Mont des Arts, **Le Dixseptième** (*see p268*) is a gem, a boutique hotel with 24 rooms. Popular with business travellers looking for the personal touch, the hotel is also an ideal destination for a romantic weekend in Brussels. Twelve of the rooms are housed in the 17th-century building that was once home to the Spanish ambassador, while the other dozen, equally spacious, are in a new block to the back. There's a bar and a period salon overlooking an inner courtyard where breakfast is served.

rooms are triple-glazed to block out the sound of the
market and nearby bars. Downstairs, the terrace of a
brasserie spreads over an enclosed forecourt.

UPPER TOWN

Moderate

Hôtel du Congrès

*42 rue du Congrès, 1000 Brussels (02 217
18 90, www.hotelducongres.be). Métro Madou.*
Rooms 80. **Map** p303 F4.

The four elegant townhouses that constitute the
Hôtel du Congrès have been beautifully renovated
to create a sleek, modern lodging with original fin-
de-siècle features. Some rooms have high ceilings,
a stunning fireplace and original cornicing, with a
simple modern bathroom en-suite. Others may not
include as many authentic features, but what they
lack in detail they make up for in space and/or tranquillity. This is particularly true of those overlooking or opening on to the back garden and split-level
terraces, where residents can breakfast in summer.

Hotel NH Brussels Du Grand Sablon

*2 rue Bodenbroek, 1000 Brussels (02 518 11 00,
www.nh-hotels.com/hotel/nh-brussels-du-grand-
sablon). Tram 92, 93, 94, or bus 95.* **Rooms** 196.
Map p301 D6.

Away from but within easy reach of the city-centre
bustle, travellers can look forward to a relaxing stay
at the calm, assured, four-star NH on pretty place du
Grand Sablon, site of the weekly antiques market.
Deluxe rooms and suites overlook the square, while
families will enjoy the connecting bedrooms of two
adapted units. All in all, a great location in a handsome building at great rates.

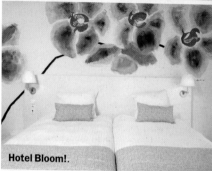

Hotel Bloom!.

SCHAERBEEK

Deluxe

★ Hotel Bloom!

*250 rue Royale, 1210 Brussels (02 220 69 05,
www.hotelbloom.com). Métro Botanique.*
Rooms 287. **Map** p305 E8.

Hotel Bloom! puts nature at the forefront. Walking
into its entrance alongside the Botanical Gardens,
you're pleasantly assailed by floral scents that waft
around the spacious lobby as the efficient staff go
about the business of checking in, checking out and
serving hundreds of guests. While the hotel they
work for emphasises its green initiatives – using
environmentally friendly energy and raising tens
of thousands of euros for SOS Children's Villages –
its customers will immediately notice another of its
hallmarks: individual art. It features in the lobby and
in every guestroom, created by budding artists from
around Europe, their biographies set alongside their
works. You'll have space to stand back and admire
them – no room is under 30sq m (323sq ft). With

ESSENTIAL INFORMATION

IN THE KNOW
ROOMS WITH A BREW

Unlike Paris or London, Brussels hasn't really gone big on the hotel bar – until now, that is. Yes, among the city's hotels are the odd stalwart – the **Métropole** (see p267), for example – but cool spots to zing back drinks haven't been the norm. Recently, though, trendy hotels such as **Aloft Brussels Schuman** (see right), with its cocktail bar and DJ nights twice a week, and the **Zoom Hotel** (see p276), with its in-house bar for sampling rare Belgian beers, have been swimming against the tide. Even at the top end of the scale there's some action: the **Dominican Brussels** (see p268) hosts a weekly DJ in its Lounge Bar, and the **Steigenberger Grandhotel** (see p275) has live jazz every weekend in its cosy Loui bar.

rooms priced at more than €300 during the week, it's an expensive option unless the firm is paying – but rates come down by more than half at weekends. Breakfasts are substantial.

Moderate

Hotel Retro

3 chaussée de Haecht, 1210 Brussels (02 210 19 90, www.hotelretro.be). Métro Botanique.
Rooms 25. **Map** p305 E8.
Occupying a stark white corner building above a busy supermarket on the edge of the Turkish quarter, the Retro does what it can with its situation – and its concept. Rated with three stars but perhaps worthy of another half-star given the comfortable furnishings and bathroom fittings, the Retro falls down on its retro – weakly conceived and barely worthy of the name. Still, it's a decent location, mere steps from rue Royale and the Botanical Gardens, and within walking distance of the city centre.

EU QUARTER
Deluxe

Silken Berlaymont Brussels

11-19 boulevard Charlemagne, 1000 Brussels (02 231 09 09, www.hoteles-silken.com/en/ hotels/berlaymont-brussels). Métro Schuman.
Rooms 212. **Map** p307 J5.
The Silken B's location in the heart of the EU district, its sleek rooms and the slick staff mark it out as a business hotel, while the modern architecture, spa (€10 surcharge) and arty streak give it a certain funkiness. Images by photographers from across the EU adorn the News Bar and, all in all, the hotel strikes the right balance between work and play. A number

of rooms have been adapted for the female business traveller, while the in-house restaurant L'Objectif with its artful modern cuisine and garden views is another draw.

Expensive

Eurostars Montgomery

134 avenue de Tervuren, 1150 Brussels (02 741 85 11, www.eurostarshotels.com). Métro Montgomery. **Rooms** 63.
The Montgomery is a lovely, small hotel in an upmarket residential area, beside a métro station six stops from the city centre. The rooms are all beautifully decorated in English country style, and come equipped with all the latest gadgets, including DVD players (DVDs can be borrowed from reception). As most guests are here on business, the restaurant only opens on weekdays. So although it's a peaceful place to stay, to be at the heart of the action, look elsewhere.

Stanhope Hotel

9 rue du Commerce, 1000 Brussels (02 506 91 11, www.thonhotels.be/stanhope). Métro Trône.
Rooms 125. **Map** p305 F6.
The Stanhope has almost doubled in size since being taken over by Norwegian chain Thon, but that has not changed its calm and intimate atmosphere. Book one of the original rooms, carved out of a row of elegant townhouses, if you want a stay that evokes an idealised 19th-century English country home. Check into a new room if you prefer antique-style furnishings, but also want modern wooden floors and high-tech bathroom facilities. The Library Bar is all varnished wood and cosy warmth, while chef Laurent Gauze creates Mediterranean flavours in the Brighton restaurant. Online deals can often bring room rates to under €100 at weekends.
▶ *In all, the Thon group runs five hotels in Brussels – including the Bristol Stéphanie (see p276) – plus three apartments for short- or long-term rental. Thon Residence EU (126 rue de Trèves, 02 204 39 13) is walking distance from the main European institutions.*

Moderate

★ Aloft Brussels Schuman

Place Jean Rey, 1040 Brussels (02 800 08 88, www.aloftbrussels.com). Métro Schuman.
Rooms 150. **Map** p308 H6.
At last! Aloft! With accommodation around the EU Quarter either expensive and staid or expensive and shiny, recently opened Aloft provides a much welcome helping of sassy. Right in the shadow of the Julius Lipsius Building, home of the EU Council, Aloft goes big on windows (large), flatscreen TVs (42in) and showers (of the walk-in spa variety). Desks are similarly spacious for tapping away at your laptop. An extra €30 on the standard rate gets you lovely views over Parc Léopold or place Jean

Warwick Barsey Hotel.
See p276.

Rey. Once the working day is done, Aloft has made a point of making its bar a destination in its own right, with its split happy half-hours from 6pm and from 8pm and DJ nights on Wednesdays and Thursdays. On Fridays, you're invited to bring and amplify your own tunes. Tech-savvy Aloft also allows you to check in by touch-screen.

Monty Small Design Hotel

101 boulevard Brand Whitlock, 1200 Brussels (02 734 56 36, www.monty-hotel.be). Métro Montgomery. **Rooms** 18.

Located in a 1930s townhouse, the Monty was utterly transformed by Thierry Hens's mix of modern and traditional. The interior sparkles with classic design items by Philippe Starck and Charles Eames, and grey and red decoration throughout sets an understated but eminently stylish tone. The 18 rooms are simple but sexy, with en-suite shower rooms, and guests seem happy to mingle around the breakfast table in the reception area. There's a front terrace and courtyard garden, as well as a fashionable lounge that adds a welcome touch of home – especially when juxtaposed with the sterility of the EU façades nearby.

Budget

New Hotel Charlemagne

25-27 boulevard Champagne, 1000 Brussels (02 230 21 35, www.new-hotel.com/fr/hotels-bruxelles/charlemagne). Métro Schuman. **Rooms** 68. **Map** p307 J4.

With several branches in Paris and Marseille, the funky New Hotel budget chain has just moved into Brussels – right in the EU Quarter, between the Berlaymont building and square Ambiorix, to be precise. With rooms at just over €50 if booked in advance, they're certainly a bargain, and comfortable with it – though a four-star status may be somewhat ambitious. Bright colours and tasteful decor feature throughout, as well as pay-for Nespresso machines. In addition to the City and superior Club Rooms, four Club Room Terrasses offer panoramic views of town from their private terraces.

IXELLES

Deluxe

Steigenberger Grandhotel

71 avenue Louise, 1050 Brussels (02 542 42 42, http://en.steigenberger.com/brussels/steigenberger-grandhotel). Métro Louise. **Rooms** 267. **Map** p305 D8.

The high-end German chain Steigenberger has taken over this luxury property, formerly the landmark Conrad, on the city's smartest shopping boulevard. Straight away, it modernised all the rooms, with creams and coffee colours. Service remains, *natürlich*, tip-top, with valet parking, shoe shine and

Zoom Hotel.

a secretary on hand if so required. Steigenberger has spiffed up the hotel bar too; the Loui hosts live jazz every weekend from September to June, and Restaurant No.77 operates daily. There's also a gym on the first floor.

★ Warwick Barsey Hotel

381-383 avenue Louise, 1050 Brussels (02 649 98 00, warwickhotels.com/barsey). Métro Louise then tram 94. **Rooms** 99. **Map** p310 F12.

As soon as you walk through the door of this luxurious boutique hotel, you know that you're somewhere really special. The interior was designed by none other than Jacques Garcia, who created an opulent reception area in his signature rich red with Napoleon III-style furnishings and neoclassical relief work. The restaurant (with occasional DJs) and rooms are similar in style, exuding a warmth and intimacy that make the Barsey a perfect winter hotel. And there's also a courtyard terrace, making it the perfect summer residence as well. Rooms on the upper floors, where you'll find the opulent suites, feature balconies with panoramic views, and all bedrooms have been positioned to receive as much natural light as possible. The only real downside is the location: set at the leafier end of avenue Louise, it's quite a hike from the centre of town, though not too far from Brussels' luxury shops. *Photos p275.*

Expensive

Agenda Louise

6-8 rue de Florence, 1000 Brussels (02 539 00 31, www.hotel-agenda.com). Métro Louise then tram 94. **Rooms** 37. **Map** p305 E9.

The Agenda Louise is an unassuming, friendly and comfortable hotel. With a quiet location just off avenue Louise and clean, spacious rooms, it's popular with families. A nice touch in each room are the framed photos of Brussels and the accompanying book giving details of the subjects in the pictures. The Agenda attracts business guests during the week – and as long as the company is happy to pay €200-plus a night, few visitors complain. Those paying from their own pocket may expect a few improvements to the breakfast.

Thon Hotel Bristol Stéphanie

91-93 avenue Louise, 1050 Brussels (02 543 33 11, www.thonhotels.be/bristolstephanie). Métro Louise then tram 94. **Rooms** 142. **Map** p305 E9.

Norwegian Thon claims to offer the biggest hotel rooms in Brussels; they certainly are spacious, all with room for a desk, the singles for a coffee table. Superior rooms have a sofa, while the club rooms can sleep up to four. There are also rooms for people with allergies. The lobby is strangely old-fashioned and slightly kitsch, with its swagged curtains and over-the-top sofas. Once you get beyond that, though, things rapidly improve.

★ Zoom Hotel

59-61 rue de la Concorde, 1000 Brussels (02 515 00 60, www.zoomhotel.be). Métro Louise then tram 94. **Rooms** 37. **Map** p305 E8.

Photography is the theme here – hence the name and the display of vintage cameras by the stylish café (where a decent breakfast is served). It's also a tasting bar for sought-after Belgian beers. Completely renovated and reopened in autumn 2014, Zoom has been

FIRST CLASS

Station hotels worth missing the train for.

Those travelling to Brussels by Eurostar from London set off from a station impressively recreated in its original dramatic Gothic-Revival style. Forming part of the fabulous façade, the striking five-star St Pancras Renaissance defines the railway hotel – exciting, lavish yet relaxed, much like the travel of the steam-palace era in which it was built.

Until recently, though, arriving at Brussels Midi was a rather less impressive experience. These same travellers would high-tail it out right away by taxi or pré-métro, avoiding the down-at-heel local bars and cheap hotels. Many of these low-grade lodgings still exist, awaiting the unsuspecting budget traveller on and off adjoining avenue Fonsny. But the relandscaping around place Victor Horta beside Midi station has created a neat pedestrianised zone, the ideal location for a sleek, modern railway hotel such as the four-star **Pullman Brussels Centre Midi** (see p278; pictured), designed by Jean-Philippe Nuel. With a Eurostar meeting room, gym and sauna, fine wines at La Vinoteca and Italo-Gallic cuisine at the Victor Restaurant, not to mention in-room Bose docking stations, Nespresso machines and CO Bigelow smellies in the bathroom, the Pullman is a work-centred, comfortable hub that means you need only see Brussels from its spacious windows.

Round the corner on avenue Fonsny, the **Park Inn by Radisson Brussels Midi** (see p279) was the first at Midi station to offer contemporary comfort to the business traveller. An expansive meeting space, fine views from the seventh-floor gym and a decent steak restaurant are only part of the attraction – the guestrooms are plush and tasteful, and also feature super-fast Wi-Fi. OK, this may be par for the course in Amsterdam or Copenhagen, but it wasn't that long ago that Midi could only provide a dingy welcome to Brussels.

Georges Nagelmackers, the Belgian who conceived of the Orient Express after being inspired by Pullman's service in the US, would surely have approved. His iconic train used to pull out of Paris, not Brussels.

But in 2014, its contemporary counterpart, the Venice Simplon-Orient-Express, was rerouted to make Midi station a new destination on its roster of glamour.

The Belgian capital is unique in that its main three stations are connected with one straight railway line that slices through its heart. A simple change of platforms at Midi means you can get to Gare Centrale and Gare du Nord in a few minutes, through the busiest train tunnel in the world. The price for this convenience – the North-South Connection, created after World War II – was the demolition of houses along one side of rue de la Madeleine. The line runs below soulless boulevards Pachéco, de Berlaimont, de l'Impératrice and de l'Empereur, before finally emerging at the third of the three hub stations, Gare du Nord, situated close to the city's red-light district.

In between Midi and Nord lies the Horta-designed Gare Centrale, a short walk from downtown shops and offices. For Eurostar tourists, jumping on to one of 1,000 national trains a day from Midi to Centrale means that you emerge an eight-minute walk from Grand'Place. And for hoteliers, Gare Centrale is a prime site, and sight, backdropped by Horta's elegant sweeping façade.

Alongside now stands **9Hotel Central** (see p268), all bare-brick industrial cool, designed by Castel Veciana of Barcelona. Appealing to the discerning urban single traveller or couple with its 24-hour bar and loft-like lodgings, it also caters to the visiting creative with its communal working space, business corner and lounge music.

Slap bang opposite the main entrance to Gare Centrale, the Hilton chain opened its **Brussels Grand Place** (see p270) in November 2014. The former Marriott has been converted into a business-oriented hub with 224 sleek rooms, a 24-hour gym and 17 meeting rooms and events spaces, including two grand ballrooms. Food-wise there's steak or trout available in Le Bar, North Sea sole or grey shrimp bisque in L'Épicerie restaurant, and made-to-order omelettes for breakfast.

much talked about for its concept and comfort, the rooms spacious and tastefully furnished, offset by contemporary Belgian photography. Given the location, one tram stop from Louise métro station, it's no surprise that standard weekday rates are €200-plus – but weekend ones can be half that, a real bargain.

Budget

Rembrandt

42 rue de la Concorde, 1050 Brussels (02 512 71 39, www.hotelrembrandt.be). Métro Louise then tram 94. **Rooms** 12. **Map** p305 E8.

There's something rather quaint about this favourite cheapie, with a reception that closes at 10pm and a breakfast room filled with twee china ornaments and gilt-framed still-lifes. The rooms are similarly homely, featuring high ceilings, flowery wallpaper, old dark wood furniture and framed prints on the wall. Two cats complete the picture. All in all, clean, quirky, great value and well located.

ST-GILLES

Deluxe

★ Manos Premier

100-106 chaussée de Charleroi, 1060 Brussels (02 537 96 82, www.manospremier.com). Métro Louise. **Rooms** 50. **Map** p305 D8.

With its ivy-clad front dotted with fairy lights, there's something undeniably romantic about the Manos Premier. It's a converted townhouse with just 50 rooms, so when you step inside it feels like you're entering someone's home (which is not surprising, since it's been run by the same Greek family for more than three decades). While the rooms are comfortable and elegantly fitted, with antiques and Louis XVI-style decor, the hotel's real attractions lie elsewhere. The Kolya restaurant, open for lunch and dinner, has a lovely conservatory; there's a great African-themed bar with striped carpets, curvy velvet armchairs and leopard skin; and the spacious, terraced garden is a real oasis of peace. There's even a fully equipped gym. The icing on the cake, however, is the magnificent, Moorish-styled hammam, with a jacuzzi and sauna.

▶ *The hotel's plainer, four-star sister, the Manos Stéphanie, is located along the street at 28 chaussée de Charleroi (02 539 02 50, www.manosstephanie. com). A newer, funkier branch, Be Manos (23-27 square de l'Aviation, 02 520 65 65, www.bemanos. com) lies between the city centre and Midi station.*

Expensive

Pullman Brussels Centre Midi Hotel

1 place Victor Horta, 1060 Brussels (02 528 98 00, www.accorhotels.com). Métro/pré-métro Gare du Midi. **Rooms** 237.
See p277 **First Class**.

Vintage Hotel

45 rue Dejoncker, 1060 Brussels (02 533 99 80, www.vintagehotel.be). Métro Louise. **Rooms** 29. **Map** p305 D8.

The Vintage is fabulously retro, all swirly wallpaper and Eames chairs. Pride of place, though, goes to the gleaming, Elvis-era Airstream caravan in the forecourt, the largest and most lavish of the artefacts garnered at various auctions and car-boot sales by hoteliers Isabelle and Fabian Henrion. The other unusual feature is the wine bar, expertly stocked by Belgian vintners Ad Bibendum, but looking for all the world like the spaceport waiting room in *2001*.

Moderate

Pantone Hotel

1 place Loix, 1060 Brussels (02 541 48 98, www. pantonehotel.com). Métro Hôtel des Monnaies, or tram 92, 97. **Rooms** 61. **Map** p305 D9.

Michel Penneman and Olivier Hannaert have created a contemporary hotel according to the Pantone colour-matching scheme. Limes, mauves and deep reds splash bright hues over the guestrooms and public areas, each given its respective catalogue number in the iconic canon of Pantone. Light, spacious rooms provide a fitting backdrop and feature comfortable beds and pillows. Facilities and amenities are otherwise fairly sparse but, given the mid-range price bracket and location 300m from avenue Louise, you're getting something to write home about.

Park Inn by Radisson Brussels Midi

3 place Marcel Broodthaers, 1060 Brussels (02 535 14 00, www.parkinn.com/hotel-brussels). Métro/ pré-métro Gare du Midi. **Rooms** 142. **Map** p304 A8. *See p277* **First Class**.

Budget

Les Bluets

124 rue Berckmans, 1060 Brussels (02 534 39 83, www.bluets.be). Métro Hôtel des Monnaies. **Rooms** 8. **Map** p304 C9.

This place is as colourful as the couple who run it: an eccentric Belgian-English lady and her Colombian husband. Set in a building dating from 1864, Les Bluets has been a hotel for more than 30 years and has acquired a fair amount of decorative features in that time. Every room is crammed with antiques, kitsch holiday souvenirs and what look like jumble-sale buys, while plants and flowers spill out from balconies and bathrooms. Nothing is standard – the decor, the room sizes or the amenities. Smokers and noisy young people are not welcome as guests. Check-in is from 11am to 10pm, and cash payments are preferred.

BED & BREAKFAST

B&Bs in Brussels (also known as *maisons* or *chambres d'hôtes*) are traditional in that they involve staying in someone's house – it's not a euphemism for a cheap hotel. Be prepared to respect the owner's foibles and accept that hotel-style services are not on offer. The appeal lies in the chance to stay with Belgians.

Bed & Brussels

02 646 07 37, www.bnb-brussels.be.

B&Bs throughout Brussels can be booked through this friendly agency that visits homes regularly. The

Pantone Hotel.

website has plenty of pictures and allows you to see a 360-degree panorama of the place you're booking. Weekly rates and longer rentals are also available.

Chambres en Ville

19 rue de Londres, Ixelles, 1050 Brussels (02 512 92 90, www.chambresenville.be). Métro Trône. **Rooms** 3; **studios** 2. **No credit cards. Map** p305 F7.

There's no better endorsement than word of mouth, and much of Philippe Guilmin's custom comes via recommendations. You could easily walk past the ordinary front door, behind which lies a very attractive, good-value place to rest your head. The sympathetic, erudite and competently English-speaking Guilmin is hospitality itself, his three rooms individually decorated and boasting spacious en-suite bathrooms. The rooms feature stone or stripped wooden floors, high ceilings and windows, wall hangings and homely touches such as fresh flowers. The large breakfast table is often shared with Guilmin's cosmopolitan clientele – middle-aged academics, art historians, Brussophiles – pleased with the proximity to the restaurants of Ixelles, the Royal Quarter, a métro station, and peace and quiet. An across-the-board rate of €110, with breakfast, increases to €120 if you're only staying one night. The third-floor studios are rented by the week, fortnight or month.

Sweet Brussels

78 avenue de Stalingrad, Grand'Place & Around, 1000 Brussels (0486 259 137 mobile, www.sweetbrussels.be). Pré-métro Lemonnier. **Rooms** 3; **apartments** 2. **Map** p304 B6.

This luxurious B&B, all high ceilings, parquet floors and filled with natural light, is refined down to the fresh juices at breakfast. Considering they contain fridge-freezers and four-hob cookers, the apartments are a steal at a similar price to the rooms. Attractive rates are offered for longer-term stays. Box-spring beds are fitted throughout, as well as wide flatscreen TVs. Convenient for Midi station, on the main drag to the city centre, Sweet Brussels also stands close to side streets that become a little edgier after dark – have your wits about you if coming back round the houses from a night out.

YOUTH HOSTELS

With the arrival in Brussels of one of Germany's big hostel/hotel chains, Meininger, which set up in a huge former brewery by the canal, the days of curfews and institutionalised bedding seem quaint. Three hostels in Brussels are affiliated with Hostelling International (www.hihostels.com) – two belong to the French-language Walloon organisation Les Auberges de Jeunesse (www.lesaubergesdejeunesse.be/en_us), one to its Flemish counterpart, Vlaamse JeugdHerbergen (www.jeugdherbergen.be/en). All have had to move with the times, but still require everyone to be out of their rooms from late morning to mid afternoon.

Bruegel (YHI)

2 rue du St-Esprit, Marolles, 1000 Brussels (02 511 04 36, www.jeugdherbergen.be/en/overview-brussel). Métro Gare Centrale. **Beds** 135. **Map** p301 C6.

This hostel is set on a pleasant church square near the Sablon, a short walk from the Gare Centrale and the Grand'Place. Another bonus is the fact that nearly a third of the rooms are en-suite, and 26 are one- or two-bedded. Reception operates until 1am, but checked-in guests can access the building 24/7. And with the late-opening Backpacker Bar, there's always time for a nightcap.

Centre Vincent Van Gogh (CHAB)

8 rue Traversière, St-Josse, 1210 Brussels (02 217 01 58, www.chab.be). Métro Botanique. **Beds** 100. **Map** p306 F2.

Currently undergoing major changes, this hostel is often used by school groups visiting the European Parliament. Housed in two buildings, the Van Gogh makes up for its bare rooms with a programme of entertainment. As well as occasional live music, there's a billiard room and book exchange. Those travelling in smaller groups may do better elsewhere in town. Lock-out is between 11am and 3pm.

★ Meininger Hotel Brussels City Center

33 quai du Hainaut, Molenbeek, 1080 Brussels (02 588 14 74, www.meininger-hotels.com/ en/hotels/brussels). Métro Comte de Flandre. **Beds** 719. **Map** p302 A3.

Offering the comforts of a budget chain with the facility to offer youth groups communal lodging, the Meininger generally creates its properties from centrally located, large institutional buildings – in this case, the former Belle-Vue brewery overlooking the canal. With no lock-outs or membership requirements, Meininger treats visitors as travellers to be catered for rather than numbers to suit a system. Original art on the walls of the public areas – the old brewery acted as an exhibition centre before its latest conversion – adds a little colour to the red-brick surroundings. Officially located in the otherwise soulless borough of Molenbeek, the Meininger stands a short walk from the bar hub of rue de Flandre over the canal.

Sleep Well Youth Hotel

23 rue du Damier, Grand'Place & Around, 1000 Brussels (02 218 50 50, www.sleepwell.be). Métro/ pré-métro Rogier or De Brouckère. **Beds** 250. **Map** p303 D3.

This 'youth hotel' feels less institutionalised than youth hostels. Private doubles now feature flatscreen TVs and fridges (and no lock-out times except from 11am to 3pm), while the bright communal rooms (sleeping up to six) feel less like dormitories. All sleeping units have private showers. Film nights, board games, table football and cycle rental are other features – plus a location behind the shopping street of rue Neuve and a five-minute walk to the Grand'Place.

Getting Around

TRAVEL ADVICE

For up-to-date information on travel to a specific country – including the latest on safety and security, health issues, local laws and customs – contact your home country government's department of foreign affairs. Most have websites with useful advice for would-be travellers.

AUSTRALIA
www.smartraveller.gov.au

CANADA
www.voyage.gc.ca

NEW ZEALAND
www.safetravel.govt.nz

REPUBLIC OF IRELAND
foreignaffairs.gov.ie

UK
www.fco.gov.uk/travel

USA
www.state.gov/travel

ARRIVING & LEAVING

By air

Brussels Airport
0900 700 00, www.brussels airport.be.
Brussels' main airport is located at Zaventem, 14 kilometres (nine miles) north-east of the capital, and there are good road and rail connections into the city centre. You'll find the information desk (open 6am-10pm daily) in the check-in area. Hotel information and a phone link for reservations are in the arrivals section. Hotel shuttle buses run from level 0, platform E.

A train service (02 528 28 28, www.belgianrail.be), runs to Gare du Midi, Gare Centrale and Gare du Nord. Tickets cost €8.50, first-class €10.30. There are six trains an hour from 6am to midnight; journey time is 20mins. Women travelling alone at night are safest to alight at Gare Centrale.

The **Airport Line bus No.12** (070 23 2000, www.stib.be) leaves the airport three times an hour between 5.30am and 8pm Mon-Fri, making six stops on its way to the EU Quarter; it costs €4.50 (or €6 from the driver). Outside of these times you need to take the No.21, which stops four times on the way to the EU QUarter.

De Lijn bus 471 (070 220 200, www.delijn.be) also travels between Brussels Gare du Nord and the airport; a single ticket costs €3 (or €4.50 from the driver). A **Brussels Airlines Express** bus (052 33 40 00) runs hourly to Antwerp from 4am (6am Sun) to midnight and costs €10 for a single ticket.

Taxis wait by the arrivals building and should display a yellow and blue licence. The fare to central Brussels is around €40 – many accept credit cards but check first.

Wheelchair users can book a taxi from **Taxi Hendriks** (02 752 98 00, www.hendriks.be).

Car rental desks located in the arrivals hall are generally open from 6.30am to 11.30pm daily.

Charleroi Airport
07 815 27 22, www.charleroi-airport.com
Budget airlines use this airport, 55 kilometres (34 miles) south of Brussels. Local bus A connects with arrivals and runs the 20-minute journey to **Charleroi** train station, where a half-hourly train takes 50 minutes to reach Brussels (combined ticket with city transport €14.40).

Brussels City Shuttle (07 135 33 15, www.voyages-lelan.be) runs a bus (€10 one-way) from Charleroi airport to Brussels Gare du Midi. Journey time is about an hour. The taxi rank outside Charleroi airport is chaotic and unreliable. The standard price to Charleroi station is €20, and to Brussels around €100, but agree a price beforehand.

By rail

There are up to ten Eurostar trains a day between London St Pancras and Brussels Midi, with a journey time of one hour 50 minutes. Check in at least 30 minutes before departure.

Eurostar St Pancras
08432 186186, www.eurostar.com.

Eurostar Gare du Midi
02 528 28 28, www.eurostar.com.
Open 8am-8pm daily. **Map** p304 A7.

By car

To drive to Brussels from the UK, Eurotunnel can transport you and your vehicle from the M20 near Folkestone to Coquelles near Calais in 35 minutes. There are motorway connections to Brussels from there. Eurotunnel is a 24-hour service with up to three trains an hour 7am-midnight and one every two hours during the night. There are facilities for the disabled. Tickets can be bought from a travel agent, Eurotunnel's website or call centre, or, more expensively, on arrival at the tolls. Hertz and Eurotunnel operate a Le Swap rental system for left-hand and right-hand drive hire cars in France and the UK.

Eurotunnel
UK 08443 353535, www. eurotunnel.com. **Open** 8am-7pm Mon-Fri; 8am-5.30pm Sat & Bank Hols; 9am-5.30pm Sun. Ticket prices depend on the time and length of travel, with cheaper fares available for advance booking. Fares start from £73 single. There are discounts for frequent travellers.

By coach

Eurolines (UK)
08717 818 178, www.eurolines. co.uk. **Open** 24hrs daily.
A return fare from London to Brussels starts at around £60 with advance booking discounts and cheaper rates for children and senior passengers.

Eurolines (Brussels)
80 rue du Progrès, Schaerbeek (02 274 13 50, www.eurolines.be). Métro/pré-métro Gare du Nord. **Open** 9am-6pm Mon-Fri; 9am-5pm Sat. **Map** p303 D2.
Eurolines buses depart from CCN Gare du Nord (80 rue du Progrès) and offer services to 600 destinations in 33 countries. A return ticket to London Victoria costs from €37 with the journey taking around seven hours.

PUBLIC TRANSPORT

The city's cheap, integrated public transport system is made up of métro, rail, buses and trams, with tickets allowing for any changes en route up to an hour. A map is invaluable, as stations are not well signposted.

Métro, trams & buses

The public transport network in the capital is run by **STIB/ MIVB** (Société des Transports Intercommunaux de Bruxelles). Maps and timetables are available from information centres at Gare du Midi, Porte de Namur and Rogier. **De Lijn** runs suburban buses from its main Gare du Midi terminal. Public transport operates from around 5.30am to midnight, depending on the location.

De Lijn
070 220 200, www.delijn.be. **Open** *phone only* 7am-6pm Mon-Fri; 10am-6pm Sat. Flemish buses operating from Brussels and around Flanders. Fares are based on time of journey. The cost of a ticket is €3 for 60 minutes during which you can make unlimited changes. After 60 minutes, you can complete your journey but can no longer change.

STIB/MIVB
BOOTIK Porte de Namur (07 023 20 00, www.stib.be). Métro Porte de Namur. **Open** 8am-6pm Mon-Fri; 10am-6pm Sat. **Map** p305 E7.

Tickets, lines & passes

Tickets are sold at métro and rail stations, on buses and trams, at STIB info centres and at newsagents. Points of sale for monthly passes are métro Porte de Namur, Gare du Midi, Rogier and Merode, SNCB stations and online. Tickets must be validated, by using the machines at métro stations and on trams and buses at the start of the journey. They are then valid for one hour on all forms of transport and with unlimited changes, but require revalidating each time.

A new electronic system of ticketing is slowly being introduced across the STIB network so there are currently two types of ticket; **Jump** is a card system offering single, five or ten journeys as well as one- or three-day passes – validate these in the orange machines. **MOBIB** is the new electronic system – touch the card on the red reader to validate the

fare. A MOBIB card requires a €5 refundable deposit and a passport photograph. Fares for MOBIB are slightly cheaper than Jump.

The **Brussels Card** for tourists offers unlimited public transport for one, two or three days, plus admission to 30 museums, for €22, €29 or €35 respectively. Children under six travel free if accompanied by an adult with a valid ticket.

A **night bus** service, NOCTIS, was introduced in 2007. The 11 routes run on Friday and Saturday only and end at 3am. A single journey is: Jump €2.10, MOBIB €1.60 or €2.50 from the driver.

Métro stations are indicated by a white letter 'M' on a blue background, while red and white signs mark tram and bus stops. Brussels is served by four métro lines (1, 2, 5, 6), plus two pré-métro underground tram lines (3, 4) running north–south through town, linking Gare du Nord and Gare du Midi, and pré-métro 7 linking Laeken and Uccle.

Fares

One journey
Jump €2.10 or €2.50 (from driver), MOBIB €1.60.

Ten journeys
Jump €14, MOBIB €11.30.

One day
Jump €7.50, MOBIB €4.20.

Three days
Jump €18, MOBIB €9.20.

Belgian railways

SNCB (02 528 28 28, www. belgianrail.be) runs an efficient, cheap national rail system. Most tourist spots are an hour or so from Brussels. Tickets can be bought online and printed at home or at the station, but leave plenty of time for queues.

Brussels has three linked mainline stations: **Gare Centrale** ('North Station', 1km from the Grand'Place), **Gare du Midi** ('South Station') and **Gare du Nord** ('North Station'). All have baggage facilities. Midi's left luggage office is by the Eurostar terminal. *See p286* **Lost Property**.

Disabled travel

For those travelling outside Brussels by train or on certain bus services, the disabled passenger pays and any accompanying person travels free. Contact the train station in advance for travel with a wheelchair,

which is carried free. There are also reductions for the blind (call SNCB for details; *see left*).

TAXIS

Ranks are found by mainline stations and at strategic points such as Porte de Namur, place d'Espagne, the Bourse and De Brouckère.

Taxis can take up to four people and the tip is included in the meter fare. If you have a complaint to make against a driver, or you've lost an item in a taxi, record the registration number of the vehicle and contact the taxi service of the Ministry of Brussels Capital Region on 0800 147 95 or www.brusselstaxi.be. The clock starts at €2.40 (€4.40 after 10pm) and is then charged at €1.80 per kilometre if the journey is inside the 19 communes – €2.70 outside.

Autolux
02 411 41 42, www.autolux.be.

Taxis Bleus
02 268 00 00, www.taxisbleus.be.

Taxis Verts
02 349 49 49, www.taxisverts.be.

DRIVING

It's not easy driving around Brussels. You're better off taking public transport or walking. Dents on the right side of many cars show the damage caused by the *priorité à droite* rule, the reason for so many accidents. Cars must give way to any vehicle from the right, even on a major road, unless marked otherwise. A white sign with a yellow diamond on your road means cars from the right must stop for you.

A comprehensive tunnel system links major points in the city, making it possible to traverse Brussels without seeing the light of day. The inner ring is a pentagon of boulevards (marked with signs showing a blue ring on which the yellow dot is your current location). The outer ring is a pear shape, divided into an east and west motorway ring.

The speed limit on motorways is 120kph (75mph), on main roads 90kph (56mph), and in built-up areas 50kph (31mph). There are no tolls on Belgian roads. The wearing of seat belts is compulsory in the front and rear of the car. The legal maximum blood alcohol level is 0.5g/l (approx one glass of wine).

A driving licence from your home country is acceptable if you're staying less than 90 days in Belgium.

ESSENTIAL INFORMATION

If your car is towed, go to the nearest police station to get a document releasing it. Police may give you the document free of charge or demand a nominal fee, depending on the area of town. They will then give the address of the garage holding your car. Present the police letter there and pay another fee – the sum can vary – to get your car back. On-the-spot fines are common for speeding.

It takes 40 minutes to reach Antwerp, 50 minutes to reach Ghent, and 90 minutes for Liège and Bruges. Calais and Amsterdam are two-and-a-half hours away, Paris three hours. Names are signposted in two languages (except in Flanders); Antwerp is given as Anvers/Antwerpen, Ghent is Gand/Gent, and Bruges is Bruges/Brugge.

For information on importing a car, registering a vehicle or getting a licence in Belgium, see www.mobilit.belgium.be.

Breakdown services

Royal Automobile Club de Belgique
24hr emergency service 02 287 09 00, enquiries (8.30am-5pm Mon-Fri) 02 287 09 11, www.racb.com.

Tourist Club Belgique (TCB)
24hr emergency service 070 344 777, enquiries (9am-5pm Mon-Fri) 02 233 23 27, www.touring.be.

Car hire

To hire a car, you must have a full current driving licence (normally with a minimum of one year's driving experience) and carry a passport or identity card, as well as a credit card in your name. The major car hire companies can be found in the arrivals hall of Zaventem airport and at Gare du Midi. Hire rates at the airport can be steeper than those you'll be quoted in town.

Avis
070 223 001, www.avis.be.

Budget
02 789 86 64, www.budget.be.

Europcar
02 348 92 12, www.europcar.be.

Hertz
02 717 3201, www.hertz.be.

Repairs & services

Carrosserie Européenne
933 chaussée d'Haecht, Evere (02 231 00 69, www.carrosserie-

europeenne.be). **Open** 7.30am-noon, 1-6pm Mon-Thur; 7.30am-noon, 1-5pm Fri.
Also check *auto-carrosseries – reparations/Carrosserie herstellingen* in the *Yellow Pages.*

CYCLING

Cycling on the main roads in central Brussels can be a daunting prospect. However, cycling the back streets and out of town is generally safe. Lanes are shown by white lines and are less secure than the cycle tracks, which are separated from the traffic. Some city lanes go against the flow of traffic. A map of local lanes and tracks can be found at **Pro-Vélo**.

In Brussels city, the rent-a-bike scheme **Villo!** allows you to rent a bike from any of 346 bike stations.

Pro-Vélo
15 rue de Londres, Ixelles (02 502 73 55, www.provelo.org).
Organises guided tours at 2pm (Dutch), 2.30pm (French) on Sundays from April to October. Tours cost €10 for half a day, €13 the whole day. Bike hire costs €8 half-day, €10 whole-day.

Villo!
078 05 11 10, www.villo.be.
Villo! is an urban cycling scheme that allows you to hire a city bike for any period. For visitors there is an option of a one or seven-day basic registration (€1.60 or €7.65) bought from any of the stations using your bank debit card. You are then able to use the bikes when you like, using a pin number. The first 30 minutes are free, then start from 5c for the next 30 minutes and €1 for the next hour. Bikes can be picked up and dropped off at any of the stations – maps are on the stations or there are apps available for WAP and iPhones. See website for details.

WALKING

The centre of town, although uneven, is easy to navigate, with many traffic-free streets around the Grand'Place. The only real slog is the walk up to the Upper Town. The **Institut Géographique National** (02 629 82 82, www.ngi.be) has maps of trails outside the centre.

GUIDED TOURS

Bus tours

There are two main hop-on-hop-off bus tour companies, both offering

24hr tickets. They also both run day trips to Antwerp, Bruges and Ghent.

For pre-booked groups, **Brukselbinnenstebuiten** (02 218 38 78, www.brukselbinnenstebuiten.be) is a non-profit association running small bus tours with local guides. Prices start at €190 for a half-day. They also organise walking tours. **ARAU** (*see below*) runs an art nouveau bus tour with an English-speaking guide.

Brussels City Tours
02 513 77 44, www.brussels-city-tours.com.
Tours with themes: half-day city and chocolate tour €31; €28 reductions.Half-day Waterloo €39; €36 reductions. Buses run every 30 minutes 10am-4pm Mon-Fri, Sun; 10am-5pm Sat. The best place to join these tours is at the Bourse.

Visit Brussels Line
www.city-discovery.com.
Tickets €17.99; €9.99 reductions. Buses run every hour 10am-4pm daily. Join at Gare Centrale.

Walking tours

Be.guided (mobile 02 495 538 163, www.beguided.be) is a walking tour service. All guides are recognised by Tourism Flanders and walks are led by enthusiastic guides.
Brussels Walks or **Klare Lijn** (0493 50 40 60 mobile, www.brusselswalks.be) organises walks (€120 per guide for a 3hr walk, €210 per guide for an 8hr tour) starting at the BIP tourist centre (*see p289*). See website for dates.
ARAU (02 219 33 45, www.arau.org) organises themed walks with an English-speaking guide – see website for details. Walking tours cost €10.

Boat tours

Between May and September there are canal and river cruises in and around Brussels (www.brusselsbywater.be). These include a trip on the Brussels sea canal. Boarding is at 6 avenue du Port (métro Yser).

River Tours
84 boulevard d'Ypres, 1000 Brussels (02 218 54 10, www.rivertours.be). **Brussels canal tour** (50mins) 10am, 11am, 2pm, 3pm, 4pm Tue-Sun. **Tickets** €4; €3 reductions. **Waterbus to Vilvoorde tour** (55mins). Hourly except 1pm 10am-5pm Tue-Thur. **Tickets** €3; €1.50 reductions. **No credit cards.**

Resources A-Z

AGE RESTRICTIONS

In Belgium, you have to be 18 years old to vote or get married, and 16 to smoke, drink and have sex. For driving, the minimum age is 18 (but car hire firms won't rent to under-21s).

BUSINESS

Chambers of commerce

American Chamber of Commerce 60 rue du Trône, 1050 Brussels (02 513 67 70, www.amcham.be).
British Chamber of Commerce 11 boulevard Bischoffheim, 1000 Brussels (02 540 90 30, www.britcham.be).

Conferences & seminars

Brussels International 02 800 3746, www.brusselsinternational.be. This non-profit regional public service organisation is supported by the City of Brussels and its services are free of charge.
Management Centre Europe 118 rue de l'Aqueduc, 1050 Ixelles (02 543 21 20, www.mce.be). This international business and training organisation can put together a variety of large seminars and conferences.

Couriers

DHL 02 715 50 50, www.dhl.be.
FedEx 02 752 75 75, www.fedex.com/be.
UPS 078 250 877, www.ups.com.

Office services

Papeterie du Parc Léopold 177 rue Belliard, 1040 Brussels (02 230 69 12, www.parcleopold.com). This top-notch stationers is located in the EU Quarter.
Regus 02 234 77 11, www.regus.be. International company that rents out fully equipped offices; there are six locations around Brussels.

Secretarial services

Manpower 02 218 36 00, www.manpower.be.
Tempo Team 02 250 32 51, www.tempo-team.be.

Translators & interpreters

Aplin 02 808 07 65, www.aplin.be.

CONSUMER

To complain about shops selling faulty merchandise or for general consumer protection issues, contact **Economie** (0800 120 33, www.mineco.fgov.be).
If you're dissatisfied with the hygiene standards in a restaurant, café, food store or supermarket, contact the **Federal Agency for the Safety of the Food Chain** (02 211 82 60, www.afsca.be).
To complain about a taxi driver, call the taxi service of the **Ministry of Brussels Capital Region** on 0800 940 01. Operators can take your call in English; note the number of the taxi to lodge a complaint.

CUSTOMS

The following customs allowances apply to those bringing duty-free goods into Belgium from outside the European Union:

● 200 cigarettes or 100 cigarillos or 50 cigars or 250g (8.82oz) tobacco.
● Two litres of still table wine and either one litre of spirits/strong liqueurs (over 22% alcohol) or two litres of fortified wine (under 22% alcohol)/sparkling wine/other liqueurs.
● 500g coffee or 200g coffee extracts/essences.
● 50g perfume.
● 250ml toilet water.
● 100g tea or 40g tea extracts/essences.
● Other goods for non-commercial use up to a maximum value of €300 for land/sea arrivals, €430 for air arrivals.

If you're travelling from an EU member state, you're allowed to bring in as many duty-paid goods as you can carry. But if you bring more than 110 litres of beer, 90 litres of wine, ten litres of spirits and 800 cigarettes, you may be asked to pay an additional tax. There's no limit to the amount of foreign currency that can be brought in or out of Belgium.

DISABLED

New buildings in Brussels are required by law to be fully accessible to people who are not fully mobile, and most of the city's large hotels are wheelchair-friendly. That said, the cobbled pavements are very uneven (tactile pavement slabs are installed at all road crossing points) and there are lots of steep hills to negotiate. The city's many older buildings are often not equipped to handle disabled visitors.
Public transport is increasingly well adapted for disabled passengers – all trams and buses now have low-level platforms for access, and new buses have retractable ramps. Many métro stations are also equipped for wheelchairs. An **STIB minibus** (02 515 23 65, www.stib.be) with vehicles equipped for wheelchairs, is available to transport disabled travellers door-to-door 6.30am-11pm for the same price as a métro ticket (book in advance). STIB has

---

LOCAL CLIMATE

Average temperatures and monthly rainfall in Brussels.

	High (°C/°F)	Low (°C/°F)	Rainfall (mm/in)
Jan	7/45	2/36	53/2.1
Feb	10/50	2/36	43/1.7
Mar	13/55	4/39	49/1.9
Apr	17/63	6/43	53/2.1
May	20/68	9/48	65/2.6
June	23/73	12/54	54/2.1
July	25/77	15/59	62/2.4
Aug	26/79	16/61	42/1.6
Sept	23/73	12/54	54/2.1
Oct	20/68	8/46	60/2.4
Nov	14/57	4/39	51/2.0
Dec	7/44	3/37	59/2.3

also installed braille information panels and floor-level tactile guides in all métro stations.

ELECTRICITY

The current used in Belgium is 220V AC. It works fine with British appliances (which run on 240V), but you'll need an adaptor. American appliances run on 110V and you'll need to buy a converter. Good hotels should be able to supply adaptors and converters.

EMBASSIES

It's advisable to call to check the opening hours of the embassies listed below (different departments within the embassies often keep different hours). You may also need to make an appointment. In emergencies it's worth ringing after hours; there may be staff on hand to deal with crises. For embassies not listed here, check the *Yellow Pages* or visit www.brussels.angloinfo.com.

American Embassy 25 boulevard du Régent, 1000 Brussels (02 508 21 11, http://belgium. usembassy.gov).
Australian Embassy 56 avenue des Arts, 1000 Brussels (02 286 05 00, www.eu.mission.gov.au).
British Embassy 10 avenue d'Auderghem, 1040 Brussels (02 287 62 11, www.gov.uk/ government/world/belgium).
Canadian Embassy 2 avenue de Tervuren, 1040 Brussels (02 741 06 11, www.ambassade-canada.be).
Irish Embassy 180 chaussée d'Etterbeek, 1040 Brussels (02 282 34 00, www.embassyofireland.be).
New Zealand Embassy Level 7, 9-31 avenue des Nerviens, 1040 Brussels (02 512 10 40, www. nzembassy.com/belgium).

EMERGENCIES

Emergency 112
Police 101
Fire brigade/Ambulance 100
Belgian Red Cross 24-hour ambulance service 105
Belgian Poison Control Centre 070 245 245, www.poisoncentre.be

GAY & LESBIAN

English-speaking Gay Group in Brussels www.eggbrussels.be. Hosts informal parties every month for people of all nationalities.
International Lesbian & Gay Association 02 609 54 10, www.ilga-europe.org.

Network of international bodies that campaign to end discrimination against gays and lesbians.
Rainbowhouse 02 503 59 90, www.rainbowhouse.be.
A meeting and information point.
Tels Quels Helpline 02 502 00 70, 02 511 31 48, www.telsquels.be. This collective organises events and activities for parents, students, singles and other groups.

HEALTH

Belgium has an excellent healthcare system, with a ratio of one doctor for every 278 people and well-run, modern hospitals. You'll also find that many doctors speak English.

Accident & emergency

The following hospitals can provide 24-hour emergency assistance. Call 105 for the Red Cross 24-hour ambulance service.

Cliniques Universitaires St-Luc 10 avenue Hippocrate, Woluwe-St-Lambert (02 764 11 11, www.saintluc.be). Métro Alma.
Hôpital Brugmann 4 place van Gehuchten, Laeken (02 477 21 11, www.chu-brugmann.be). Métro Houba-Brugmann.
Hôpital Erasme 808 route de Lennik, Anderlecht (02 555 31 11, www.erasme.ulb.ac.be). Métro Erasme.
Hôpital St-Pierre 322 rue Haute, Marolles (02 535 31 11, www. stpierre-bru.be). Métro/pré-métro Porte de Hal or bus 27, 48.
Hôpital Universitaire des Enfants Reine Fabiola Paediatric emergency room, 15 avenue Jean-Jacques Crocq, Laeken (02 477 33 11, www.huderf.be). Métro Houba-Brugmann.

Complementary & alternative medicine

Acupuncture, chiropractic medicine, homeopathy and osteopathy are recognised, but alternative medicine in Belgium still lags behind many other European countries. See www.homeopathy-unio.be for details of doctors and dentists who subscribe to homeopathic principles. There are homeopathy sections in many pharmacies.

Contraception & abortion

Condoms are sold at most chemists and supermarkets (but condom vending machines are not very widespread). Birth-control pills

can be bought at pharmacies with a doctor's prescription.
Abortion is legal up to the 12th week of pregnancy. After that, in cases of foetal abnormality or health risks to the mother, the agreement of two independent doctors is required.

Dentists

Dental care in Belgium is of a high standard. The Health Unit at the American Embassy (02 508 22 25) can provide a list of English-speaking dental practitioners, as can the Community Help Service helpline (02 648 40 14). Call 02 426 10 26 for a current list of dentists on duty at evenings and weekends.

Doctors

Call 02 479 18 18 to find a doctor or click on www.mgbru.be. You're free to choose any doctor, no matter where you live, and you don't need a referral. You can often walk in without an appointment during weekday office hours. If you're too sick to go into the surgery, some doctors will make house calls. After hours, you can often reach your doctor (or one on call) through an answering service. Even if you're insured, expect to pay for your visit on the spot in cash. Keep receipts to claim reimbursement from your insurance company.

Hospitals

Outpatient clinics at private or university hospitals have a good reputation for their state-of-the-art technology, but often suffer from bureaucracy and crowded waiting rooms. Despite the drawbacks, they have a concentration of specialists in one place, as well as laboratory and X-ray facilities.
For details of Brussels' emergency hospitals, *see left*. A full list is available at www.hospitals.be.

Opticians

There are many opticians in Brussels. The American Embassy (02 508 22 25) can provide a list of English-speaking ones.

Pharmacies

Pharmacies (*pharmacies/apotheeks*) in Belgium are clearly marked with a green cross. Most are open 9am to 6pm weekdays, plus Saturday morning or afternoon. For the nearest

ESSENTIAL INFORMATION

pharmacy on weekend or night duty, phone 0900 105 00, or enter your postcode at www.pharmacie.be.

STDs, HIV & AIDS

See also below **Helplines**.

Aide Info SIDA *02 514 29 65, www.aideinfosida.be.*
Le Centre Elisa *11 rue des Alexiens, 1000 Brussels (02 535 30 03, www.stpierre-bru.be/fr/service/ autres/elisa.html).*
Anonymous HIV and STD tests.

HELPLINES

Brussels' large foreign community has established an extensive network of support groups. Unless indicated in the listings, the groups below are for English speakers.

Aide Info Sida *0800 20 120.*
Open 6-9pm Mon-Fri.
Alcoholics Anonymous *02 216 09 08, www.aa-europe.net/ countries/belgium.htm.* **Open** 24hrs daily.
Community Help Service (CHS) *02 648 40 14, www.chs-belgium.org.* **Open** 24hrs daily.
Drugs Information *02 227 52 52.* **Open** 24hrs daily.
Rape Crisis *02 534 36 36.*
Open 9.30am-5.30pm Mon-Fri.
Suicide Prevention *0800 32 123.*
Open 24hrs daily.
Victim Support *02 537 66 10.*
Open 9am-5pm daily.

ID

Belgium has an identity card system; citizens are expected to be able to show their card and thus prove their identity at any time. As a visitor, you're also expected to carry some sort of photographic ID, such as your passport, with you at all times.

INSURANCE

As members of the EU, the UK and Ireland have reciprocal health agreements with Belgium. You'll need to apply for the necessary European Health Insurance Card (EHIC) at home first. British citizens can obtain this by calling 0300 330 1350 or online at www.ehic.org.uk. Try to get the EHIC at least two weeks before you travel.

For long-term visitors, after six months in residence you're eligible for cover under Belgium's basic health insurance system, the *mutuelle*. You're allowed to choose whichever *mutuelle* best meets

your needs. For phone numbers, consult the local *Yellow Pages* under 'Mutualités/Ziekenfondsen'.

INTERNET

Central Brussels has few internet cafés, though some small telephone cabin shops offer internet access. Many bars, cafés and hotels offer free Wi-Fi. Retailer **Fnac** (www. fnac.be) has a cybercafé.

LEFT LUGGAGE

All the main train stations offer left-luggage offices, open 6am-midnight. Smaller stations have coin-operated lockers.

LIBRARIES

Bibliothèque Royale de Belgique *4 boulevard de l'Empereur, Upper Town (02 519 53 11, www.kbr.be).*
This is the state library, holding everything that's published in Belgium, as well as various foreign publications. Details of the library's enormous catalogue are accessible on the website.
ULB (Université Libre de Bruxelles) *50 avenue Franklin Roosevelt, Ixelles (02 650 21 11, www.bib.ulb.ac.be).*
Although the ULB library is intended for students at the university, it's also open to non-students. It has a large collection of material in English in various media, accessible via the website.

LOST PROPERTY

Report lost belongings to the nearest police station or police HQ at 30 rue du Marché au Charbon, Lower Town (02 279 79 79); bear in mind that you may have trouble finding an English speaker. You must ask for a certificate of loss for insurance purposes. If you happen to lose your passport, contact your embassy or consulate (*see p285* **Embassies**). Below are details for items lost on public transport.

Airlines

Aviapartner *02 723 07 07, www.aviapartner.aero.* **Open** *Phone enquiries* 6am-10pm daily.

Airport

Brussels Airport *0900 700 00, www.brusselsairport.be.* **Open** 7am-10pm Mon-Fri; 7am-8pm Sat, Sun.

Métro, buses & trams

STIB/MIVB *BOOTIK, Porte de Namur, Ixelles (07 023 20 00).* **Open** 8am-6pm Mon-Fri; 10am-6pm Sat. Lost property office located at Porte de Namur métro.

Rail

For articles left on a train, enquire at the nearest station or check with the main rail lost property office at **Gare du Midi** (02 224 88 62). The www.b-rail.be website has an online form to register any losses.

Taxis

If you have the number of the taxi where you left your item, or want to report an item that you've found in a taxi, call the taxi service of the **Ministry of Brussels Capital Region** on 0800 147 95. There's an online form to register loss at www.brusselstaxi.be.

MEDIA

Most newsagents and kiosks in Brussels stock leading papers and magazines from Britain, France, Germany, the Netherlands and elsewhere (including the US). The local press is still surprisingly broad, and runs the gamut from the conservative (*De Standaard*) to the more outrageous (*Humo, Ché*). Belgians are even more spoilt for choice when it comes to TV and BBC is easily available. Nearly all households receive around 40 channels, many from overseas.

Newspapers

La Dernière Heure
www.dhnet.be
Popular right-leaning French-speaking tabloid.
L'Echo
www.lecho.be
Pre-eminent French-speaking business paper in Belgium.
Het Laaste Nieuws
www.hln.be
Once renowned as the traditionally liberal Flemish daily, *HLN* also takes an interest in the seamier side of life.
La Libre Belgique
www.lalibre.be
Catholic French-language daily with a serious tone and look.
Metro
www.metrotime.be
This free paper is available at most métro stations in French (green) and Dutch (blue).

ESSENTIAL INFORMATION

De Morgen
www.demorgen.be
Once the staple of socialist workers, *De Morgen* has evolved into a more general left-wing Flemish daily.
Politico Europe
www.politico.eu
This weekly English-language paper specialises in the workings of the EU.
Le Soir
www.lesoir.be
The most widely read francophone daily is an independent-minded, quality broadsheet. Wednesday's issue comes with *MAD*, an indispensable supplement featuring the week's listings.
De Standaard
www.standaard.be
The biggest Dutch-speaking daily takes few risks, opting for a conservative Catholic angle on most issues.
Vlan
www.vlan.be
Thousands of ads – from property to cars, jobs to junk – appear in this paper every Sunday.

Magazines

The Bulletin
www.xpats.com
Since 2012, the city's English-language weekly has only existed online. Has insider tips on expat life.
Dag Allemaal
www.dagallemaal.be
Dutch-language TV and radio listings magazine.
Kiosque
Twitter: @Kiosque
Pocket-sized, French-language monthly listings magazine with small English section.
La Libre Match
Joint venture between *Paris Match* and *La Libre Belgique*.
Le Vif-Express/Knack
www.levif.be
These sister publications in French and Dutch are the country's only news magazines.

Radio

To keep anglophone pop/rock music at bay, radio stations receiving subsidies must make at least 60 per cent of their music broadcasts in the language of the region from which the station is funded. Commercial stations are free to play as they choose. Frequencies for stations differ in other parts of the country.

French-speaking radio includes **Bruxelles-Capitale** (99.3 MHz), the Brussels-only news station; **La Première** (92.5 MHz), state-owned

and solid; **Radio Contact** (102.2 MHz) and **Radio 21** (93.2 MHz), both popular and poppy; and **Musique 3** (91.2 MHz), classical.

Flemish radio stations include **VRT 1** (91.7 MHz), classical and talk; **VRT 2** (93.7 MHz), Top 40 and oldies; **VRT 3** (89.5 MHz), high culture; and **Studio Brussel** (100.6 MHz), alternative rock and indie.

Television

Cable TV gives Belgians easy access to BBC1 and BBC2, CNN and MTV, as well as channels from France, the Netherlands, Germany, Spain, Portugal and Italy. The main Belgian TV channels include **Kanaal 2**, showing anglophone series and films in their original language; and the state-run **RTBF1 & 2**. The Flemish version is **VRT**.

MONEY

There are euro banknotes for €5, €10, €20, €50, €100, €200 and €500. Coins are worth €1 and €2, plus 1, 2, 5, 10, 20 and 50 cents.

ATMs

ATMs are somewhat difficult to find in the city centre. Gare du Midi has ATMs at the bottom of the Eurostar escalator. As well as using a debit card to withdraw euros, you can also obtain a cash advance on most major credit cards from ATMs. Just keep in mind that cash advance fees can be steep.

Banks

Most banks are open from 9am to 3.30pm or 5pm, Monday to Friday. A few open half-days on Saturdays. Some close for lunch. There will usually be a staff member who speaks English.

Bureaux de change

Banks are the best places to exchange currency. After banking hours you can change money and travellers' cheques at bureaux de change in the centre of town (the money exchange at 88 rue Marché aux Herbes, just off the Grand'Place, is open 10am-7pm Mon-Sat, closed Sun) or at offices in the Gare du Midi (7am-8pm Mon-Fri, 8.30am-8pm Sat, 9am-6.30pm Sun) and Gare Centrale (8am-7.30pm Mon-Fri, 9am-6pm Sat, 10am-5pm Sun). Several banks at the airport give cash advances on credit cards, and convert currency. Most open early and close at 10pm.

Credit/debit cards

Most large shops, restaurants and hotels accept credit cards, including Visa, Mastercard and American Express. Debit cards from other European countries are accepted in most places.

Report card thefts immediately to the police and to the 24-hour services listed below.

American Express *02 676 21 21, www.americanexpress.com.*
Diners Club *02 626 50 24, www.dinersclub.com.*
Mastercard *001 800 307 7309 (toll-free), www.mastercard.com/be.*
Visa *070 344 344, www.visa europe.com.*

Tax

Belgian VAT (TVA) is 21 per cent, but if you're a non-EU resident wanting to make a purchase of more than €125 and plan to take the purchase out of the country within three months, you can buy tax-free. Look for the 'Tax-Free Shopping' logo on shop windows. Bring your non-EU passport to make a purchase and you will be given a Tax-Free shopping cheque that can be stamped by customs officials at the airport and then cashed at the Europe Tax-Free shopping desk (make sure you allow plenty of time at the airport for extra queues).

Shopping tax-free in shops without the Tax-Free logo is more complicated, but usually still possible. You need to request an itemised invoice at the shop and have it stamped by a customs agent when you leave Belgium. Then mail the invoice to the shop, which will send you the refund. This works best if you happen to be flying out of Zaventem – customs officials at Charleroi airport are notoriously impossible to locate.

OPENING HOURS

Many offices close for lunch or close early on Friday, although this is not official. Most shops open from 9am to 6pm, though certain grocery stores and supermarkets remain open until 9pm. Department stores tend to stay open until 9pm one day a week, usually Friday. For late-opening shops, look out for a 'Night Shop' sign.

Most museums are open 9am to 5pm Tuesday to Saturday, and sometimes on Sunday. Nearly all are closed on Monday. Several only open from Easter Sunday to September.

ESSENTIAL INFORMATION

It's wise to call the museum, particularly if it's a smaller one, before visiting.

For banking hours, *see p287* **Money**; for post office hours, *see below* **Postal services**.

POLICE STATIONS

For the police, call 101. The central police station in Brussels is situated at 30 rue du Marché au Charbon (02 279 79 79, www.polbru.be). For other emergency numbers, *see p285* **Emergencies**.

POSTAL SERVICES

Post offices are generally open from 9am to 5pm Monday to Friday, but times can vary. The central office at place de la Monnaie is open until 7pm. Queues in post offices can be long and slow, though a ticketing system is now in place.

Letters mailed to the UK and other European countries usually take two days; the US takes about five days. A letter weighing up to 50g costs €1.20 to any country in Europe. A letter up to 50g to any country in the rest of the world costs €1.42. Price is determined by the size of the envelope. Stick to using local Belgian envelopes, as non-standard sizes – even if different by only a fraction of an inch – can send the cost of postage soaring. Staff will measure to ensure the correct dimensions. Sending a postcard is the same price as a letter.

For postal information and to find the nearest post office to you, refer to the www.post.be website.

Central Post Office *1 boulevard Anspach, Lower Town (02 226 97 00). Métro/pré-métro De Brouckère*. **Open** 8.30am-6pm Mon-Fri; 10.30am-4pm Sat. **Map** p301 C3.

Packages

Packages weighing more than 2kg (4.4lbs) are taken care of by Kilopost or Taxipost, managed by La Poste (www.post.be). Just take any package weighing up to 30kg (66lbs) to the nearest post office. *See also p284* **Couriers**.

RELIGION

Many churches and synagogues hold services in English. For places away from the city centre, it's best to call for directions. See the 'Religious Services' section at www.xpats.com for a full list.

Holy Trinity Church *29 rue Capitaine Crespel, Ixelles (02 511 71 83, www.holytrinity.be). Métro Louise*. **Map** p305 D8. Holy Communion in English is on Sundays at 9am and 10.30am, with Evening Praise at 7pm. An African-style Afternoon Praise is held at 2pm.
Beth Hillel Reform Synagogue of Brussels *80 rue des Primeurs, Forest (02 332 25 28, www.beth-hillel.org). Bus 54 or tram 52*. **Services** 7pm Fri; 10.30am Sat.
Grande Mosquée de Bruxelles & Centre Islamique *14 Parc du Cinquantenaire, EU Quarter (02 735 21 73, www.centreislamique.be). Métro Schuman*. **Map** p309 K5.
International Protestant Church *40 avenue des Héros, Auderghem (02 673 05 81, www.ipcbrussels. org). Métro Herrmann-Debroux, then bus 41*. **English service** 11.15am Sun.
Quaker House *50 square Ambiorix, EU Quarter (02 230 49 35, http:// qkr.be). Métro Schuman*. **Map** p307 J4. **Meetings** 11am Sun; 12.30pm Wed.
St-Nicolas *1 rue au Beurre, Lower Town (02 267 51 64). Métro/ pré-métro Bourse*. **Map** p305 E6. **Mass in English** 10am Sun.
Our Lady of Mercy Parish *10 Place de la Ste-Alliance, Uccle (02 354 53 43, www.olm.be). Bus 43*. **Mass in English** 5pm Sat; 10am Sun.

SAFETY & SECURITY

While generally safe, Brussels is starting to gain some of the less desirable attributes of a big city. Pickpockets and bicycle thieves have become part of the city's landscape, especially in crowded tourist areas during the day, and after dark in the grey streets downtown between Grand'Place and the Gare du Midi. Gangs of pickpockets work the major railway stations, the pré-métro tram serving Midi and incoming international trains. Take the sort of precautions you would in any big city. *See also p285* **Emergencies**.

SMOKING

Smoking in confined public places is banned by law. This amounts to no smoking in train stations (except on open-air platforms) or public buildings such as town halls and theatres. In 2007, a law came in that banned smoking in restaurants if the establishment can't provide a separate smoking area.

STUDY

Brussels is a major European study centre. The city is home to universities that teach in French and Dutch, and many that offer courses in English.

Language schools

Classified ads on www.xpats.com and www.expatica.com are full of people willing to exchange conversation or teach one-to-one. There are numerous language schools in Brussels. The **Alliance Française** (02 788 21 60, www. alliancefr.be) is the leading French-language school, while the major international schools include **Amira** (02 640 68 50, www.amira.be), **Berlitz** (02 649 61 75, www.berlitz. be) and **Language Studies International** (02 217 23 73, www. lsi-be.net). **Fondation 9** (02 627 52 52, www.fondation9.be) offers lessons in all EU languages.

Universities

The two main Brussels universities are split according to language but have large numbers of foreign students. The French-speaking **Université Libre de Bruxelles** or ULB (50 avenue Franklin Roosevelt, Ixelles, 02 650 21 11, www.ulb.ac.be) is the largest with 18,000 students, a third of whom are foreign. The Dutch-speaking **Vrije Universiteit Brussel** or VUB (2 boulevard de la Plaine, Ixelles, 02 629 21 11, www. vub.ac.be) has 9,000 students and two campuses. Although most courses are taught in Dutch, there are a number of English-language postgraduate degrees. **Vesalius College** (2 boulevard de la Plaine, Ixelles, 02 614 81 70, www.vesalius. edu) is part of the VUB.

There are also excellent centres of art and design. The most famous is the **Ecole Nationale Supérieure des Arts Visuels de la Cambre** (21 Abbaye de la Cambre, Ixelles, 02 626 17 80, www.lacambre.be). It offers courses in architecture, graphic design and fashion. The **Académie Royale des Beaux-Arts de Bruxelles** (144 rue du Midi, Lower Town, 02 506 10 10, www.arba-esa.be) is best known for painting and sculpture.

TELEPHONES

Belgacom is the major operator. For a longer stay, sign up for one of its special packages for free or cheaper calls to a country of your choice (visit www.proximus.be or call 0800 558 00 for English customer service). **Telenet** (0800 660 46, www.telenet.be) is the main rival and also offers a range of services with competitive deals. For a short-term stay, you can use one of the many telephone cards available to buy in newsagents, post offices and supermarkets.

Dialling & codes

To make an international call from Belgium, dial 00, then the country code, then the number.

Australia 61
Canada 1
France 33
Germany 49
Ireland 353
New Zealand 64
Netherlands 31
UK 44
USA 1

When in Belgium, dial the city code and number (Antwerp 03, Bruges 050, Brussels 02, Ghent 09, Liège 04), even when in the city itself. To call Belgium from abroad, first dial the international access code, then 32, then drop the 0 of each city code. See www.goldenpages.be or www.whitepages.be for telephone listings. 0800 numbers are free to call within Belgium.

Public phones

Public telephone booths are a rarity since the mobile phone revolution, but look in stations, post offices and other typical locations. There are several close to the Grand'Place, around place de Brouckère and the Bourse. Many public phones accept only prepaid telephone cards – coin phones are rare. You can buy phone cards at newsstands, post offices, train stations and supermarkets.

Operator services

Operator assistance 1324 (all languages).
Directory enquiries 1405 (English enquiries for numbers).

Mobile phones

Belgium is part of the GSM mobile network. You can rent GSM phones at the airport or from some car hire agencies. The rental fee is usually low but the cost per call is high. Network providers include **Proximus** (0475 15 60 30, www.

proximus.be), **Mobistar** (0495 95 95 00, www.mobistar.be) and **Base** (0486 19 19 99, www.base.be).

TIME

Belgium is on Central European Time, one hour ahead of GMT, six hours ahead of US Eastern Standard Time and nine hours ahead of US Pacific Standard Time. Clocks go back an hour in the autumn and forward an hour in the spring.

TIPPING & VAT

Service and VAT are included in hotel and restaurant prices, though people often throw in a few extra euros if the service has been exceptional. Tips are also included in metered taxi fares, but taxi drivers expect extra tips from foreigners. At cinemas and theatres, tipping the attendant a few cents for a programme is expected.

TOURIST INFORMATION

For visitors from the UK, the websites for Brussels and Wallonia are www.belgium theplaceto.be and www.visit flanders.co.uk. For tourist information tailored to the US market, see www.visitbelgium.com.

Brussels Info Point (BIP)
2-4 rue Royale, Upper Town (02 563 63 99, bip.brussels/en). **Open** 10am-6pm daily. **Map** p305 E6. There's also a small tourist office in the Hôtel de Ville on Grand'Place (same contact details as above).

VISAS & IMMIGRATION

EU nationals and citizens of Iceland, Monaco, Norway, Liechtenstein and Switzerland can enter Belgium without a visa or a time limit. EU nationals only need to show a valid national ID card to enter. Citizens of Australia, Canada, New Zealand, Japan and the United States, among other countries, are permitted to enter Belgium for three months with a valid passport. No visa is needed. For longer stays, they must apply for a Schengen type D visa from the Belgian consulate in their own country before entering Belgium. *See right* **Working in Brussels** for more information on long stays.

WHEN TO GO

Winters tend to be quite cold and damp, sometimes with considerable

snowfall. Summers are generally warm. Rain can fall all year round. The biggest drawback to visiting Brussels in the winter are the short days – the sky is dark until 8.30am and after 4pm during the shortest months. *See also p284* Local Climate

Public holidays

Belgian public holidays are: New Year's Day (1 Jan); Easter Sunday; Easter Monday; Labour Day (1 May); Ascension Day (6th Thur after Easter); Pentecost Whit Monday (7th Mon after Easter); Belgian National Day (21 July); Assumption (15 Aug); All Saints' Day (1 Nov); Armistice Day (11 Nov); and Christmas Day (25 Dec).

If a holiday falls on a Tuesday or Thursday, most offices, by tradition, will 'make the bridge' (*faire le pont/de brug maken*) and observe a four-day weekend. The French and Flemish communities celebrate separate regional holidays – 11 July for the Flemish-speaking community, 27 September for the French-speaking community.

WOMEN

Downtown Brussels during the daytime is open and female-friendly. After dark, unaccompanied women should avoid the gloomier areas towards the Gare du Midi and Gare du Nord. *See also p288* **Safety & security**.

WORKING IN BRUSSELS

EU nationals and citizens of Iceland, Norway and Liechtenstein don't require a work permit. However, they are required to register and get a residence permit. To register, you must go to the town hall of the *commune* where you're living. For a list of *communes*, see www.bruxelles.irisnet.be. If you live or work in Belgium, you must carry your Belgian identity card (*carte d'identité/identiteitskaart*) with you at all times. If you don't have one, carry your passport.

Non-EU citizens do need a work permit, which is usually granted to the employer. For more information about the different types of work permit, see the official Brussels Region website (www.bruxelles. irisnet.be) or the federal Office des Etrangers (www.ibz.be/code/fr/loc/etrangers.shtml).

Working illegally isn't advised. For employment laws, see www.meta.fgov.be.

ESSENTIAL INFORMATION

Vocabulary

Although officially bilingual, Brussels is a largely French-speaking city. For this reason, we have usually referred to Brussels's streets, buildings and so on by their French name. In town, street signs are given in both languages (as they are on our street maps, starting on page 300).

French is also the language of Wallonia (the south), while Flemish, a dialect of Dutch, is the language of Flanders (the north). In the **Escapes** chapter (*see pp202-235*) we use Dutch for place names in Flanders.

English is widely spoken in Brussels and Flanders, but attempts to speak French in Flanders will fall on deaf ears at best. Simply put, the Flemings won't speak French and the French can't speak Dutch. Words and phrases are listed below in English, then French, then Dutch – with pronunciation for Dutch given in brackets.

USEFUL EXPRESSIONS

Good morning, hello bonjour *hallo* ('hullo'), *dag* ('daarg')
Good evening bonsoir *goedenavond* ('hoo-dun-aav-ond')
Good night bonne nuit *goedenacht* ('khoo-dun-acht')
Goodbye au revoir *tot ziens* ('tot zeens'), *dag* ('daarg')
How are you? comment allez-vous? *hoe maakt u het?* ('hoo markt oo hut')
How's it going? ça va? *hoe gaat het?* ('hoo hart hut')
OK d'accord *okay* ('okay'), *in orde* ('in order'), *goed* ('hoot')
Yes oui *ja* ('yah')

No non *nee* ('nay')
Please s'il vous plaît *alstublieft* ('als-too-bleeft')
Thank you/thanks merci *dank u* ('dank oo'), *bedankt* ('bur-dankt')
Leave me alone laissez moi tranquille *laat me met rust* ('laat mu mat rust')
How much?/how many? combien? *hoeveel?* ('hoofail'), *wat kost het?* ('vot cost hut')
I would like... je voudrais... *ik wil graag...* ('ick will hraak')
My name is... je m'appelle... *mijn naam is...* ('mine narm iss')
Left/right gauche/droite *links/rechts* ('links'/'reckts')
Open/closed ouvert/fermé *open/gesloten* ('open'/'he-slo-tun')
Good/bad bon or bonne/mauvais or mauvaise *goed/slecht* ('hoot'/'sleckt')
Well/badly bien/mal *goed/slecht*
Stamp timbre *postzegel* ('postzehel')
Toilet WC *toilet* ('twalet')
Do you know the way to... est-ce que vous savez où se trouve... *weet u de weg naar...* ('vait oo de veg nar...')

LANGUAGE EXPRESSIONS

Do you speak English? parlez-vous anglais? *spreekt u Engels?* ('spraykt oo engels?')
I don't speak French/Dutch je ne parle pas français *ik spreek geen Nederlands* ('ick sprayk hain nay-der-lants')
Speak more slowly, please parlez plus lentement, s'il vous plaît *kunt u wat trager spreken, alstublieft* ('kunt oo waht tra-her spray-cun, als-too-bleeft')
I don't understand je ne comprends pas *ik begrijp het niet* ('ick be-gripe hut neet')

ACCOMMODATION

Do you have a room... avez-vous une chambre... *heeft u een kamer...* ('hay-ft oo an kam-er')
...for this evening/for two people? pour ce soir/pour deux personnes? *voor vanavond/voor twee personen?* ('vor vanarfond/vor tway per-sone-an')
Double bed un grand lit *een tweepersoonsbed* ('an tway per-sones-bed')
With bathroom/shower avec salle de bain/douche *met badkamer/douche* ('mat bat camer/doosh')
Expensive/cheap cher/pas cher *duur/goedkoop* ('doer/hoot-cope')

EATING OUT

I would like to reserve a table... je voudrais réserver un table... *ik zou graag een tafel reserveren...* ('ick zoo hraak an ta-full ray-sir-va-run')
...for two people/at eight o'clock ...pour deux personnes/a vingt heures ...*voor twee personen/ om acht uur* ('for tway per-sone-an/om acht oor')
Can I have the bill, please? l'addition, s'il vous plaît *mag ik de rekening, alstublieft?* ('mach ick de ray-cun-ing, als-too-bleeft')
Two beers, please deux bières, s'il vous plaît *twee bieren/pilsjes/pintjes, alstublieft* ('tway beer-an/ pils-yes/ pint-yes, als-too-bleeft')

NUMBERS

zero zéro *nul*; **1** un/une *een*; **2** deux *twee*; **3** trois *drie*; **4** quatre *vier*; **5** cinq *vijf*; **6** six *zes*; **7** sept *zeven*; **8** huit *acht*; **9** neuf *negen*; **10** dix *tien*; **11** onze *elf*; **12** douze *twaalf*; **13** treize *dertien*; **14** quatorze *veertien*; **15** quinze *vijftien*; **16** seize *zestien*; **17** dix-sept *zeventien*; **18** dix-huit *achttien*; **19** dix-neuf *negentien*; **20** vingt *twintig*; **30** trente *dertig*; **40** quarante *veertig*; **50** cinquante *vijftig*; **60** soixante *zestig*; **70** septante *seventig*; **80** huitante *tachtig*; **90** nonante *negentig*; **100** cent *honderd*; **thousand** mille *duizend*; **million** million *miljoen*.

DAYS & MONTHS

Monday lundi *maandag*; **Tuesday** mardi *dinsdag*; **Wednesday** mercredi *woensdag*; **Thursday** jeudi *donderdag*; **Friday** vendredi *vrijdag*; **Saturday** samedi *zaterdag*; **Sunday** dimanche *zondag*.
January janvier *januari*; **February** février *februari*; **March** mars *maart*; **April** april *april*; **May** mai *mei*; **June** juin *juni*; **July** juillet *juli*; **August** août *augustus*; **September** septembre *september*; **October** octobre *oktober*; **November** novembre *november*; **December** décembre *december*.

MENU ESSENTIALS

Most menus in Brussels are in French; many restaurants in the centre will also have versions in Dutch and English.

Cooking type (la cuisson)

bleu all but raw; **saignant** rare; **rosé** pink (for lamb, duck, liver and kidneys); **à point** medium rare; **bien cuit** well done.

Meat (viande)

agneau lamb; **andouillette** sausage made from pig's offal; **biche** venison (doe); **boeuf** beef; **boudin noir/boudin blanc** black or white pudding; **caille** quail; **canard** duck; **confit de canard** preserved duck leg; **magret de canard** duck breast; **caneton** duckling; **cerf** venison (stag); **cervelle** brain; **cheval** horse; **chevreuil** venison; **dinde** turkey; **escargot** snail; **faisan** pheasant; **foie** liver; **gésier** gizzard; **gibier** game; **cuisses de grenouille** frog's legs; **jambon** ham; **jambonneau** ham (normally knuckle) on the bone; **langue** tongue; **lapin** rabbit; **lard**

bacon; **lardon** small cube of bacon; **lièvre** hare; **oie** goose; **perdreau** young partridge; **perdrix** partridge; **pied** foot/trotter; **pintade/pintadeau** guinea fowl; **porc** pork; **poulet** chicken; **ris** sweetbreads; **rognon** kidney; **sanglier** boar; **saucisse** sausage; **tripes** tripe; **veau** veal; **volaille** poultry/chicken; **suprême de volaille** chicken breast.

Fish & seafood (poissons & fruits de mer)

crustacé shellfish; **anguille** eel; **bar** sea bass; **barbue** brill; **brochet** pike; **cabillaud** cod; **carrelet** plaice; **coquilles St-Jacques** scallops; **colin** hake; **crevette** shrimp; **crevettes grises** tiny sweet shrimps; **daurade** sea bream; **écrevisse** crayfish (freshwater); **eglefin** haddock; **espadon** swordfish; **flétan** halibut; **hareng** herring; **homard** lobster; **huître** oyster; **langoustine** Dublin Bay prawn/scampi; **limande** lemon sole; **lotte** monkfish; **loup de mer** similar to sea bass; **maquereau** mackerel; **merlin** whiting; **merlu** hake; **morue** dried salt cod; **moule** mussel; **palourde** clam; **plie** plaice; **poulpe** octopus; **raie** skate; **rouget** red mullet; **roussette** rock salmon/dogfish; **St-Pierre** John Dory; **sandre** pike-perch; **saumon** salmon; **scampi** prawn; **seîche** squid; **thon** tuna; **truite** trout.

Vegetables (légumes)

ail garlic; **artichaut** artichoke; **asperge** asparagus; **aubergine** aubergine/eggplant; **betterave** beetroot; **céleri** celery; **céleri rave** celeriac; **cèpe** cep mushroom; **champignon** mushroom; **chicon** chicory/Belgian endive; **chou** cabbage; **choucroute** sauerkraut; **choufleur** cauliflower; **cresson**

watercress; **échalote** shallot; **épinards** spinach; **fève** broad bean/fava bean; **frisée** curly endive; **girolle** pale wild mushroom; **haricot** bean; **haricot vert** French bean; **morille** morel mushroom; **navet** turnip; **oignon** onion; **pleurote** oyster mushroom; **poireau** leek; **poivron vert/rouge** green/red pepper/bell pepper; **pomme de terre** potato; **truffe** truffle.

Fruit (fruits)

ananas pineapple; **banane** banana; **cassis** blackcurrant; **cerise** cherry; **citron** lemon; **citron vert** lime; **fraise** strawberry; **framboise** raspberry; **griotte** morello cherry; **groseille** redcurrant; **groseille à maquereau** gooseberry; **marron** chestnut; **mûre** blackberry; **myrtille** blueberry/bilberry; **pamplemousse** grapefruit; **pêche** peach; **poire** pear; **pomme** apple; **prune** plum; **pruneau** prune; **raisin** grape.

Desserts (desserts)

crème anglaise custard; **crème chantilly** whipped cream; **dame blanche** vanilla ice-cream with hot chocolate sauce; **feuilleté** layers of puff pastry; **gâteau** cake; **glace** ice-cream; **glacé** frozen or iced; **île flottante** soft meringue floating on custard sauce; **macédoine de fruits** fruit salad; **massepain** marzipan; **mignardises** small biscuits or cakes to accompany coffee; **soufflé glacé** iced soufflé.

Herbs & spices (herbes & épices)

aneth dill; **basilic** basil; **cannelle** cinnamon; **cerfeuil** chervil; **ciboulette** chive; **citronelle** lemongrass; **estragon** tarragon; **fenouil** fennel; **muscade** nutmeg; **persil** parsley; **romarin** rosemary; **sauge** sage; **thym** thyme.

General

amande almond; **beignet** fritter or doughnut; **beurre** butter; **chaud** warm/hot; **chèvre** goat's cheese; **cru** raw; **farci** stuffed; **frites** chips; **froid** cold; **fromage** cheese; **fumé** smoked; **gaufre** waffle; **gelée** aspic; **haché** minced; **lentille** lentil; **miel** honey; **moutarde** mustard; **noisette** hazelnut; **noix** walnut; **nouilles** noodles; **oeuf** egg; **pain** bread; **pâtes** pasta; **poivre** pepper; **potage** soup; **riz** rice; **sel** salt; **sèche** dry; **sucre** sugar; **thé** tea; **végétarien(ne)** vegetarian.

ESSENTIAL INFORMATION

Further Reference

BOOKS

Art & architecture

Meuris, Jacques
René Magritte
The world of the surrealist
painter, in words and pictures.
Rombout, Marc
Paul Delvaux
Excellent selection of colour
plates, plus biographical text.
Shimomura, Junichi
*Art Nouveau Architecture,
Residential Masterpieces
1892-1911*
This selection of photographs
of the Musée Horta would be a fine
addition to anyone's coffee table.
White, Christopher
Pieter Paul Rubens: Man and Artist
A lavishly illustrated look at the
Antwerp-born artist.

Fiction, drama & poetry

Baudelaire, Charles
Amoenitates Belgicae
A scathing look at the Belgians
and their culture.
Brontë, Charlotte
The Professor
Charlotte Brontë's first novel
was set in Brussels.
Villette
Brussels was the model for the
town of Villette in her final novel,
based on her experiences there.
Claus, Hugo
The Sorrow of Belgium
Milestone novel, set during the
Nazi occupation, by a major
Flemish-language novelist.
Conrad, Joseph
Heart of Darkness
Conrad's masterpiece features
early scenes in a corrupt, cheerless
Brussels, unnamed but still
clearly identifiable.
Hergé
The *Tintin* books
Belgium's most famous author
needs only one name, where others
require two, and no introduction.
Hollinghurst, Alan
The Folding Star
Fictional art history and sexual
obsession in a dreary city in
northern Belgium.
Martin, Stephen (ed)
*Poems of the First World War:
Never Such Innocence*
An anthology, with poems about
the battlegrounds of Flanders.

Maeterlinck, Maurice, et al
*An Anthology of Modern
Belgian Theatre*
Works by Maeterlinck,
Crommelynck and de Ghelderode.
Meades, Jonathan
Pompey
Portrait of Belgium's imperial
escapades in the Congo.
Royle, Nicholas
Saxophone Dreams
A magical-realist adventure set in
the landscapes of Belgian surrealist
Paul Delvaux, including a role for
Delvaux himself.
Sante, Luc
The Factory of Facts
An autobiographical account
of growing up in Belgium in
the 1950s.
Simenon, Georges
Maigret's Revolver
Simenon was prolific but always
maintained the quality of his writing.
Any title by the Liège-born master
of the crime/detective fiction genre
is worth a read.
**Thackeray, William
Makepeace**
Vanity Fair
The middle section describes the
social scene in Brussels on the eve
of the Battle of Waterloo.
Yourcenar, Marguerite
Zeno of Bruges
The wanderings of an alchemist
in late medieval Europe.

Food & drink

Hellon, John
Brussels Fare
Delicious recipes from various
Belgian restaurants.
Webb, Tim
*Good Beer Guide to Belgium
& Holland*
Excellent guide for beer lovers
from the Campaign for Real Ale.
Wynants, Pierre
Creative Belgian Cuisine
Anyone who ate at the wonderful
Comme Chez Soi will need no
further encouragement.

History & politics

Since Belgium did not exist as
an entity until 1830, few books
deal specifically with its history.
Instead, the determined reader
should search for books about
Spain, Austria, the Netherlands
and so on.

Glover, Michael
*A New Guide to the Battlefields
of Northern France and the
Low Countries*
Waterloo is covered here, alongside
the World War I battlefields.
Kossman, EH
The Low Countries
Dull but informative history of
Belgium 1780-1940.
Parker, Geoffrey
The Dutch Revolt
Excellent history of the decline
of the Spanish empire in the
16th century.

Travel

Bryson, Bill
Neither Here Nor There
Belgium and Brussels fill two
amusing, if predictable, chapters
of Bryson's European travels.
Pearson, Harry
A Tall Man in a Low Land
Entertaining and affectionate
travelogue.

WEBSITES

www.agenda.be
Comprehensive listings
(in French and Dutch).
http://belgianbeerboard.com
Readable Belgian beer site.
www.belgiumtheplaceto.be
The official tourist site for
Brussels and Wallonia.
www.ebrusselshotels.com
Descriptions, reviews, prices
and photos of the city's hotels.
www.expatica.com
Expat website.
www.resto.be
Excellent site with a detailed
search engine and customer
reviews of restaurants
around Belgium.
www.trabel.com
Travel information and
photographs of Belgian
destinations.
www.visitbelgium.com
Hotels, beer and chocolate,
all on one site.
www.visitbrussels.be
The city's own site, with online
sales of the Brussels Card.
www.visitflanders.com
Official tourist guide for
Brussels and Flanders.
www.xpats.com
Web page for the former print
weekly magazine *The Bulletin*.

Index

INDEX

Bags packed, milk cancelled, house raised on stilts.

You've packed the suntan lotion, the snorkel set, the stay-pressed shirts. Just one more thing left to do – your bit for climate change. In some of the world's poorest countries, changing weather patterns are destroying lives.

You can help people to deal with the extreme effects of climate change. Raising houses in flood-prone regions is just one life-saving solution.

**Climate change costs lives.
Give £5 and let's sort it *Here & Now***

www.oxfam.org.uk/climate-change

Oxfam is a registered charity in England and Wales (No.202918) and Scotland (SCO039042). Oxfam GB is a member of Oxfam International.

Be Humankind ⊗ Oxfam

INDEX

Maps

Bozar

Casino

Parc de Bruxelle
Warandepark

Cathédrale
Kathedraal

Gare Centrale
Centraal Station

Royale
gsplein

Grand'Place
Grote Markt

Coudenberg
e Coudenberg

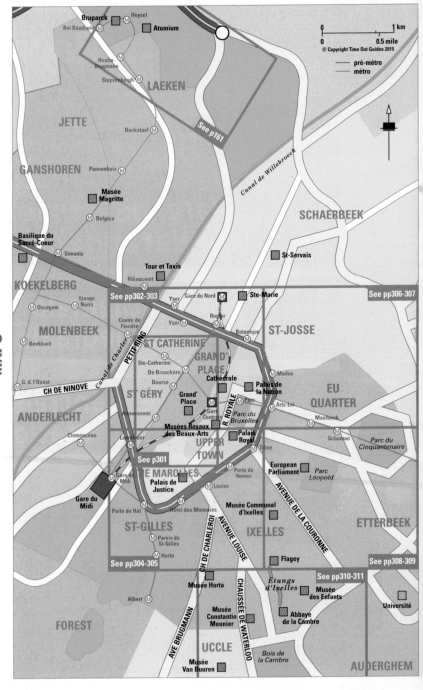

MAPS

0   0.5   1 km
0   0.5 mile
© Copyright Time Out Guides 2015

—— pré-métro
—— métro

Bruparck
Heysel Ⓜ
Roi Baudouin Ⓜ
Atomium

Houba-
Brugmann Ⓜ
Stuyvenbergh Ⓜ
LAEKEN
See p161

JETTE
Canal de Willebroeck

Bockstael Ⓜ

GANSHOREN
Pannenhuis Ⓜ
SCHAERBEEK

Musée
Magritte
Belgica Ⓜ

Basilique du
Sacré-Coeur
Simonis Ⓜ
St-Servais
KOEKELBERG
Ribaucourt Ⓜ
Tour et Taxis
Gare du Nord Ⓜ
Ste-Marie
See pp306-307

Etangs
Noirs Ⓜ
See pp302-303
Yser Ⓜ
MOLENBEEK
Ossegem Ⓜ
Comte de
Flandre Ⓜ
Yser Ⓜ
Rogier
Botanique Ⓜ
ST-JOSSE

Beekkant Ⓜ
ST CATHERINE
Ste-Catherine Ⓜ
GRAND'
PLACE
Madou Ⓜ
EU
QUARTER

G. d. l'Ouest Ⓜ
De Brouckère Ⓜ
Cathédrale
Palais de
la Nation
Arts-Loi Ⓜ

CH DE NINOVE
Canal de Charleroi
PETIT RING
Bourse Ⓜ
ST GÉRY
Grand'
Place
R. ROYALE
Parc du
Bruxelles
Maelbeek Ⓜ

ANDERLECHT
Aumale Ⓜ
Gare
Centrale Ⓜ
Schuman Ⓜ
Parc du
Cinquantenaire

Clemenceau Ⓜ
Lemonnier Ⓜ
Musées Royaux
des Beaux-Arts
Palais
Royal
UPPER
TOWN
See p301
Trône Ⓜ

LES MAROLLES
Gare du
Midi
Palais de
Justice
Porte de
Namur Ⓜ
European
Parliament
Parc
Léopold

Gare du
Midi
Louise Ⓜ
AVENUE DE LA COURONNE
ETTERBEEK

Porte de Hal Ⓜ
Hôtel des Monnaies Ⓜ
Musée Communal
d'Ixelles
See pp308-309

ST-GILLES
IXELLES

Parvis de
St-Gilles Ⓜ
AVENUE LOUISE
Flagey
See pp304-305
Horta Ⓜ

CH DE CHARLEROI
Étangs
d'Ixelles
See pp310-311

Musée Horta
CHAUSSÉE DE WATERLOO
Musée
des Enfants
Université

Albert Ⓜ
Musée
Constantin
Meunier
Abbaye
de la Cambre

FOREST
AVE BRUGMANN
UCCLE
Bois de
la Cambre
AUDERGHEM

Musée
Van Buuren

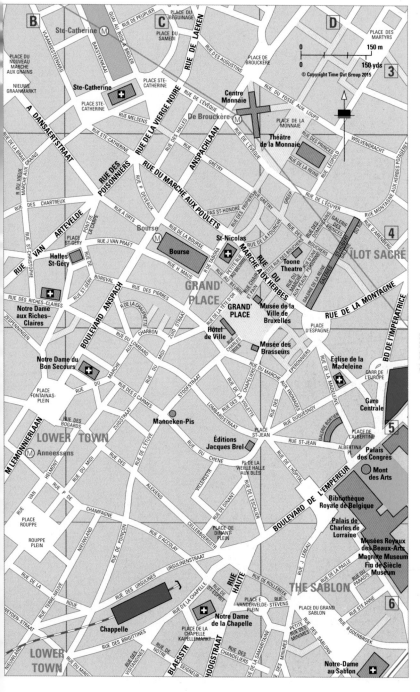

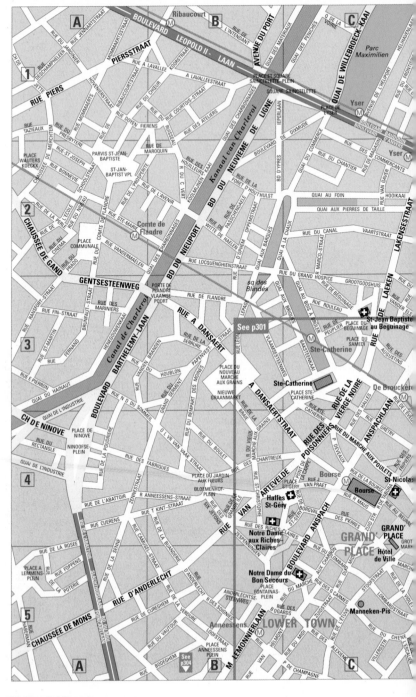

MAPS

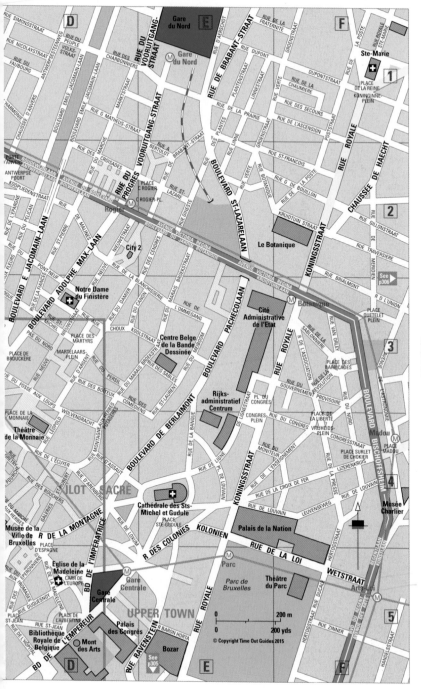

MAPS

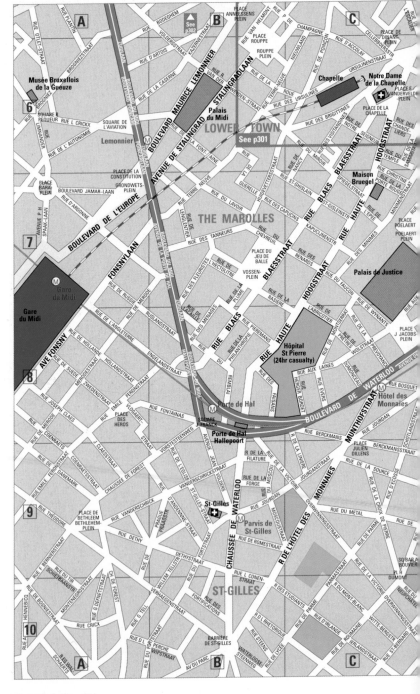

MAPS

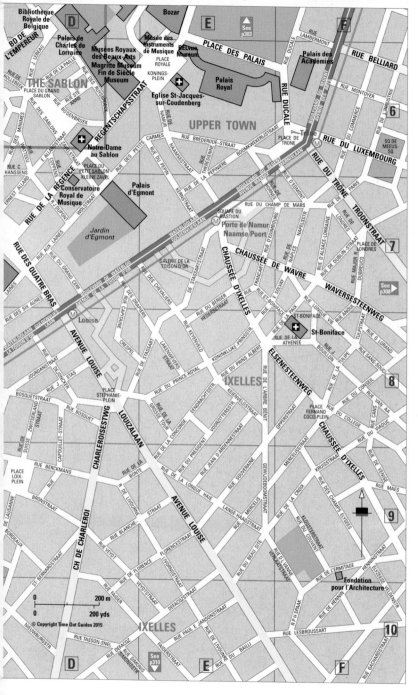

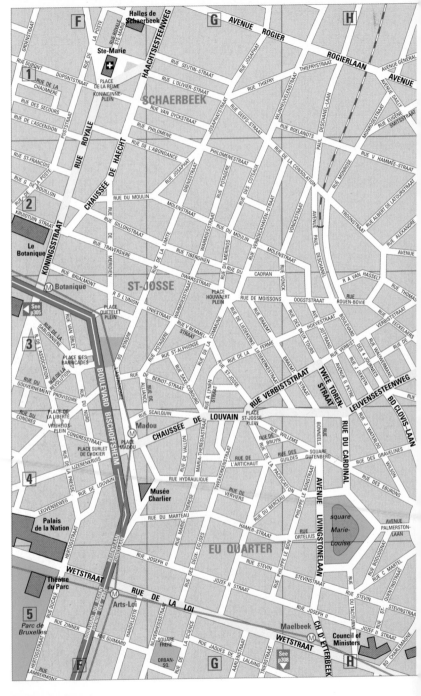

MAPS

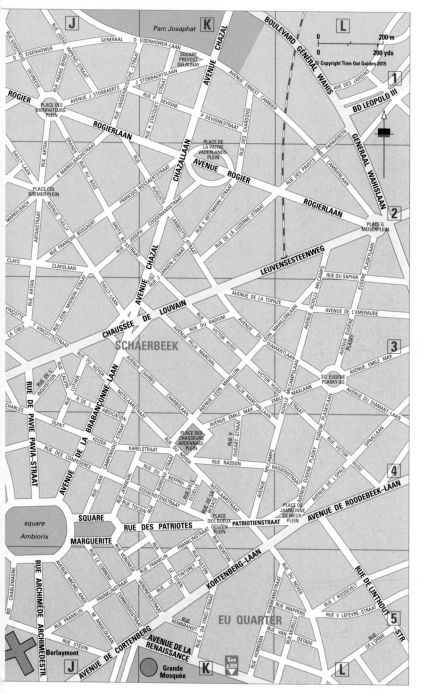

MAPS

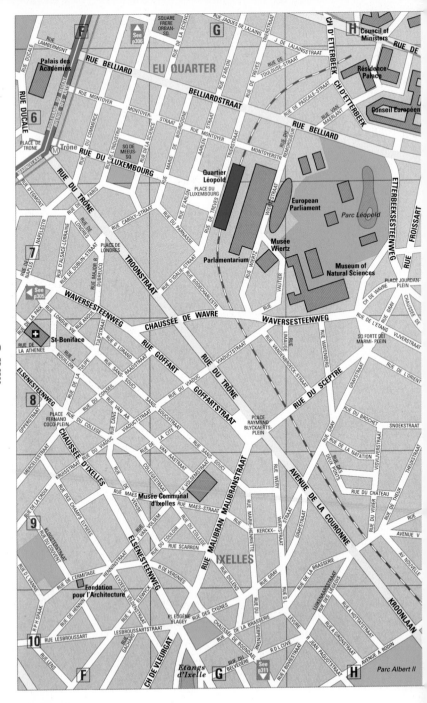

MAPS

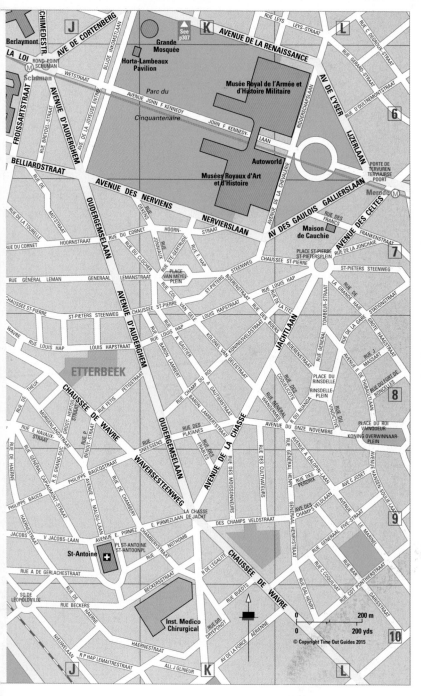

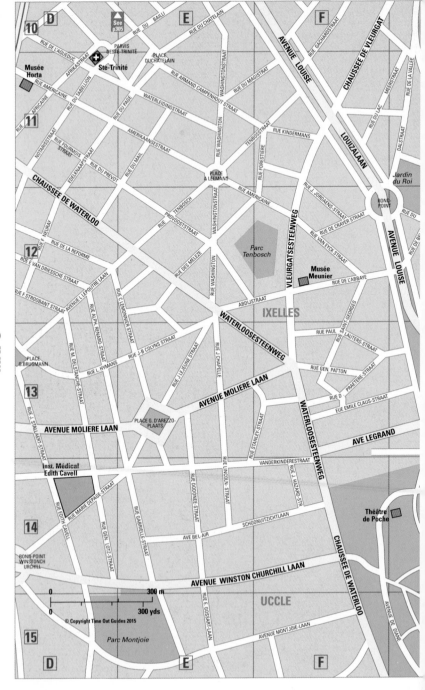

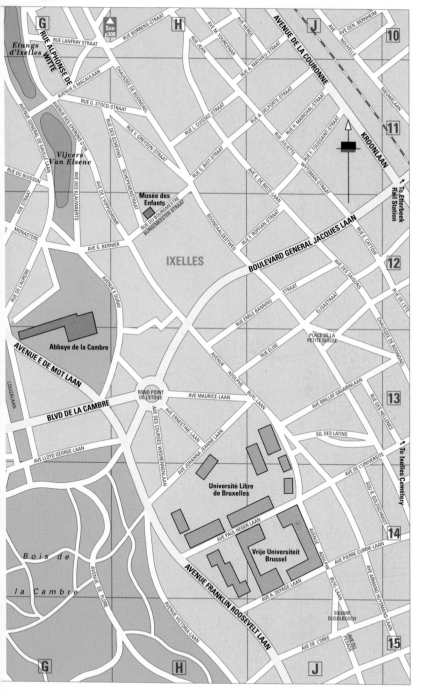

MAPS

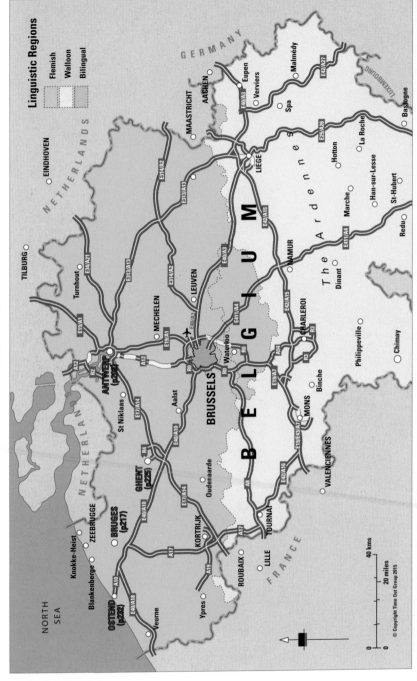

Street Index

STREET INDEX

Made with

Copenhagen

INSIDE
PULL-OUT
MAP

with

**2015
guidebook
on sale now**
Written by
local experts

100%
locally
sourced
ingredients

Keep up, join in Time Out

STREET INDEX

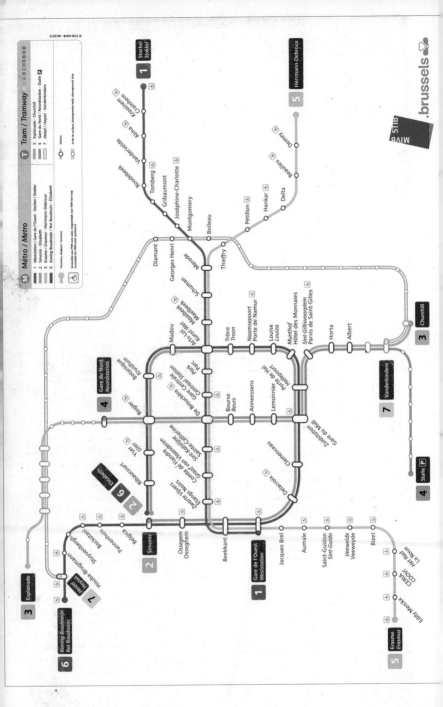